WARS, INTERNAL CONFLICTS, AND POLITICAL ORDER

SUNY Series in Israeli Studies
Russell Stone, Editor

WARS, INTERNAL CONFLICTS, AND POLITICAL ORDER

A Jewish Democracy in the Middle East

GAD BARZILAI

State University of New York Press

Published by
State University of New York Press, Albany

© 1996 State University of New York

All rights reserved

Printed in the United States of America

No part of this book may be used or reproduced
in any manner whatsoever without written permission.
No part of this book may be stored in a retrieval system
or transmitted in any form or by any means including
electronic, electrostatic, magnetic tape, mechanical,
photocopying, recording, or otherwise without the
prior permission in writing of the publisher.

For information, address State University of New York
Press, State University Plaza, Albany, N.Y. 12246

Production by E. Moore
Marketing by Theresa Abad Swierzowski

Library of Congress Cataloging-in-Publication Data

Barzilai, Gad.
    Wars, internal conflicts, and political order : a Jewish democracy
in the Middle East / Gad Barzilai.
       p.   cm. — (SUNY series in Israeli studies)
    Includes bibliographical references and index.
    ISBN 0-7914-2943-1 (HC : acid free). — ISBN 0-7914-2944-X (PB :
acid free)
    1. Israel—History, Military. 2. Israel-Arab conflicts. 3. War
and society—Israel. 4. Politics and war. 5. Democracy—Israel.
I. Title. II. Series.
DS119.2.B36 1996
956.9405—dc20   95-37349
                                                                          CIP

10 9 8 7 6 5 4 3 2 1

Contents

Preface   vii

Acknowledgments   ix

PART ONE: A CONCEPTUAL FRAMEWORK

1. Democracies in Wars and
   Severe National-Security Crises:
   Theoretical and Comparative Aspects   3

PART TWO: A DEVELOPING DEMOCRACY DURING THE FIRST STAGES OF NATION-BUILDING

2. The Suez Campaign: Ideological Rift,
   Preemptive War, and a Dominant Party   27

3. The Six-Day War: Political Crisis and War of Consensus   59

PART THREE: POLYARCHY DURING TERRITORIAL STATUS QUO

4. Dissent and Consensus in the War of Attrition   83

5. The Power Illusion Smashed and
   National Security Affairs (Partly) Democratized   102

6. War of Initiative and Political Polarization   123

7. Israeli Society and Politics during the Gulf War   156

8. The Inter-Communal Conflict of the Intifada
   and the Israeli Regime (1987–93)   171

PART FOUR: BOOK FINDINGS IN
COMPARATIVE AND THEORETICAL PERSPECTIVE:
FROM A WARTIME SOCIETY TO A CIVILIAN SOCIETY

9. The Long-Term Effects of Wars
   and the Emergency Situation   185

10. Final Conclusions: Establishing a Civilian Society   219

Notes   225

Bibliography   277

Subject Index   291

Name Index   299

Preface

The purpose of this book is to explain national consensus and dissent in Israel by analyzing the effects of the protracted national security crisis and the Arab-Israeli wars since 1949. The book deals with two major questions. What were the principles in the Israeli political spectrum regarding military force, and how did those outlooks develop? And, how did these concepts influence the sociopolitical order? I will examine how contrasting political dilemmas and attitudes regarding (conventional) military force interacted with characteristics of wars and military operations, state apparatuses, fear responses, threat concepts, cultural values (mainly those affecting political behavior), and political structures (primarily ruling coalitions).

Part one begins with the political origins and implications of national consensus and dissent during security crises in democracies. After a theoretical discussion and the requisite comparative examination of various states and societies, I will clarify the Israeli setting and offer my basic arguments. The last two sections provide two fundamentals to the understanding of this book: the political importance given to Jewishness in the Israeli nationality and the contribution of the prestatehood (Yishuv period, 1919-48) to the formation of the Israeli discourse regarding military power. Each one of the chapters in Parts two and three presents a concrete sociopolitical analysis, based on primary sources, of an international conflict.

Part two deals with the Israeli democracy prior to its occupation of territories in 1967. It dwells on a society in a stage of nation-building characterized by an intensive mobilization of the public by the Jewish state's apparatuses, and assorted party organizations, primarily Mapai and its agencies.

Part three examines consensus and dissent regarding military force and the issue of war while a territorial status quo, due to a military occupation, prevails. I submit that, above the military aspects of the occupation and the issues of strategy, which have often been underscored in literature about Israel, the main impact of the 1967 War was on the structure and culture of the Israeli political setting. Furthermore, contentions about military force were not an "objective" articulation of "security" dilemmas, but a central political reflection, and also a prime cause of the polarization, fragmentation, and emergence (sometimes, revival) of political extremism in Israel. Thus, the question of how the society and state reacted to warfare is even more crucial. I do not see the post-'67 wars as isolated cases. Rather, I defer to a compound historical process of two different dimensions: on the one hand, functional adaptability to emergency conditions and, on the other hand, growing destructive effects of the protracted warfare situation on democratic tenets in Israeli politics.

This book's main concern is not how wars were conducted militarily, but rather how a society was mobilized, managed, and touched by adverse security conditions. In this study, I intertwine the practice of the Arab-Palestinian-Israeli conflict and the application of the theory of primary-conflict studies to show how internal political conflicts, national consensus, international conflicts, and a state's legitimacy are linked. As shall be more specifically argued and empirically analyzed, political order in democracies, including in Israel, is not a direct result or a mere reflection of wars. In contradiction to main intellectual streams in social science, this book submits that consensus and dissent in times of international military emergency are to a great extent internal political phenomena strongly influenced by internal causes. In contrast to most studies about the Arab-Palestinian-Israeli conflict, and military conflicts on the whole, this book does not aim to examine military events as such. Instead, I investigate the much broader context of internal political processes and the blurred, overlapping boundaries between international and domestic affairs. Finally, Part four will hone general empirical and theoretical claims and suggest how to further understand the nature and ramifications of national consensus and dissent, especially in time of war.

Acknowledgments

The origins of this book are in my Hebrew work about the Israeli political regime in wartime (*A Democracy in Wartime: Conflict and Consensus in Israel*; Tel Aviv: Sifriat Poalim, 1992). Ms. Yeudit Yilon helped me to translate the chapters from the Hebrew book into English. Ms. Suzanne G. Kelley assisted in proofreading and made useful suggestions on how to improve the English prose. Mr. Avi Rembaum has assisted me in making additional improvements to the English style. I have extensively revised all of the chapters and, in addition, have written entire new chapters as well as new sections in chapters.

I would like to acknowledge the helpful remarks of many of my colleagues in the Department of Political Science, Tel Aviv University; Professor Ilan Peleg from the Department of Government and Law, Lafayette College; and four anonymous referees. The Department of Political Science at Yale, headed by Professor Bruce M. Russett, provided an excellent intellectual environment to work on the manuscript while I visited at Yale in 1993–1994. In addition, I appreciate the helpful comments of the series' editors, Clay Morgan and Professor Russell Stone. I alone bear full responsibility for the content of this book and sincerely hope it will foster scholarly debates about the politics of conflicts, in general, and the nature of the Israeli political regime, in particular.

Part One

A Conceptual Framework

1 Democracies in Wars and Severe National-Security Crises: Theoretical and Comparative Aspects

Political Dilemmas Surrounding the Use of Armed Force

To understand political processes, we must examine the phenomena of national consensus and dissent regarding armed force, and especially wars. Consensus and dissent affect, and are affected by, relations between society and ruling apparatuses, and they have a resounding impact on the foundations of political regimes. Consensus and dissent have highlighted the importance of social rifts, the divisiveness of political power foci, the political behavior patterns of the state—its apparatuses and populations, and the degree of legitimacy accorded political regimes and administrations. Thus, for example, the Algerian War (1954–62) brought about some very basic changes in the structure of France's political regime. Similarly, the Vietnam War (1964–73) was a factor leading to a profound rethinking of U.S. foreign and defense policies, and the narrowing of the president's constitutional war powers.[1]

Many studies have focused on an analysis of how wars were launched and how they were conducted (and ended). Only a few studies have asked what effect wars have, and how other possible variables affected politics in democracies during and subsequent to wars. Even these few studies have produced only partial findings.[2] We need but turn to history to learn the extent of the impact of wars. Wars have helped forge consensus, but they have also caused bitter conflicts in domestic politics. In analyzing these influences, I shall first discuss how consensus is formed.

Since World War I, the outbreak of war has generally brought political consensus to democratic regimes. I have researched thirteen such instances, starting with World War I ("instance" refers to a democracy participating as a belligerent in a given war)[3] and in twelve of these instances no overt political opposition arose in response to the war engagement. At most, these instances furnish evidence of only a weak protest by small opposition groups. Also, wars have displaced controversial topics to the bottom of the national agenda. On occasion, as for example in Britain in 1915, such consensus is accompanied by public enthusiasm that heightens political awareness, in contrast to the political apathy of most of the population of any given democracy in peacetime.

Keen interest in the use of armed force is also evidenced by mass volunteering for the military and for support jobs on the home front. Here, consensus in using armed force is of utmost importance, much like conferring a seal of legitimacy on the regime's decision to go to war. And even more important, consensus, no matter how engendered, is helpful for the mobilization of resources that may enable a military victory, at the same time prodding the civilian hinterland to adapt to a state of war. And when both fighting forces and home front stand united, there is less danger that their common motivation for shouldering the burden of war effort will be eroded.

In these political and administrative pursuits of war preparations and management, an ability to forge consensus is a critical component of state power. Social consensus in total or protracted wars, which, in the face of the potential erosion of the population's steadfastness and motivation, particularly when involving a fair measure of solidarity, enables the defense burden to be borne more easily. Thus, for example, Britain's success in the war against Nazi Germany was greatly helped by the prevailing national consensus. It saw Britons through massive air raids and very heavy losses, keeping national morale at a high level. Consensus also fueled an unprecedented nationwide economic and military mobilization, greater than that of Britain during World War I.[4] But consensus also has authoritarian and antidemocratic aspects; it legitimizes massive state interference in social and political life during security crises. The political establishment imposes compulsory recruitment of people and economic resources by controlling information and by curtailing individual freedoms, that is, freedom of expression, association, and demonstration. The state's broadening reach promotes the emergence of exacting sociopolitical norms endorsing severe sanctions against the opponents of the war.

Hence, my contention is that, in essence, wars and the liberal principles of democracy are mutually incompatible. Yet we still lack sufficient explanation as to the how and why of the transition, in democracies, from pluralism in peacetime to consensus during war.

Dissent can also accompany the use of military force. There are several instances of wars producing consensus only for a limited time. As hostilities have worn on, even agreed wars have aroused dissent. Of the twelve wars launched since World War I, six came to be disputed in the course of time.[5] Extensive public opposition took place in France and Britain during World War I, especially during and after 1916. European statesmen and generals had predicted an end to the war in six months, yet there was no sign of any abatement of the hostilities. Then again, both France and Britain numbered their losses in the hundreds of thousands. Another, albeit less influential, factor was the severe rationing instituted in both countries, giving rise to widespread and vociferous demand to end the fighting.

Similar, even more clamorous instances of dissent occurred after World War II.[6] The evolution of the electronic media as a means of political criticism; the increasing potency of war weapons; the greater awareness of the deadliness of war, paralleled by more insistent objection to the use of military force; and the burgeoning of political protest in Western political culture all operated to render war the subject of open opposition. Public dissent thus developed in Britain in the course of the Suez Campaign (1956); in France during the Indochina War (1946–54) and the Algerian War (1954–62); and in the United States during the Korean War (1950–53) and most notably during the Vietnam War (1964–73).

The events of those years indicate that wars can produce societalwide political and social rifts that are divisive to the point that the legitimacy of the administration and the regime are called into question. France experienced this during the Algerian War and the United States during the Korean War, all at the hands of right-wing radicalist groups. Left-wingers lambasted the U.S. administration and its values during the Vietnam War. Thus, dissented wars have dealt severe blows to political stability.[7]

Disputes over the use of armed force have been far more intense than others in democracies. This is because a broad spectrum of groups have clearly understood how strongly the issue ultimately affects public and individual security. Costly victories or losses have sometimes resulted in the ouster of the incumbent administration and a rethinking of the regime's ideological bent. This happened in Britain following the Suez Campaign and in France during the Algerian War. And even where controversial wars have not resulted in the replacement of regimes or ruling elites, debates have often arisen over the use of armed force.

Western democracies, with their attributes of cooperation between political elites, willingness to compromise, and the political apathy of their publics, have sustained profound changes both during and after wars. They have known social rifts (France and the United States), political violence (France, Britain, and the United States), and processes of delegitimization of the administration (France, Britain, and the United States) and of the regime (France and the United States). They have experienced increasing difficulties in maintaining effective government (the United States, France). All of these situations have stemmed mainly from the public controversies conducted by numerous political groups during the wars of Korea, Suez, Indochina, Algeria, and Vietnam.[8]

The causes of such sociopolitical changes have not been researched well enough. To assert, as research literature does, that "unenforced" and "unjust" wars tend to be controversial is simply begging the question why? The issue of when wars may be deemed unenforced and unjust must be examined in its own right, in the context of a given state, with a given political, social, and cultural infrastructure. Before the arguments of this book are presented more fully, however, critical analysis of the literature is required.

Research Studies on the Issue of Democracies in War: Explanation of the Pre-Paradigm[9]

The study of this subject has been largely distorted by the (erroneous) premise that war leads directly to consensus in democracies and that it is not connected to values, images, attitudes, political concepts, or structures. This error derives from three postulates.

First, war generates among civilians images of common fate and the impression that defeat in war will wreak havoc on their lives. They are therefore prepared to take part in the war effort and cooperate with one another until the common goal of victory is achieved. Second, in addition to this expedient solidarity with the state, they may come to identify with the political establishment by reason of political and ideological support for its war aims. Third, people aspire to assimilate into society and externalize aggression, thereby lending definition to their personal identity that is essential to their sanity. War allows aggression to be externalized and provides the individual with a social mechanism for assimilation. The authorities exact obedience, and a pervasive atmosphere of national excitement is generated by the war, enabling the individual to submerge into the collective and to express aggression in the guise of the discharge of a national obligation.[10]

Based on this premise, the social sciences have evolved a cause and effect approach. Studies in social psychology, criminology, communications, political sociology, and political science have determined that war, as an exogenous factor, produces unity in endogenous politics (outstanding researchers of this school include G. Simmel and L. A. Coser).[11]

I show the "cause and effect" approach to be too simplistic, based on faulty reasoning, and therefore fails to adequately explain the important effects of wars and protracted emergency situations on democracies.

A broadly encompassing study that represents something of a departure from that approach is that of P. A. Sorokin. Having scrutinized political events up to and including the third year of World War II, he concluded that the effect of wars on public behavior in democracies is contingent on four factors: (1) the extent of popular support for the goals of the war; (2) the degree to which the lives and safety of the population are threatened during hostilities; (3) the damage liable to be caused (Sorokin does not specify to whom) by defeat in war; and (4) the potency of the "sense of allegiance, patriotism and morale of the population." Sorokin alludes to the existence of other possible factors but without specifying what they are, except in one instance, namely, government interference in the life of the individual. His argument is that in total wars, those whose undertaking demands an especially wide-ranging mobilization of resources, and that seek the enemy's ignominious defeat, the public refrains from opposition. In such times, governments habitually step up their interference: in social life (restrictions on freedom of association); the economy (higher than normal rates of taxation); culture (censorship); and the political setting (by using propaganda, searches, and arrests). The result, says Sorokin, is a curtailment of individual freedoms, which hinders any effective opposition.[12]

Michael Stohl, a sociologist who focused on the research of war, elaborates on this conclusion. He claims that since the American-Spanish War (1898) until the midst of the Vietnam War (1970) the U.S. federal administration made extensive use of "governmental violence," meaning that it manipulated information and even resorted to physical violence against the opponents of war. Stohl's conclusion was innovative mainly in that it offered evidence that the state uses undemocratic means to ensure "free" support.[13] This is in line with the elitist view of political phenomena, in general, and wars, in particular, whereby wars are taken advantage of or initiated by political regimes in order to realize the vested interests of the ruling elite and to secure obedience and sociopolitical order. Importance is here ascribed to the military elite and their relationship with defense industries and to the civilian elite.

The elitist school emphasizes two main issues. The first topic is the importance of armies, security organizations, and experts on violence for the emergence of military juntas or democratic regimes intent on war. Militarism is explained by the weight of armies as bureaucratic organizations controlling information sources and highly skilled in the use of violence. It is these organizational features that enable armies to exert so decisive an influence on the architects of policy, whether in formal or informal frameworks. The army is particularly influential in times when the policymakers are, or claim to be, confronted with security threats.

Harold D. Lasswell has illuminated the cultural aspects of such military-civilian relations. He particularly stressed the mutual influence exerted by uncertainty, expertise, and processes of militarism. Uncertain crisis situations cause civilian elites to collate information deemed crucial in order to reduce the insecurity generated by uncertainty. Since the army has control of what is believed to be relevant information, military personnel gradually come to control the regime's power foci. This process gradually changes the whole fabric of society into a military society.[14]

The second issue, notably pioneered by Wright C. Mills, concerns the military-industrial complex. Mills determined that both political elites and military industries are guided by economic interests. Both types of organization aspire to initiate wars and security crises in order to justify their mass production of weapons and forestall opposition to territorial expansion. The aspiration to financial and political power is what guides the state to authorize the deployment of armed force and incite an arms race. This leads to a dovetailing of interests between civilians and the military. The general public, mistakenly viewing the use of armed force as dictated by objective considerations of national defense, unknowingly supports needless acts of violence.[15]

The importance of socioeconomic factors in explaining the nature of military force has been strongly emphasized by Marxists and neo-Marxists. The Marxists' main contention is that war is a result of basic tensions between socioeconomic classes. War is meant to serve the bourgeoisie, since it diverts the attention of the proletariat from its true problems while enabling the bourgeoisie to conquer new markets (always excepting proletarian wars whose purpose is the destruction of the bourgeoisie). While the Marxist school confined itself mainly to shedding light on the causes of war, the neo-Marxist approach shifts the focus of attention to war's repercussions. The ability to deploy and the actual deployment of armed force are considered the means whereby political and military elites control the masses. Armed force is exerted against "external" enemies with a view to convince the public that support for the state is vital to its security, whereas, in fact, armed force can be of service to none but the ruling elite.

Common to both these approaches is the essential argument that warfare is intended to gloss over the bitter realities of the class stratification of society. Both also hold that to the extent that wars do produce consensus, it is due to the intervention of the state into society. Moreover, both deny the possibility that wars can be consented to by the public.[16]

Both approaches are defective mainly in that they fail to appreciate international affairs and the mutuality between international relations and domestic politics. Another serious deficiency is their neglect of various political factors that may be relevant to an analysis of the phenomena of consensus and dissent. Thus, they deal only very slightly with the dispersal of political powers and the dynamic change in political power foci. They moreover concentrate so narrowly on the structural aspects of, primarily, state control of the mechanisms of oppression (army and bureaucracy, for example) as to exclude historical analysis of the evolution of ideologies and political attitudes. Any light they are able to shed on the world of politics is thus somewhat one-sided.[17]

This deficiency has been partially corrected by Theda T. Skocpol's study. She has endeavored to apply some tenets of the Marxist thinking to an understanding of the causes of revolutions. In her book *States and Social Revolutions*, she starts out by stressing that the mutual influences exerted by international relations and domestic politics must be studied if we are to understand how the autonomous state behaves toward society. Skocpol zeroes in on the French Revolution of 1789, the Russian-Bolshevik revolution of 1917, the Russian-Stalinist revolution of the twenties and thirties, and the Sino-Maoist revolution of the forties. Her conclusions, however, are difficult to apply to modern reality in Western democracies and in other, more formal democracies like Israel.

Skocpol claims that interstate rivalries have been exploited by revolutionaries to mobilize mass support for their cause. In principle she maintains that the state has absolute autonomy in matters of security and that the ruling elites are utterly indifferent to the public and are primarily engaged in recruiting mass support for their aims. Subjected to the test of Israeli realities, however, some of her conclusions must be refuted. Michael N. Barnett examined Israeli policy in the mobilization of resources and preparation for war from 1967 to 1977. In a study scrutinizing mainly the economic aspects of the issue, he found, contrary to Skocpol, that the state did not enjoy absolute autonomy in matters of national security but that Israel's political elites and its military had to reckon with serious social and public constraints.[18] Some of Skocpol's assertions are true of Israel, insofar as they concern the harnessing of the international environment to the needs of the deployment of armed force with a view to attaining international and domestic political goals.

By contrast, other pluralist-liberal researchers have focused on the structure of public opinion and attitudes. Mainly they contend that the level of sociopolitical order in time of war depends on the breadth of the basic consensus regarding the fundamental prewar goals of the political community. They particularly underline that consensus will be generated in relation to two key issues: that the oncoming danger is a threat to the survival of the entire population and that the use of military force will, at reasonable cost, attain the goal of social preservation. Thus, according to these studies, modes of response to war have been determined by the cohesiveness of the political communities.

The weakness of this argument is that it provides no clear definition of mutual relations between organizations, attitudes, culture, attributes of the use of armed force, and modifications of the solidarity that becomes an essential precondition of national consensus.[19] These studies, moreover, ignore the importance of the state as the architect of sociopolitical order. Another major drawback lies in their liberal premise, adopted without empirical proof, that human societies incline to form consent, deriving from free dialogue between groups and individuals consciously formulating a clear-cut understanding regarding given goals.

Affinities of intellectual influences have existed among the different schools of thought. Marxists and neo-Marxists have also dealt slightly more with the premises of a cause-and-effect approach and of the pluralist paradigm that posits that war, as an exogenous cause, exerts great influence on domestic politics. The pluralist school on the other hand has begun to focus increasingly on factors of intrasocial tension as affecting mutual relations between military force and consensus and dissent. A corollary of this idea has been the diversionary theory, according to which in Western democracies the chief executive tends to boost popularity and forge consensus in the domestic front through the deployment of military force against external enemies.[20]

These various studies could not suggest an all-encompassing conclusion as to the effects of war on democracies. They do not suggest a comprehensive analysis of societies and politics during war. They do not consider consensus and dissent but only examine certain of their aspects. Also, they do not distinguish between the effect of different types of wars on domestic politics or the differences between interethnic disputes and interstate wars.

Other possible explanations regarding the origins of political order during war can be found in schools of thought that concentrate on political order in Western democracies.

The Consensus Concept and the Dissent Concept

In light of accelerated industrialization, economic development, and the accruing of national wealth in the wake of World War II, especially in the United States, there evolved a consensus concept, whereby Western democracies tend to have political stability. It has been explained as deriving from the impression that (1) politics in

Western democracies are based on compromise and pragmatic decisions; (2) despite rivalry with communist regimes, Western democracies are at a postwar and postindustrial stage; they sustain affluent societies, which derogate the value of ideology; and, (3) social groups succeed in realizing their interests, thus ideological polarity narrows. Stability, then, was conceived as a natural product of liberal, democratic society. Of itself, war was not deemed capable of causing significant changes in the general stability-seeking nature of society.[21]

But the Vietnam War, the black riots, and the student riots of the sixties and the seventies combined to produce a concept of dissent, whereby widespread public controversy became a most conspicuous feature. The consensus regarding the war in its first four years (1964–68) began weakening in March 1968, when the peace movements began rallying extensive support. Later, after 1970, the demonstrations grew in size and frequency. The outbreak of (partly violent) riots against the political establishment during a time of economic affluence led scholars to a number of conclusions.

Redeemed from their former status as expressions of violence, demonstrations came to be defined as manifestations of distinctly sociopolitical protest. Extra-parliamentary struggle was perceived as taking part in the decision-making processes. Studies gradually began being published, such as those of Daniel Yankelovich and Amitai Etzioni, asserting that in the democratic West, a politics-of-conflict was evolving, characterized by attempts on the part of broad strata of the public to intervene in decision-making processes, including its desire to be consulted in shaping the nation's foreign and defense policies.[22]

The explanation of the new political culture featuring both struggle between elites and nonruling groups and social strife involved three primary factors: (1) the effect of the electronic media, especially television, on enabling extra-parliamentary groups to influence decision-making processes; (2) claims of mismanagement and other psychosocial grievances, including the sense of relative deprivation and dissatisfaction with and alienation from the political establishment; (3) wars whose aggressive goals engendered ideological and moral dilemmas that have created and accommodated the expression of severe rivalries, primarily between competing economic and political elites, or between them and weak social groups. Yankelovich and Jerome H. Skolnick examined the political behavior of students and radical left-wing political groups in America.

They saw the Vietnam War as a catalyst in the processes of protest and even alienation. They stressed, however, that the main source of dissent was hostility toward and alienation from the U.S. political establishment.[23]

These and other studies fail to deal comprehensively with problems of sociopolitical order in democracies in the context of wars and national security crises. They disregard certain fundamental problems, such as whether the fragmentation of political power also significantly affected consensus and dissent. But more important, the studies are deficient in their inability to show mutual affinities between the various factors of domestic politics or indicate whether mutual interaction can be discerned between domestic political variables and characteristics of wars.

Attempts to interpret the complexities of issues of national security and sociopolitical order have revealed conceptual differences regarding national consensus and dissent. One school asserts that these notions have no social reality since individuals make no volitional, conscious choice between alternative values and principles; rather, their behavior is molded by the state or its central political organizations (the neo-Marxist and elitist approach).

Another version declares consensus and dissent to be a product of the free exchange of views between individuals and groups in a given political community, free from massive political intervention in its affairs by the state (the pluralistic approach). A third claim is that consensus will form to the extent that a political regime can adapt itself to the values of a given population. Where the values of the regime do not match those of the population, conflicts will arise (the system concept). Yet another view sees consensus as the product of the propertied bourgeois class interested in creating a false show of national brotherhood, thereby forestalling any change in the infrastructure of relations that enables it to exploit the proletariat (the Marxist theory). Finally, another approach, by contrast, defines consensus as a reflex to extraneous states of war (the cause-and-effect approach).[24]

All approaches view consensus and dissent as independent variables in explaining the foundations of the nation-state. Their main question was how do consensus and dissent affect the state? Whereas the general and main question in this book is how are consensus and dissent affected by wars? Formulated in reverse, the question assumes vital importance for the proponents of all intellectual approaches.

I do not focus on the state or its direct power apparatuses as such (bureaucracy, courts, army, mass media, police, educational systems, and economic organizations). This book will, however, try to clarify processes in the political setting, including the involvement therein of institutional power apparatuses. For example, I do not ask what is central to the experience of the modern state: the gaining of legitimacy or the mechanisms of compulsion operated by autonomous states. Instead, the book will determine how a diverse range of public dispositions toward its ruling bodies' legitimacy and policy gives shape to consensus and dissent.

Two different types of definitions shall be applied in this book to the terms consensus and dissent. The first is an operative-instrumental definition, which enables the accumulation of findings and analyses of phenomena, and the second is substantive-contextual, which is based on the research. A substantive-contextual label will be proposed in the conclusion of this book, following an analysis of the sociopolitical aspects of Israel's wars. I shall now, however, define the notions of consensus and dissent in operative-instrumental terms.

Political Order: A Framework for Debate

Consensus is not necessarily a corollary of a situation in which the public knows of, correctly understands, and accepts a governmental policy. The definition is that consensus is a condition in which the public does not reject a certain sociopolitical situation. Thus, I am treating passivity as consensus. My use of the term "consensus," therefore, does not suggest that in the political world true debate or negotiation necessarily occurs among the public or between the public and the political elites. In my view, such debate or negotiation can neither be presupposed nor automatically excluded.

Dissent, on the other hand, is any situation in which conflict between different positions finds political-behaviorist expression. This book focuses on controversies on the parliamentary plane and on the extra-parliamentary plane. The analysis of public opinion trends, by contrast, takes second place, as having only a limited effect on the features and import of deliberations regarding military power. Underlying this book are a number of fundamental claims that let us hurdle value-oriented judgments.

A. Consensus and dissent are neither "negative" nor "positive" since each has diverse, even contradictory, meanings for society and politics. Conflict is neither a "deviation" nor a "depravity" but, on the contrary, a phenomenon that can lead social and political developments in a more useful and equitable direction. Consensus is also neither natural nor necessarily desirable in politics, as it sometimes precludes the probing discussion of social and political options that are vital to better public policy-making.

B. Sociopolitical order is not one dimensional. Consensus and dissent will usually intertwine, and they will find various forms of expression among groups and organizations. Accordingly, an analysis of the foundations of consensus and dissent calls for a systematic study that traces processes of interaction between organizations and cultural political components.

C. There are various levels of sociopolitical order. One is basic consensus. In this, a certain society can exist as a political system maintaining mutual relations that are identifiably closer than those outside the political system. Basic consensus is a sum achieved by combining organizations with political values and attitudes. Ardent value-derived dissent, organizational factionalism, class divisiveness, and too many conflicting attitudes will hamper a society's maintenance of its qualities as a political system.

D. War both affects and derives from a given political system. Accordingly, any analysis of sociopolitical order mindful of the effects of wars and security crises entails historical scrutiny of the processes and trends in domestic and international politics. Only in this way is it possible to discover how, and indeed whether, a state of war has affected the society and its politics, while admitting the repercussions of other processes not necessarily connected with states of war.

E. The various effects of wars and national security crises are often neither direct nor immediate. They depend on basic properties of society and domestic politics. Emphasis in research must not be placed on war as a stimulus and sociopolitical order as a response. What should be underlined, however, is the importance of the constant interaction between domestic and international politics, and between politics and military power, assuming that all these are indiscreet, not overlapped by frequent, multidirectional influences.

The Field of Research

Israel is well suited to the elucidation and analysis of features of sociopolitical order in democracies in national security crises and wars. The ongoing state of emergency has complicated the evolution of her political regime and the emergence of patterns of consensus and dissent. From 1920 to 1921, the Yishuv was embroiled in an ongoing military struggle. The founding of the state (May 15, 1948) merely aggravated the Arab-Palestinian-Israeli dispute. Up to the present, Israel has engaged in six interstate wars (including the War of 1948 and the Lebanese War, which also took on an interethnic face). In addition, she was passively involved in the Gulf War (1991). Since 1987, moreover, she has been immersed in a protracted and violent interethnic warlike struggle, the Palestinian Intifada. This conflict has not been completely resolved by the Israeli-PLO (Palestine Liberation Organization) interim agreement (September 1993). Yet, that agreement has, at least for a while, reduced the level of strife.

This book deals primarily with interstate wars and dilemmas. To analyze Israeli attitudes toward Israeli Arabs, Palestinians, and the Intifada we must grapple with theories other than those presented here. My relatively limited analysis of the Intifada also stems from another reasons. This book is based on extensive historical documentation, including inside information on political organizations. As of 1996, documentation of Israeli politics during the Intifada were incomplete.

In the following chapters I examine the emergence of consensus and dissent in wars of various types, preventative wars (the Six-Day War, the War of Attrition, the Yom Kippur War); a partly offensive war (the Sinai Campaign); and an aggressive war (the Lebanese War). The distinctions among Israel's wars enable us to analyze how those wars have affected the development of the political regime. From such a study can come much information on the basic features of democracies and on diverse types of national security crises. All, of course, while bearing in mind the features particular to Israel.

The Israeli Society at War: Relevant Research Literature

Not until after the Yom Kippur War (1973) did scientific literature begin to focus on the possible effects of war on Israeli democracy and internal politics. A broad consensus during the War of Independence (1948), the gratification afforded many Israelis by Israel's military and diplomatic cooperation with France and Britain over the Sinai Campaign (1956), and the public's show of solidarity during the Six-

Day War (1967) produced the erroneous impression that wars necessarily bring about national unity. Accordingly, consensus was considered to be a foregone conclusion in relation to national security issues and especially in the deployment of military force. One of the components of the consensus cited to support this conclusion is the need to defend the existence and security of the state.[25] The Sinai Campaign, to be sure, was questioned (mainly by the left-wing Mapam), the controversy aired publicly once the fighting had ended and during the debate over the withdrawal from Sinai and the Gaza Strip. But these important issues remain unilluminated by research. The broad consent during the Six-Day War merely reinforced the rejection of the need to investigate controversies over Israeli use of force.

Attitudes and political events during the 1956 and 1967 wars did not reflect opposition from the political center to Israel's security policy, but only latent controversy over the use of military power. A major reason was the structure of the political system, which in those years was extremely centralist and characterized by the rule of the then-dominant and ruling party, Mapai. As a result, researchers focused on Mapai and its salient features and viewed the analysis of its opposition as unimportant.[26] This research trend persisted throughout and beyond the termination of the War of Attrition (1969–70).

The only major political resistance to the security policy during that war came from the periphery of the political system, and the war was therefore conceived, on the whole, as having the consent of the general public. The fact that during the war a gradual erosion occurred in the public's fighting spirit was not apparent in the early seventies and was not verified until later.

The Yom Kippur War (1973) led to a change in political and social research about Israel. Protest groups formed, and their public expressions of lack of faith in the security-military establishment and the political leadership attested to the onset of changes to come in the political culture. The vigorous endeavors of extra-parliamentary mass movements ("Gush Emunim," 1974, and of "Peace Now," 1978) and the violent resistance to the evacuation of Yamit in April 1982 illustrate some of the shifts in Israeli politics. National security matters were ideologized, political power foci were dispersed more than in the past (due to the loss of dominance of the Labor Party) and the public increasingly participated in national decision-making processes.

18 *A Conceptual Framework*

During the Lebanese War (1982–85) there was significant public contention to political goals, military targets, and war moves. It generated scientific interest in that conflict's impact on Israeli society and politics. Researchers claimed that the national debate following the Lebanese War over the use of military force was one of the highest costs of the war. As a result, those researchers determined that basic national solidarity was undermined. Academic discussions were conducted on the most poignant questions, asking what is a just war? Under what circumstances, if any, is military disobedience permissible in the course of war from a moral, political, and legal point of view?

In the course of the military struggle against the Intifada (1987–93), academic circles widely expanded their study of the possible mutual relations between democratic regimes and states of national emergency. Due to the difficult political and security realities of this dispute, attention was drawn to the risk to valuational, social, military, and political features liable to come about as a result of an internal, political interethnic conflict.[27]

At the same time, research literature made no attempt at methodically singling out features of Israel's wars and the long-standing conflict to explain significant changes in Israel's democratic regime. Attention was directed mainly at the hawk-dove alignment and aspects of the extra-parliamentary opposition. No research focused on the creation of sociopolitical order, the structure of the party setting and political communications, or the differences in attitude between the various elites and the nonruling groups on topics of military force. And almost no attention was paid to the way democratic values, such as freedom of expression, interacted with national security requirements.[28] Subsequent chapters deal with these matters. I shall now outline my principal arguments regarding Israel:

A. Since 1949, there has existed a constant, alternately latent, and undisguised pattern of controversy over how military force is to be conceived and deployed. Differing perceptions drive this controversy as a political phenomenon, in general, and in the context of the Arab-Palestinian-Israeli conflict, in particular. Beyond modifications of style, secondary political changes, or historical events (such as the Egypto-Israeli peace agreement of 1979), no intrinsic alterations took place until the beginning of the nineties in the ingredients of the controversy.

B. Israeli society stands divided on the subject of military force. Although all of Israel's wars have been controversial, that fact is not always mirrored in political behavior. A deep gap exists between the infrastructure of any dispute and the externals of political behavior and consensus. This assertion should not detract from the distinctiveness of some events, for example, the Lebanese War, as events of traumatic impact on Israel's sociopolitical order.

C. Through wars and their attendant political crises, Israel's consensus/dissent balance has been molded by the changing and continuous, multidirectional influences exerted by organizations, political values, attitudes, and behavior. Particular importance attaches to the political dilemmas over armed force, organizational interests to preserve national stability or to challenge it, the state's control and use of information, the divisiveness of political power centers, cognitive reactions and fears, and social sanctions and norms.

D. The mutuality alleged in this book is not the result of one time historical developments. Instead, it is a regularly recurring pattern that shaped Israel through to the early 1990s, producing a fighting society so disunited and polarized as to be in imminent danger of utter breakdown.

E. By juxtaposing the findings here with theories and experiences of other political regimes, I am able to determine what conditions are essential and sufficient in order for Israel to become a civilian society.

Jewish Democracy in Israel

This book focuses on the Jewish political system in Israel (within the pre-1967 borders). I shall not deal with minority populations, since they have their own politically distinguishing features. The Jewish public itself, constantly preoccupied with the legitimacy of a Jewish state, lends itself to no single, common, clear definition of its affinity to the state and its territory.

Three fundamental concepts prevail among the Jewish public on this subject: one declines to recognize Israel as a lawful state. This concept belongs to certain peripheral, usually extra-parliamentary groups found in the "left wing" (that is, the most moderate regarding the Arab-Israeli conflict) of the system. Many of these groups (such as Matzpen) maintain a socialist-communist ethos. Making common cause with them are outer, ultraorthodox-religious groups (preeminent among which is Naturei Karta). Israeli journalists define the proponents of this concept as "anti-Zionist" or "non-Zionist." Another concept casts doubt on the legitimacy of Israel's Jewish foundations, based as they are on nonseparation of state and religion. However, that concept does recognize, in practice, the legitimacy of the state of Israel. Here, on the one hand, the demand is voiced that Israel base itself on secular nationality, without preconditions of Jewishness or religious affiliation. This concept, found among "left wing" groups (Mapam, Ratz, Siah, or groups supporting the Progressive List, for example), also prevails in the "right wing" of the political system (where the "Canaanites" are its sole outstanding adherents). But this concept gives rise, on the other hand, to the demand that Israel be governed as a Jewish-Halakhic state through, primarily, the very considerable bolstering of the national status of orthodox Judaism. This concept is championed by both the Ashkenazi and the Sephardi camps of Jewish orthodoxy, and especially by Agudath Israel. In terms of the third concept, that of the vast majority (some 94 percent of the Jewish population), the Jewish state, from the fifties to the late eighties, is seen as legitimate.[29]

Another important attribute of the Jewish public is its only partial identification with certain elements of democracy. The eighties and the early nineties recorded some increasing support for the replacement of the democratic regime by an authoritarian one. The trend encompassed various age brackets. Accordingly, Israel may be said to lack any comprehensive awareness of the supreme importance of individual and minority rights. The majority, however, still favors free elections, as well as preservation of the principle of majority rule.[30]

Israeli democracy, then, is more a matter of form than substance. Constantly bubbling up in this wartime society are political dilemmas relating to the use of armed force, some of them traceable to the Jewish Yishuv era. The contributions of controversies during the thirties and forties to Israeli politics will be analyzed in the following section.

Ethics and Violence: Toward Realization of the Vision of Independence

Political dilemmas over armed force first found expression in the Yishuv of Eretz Israel/Palestine in the twenties. In 1929, the main worry of the Yishuv was whether to rely on its own strength for defense against Arab rioters or whether, in view of its meager resources, to call for the protection of the Mandatory-British regime. But massive, violent Arab riots broke out in 1929 and were followed by the Great Arab Uprising of 1936–39. During and after these troubles the British authorities did little to protect the Jews. Hence, Jewish political elites unanimously concluded that the Yishuv must defend itself. This basic outlook was shared by both the Mapai and Revisionist camps.

But the political dilemma centered around the deployment of armed force. A dispute evolved between the Revisionist Party and the radical military underground movements, Etzel and Lehi, and the leadership of the Mapai "organized Yishuv" and its military organization, the Haganah. It focused on three issues. First, was it morally right to initiate military actions against Arab population centers to prevent attacks against Jews? Second, how effective was the policy of "restraint," the defense strategy consisting exclusively of military operations in retaliation to attacks on Jews? Conversely, to what extent would "response," the offensive strategy of Jewish actions against Arabs, prevent attacks on Jews? And third, how damaging would using armed force be to the Yishuv's relations with the Mandatory regime and its chances of gaining political independence. These debates thus exposed a pivotal political dilemma: in the absence of sovereignty, how was an interethnic dispute to be conducted?[31]

The concerted assault of the Arab states on May 15, 1948, quelled arguments between those for "restraint" and the advocates of "response." Fear of annihilation and the desire to establish the minimal geostrategic conditions for its preservation, produced a consensus, in principle, for the vital necessity of deploying armed force. A consensus likewise emerged on the principal aims of the War of 1948, which the Jewish Yishuv designated the War of Independence: to secure the existence of the Jewish state and to join western Galilee, Jerusalem, and the whole of the Negev to its territory.[32] Toward the end of the war, as politicians deliberated on the possibility that Israel might agree to an armistice with Jordan (April 1949), the old debate resurfaced of whether to exercise military force or not? But whereas in the past the issue was what military action to take against attacks by Arab rioters, it now transformed into how, for future prospects of peace, to bring hostilities to an end.

The deliberations of the Provisional State Council and the Knesset reflected two basic approaches. The first, held by dominant

Mapai, viewed armed force only as an adjunct to diplomatic efforts, with no, or very limited, strategic value.

Armed force, they said, was essential for beating off military attacks, to found the state, and to establish boundaries to meet the minimal requirements of survival. But it was not a means for resolving the Israeli-Arab conflict. Peace was the diplomatic goal, but imposing a "peace" by military means was undesirable. On three counts, diplomacy was held preferable to armed force. First, coexistence could not be achieved militarily. Thus not even the enemy's defeat would help implement a real peace. Second, its inherent destructiveness rendered the use of armed force immoral, unless responding in self-defense only. Third, using armed force solely to wring a peace agreement would trigger military intervention by the superpowers (Britain, the Soviet Union, the United States) against Israel. The then-Premier and Defense Minister Ben-Gurion, reviewing the security situation before the Provisional State Council (June 17, 1948), pointed out that Israel must remain aware of its small size:

> I know there are limits to our strength, and we must be aware of this . . . which is why we have taken care, this past six months, not to become embroiled in a military clash with England. . . . We have enough on our hands with the military campaign against the kings of the Arab world. We were not eager for this military campaign either—the Arab rulers imposed it on us.[33]

During debates (April 21, 1949) on the armistice agreement with Jordan, Ben-Gurion explained to the Knesset why, despite limited military achievements, Israel must end the war and not inflict final defeat on the enemy. He argued that peace would produce certain crucial political objectives that expressed the core of the Zionist vision (such as, the founding of a haven for the Jewish people and the absorption of immigration):

> In our view, peace, even if only for half a year, is better than non-peace for half a year, because it will enable us to bring more Jews to Israel. . . . No one in this world will look out for our interests. . . . No state anywhere in the world is concerned about us. The world can live without us even if the entire Jewish race is eliminated from earth. . . . Thus, we measure, and

will continue to measure, every political step by a single yardstick: does it widen Israel's options and absorption capability, does it strengthen her security, does it increase the population's living standards, does it bring closer the fulfillment of the vision that pulsates in the heart of the Jewish people, . . . and we say: we do not want to fight them if they do not fight us.[34]

In contrast, the Revisionist Party, which articulated Zeev Jabotinsky's vision, opposed the idea that armed force was meant to be used for survival purposes only. War was also a means of achieving a maximal political, ideological, and security goal—"the liberation of all the territories of Eretz Israel."[35] Consequently, those politicians (most prominent of whom were Arieh Altman, Menachem Begin, Uri Zvi Greenberg) acted to promote this ideology, hoping to gain control of at least the West Bank, which they deemed a part of Eretz Israel and a security-military stronghold. Without that territorial minimum, they believed, there was no use pretending to national objectives, since the state would then face the graver threat of extinction. Thus Altman, addressing the Provisional State Council on September 27, 1948, attacked Mapai's position on the issue of war:

> And if a minimum, and by minimum I mean that which we cannot forgo and for which we are prepared to fight—then it must be the whole of western Eretz Israel . . . without which we have nowhere to settle the millions, . . . and because after the past year's war experience we shall not, in terms of our defense, be able to tolerate that any part of western Eretz Israel shall serve, whether in the shape of the Mufti's state or in the shape of annexation to Abdallah, as a springboard for assaults on us, . . . because for the Arab part, in no matter what combination, whether attached to Transjordan or camouflaged as an independent state, the purpose is one and the same: to embitter our lives, rather than to create any possibility of life for the Arab public resident there.[36]

Hence, the basic controversy over using armed force found expression with the transition from the Yishuv era to the sovereign state era. The 1949 armistice agreements that terminated the War of Independence did not establish peace between Israel and the Arab states. The dual features of this neither-peace-nor-war situation of the fifties were fedayeen operations, and the ever-present threat of an outbreak of war. Israel's political system reviewed possible options in response to the perception of a constant menace to her existence along with acts of terror against the population. The Revisionist Party's successor Herut, for example, wanted to go to war so that a peace agreement could subsequently be enforced but not before the West Bank was "liberated"; meanwhile, Mapam and Maki (the Israeli Communist Party) proposed a strategy of political initiatives and military passivity. The issue of military force thus evoked diametrically opposing views in the political system.

Part Two
A Developing Democracy during the First Stages of Nation-Building

2 The Suez Campaign: Ideological Rift, Preemptive War, and a Dominant Party

Introduction

This chapter begins with an analysis of contentions regarding armed force, while focusing on two parties opposed to the Israeli national security concept, the politically right-wing Herut and the left-wing Mapam, formerly the socialist "Hashomer Hatzair."[1] This perspective enlightened the foremost political dilemmas of the fifties over the question of war. Then, there is an analysis of Israel on the eve, in the course of, and immediately after the Suez War ("The Suez Campaign"). This is a paradoxical case study. The war was ideologically controversial, yet the Israeli political system experienced national consensus. Chapter 2 submits that the structure of the political system, based on the rigorous intervention of the state's apparatuses in social processes, and the hegemony of the dominant political party Mapai, was one of two leading causes of consensus. The other was fear responses and their interactions with threat concepts and political values.

Patterns of Controversy over the War Issue

Four distinct political concepts of the war issue prevailed prior to Suez, each expressing a differing view of armed force. Each was maintained by at least one political party in the political system.

Military Passivity

Maki, a periphery, marxist-oriented party rejected any military action other than in a "war of defense." According to Maki, the Arab/Palestinian-Israeli conflict resulted from Israel's denial of the Palestinian's right to a homeland. Both wars and fedayeen activities, they claimed, would evaporate on two essential conditions: that Israel consent to the return of the Palestinian refugees or compensate those not so electing and that she originate peace based on the Partition Plan of November 29, 1947. Any belligerent initiative was thus deemed superfluous and inadmissible, except an Israeli response to a military attack liable to result in her destruction.[2]

Partial Military Passivity

Mapam theorized that the "shaky peace" between Israel and the Arab states was preferable to war. Mapam's approach, stemming largely from the Marxist-Leninist ethos, was partly moral and partly expedient. War was not the proper way to solve disputes, and war would in any case not settle Israel's security problems. It could only claim more victims and put Israel at greater risk of involvement in a third world war. But with the Arab states stockpiling and the fedayeen attacking, Mapam proposed a two-pronged security policy—the development of the strength of the Israel Defense Forces (IDF) and the use of rigorously selected reprisals. War was to be avoided unless it was a response to an attack or initiated by Israel to thwart an immediate threat to her existence.[3]

Partial Military Activism

Although Ben-Gurion believed that the whole conflict could not be militarily resolved, he did not exclude the opening of military operations. War could justifiably and profitably be initiated to deflect a definite attack on the state. His position in the fifties, and thus the position of Mapai, was that Israel should consider launching a war when a menacing concatenation of political and military events threatened to destroy Israel. Then, diplomacy would be useless in averting the danger, whereas by a preemptive strike, Israel could enjoy the advantage of surprise. Other than that, Ben-Gurion preferred the use of limited armed force, especially for daily security. For him, this controlled initiation of military force would preserve Israel's deterrence vis-à-vis the Arab states, reduce the frequency of fedayeen activity, lower the expectations of the Israeli political and military elites for belligerent initiatives, and project an image of a firm security policy aimed at ensuring public popularity and electoral support. Mapai, as the governing party, gave greater weight to considerations of expediency than to pure ideology and morality. Mapai's approach had the support of Ahduth Haavoda, the Progressives, the religious parties of Hapoel Hamizrahi and Hamizrahi (the National Religious Front), and the religious-orthodox parties of Agudath Israel and Poalei Agudath Israel.[4]

Military Activism

The Herut Party ideology justified the extensive use of military initiatives. The political and military realities of the Middle East, said Herut, rendered it vital at all times to initiate wars against Arab states (Jordan specifically), so as to significantly improve Israel's military-security toeholds, impose peace agreements, and "redeem" the territories (Judea, Samaria, and the East Bank of the Jordan River) of Eretz Israel.[5] The General Zionists concurred but stressed military activism as a principle dictated by pragmatic considerations of national security, while soft-pedaling the "whole Eretz Israel" motif.

How much public support did each approach inspire? Public opinion polls did not become popular in Israel until the seventies. But national security and, especially, the use of armed force were fervent topics heading the public agenda. Some indication can thus be extrapolated from the results of the first three Knesset elections (1949, 1951, and 1955). The passive approach of the non-Zionist left carried the support of only 2 percent of the Jewish population. The semipassive military approach of the Zionist left could claim the support of about 7 percent. But the semiactivist military approach of the Labor camp reaped in 62 percent of Jewish votes. Military activism was advocated primarily by the Israeli right, accounting for about 12 percent of the Jewish public; another 13 percent, predominantly liberals, favored military hawkishness but did so out of military-security considerations without subscribing to the Jabotinski doctrine. And 4 percent, including supporters of ethnic-based parties, did not clearly favor any one approach.

Egypt's nationalization of the Suez Canal and her blockade of the Tiran Straits (July 26, 1956), as well as fedayeen attacks launched mainly from Jordan, put the option of declaring war against Egypt and Jordan high on the national agenda. Political debates between the advocates of the different approaches consequently focused on three principal issues: (1) was it moral to initiate the use of armed force? (2) was an Israeli-initiated war, in fact, an appropriate and inevitable means of resolving the conflict? and, (3) what should be Israel's war objectives? It is interesting to note that these questions remain the fundamental issues of today.

The Suez Campaign embodied partial military activism. As such, it enlisted the support of Mapai, Ahdut Haavoda, the General Zionists, the Progressives, and the religious parties. Herut objected to the timing of the Suez initiative and also to its conclusion before the occupation of the territories of Eretz Israel. Mapam and Maki were against engaging in what they deemed a war of offense.

The Zionist Political Right—Attitudes of Herut: In Favor of "Realization Campaigns"[6]

Herut believed that by means of an Israeli-initiated war, to be conducted under favorable political and military conditions ("propitious opportunities," they called it), Israel would be able to quash the Arab states' ability and will to fight. Such a war would achieve three principal aims: Arab regimes would be toppled and a political alliance formed with minorities in the Arab states as, for example, the Christian Maronites in Lebanon; Israeli sovereignty would be extended over more of the territories of Eretz Israel (meaning, primarily, the West Bank); and the Arab states would have perforce to consent to peace with Israel.[7]

Under the political influence of Menachem Begin and Yochanan Bader, the military-activism approach assumed certain ideational features. The Israel-Arab dispute was conceived as a constant, and its threat was an enduring consequence of the Arab world's inevitable, historical clash with Zionism. Israel was depicted as a "bayonet-surrounded" state, its population inhabiting a "defensive ghetto." Herut then concluded that there was nothing for it to do but to proceed to an initiated war so as to prevent Israel's very destruction: "Ours is not an alternative between peace and war but between seizing the initiative ourselves and improving the terms of the struggle, or handing the initiative over to others."[8]

On October 25, 1956, Egypt, Syria, and Jordan formed a joint army command, and the Herut Party gave vent to its fear of annihilation and its despair of any solution to the conflict other than through armed struggle, "The Government of Israel owes the public an answer—is it really waiting until the noose finally tightens around our neck?"[9] Arab military forces, it warned, would invade the country from the region of Hebron, cutting off the southern part of Israel from the center. And the south, according to Herut, faced danger at the hands of fedayeen units infiltrating from the Gaza Strip and of "the tyrant Nasser, who is plotting to destroy Israel and who constitutes the greatest danger to her existence since Hitler."[10] The possible risk of an invasion by Syrian armies into northern and central Israel was given less weight. Finally, Britain's support for Jordan, the entry of Iraqi armed forces into that country, and Egypt's arms deal with Czechoslovakia led to the only logical conclusion—that Egypt and Jordan were Israel's most dangerous enemies.[11]

Israel, it followed, must await a propitious opportunity for initiating a war in order to set new borders. Such borders would offer greater security than the armistice frontiers that Herut deemed immoral and meaningless in the face of the inevitable threat to Israel. The fight for new borders would also allow Israel to liberate the territories of Eretz Israel that "awaited redemption," thereby renewing the historical bond between the Jewish people and its land. On these grounds, Herut designated the possible war a "liberation campaign."[12] Moreover, limited military operations were considered ineffective for no sooner was such an operation concluded than enemy army units and fedayeen returned to the border areas, dispatching even more squads to perpetrate further attacks. A war of initiative was, thus, considered the means for solving Israel's defense needs.

Herut distinguished between strategy (the initiated-war policy) and tactics (when to initiate the war). The party pointed to the prospects of an alliance between Israel and one of the foreign powers as a promising situation suitable to the massive deployment of armed force. It disagreed with the prevailing policy of nonalignment with the superpowers and endeavored to reinforce Israel's diplomatic ties with Western-bloc countries (mainly the United States and France). An alliance with Western states, Herut presumed, would enable procuring arms and equipment. The party also favored political cooperation based on a shared interest in preventing the spread of communism in the Middle East. In particular, Menachem Begin presumed that collaboration with France was very possible, especially since Egypt had nationalized the Suez Canal, thereby severely damaging French interests in the Middle East.[13]

In September and October 1956, the party felt that circumstances presented a timely opportunity for opening hostilities against Egypt and Jordan. With his regime teetering on the brink, Nasser would be hard put to wage war against Israel. And as Egypt's status in the Arab world declined, her sister states were unlikely to hasten to her assistance in her hour of need. Coups d'état attempted against King Hussein were construed by Herut as denoting Jordan's internal weakness. Meanwhile, on the global plane, the presidential elections in the United States and the Soviet intervention in Poland and Hungary were all perceived as conducive to Israel's launching of a war.[14]

With the failure of the Qalqilya operation (a large military activity against Jordanian police and military forces on October 11, 1956), the party reemphasized that limited military goals were not sufficient and that the instability of the Jordanian regime should be seized for initiating a war and occupying the territories.[15] The Herut organ declared, "The Israeli public, regardless of political stream or party, stands stoutly behind all firm resolve to break the noose and exploit this historic, propitious opportunity to rout the enemy, as he flounders in his domestic vortex of spilled blood."[16]

On October 28, 1956, the Israeli call-up for the Suez Campaign went into effect. Herut presumed that the call-up's purpose was to keep Arab states from intervening in the internal affairs of Jordan. The clause in the government communiqué of October 29 that spoke of mobilizing militarily in order to "safeguard our borders" drew particularly harsh criticism. Herut complained that Israel was depriving herself of the element of surprise and inviting international pressure that would ultimately prevent a military operation. Neither Herut leader Menachem Begin nor any other prominent party member was aware, until noon of October 29, that the IDF was poised to invade the Sinai Peninsula in a joint operation with France and Britain. While Herut militated for the massive deployment of armed force, especially against Jordan, the government planned the Suez Campaign in order to solve Israel's southern frontier problems. Herut was completely surprised by the outbreak of the war.[17]

Herut, however, was not the only party taken aback by the news of the Suez Campaign. Mapam leaders, apprised of the plan just one day prior, had precious little time to decide how to react.

The Zionist Left—Mapam's Positions: Defensive War Only

Mapam embraced one of the basic tenets of Marxism-Leninism, that war was an expression of the ills of the bourgeois-capitalist state. War served the bourgeois, who sought additional economic power with which to exploit the proletariat. But arguing that war was undesirable, Mapam also held that in political circumstances of conflict, when war was a real eventuality, the use of military force must not necessarily be ruled out in every situation. This premise also mirrored the Marxist-Leninist view whereby the workers need not always refrain from war, since they must sometimes resort to armed force to realize their goals.

Mapam adjusted the Marxist-Leninist distinction between just and unjust wars to suit its political concepts. Marxism-Leninism categorized a war as just if, and to the degree, that it was meant to overthrow bourgeois capitalist regimes. What were the political implications of such an ideological statement? Despite its harsh socialist criticism of bourgeois elements in the Israeli political regime, Mapam was a Zionist party. Especially since the mid-fifties, Mapam deemed Israel to be a political framework enabling the accomplishment of rightful social goals. Mapam members were not alienated from the political regime.[18] Military attack by the Arab states was considered an attack by the Arab feudalist bourgeoisie against the Jewish and Arab working class in Israel; it was this working class that bore the brunt of the military and economic burden of the Arab-Israeli wars.

A defensive military stance against "outside attack" was therefore justified by Mapam as an exception to the principle that all war is wrong. As Mapam leader Mordechai Bentov put it, "There is no just war, only just self-defense."[19] Just self-defense was also any war that Israel was constrained to initiate after all political and limited military means for averting an imminent threat to her existence had been exhausted and had failed.[20]

According to Mapam, morality dictated that military power was a factor in broaching diplomatic initiatives with a view to promoting peace on the interethnic plane and ensuring the relief of the plight of the Arab refugees. Success in peacefully resolving the interethnic problem, defined as the hub of the dispute, would foreshadow the diplomatic resolution of the conflict as a whole.[21] Considerations of expediency likewise led to the rejection of the preventive strike policy. In Mapam's opinion, it was not within Israel's capacity to militarily impose a peace agreement on the Arab states. A military victory by Israel would merely intensify the Arabs' hatred and determination to destroy Israel. Even Israel's invidious situation following the Czech-Egyptian arms deal and the blockade of the straits was considered not as bad as war. Awareness of Israel's small size motivated the party's adherence to the principle of self-restraint. It was in this spirit that Mapam's leader, the then-Minister of Health Israel Barzilai, declared, about two weeks before the Suez Campaign was launched, "Israel will not initiate a war, and even a strained and miserable peace is preferable to victory in war."[22]

Mapam's advocacy of a nonaligned foreign policy constituted an important dimension in its approach. The Czech-Egyptian arms deal and the Soviet Union's revelations at the Twentieth Conference of the Communist Party (February 1956) of the terrors of the Stalinist regime heightened opposition to sole reliance on Soviet aid. Yaakov Hazan expressed the majority view at the party center on August 15, 1956:

> The Socialist Bloc effectually faces moral and political downfall. . . . Here they have supported the reactionary forces. We shall have to explain all this. . . . When I meet them, I shall tell them straight that this is one of their sins, that they armed Nasser against us.[23]

Israel should aspire, as Yaakov Hazan put it, "To adopt an independent line without reference to this or that axis."[24] Thus Mapam hoped that Israel's policy would secure from the West the arms needed for fighting the Egyptian army, without risking involvement in the "cold war." A war of offense, by contrast, was defined as exceedingly detrimental to the Israeli interest of forging a nonaligned policy. An attack on Jordan, Mapam assessed, would unleash British forces against the IDF, with a resultant undermining of all of Israel's relations with the West, and an embargo on arms shipments to her as well. Finally, to launch war against Egypt was to invite Soviet active military intervention in a war against Israel.[25]

Domestic politics pivoted around attitudes toward the war issue. Seeking to right the wrong done by the War of 1948, Mapam wanted to rehabilitate the Palestinian refugees. Its ideological advocacy of a state with binational characteristics explains its affinity and sensitivity toward the Arabs of Israel, a tenet that also had a practical political aspect. Arab votes were particularly important to Mapam following the 1954 rift, when the party lost about 40 percent of its electoral strength to Ahduth Haavoda. It was feared that ready support for a war of initiative would severely erode the sympathy of the Arab minority for Mapam. The Israeli Arabs' situation, moreover, must be improved by developing interethnic ties between Jews and Arabs throughout the entire Middle East. But if war broke out, laws and regulations restricting Arab rights in Israel were likely to be enforced. For this reason, too, Mapam felt that military force should be avoided.[26]

The argument that a shipping blockade and fedayeen attacks constituted a *casus belli* was rejected outright by Mapam.[27] Israel's policy on shipping, said Mapam, must be based on "nonintervention in relations between Egypt and the powers, while insisting on the principle of freedom of shipping."[28] As for reprisals, Mapam wanted them executed by small military detachments, targeting only fedayeen departure bases. The danger of escalation toward war would thus be avoided, while reducing the risk of harming Arab civilian populations. At cabinet sessions, Minister Barzilai stressed the precept of "superficial penetration reprisals," while Meir Yaari bemoaned the scope of the reprisals: "The frequency of our responses fills me with concern. Public opinion is forming against us, since for every three or five Jews we kill fifty (Arabs)."[29]

Mapam formed part of Ben-Gurion's governments, including the one that resolved to initiate the Suez Campaign. How, then, did the Israeli left react to the military offensive, and why? What was Mapai's approach to the use of military force, and how did it lead to war? How did the political system in general respond to the outbreak of hostilities?

Mapai as Ruling Party, Decision-Making Processes, and Patterns of Political Participation

In December 1955, the IDF General Staff and the Ministry of Defense completed a plan to occupy the Straits of Tiran. At a cabinet meeting on December 15, this proposal was rejected by a majority vote of the National Religious Party (NRP), the Progressive (Liberal) Party, and Mapam, and Mapai moderates Moshe Sharett, Zalman Aran, Kadish Luz, and Pinhas Sapir. However, the camp opposing the use of armed force dwindled in 1956. The Mapai majority favored military operations even without an immediate danger to the state. In September and October 1956, the prevailing view in Mapai was that the shipping blockade, the fedayeen attacks, and the Egyptian military buildup all indicated that, in a space of only months, Egypt intended to launch an annihilating war on Israel. War was, therefore, justifiable; political and military considerations would dictate when hostilities were to begin.[30]

The decision to include Israel in a joint military operation with France and Britain was received, without reference to any political, national or party forum, by Premier and Defense Minister Ben-Gurion. It was his belief that collaboration with the two powers would avert aerial bombardment of Israeli towns and assure an Israeli victory.[31] According to General Staff plans of February 10, 1956, the war was to last about three weeks, its objects being to destroy the Egyptian military infrastructure in the Sinai Peninsula, open the straits to shipping, and demolish the fedayeen bases in Sinai and the Gaza Strip. Following Ben-Gurion's decision to open the war, two items of this plan were modified on October 25, 1956, to conform to the agreement with Britain and France. The projected duration of hostilities was reset at seven to ten days, and the IDF was ordered to create a threat against the Suez Canal prior to the landing of French and British troops, scheduled for October 31.[32]

Foreign Minister Moshe Sharett was Ben-Gurion's primary foe over the view that reprisals were a routine means of demonstrating Israel's military strength. While assenting in principle to partial military activism, Sharett favored only strictly limited reprisals. These would rarely be appropriate, he affirmed, only when patently needed for purely defensive purposes or as a means of highly selective retribution. Sharett feared that broad military actions might avalanche into war, to the great detriment of Israel's international standing. He also warned against military operations designed to achieve strategic objectives, such as the opening of the straits to shipping. Ben-Gurion consequently wanted his foreign minister out. He had his way, publicly citing as the reason for Sharett's resignation the need to coordinate between the various ministries without changing basic government policy. In his diary, Ben-Gurion noted that Sharett was to blame for the increase in Herut's electoral strength. By this he meant that pressure to moderate Mapai's reprisals' concept had led to its defense policy being identified as weak, with a corresponding increase in public support for Herut's demands that Israel initiate a war.[33] But, in fact, what Ben-Gurion probably wanted was to impose upon Mapai's top brass the acceptance of the possible initiation of the war.

Sharett resigned on June 18, 1956, and was replaced as foreign minister by Golda Meir. Thereupon, all Mapai cabinet members supported Ben-Gurion's security policy. Rank-and-file members were, officially at least, not informed of the preparations for launching hostilities. Neither the political committee nor the bureau, council, or center of Mapai was convened to discuss the war matter until the fighting was over. Ben-Gurion seems to have believed he would have his party's support in any case, especially when the scope of the hoped-for military victory became known. But he worried that premature disclosure of his plans for war might reveal secret information and incite opposition from Mapai moderates.[34]

Mapam's worst fears of a resolution initiating war seemed confirmed by the cabinet reshuffle. Still, party leaders hoped to rely on the "dovish" bloc of the government. This eight-member ministerial bloc consisted of two representatives of Mapam (Israel Barzilai, Minister of Health, and Mordechai Bentov, Minister of Housing); three of Mapai (Pinhas Sapir, of Trade and Industry, Kadish Luz, of Agriculture, and Zalman Aran, of Education and Culture); two from the NRP (Moshe Shapira, of Religions and Welfare, Yosef Burg-Posts); and one Progressive Party member (Pinhas Rosen, of Justice). These, Mapam hoped, would defeat any motion to open a military campaign that might then be tabled by the cabinet's eight hawks (Premier David Ben-Gurion, of Defense; Levi Eshkol, of Finance; Golda Meir, of Foreign Affairs; Mordechai Namir, of Labor; Bekhor Shalom Shitrit, of Police; Peretz Naftali, minister without portfolio, of Mapai; Israel Bar-Yehuda, of the Interior; and Moshe Carmel, of Transport, of Ahduth Haavoda).

Mapam's restraint in not publicly challenging government policy was largely ascribable to its being a satellite of the dominant party. Cabinet sessions were the arena for broaching political dilemmas over the use of armed force. Delegates Bentov and Barzilai tried to discourage extensive reprisals, which, according to Mapam, were liable to result in war.[35] Weeks before the war, some Mapam leaders knew that France, Britain, and Israel were sounding out the possibility of jointly opening war on Egypt. But, confident they could stymie an all-out military campaign, they refrained from publicly criticizing Ben-Gurion's policy so as not to damage their relations with Mapai and be forced to withdraw from the government. Until October 30, 1956, the second day of the fighting, no move was made to convene the party's determining forums, and members were not informed of the preparations for the war.[36]

The Herut top brass, especially leader Menachem Begin, worried that the cabinet could muster a majority against initiating war, resolved to campaign publicly (mainly via Knesset deliberations) for a military strike against Jordan and Egypt. Begin was certain his party's positions had considerable support. "The masses," he declared, "are forming an unbiased opinion." He assumed, as did also prominent party members Yochanan Bader and Haim Landau, that Herut's pressures would alter Israel's defense policy.[37] But no opposition party, outside the political center, could modify Mapai's approach of partial military activism.

While military preparations went ahead, Ben-Gurion proceeded to apprise the various party delegates of his decision. Controversy being a fact of political life, the prime minister was aware of the importance of national consensus as a precondition for success. He wanted to ensure multiparty support, thus forestalling such public opposition as to force his government to deviate from its operational timetable whereby hostilities were to commence on October 29, 1956. This, then, was an interesting situation in which consensus was deemed important notwithstanding the predominance of one party. Yet what Ben-Gurion sought was not public consent in the liberal-pluralist sense of the term, but a consensus among the other political elites. The ability to secure this consensus was part of Mapai's strength. Knesset deliberations and media reporting were ruled out; secrecy was Ben-Gurion's pretext for not allowing any serious discussion, even by the cabinet.[38]

Ben-Gurion first aimed to win the agreement of the coalition parties, approaching them before the cabinet session on October 28—D-Day minus one. He would tackle the opposition only a few hours before the final preparations had been completed. His handling of each party was tailored to his assessment of whether that party would oppose or support his moves. First to be approached, therefore, on October 26, were Ahduth Haavoda members Israel Galili, Israel Bar-Yehuda, Yitzhak Tabenkin, and Yigal Alon. Aware, since mid-September of that year, that Israel was cooperating with France and Britain, these men supported the war initiative. That same day Ben-Gurion confided his decision to the religious camp—Agudath Israel and Poalei Agudath Israel (Kalman Cahana and Yitzhak Meir Levin) and the NRP (Moshe Haim Shapira and Yosef Burg), whom he deemed to be supporters of Mapai's defense policy.[39]

Several important factors secured the Zionist parties' support for the military plan. In their eyes, Egypt was planning an imminent attack on Israel. War could therefore justifiably be begun to defend Israel's existence. The military and political cooperation with the powers was an impressive political achievement in itself, and surely a guarantee of military success. Finally, Ben-Gurion's leadership on military-defense affairs was widely acknowledged, as was the expertise of the army and the military-security establishment in general.[40]

Of all the Zionist parties, Mapam alone opposed the war. Hours before the cabinet meeting, Ben-Gurion informed Yaari, Hazan, Bentov, and Barzilai, also outlining subsequent war moves, including the collaboration with France and Britain. Ben-Gurion asked the Mapam delegates to change their minds before the vote was taken. This they refused to do, while expressing their displeasure at not being told of the forthcoming war until shortly before the cabinet was due to convene.[41]

The cabinet voted in favor of initiating war, the only dissenting votes being cast, in ineffectual protest, by Mapam delegates Barzilai and Bentov. Not even a walkout by Mapam, the prime minister assessed, could blunt the sharp edge of the military surprise. Once the cabinet had opted in favor, Ben-Gurion reported the war initiative to Herut and the General Zionists (October 29, 1956). The juggernaut, he reasoned, could not now be stopped even if they opposed him, because the cabinet had consented and preparations were complete. But those two parties, that had viewed with astonishment Israel's collaboration with the Western powers, concurred under the slogan "The whole nation forms a front," meaning that, opposition or no, they would support the government during the fighting.[42]

Consensus during the Suez Campaign

Battle was joined, and Mapam's newspaper *Al Hamishmar* published an editorial setting forth its official position that although opposed to the government's policy, the party would go along with the consensus formed during the fighting:

> The storm we said could be prevented—has broken out. We shall not, at this hour, revert to the question of whether events need necessarily have taken this course. . . . What matters now

is that we are in the thick of the campaign. . . . The Arab rulers ceaselessly brandish the sword of vengeance and death over the head of Israel. . . . Nonetheless we pointed out another road that might lead to an egress from this state of siege. But now the decisive battle is upon us . . . it is imperative that we stand ready, coiled for action. The people are called to the flag.[43]

Certain party members demanded that Mapam openly declare its opposition. Heading this minority with its patently Marxist and pro-Soviet views was Yaakov Riftin. The party political committee, convening on October 30, 1956, rejected his position, summed up as, ". . . I do not think the muses of peace ought to remain silent," and upheld that Mapam must comply with the consensus for the duration of the war.[44] The party members not only refrained from voicing any criticism, they actually encouraged the masses to volunteer for the war effort, refusing also a request by Maki that they publicly oppose the Suez Campaign.[45]

Herut also had fault to find with the government's moves. It did, however, justify the war, which it perceived as an essential initiative designed to prevent a military attack by the Arab states. Begin declared on November 2, 1956, "For the purpose of this operation, no distinction need be drawn between government and opposition." What troubled Herut was the timing of the initiative that should, it was felt, have come at the latest in 1955, immediately after the Czech-Egyptian arms deals.[46]

During the fighting, both parties kept their views to themselves. Why? Had the campaign changed their attitudes to the war issue? On the contrary, both were still entrenched on their positions of the early fifties. This is evidenced by records of deliberations in party forums, articles penned by their leaders, speeches delivered by their members, and statements made in personal interviews. How was controversy avoided in the course of the Suez Campaign? In other words, how did national consensus take shape?

State and Society and the Creation of Consensus

Mapam's political behavior was considerably influenced by its membership in the government. That it preferred continued participation in government over its convictions on the war issue was shown in June 1956, when the party debated the crisis in relations between

Ben-Gurion and Sharett. At a meeting of the party's political committee on June 14, 1956, Mapam members worried over the possible resignation of Foreign Minister Sharett, who had expressed much of their own views on the use of armed force. Yaari, Hazan, and Riftin were concerned that with Sharett's departure, many more reprisals would occur, and a majority might emerge in the government in favor of launching war against Egypt and Jordan. Said Riftin, "David Ben-Gurion is an expert at ousters. Moshe Sharett was the only Mapai leader who identified with us in the debate over the war."[47] At that debate, Mapam members demanded that their party plainly state its position that the foreign minister's resignation would lead to its withdrawal from the government. But here party leaders Yaari, Barzilai, and Bentov drew the line. Even at the risk of a coalition majority forming in favor of war, they argued, Mapam must opt to stay with the government, if only to realize its social and economic goals. The party must make no move, Yaari warned, that would overlook Hashomer Hatzair's need to have Mapam take part in national decision-making processes. The political committee adopted the leadership's position whereby Mapam would not publicly claim to prevent Sharett's resigning, nor ultimately plan its own withdrawal from the government if he did.[48]

A similar problem confronted Mapam's political committee when it met on October 30, 1956, to debate the government's war initiative. Should Mapam resign from the government, or should it assume responsibility for a policy increasingly incompatible with its principles? This time, the dilemma was tougher, the war had already begun, but to withdraw might damage their public image. Reporting to the party's political committee, Yaari revealed the nature of his talks with Foreign Minister Golda Meir about the war. Meir had told him that Mapam, as a Jewish-Arab party of perceived limited loyalty to the national interest of secrecy over military operations was not privy to secret military moves. Even so, the committee resolved that Mapam would remain in the government. It thus chose to bear collective responsibility for a war it opposed in principle.[49]

Various considerations shaped this political behavior. In addition to the enjoyment of sharing governmental power, Mapam had a number of other important political goals: to improve the workers' standard of living, to foster socialist awareness, and to achieve social and economic equality. Preventing a war of offense took lower priority. Mapam's views on the war, moreover, could have greater effect if aired in cabinet discussions rather than from the opposition benches.[50] Only a minority, led by Riftin, was less concerned with cooperating with Mapai and called for the prompt resignation from the government even while fighting was still under way, both as a protest and to avoid taking collective responsibility for the war. But even they, drawn into the general atmosphere of consensus, refrained from open opposition, and only publicly aired their views after the war had ended.[51]

Thus the intragovernmental collaboration of Mapam and Mapai figured importantly in Mapam's reluctance to oppose the war. In this sense, the Israeli government was a consensus structure, meaning a political organization accommodating institutionalized cooperation patterns and preventing differences of opinion from becoming public controversy. Yet Mapam's vested interest in cooperating with Mapai was also significantly shaped by the political culture, meaning the values of consensus.

Consensus values approved of only limited opposition and pluralism during war. The various parties all feared that controversy would lead the army to view the government incapable of conducting war, and that out of public contention would spring pessimism and a defeatist attitude.[52]

As soon as the war began, all of the political parties, except Maki, and also the press and radio announced that the people were now "a single united front." Political parties and media pundits informed the public that the state was in the throes of a struggle for survival and, to avert the danger, needed not only fighting forces and weapons but also the economic backing of the civilian hinterland (in the form of taxes and special levies), as well as its moral support. The appeal was not in vain. Voluntary organizations immediately directed volunteers to assorted sectors of the economy. This volunteer spirit both demonstrated national consensus and the citizens' desire to make an active contribution toward claiming the victory.[53]

Consensus values weighed heavily with Mapam in its resolve not to resign from the government and to refrain from outright opposition to the war. The Mapam Political Committee accordingly declared, on concluding its discussion of the events of the war (November 22, 1956):

> We rejected the premise that time necessarily works against us, and we regarded every additional period of peace as another

opportunity for increasing our defensive strength. . . . Once the decision was taken to launch the Suez Campaign, there emerged a situation calling for the people to unite in order to stand fast in battle. . . .[54]

Mapam's anxiety that its public image as a Zionist party remain untarnished was another factor influencing its reaction to the Suez war. Israel's cooperation with the Western powers was hailed enthusiastically by the Jewish public, who recognized it as a tremendous political achievement and a solid guarantee of a victory in battle. The excitement communicated itself to a small proportion of Mapam members, mostly young men in their thirties, holding command positions in the IDF and actively fighting. In their view, war had to be initiated to prevent imminent invasion by Egypt.[55] The leaders of Mapam knew just how all-pervasive and enthusiastic the concurrence over the war was.[56] They accordingly determined that any deviation by their party from the consensus values would be construed, by most of the public, as anti-Zionist, thus undermining the war effort and jeopardizing Israel's survival. Sharing these misgivings, Yaari believed that overt opposition to the war would indeed cause Mapam heavy political damage:

And after all, we are all in the same boat. We will not detach ourselves from the people. . . . To turn away would at once mean the end of Mapam.[57]

Mapam's concerns were also affected by the erosion of its electoral strength. The 1954 split into Ahduth Haavoda (a more activist party regarding military issues) on the one hand and Hashomer Hatzair on the other had been politically damaging to Mapam. It lost 42 percent of its electoral strength at the Third Knesset elections (1955), while Ahduth Haavoda won greater support. Mapam therefore adapted its political behavior to the general political atmosphere. Interparty discussions of the war only erupted with the prime minister's summarizing communiqué in Knesset, on November 7, 1956, on the events of the Suez Campaign.[58]

The press, on the whole, followed suit, contenting itself with reporting developments in the field and withholding criticism of the military campaign. As the fighting drew to an end, the press also commented on the war's political implications. The Herut newspaper, however, published three critical articles during the hostilities, claiming that the war proved that the government's security policy had failed and should be replaced by Herut's defense concept.[59] A similar trend manifested itself on the extra-parliamentary plane. While political groups refrained from voicing opposition to the war, the Committee for Peace (the main extra-parliamentary group fundamentally opposed to the initiation of military action) steered clear as well of any public discussion of security issues during the fighting.[60]

Maki rejected the consensus values. It openly opposed the war, calling on the public to support its demand to immediately stop the combat.[61] Hence it was greeted by intolerance, including statements by Jewish parties that Maki's reactions to the fight were anti-Zionist and severely detrimental to the supreme national interest, and accordingly smacked of treason. Mapam's organ, *Al Hamishmar* asserted the following:

> Apart from Maki, which even now, when our people are being put to the supreme test, continues alien to our fateful campaign—all the public is united and tensed for fulfillment of the tasks at hand. This steadfastness is a credit to the workers of Israel, attesting to their full civic maturity and responsibility.[62]

And the Mapai organ, *Davar*, declared the following:

> Isolated and held in contempt were the three delegates of that disaffiliated sect, held in the thrall of extraneous views and orders, and interests so hostile as to identify with the enemies of the people and the state....[63]

The fact that political behavior was influenced by consensus values was largely due to three anxiety responses to perceived threats in the Middle East: (a) the Arab states aspired to destroy Israel (hereafter, grade-1 anxiety response); (b) the threat to Israel's existence was real and, unless deflected, would materialize in a range of months up to one or two years (hereafter, grade-2 anxiety response); and (c) the threat to Israel's existence was unquestionable and, unless repulsed would come to be in a range of days to weeks (hereafter, grade-3 anxiety response).

Grade-1 anxiety responses were common to all political parties. This level of anxiety response, characteristic of the Jewish collective in Israel, derived from the sheer persistence of the conflict.

But various developments, such as the Czech-Egyptian arms deal, elicited higher anxiety responses. There is a positive correlation between these anxiety responses and party positions on the war issue. The more intense the anxiety, the stronger the party's tendency to support a war of initiative, which, since it would procure for the IDF the advantage of surprise, was deemed the most effective means of eliminating a solid threat. And conversely, the less intense the party's anxiety responses, the more inclined it was to prefer diplomacy over a war of initiative, because the threat to Israel's existence would presumably not become tangible in the near future.

Anxiety responses thus significantly affected the shaping of the nation's security concept, and the public's support for or dissent to it. Decision makers would form an assessment of the time factor, that is, when was war expected to be launched against Israel? The more nearly their assessment coincided with the public's anxiety responses, the greater the inclination toward consensus in time of hostilities. And conversely, the more widely the two concepts diverged, the stronger the tendency for dissent to manifest itself in time of war.

In July and August 1956, as international efforts to solve the shipping problem failed; as Egypt nationalized the Suez Canal; as fedayeen attacks became more frequent and Egypt formed a joint military command with Jordan, the Israeli leadership concluded that any prospect of resolving the dispute by diplomatic means had receded, since the Arab states were using the interval to prepare for a war of annihilation. Time, it was thought, was not working in Israel's favor. Premier Ben-Gurion and Foreign Minister Meir accordingly declared that Israel had the "right to defend herself." They hinted that a preemptive strike might be taken to break the shipping blockade.[64]

Similar anxiety responses came from most parties, including members of the opposition. According to the General Zionists (a liberal party), the government ought to regard war of only limited political value. Even though it might solve security problems on the tactical level, war would create other, more serious problems even less susceptible to resolution.

Since the Czech-Egyptian arms deal became known, the General Zionists believed time was working against Israel. But they rejected the Herut argument for a preventive strike. So until mid-1956, their positions were dictated by grade-1 anxiety responses and by the assumption that the passage of time would hamper Israel's efforts to close its military-matériel gap with the Arab states. July and October events intensified the party's anxiety responses to grade-2. General Zionist leaders concluded that Israel should consider a preemptive strike against the Arab states. They supported the government resolution to go to war, in the hope that the danger to Israel's existence would be relieved. They were, moreover, greatly impressed by Israel's military cooperating with France and Britain, believing this would ensure victory.[65]

Anxiety responses of the orthodox-religious parties (Agudath Israel and Poalei Agudath Israel) were likewise shaped by regional developments. Two weeks before the fighting broke out, both parties stated that while all diplomatic means should be attempted to prevent war, "the danger of a war of annihilation is very great," and has been "steadily increasing and, if not now, will be posed in another year or so . . ." Both parties therefore viewed Israel's Suez Campaign as what Member of the Knesset (MK) Yitzhak Meir Levin called a "convenient opportunity."[66]

The Progressive Party, a liberal satellite of Labor, rejected the initiation of what it termed "preventive war" under any circumstances and expressed a grade-1 anxiety response. The whole logic of a war of initiative, it argued, lay in the premise that the enemy could be subdued and made to accept the victor's terms. However, the annals of Europe between world wars showed the futility of attempts to solve political problems with military force. Hadn't Europe failed to solve the German problem in 1918 by imposing a "peace agreement" on the defeated?[67] But anxiety responses in the Progressive Party escalated from July 1956. The events in the Middle East led it to believe that Nasser was stepping up his preparations for war on Israel, who was falling behind in the arms race. Convinced that the proposed military campaign, undertaken in collaboration with Western powers, would prove far more effective than diplomatic means,[68] the party supported Ben-Gurion. Thus grade-2 anxiety responses, developed from July to October 1956, led the Progressive Party to support the war.

Disturbed at the increasing terrorist incidents of September-October 1956, despite IDF reprisals, the National Religious Party (NRP) called for the stepping-up of reprisals:

> We appear to be at the stage that requires those whose job it is to prevent large-scale hostile action . . . to put a stop to the murderous attacks on Israeli citizens. For the hour of decision inexorably approaches.[69]

Even so, the NRP was against initiating a war. It held that "total war" (as defined by party leader Yitzhak Rafael) was not needed for preventing fedayeen attacks.[70] But on learning that Egypt and Jordan had formed a joint command, the party fell prey to fear of an immediate military invasion of Israel (grade-3 anxiety response). Convinced that only a preemptive strike could avert the danger, the party vigorously supported the Sinai Campaign, which it designated a "divinely ordained war," justifiable under religious law.[71]

Ahdut Haavoda was the first coalition party to declare that Israel was facing an imminent threat to its survival. As early as November 11–12, 1955, the party council called for the enlistment of citizens to the aid of the frontier.[72] Its anxiety aggravated by fedayeen attacks, the party announced, "The armistice is constantly being breached, night and day, as part and parcel of the method of preparing for a major war of aggression against Israel."[73] The suffering of its settlements on the Gaza Strip frontier, targeted by fedayeen attacks, led Ahdut Haavoda to resolve on June 29–July 1, 1956, "It is Israel's right and duty to prepare for attacks that our enemies are plotting against us and to take all measures to defend her existence."[74] The party thus supported the launching of the Suez Campaign.[75]

Herut was also not immune to the fear that Israel would very shortly be called upon to fight a stronger enemy whose war aim was the destruction of Israel. Party leaders gave vent to these grade-3 anxiety responses, declaring that the Arab states were creating a "siege" and a "noose" around Israel and thereby threatening her destruction.[76] But however similar the anxiety responses of Ahdut Haavoda and Herut, their basic approaches to the war issue differed. Unlike Herut, Ahdut Haavoda would approve of a war only if it was in response to an existential threat to Israel. All other reasons for war, including those that aimed at "liberating territories of Eretz Israel" and imposing a peace agreement, were unjustifiable.[77]

Mapam, unlike all the other Zionist parties, did not view the activities of July–October 1956 as resulting in an existential threat to Israel[78] and, therefore, remained adamantly against the initiation of war. Later, Meir Yaari put the position bluntly in his speech of November 22, 1956, to the unquestioning acceptance of his party:

> Time could have been on our side since danger was not in the air. Neither can we say that [Egypt] was an international base. It is claimed that 25% of weapons there were of Soviet manufacture. Does that constitute proof? Wouldn't weapons have been

found in Israel? . . . Being constantly under siege, we said we would arm ourselves and hope to be able to prevent war. The imminence of the outbreak of war has not been proven.[79]

Influenced by its own understanding of timing, Mapam deemed the war unessential and hence unjustifiable; yet while it lasted, the party did not deviate from the consensus.[80] Mapam drew a fine distinction between fundamental attitudes toward wars of offense and reactions to them while in progress. Once a war had broken out, no matter what its causes, Israel's survival was at risk; Mapam must, therefore, regard it, as long as hostilities lasted, as a war of defense. The political committee accordingly resolved on November 22, 1956, "By reason of our being placed by our enemies under encirclement and siege, the IDF campaign has become basically a war of defense."[81] The political committee's resolution thus expressed an ambivalent attitude toward the war, deeming it unjust, but its fighting was found to be moral, inasmuch as it had become essential.

Threat concepts were another important factor making for consensus during hostilities. A threat concept is the definition placed by an individual or a group on the identity and nature of the enemy, and the means for coping with it. Grade-1 anxiety, produced second-degree consensus, meaning mutual avoidance of controversy during the war, even if positions and threat concepts differed from those of the architects of the national policy. Grade-2 and -3 anxiety responses, by contrast, evoked threat concepts similar to those of the nation's leaders, helping them engender support for the government's policy.

Seven political parties—Mapai, the Progressives, Ahduth Haavoda, General Zionists, NRP, Agudath Israel, and Poalei Agudath Israel (hereafter, "the parties")—all had remarkably similar threat concepts on a number of issues. All viewed Egypt and Jordan as posing the major threat to Israel's existence. Nor were the two countries distinguishable, according to the parties, from the fedayeen detachments. Fedayeen attacks were a means deployed by the Arab states to undermine the morale of the Israeli population and help them achieve their goal of annihilating Israel.[82]

Thus, events subsequent to the Czech-Egyptian arms deal and, more particularly, the nationalization of the canal helped shape the position of various parties who viewed a war of initiative as expedient. Most perceptibly altered was the attitude of those responsible for shaping Israel's security concept. Originally dismissive of the relevance of a preemptive strike, they gradually changed their mind as Jordan and Egypt proceeded to equip their armed forces.

But it might be misleading to contend that by October 1956 the parties had adopted Herut's approach in favor of a preventive war. Their readiness to support the initiation of war was contingent on strictly defined circumstances. War, to them, was only a means of achieving tactical military goals, primarily a means of thwarting a real existential threat. Herut, however, favored the initiation of war on the grounds that it was in any event justifiable, seeing that the conflict, by its very nature, posed an undeniable threat to Israel's existence irrespective of specific circumstances.

Features of the Suez Campaign

Despite the importance of internal political variables for the formation of consensus, an analysis of the characteristics of the war is also required. By comparison to the War of Independence, the Suez Campaign was deemed a lightning war with a low casualty rating (190 fatal casualties, 0.01 percent of Israel's Jewish—and Druze—population, compared to 6,000 dead, representing 0.89 percent of the Jewish population in the War of Independence). Among the spoils of the Suez victory were the occupation of the Sinai Peninsula, the destruction of the Egyptian military infrastructure there, occupation of the Gaza Strip (where the fedayeen bases were eliminated), and the opening of the Tiran Straits. In general, the political parties were convinced that the brilliant military success thwarted the Egyptian attack and largely took the sting out of the terror problem.

The public was excited, indeed elated, at the assistance of the two powers to a small state, only recently independent. Israeli interests appeared to have gained international legitimacy and the support of world public opinion. The isolation that had encircled Israel in the fifties seemed to be lifting. The general belief was that her collaboration with France and Britain would reinforce Israel's military and political bonds with the West and that the military victory would enhance her deterrence.[83]

When Mapai's leaders announced that an end had been made of the Arab "siege" on Israel and that "the Nasser legend of Israel's elimination is over,"[84] all the Zionist parties joined in praise of the victory. The coalition applauded the decision makers for their wisdom and the military troops for their courage, while the opposition underscored the good army planning and combat capabilities but overlooked the government's contribution to the attainments of the war.[85]

Even during the fighting, news of military successes reached the civilian hinterland through the media (primarily the press), which, subject to security censorship, omitted reports of failures. The news, however, had no more than a limited effect on the formation of consensus; as previously described, consensus prevailed even before the battle. It was undoubtedly nourished, however, by media reports of military accomplishments.[86] Positive media reporting was not only the result of elite pressure. The media also censored itself so that, in deference to consensus values, it did not constitute a pressure group for the policymakers, nor did it make any distinctive input to the decision-making processes. Indeed, where dissent emerged it was only with an exceedingly confined expression.

Controversy Peripheral to the Political System

Members of Maki (the Arab-Jewish communist party) mostly expressed their views on the war issue by conventional modes of political participation: they delivered speeches in Knesset, wrote criticisms and commentaries in *Kol Haam* (the Maki newspaper), and convened public meetings ("popular assemblies"). On October 15, 1956, Maki issued a manifesto reading: "The IDF shall not pass beyond the borders of Israel! We shall not grant the imperialists their wish, we shall oppose war, we shall defend the peace." Three days later Maki staged a demonstration in Tel Aviv under the slogan, "We are for peace—against war." On October 28, the front page of *Kol Haam* was emblazoned with the headline, "Our present imperative is the struggle to preserve peace." When the call-up notice was published on October 29, Maki submitted an urgent motion to the Knesset agenda calling for "a discussion of the danger of war and how to prevent it." The speaker, however, announced that the plenary session scheduled for October 30 had been canceled due to the outbreak of hostilities, and the discussion never took place. The rules of the democracy were somewhat tabled because of the war, thus limiting political behavior.[87]

Maki declared the Suez campaign to be a wrongful war of initiative, fruit of the "militarist" Israeli government policy, which served French and British interests—to control the Suez Canal and undermine the stability of the Arab world. The party called upon the public to unite in the struggle to save the peace and upon the government to terminate the fighting and withdraw the army to the 1949 armistice lines. A number of factors contributed to Maki's willingness to publicly air its views while fighting was in progress. As an opposition group on the periphery of the political system, Maki was not included in any political arrangement for the distribution of national resources and took no part in national political decisions; nor was it made privy to security information. Its communist ideology was jarred with the political concept of dominant Mapai, and with the prevailing ideology of the Israeli political culture.[88]

Maki felt alienated from the political establishment, which partly explains its public disavowal of and opposition to the war. Maki would countenance no possibility of collaboration with any Jewish Zionist party, even the left-wing ones, on issues of war and peace, since it regarded their views as utterly erroneous. Whereas Mapam justified the war by circumstances, Maki denounced it as clearly immoral and having no redeeming features or mitigating circumstances. Defined by its members as a non-Zionist party, Maki claimed that to refrain from opposing the war was tantamount to aiding and abetting the "ruling class," to the great disadvantage of the proletariat. Mapam's positions, they said, were accordingly a political compromise and ideological digression.[89] Maki, moreover, could see no advantage to joining the consensus. Protest, on the other hand, could make the public aware of the uniqueness of Maki's views, and rally to its standard those political forces that were opposed to the government. *Kol Haam* stated,

> "National unity" ostensibly prevails now, from Herut to Mapam inclusive. Maki, on the face of it, stands outside the "national unity." . . . But below the surface, the picture is quite different. . . . Maki is the advance company, the guiding and unifying force for all those patriotic and democratic forces in Israel that oppose the war.[90]

Opposition became more pronounced after termination of the hostilities. Different political parties enunciated a challenge to the Israeli government.

The Crisis of the Withdrawal from Sinai and the Gaza Strip (November 5, 1956-March 31, 1957)

After the fighting ended, the superpowers began pressuring the Israeli government to withdraw from the Gaza Strip, the Straits of Tiran, and Sinai. Two coalition parties (Mapam and Ahduth Haavoda) and one opposition party (Herut) were opposed to withdrawal, calling for the Gaza Strip to be annexed to Israel. Both left-wing Mapam and right-wing Herut claimed that had the government acted in accordance with their views on the war issue, there would have been no foreign pressure. The crisis thus gave rise to a form of "retrospective dissent" or postfactum opposition to the war that was influenced by postwar events. It, however, reflected the different positions over the use of military force and how the war of 1956 may have modified them. I shall first discuss the views of Mapam.[91]

Some members of Mapam, in its branches and political committee, scathingly criticized their party's positions and political behavior. They thought that as soon as it learned of the projected initiation of a military campaign, Mapam should have more emphatically denounced the errors of Israel's defense policy; when the resolution to initiate the war was actually adopted, Mapam, they said, should have resigned. Others believed that Mapam had in fact acted with the courage of its convictions but that certain of its political principles needed to be modified in view of the military achievements. Was a war of initiative not justifiable, they reasoned, when there was any danger of an enemy attack if it could secure the advantage of military surprise? But most Mapam members remained entrenched in their attitudes, causing the party to declare that the war had been unjustified since it had sprung from a nonessential military initiative. Yet, they did not condemn its membership in the government.[92]

Mapam believed the war had three military objectives: (1) to liquidate the fedayeen bases; (2) to lift the blockade on Israeli shipping in the straits; and (3) to destroy Egyptian armed forces in Sinai and the Gaza Strip. There were two political objectives: (a) the overthrow of the Nasser regime in Egypt and (b) the imposition of a peace agreement on Egypt. It was considered that the war had been started to achieve political or strategic goals, such as Egypt's recognition of Israel, which, if reached through military force, were impermissible.[93] The withdrawal crisis, asserted Mapam, was directly traceable to the defects of the security policy, for the world saw Israel as an aggressor. Wrote *Al Hamishmar*:

We apparently set one small wheel in motion—but it quickly transpired that a huge universal mechanism had been activated. The cannon roared in the vastness of the Sinai desert—and blood rolled like thunder in the world's skies. This is a fact we must bear in mind when plotting our political and security path. . . . A small nation whose fate hangs in the balance . . . must be cautious and wary, and, unless constrained so to act by exigency must not arouse or invoke upon itself the dangers of today that may possibly be avoided tomorrow.[94]

Mapam's prognosis was that the United States and the Soviet Union would force an Israeli withdrawal, thus negating the military gains and the resolution of the basic causes of the conflict.[95] Why did Mapam continue in government, and why did it not openly air its views during the fighting? Party leaders pointed to the distinction between the totally unjustified war and the unjust war launched and waged under justifying circumstances. In the face of a war of the first type, they claimed, Mapam would have resigned from the government. But since the war was fought under justifying circumstances, Mapam must not resign lest, by making an exception of itself, it damage the national unity so necessary for victory. Most Mapam members saw the campaign, unjustified in itself, as having been launched in justified circumstances, since the military operation averted Egypt's war plans.[96]

How and to what extent Mapam's attitudes to the war issue were applied to the political reality depended on various factors, but they remained basically as they were before the war—diametrically opposed, especially in their ideological aspects, to those of Herut. According to Herut, the war itself was justified; it was Israel's defense policy that was basically wrong.

Herut viewed the Suez Campaign as embodying its own concept in favor of a war of offense.[97] Begin, with whom this perception originated, viewed the war as an Herut political achievement:

The moral and historic meaning of the formidable operation of our heroically glorious army—the operation of assault, advance, disseverance, flanking, encirclement and strike, the subjugation, the subdual, the liberation, the occupation and the victory—is lawful national self-defense. We have special reason to rejoice that now, after the event, the entire nation recognizes the fact.[98]

Party spokesmen stressed, however, that Mapai had chosen a bad time, a veritable emergency, in fact, rather than an opportune moment, for initiating the war. The Herut newspaper maintained the government should have attacked two or three years earlier:

> The many opportune moments we had prior to the Czech-Egyptian arms deal were missed: times when Egypt could avail herself neither of Russian arms for the military confrontation nor Russian pressure for the political confrontation.[99]

True, the government's failure to take advantage of these opportunities had not prevented either the Israeli-French-British collaboration or the military victory. But the delay in initiating war had greatly worsened Israel's international standing. Had the Soviet Union not stepped up its military and political support for Egypt in 1955, Israel would not have been under the threat of Soviet economic, political, and military sanctions, or at least not to such a degree. Herut feared the threat of superpower sanctions would force the army to withdraw, whereupon Israel would again be in peril.[100]

For Herut, political and military realities were seen in the light of its pre-Suez war concepts. Seeing that the circumstances attending that deployment of force and the objectives for which it was deployed coincided with Herut's reasons for favoring a preventative war, as well as the fact that the venture ended in victory, the party concluded that the principles of military activism had been vindicated. The victory, Begin claimed, had done away with Herut's "extreme right-wing" image.

Neither the war nor the subsequent crisis mitigated the bitter controversy over military force, which did not, however, always find full expression in political behavior. As the scheduled military pullout approached (from Sinai on January 15, 1957, and from the Gaza Strip on March 8), Mapam, Herut, and Ahduth Haavoda concentrated on trying to prevent the withdrawal, while Mapai, the ruling party, set itself to explain government policy. The focal issue on the national agenda, seen as vital to national security, was would Israel be forced to withdraw immediately? The war issue, at this stage of the political crisis, seemed irrelevant. The trend continued after the withdrawal when the national agenda highlighted economic items, such as the wage and tax-collection policy. Latent rather than extinct, these issues would once more occupy the national agenda as the 1967 War hovered on the brink.

Summary and Conclusions

As the principal means of political communication, the parties carried political messages from the public to the political elite and, more especially, from it to the public. They accordingly both shaped and gave expression to consensus and dissent regarding the war. But how influential were extra-parliamentary political groups, volunteer organizations, the army, and the media in forming consensus and dissent? Before hostilities began, the Histadruth, the Committee for Peace, and Israeli radio and press reflected interparty controversy on the war question but not during the fighting. The Histadruth, which since independence had not taken a direct hand in shaping the security concept, now joined the consensus, as did, for the most part, the media. Mapai's political dominance, its control of the state media, and especially its hegemony in the Histadruth all helped promote consensus. Few groups could oppose Mapai. The Committee for Peace fell silent during the war when, on the strength of ideological differences, Mapam members refused to cooperate with Maki delegates. Several organizations urged the public to volunteer, also reflecting consensus.

The army senior command, which tended to support Mapai's political concepts, also supported the war. Since Israel is a "democracy in uniform," various attitudes in the political system were echoed in the military, whose loyalty, however, was given primarily to Mapai. This is why, for the duration of the hostilities, the military shared in the Suez Campaign consensus.[101]

Each political party had its own fairly ideological cohesive leadership and strongly influencing party power centers and internal apparatus. Any party leadership could thus easily come out in favor of consensus during war without risking meaningful opposition in its ranks. In Mapam, a minority that opposed remaining in the government was dissuaded from seceding. Mapai accepted Ben-Gurion's decision to initiate war even though neither the war itself nor the preliminary negotiations with Britain and France had been discussed (much less approved) at any party forum.[102]

Mapai's dominance of the political system also significantly helped create consensus. Since no government or coalition could be formed without Mapai and its prime ministership and foreign affairs, defense, education, and finance portfolios, most parties, representing some 80 percent of the Jewish population, were sure to support it. The tribute exacted from satellites such as Mapam was cooperation with Mapai in the government, the Knesset, the Histadruth, and the municipalities. Mapai could thus forge consensus on matters of national security as well. The other parties' strong tendencies to conform were also helpful to Mapai. Maki, a peripheral party, was powerless to create opposition at the hub of the political system. Mapai enjoyed extensive public support, having fostered a widespread belief that the best experts on national security were to be found in its cadres; people were generally satisfied with the way it functioned before and during the fighting as ruling party, so that dissent could hardly trickle in from the periphery to the center of the system.

The war was a response to the remorseless ambition of the Arab states to destroy Israel. Its declared aims, perceived as just because of Israel's frustrative intent, had the support of all parties excepting Maki.[103] A broad consensus also extended to military war moves, which the majority considered justifiable, being part of the struggle against a quantitatively stronger enemy. Claims by Maki that during and immediately after the war Israeli soldiers and security personnel had perpetrated acts of robbery and murder in the Gaza Strip were not reported by the media, nor did they find any echo in the political system. The success attending military operations was also significant in helping Mapam and Herut to decide against offering any public opposition while the fighting lasted. Mapam, as a government member, wanted to share the credit for the military victory, while Herut planned to argue that the military-activism approach to war was vindicated by the victory. This chapter has shown that the features of the war itself were overshadowed by the elements of the political system.

Conspicuous among the immediate political factors directly producing consensus were party positions on the war issue, anxiety responses, and threat concepts prior to and during the war, as well as consensus values and consensus structure. In Mapai, NRP, Ahduth Haavoda, the Progressive Party, Agudath Israel, Poalei Agudath Israel, the General Zionists, and Herut, anxiety responses and threat concepts were the prime causes of their support of the war.

Most important were their anxiety responses that, together with members' notions as to the effects of time on the conflict, were largely instrumental in shaping the party threat concepts. Consensus values were also significant, as reflecting the political culture of a society in wartime, a nation under siege, fighting for its life, and that regarded preparation for war as a sine qua non for its survival.

The NRP, the Progressives, and Ahduth Haavoda were also influenced by being members of the government.

Their consensual behavior was secondarily guided by their desire to take part in the decision-making process, their dependence on the dominant party, and Ben-Gurion's leadership. But, basically, these parties followed their own threat concepts and anxiety responses. The progress of the campaign merely confirmed the justice of their political position. As for Mapam, by virtue of consensus structure and consensus values, it did join the general public trend in the course of the hostilities.

There were other immediate factors that, although secondary, were still important for the formation of the consensual political order:

1. Even those media figures who resisted the war were pressured by consensus values. They therefore refrained, while the fighting lasted, from overtly opposing the war. At that time, Israel had no such entity as the "fighting press" that came to the fore in the eighties, posing an opposition to the political establishment even in the course of wars.

2. Ben-Gurion was adept at overcoming ideological rivalries, especially with Herut, to elicit the cooperation of all Zionist party leaders. His was a distinctive brand of leadership, especially considering the dominant status of Mapai.

3. The public was not vouchsafed all information pertinent to the circumstances in which hostilities commenced or how they were conducted. General information on war aims and general news on Israel's cooperation with the powers did reach the leaders of the various parties. A "blackout" was imposed, however, on the war preparations, after the military censor reached an agreement with the Israel Daily Press Editors' Committee that news of arms shipments from France to Israel would not be published. This restraint, plus the fact that news of developments was sprung on party leaders only shortly before the outbreak of hostilities, helped forge the consensus Ben-Gurion wanted. As the parties now had no time to convene their institutions before the fighting started, no significant public criticism could or would be voiced against Israel's security policy.

The political activity of the public, including Maki's supporters, did not, during the war and the subsequent crisis, exceed the bounds of routine and conventional participation. This was due to a high level of political institutionalization, reflected in the centrality of the parties as virtually the sole vehicle of political life.

Herut staged demonstrations against the withdrawal from Sinai and the Gaza Strip, an unconventional move in itself in the fifties, when demonstrations on security affairs were an almost unheard-of departure. But this political activity, too, was strictly party-controlled. The eight Herut-inspired demonstrations were not expressions of an extra-parliamentary movement. They were, on the contrary, party-orchestrated activities designed to confer a seal of public legitimacy on Herut's positions by means of allegedly spontaneous mass support.[104]

Since public attitudes found expression through political parties, the consensus during hostilities may be said to have encompassed some 95 percent of the Jewish population—making it practically unanimous. Dissent was engineered and expressed primarily through Mapam and Herut at the secondary centers of the political system and Maki at the periphery, expressing after the war, the views of about 20 percent of the public.[105]

3 The Six-Day War: Political Crisis and War of Consensus

Introduction

Chapter 3 discusses the attitudes and structures of the debates on military force between 1957 and 1967 and the effects of both the 1956 war and the national party structure on the diversity of these attitudes. It explains the sociopolitical anatomy of political dissent during the waiting period. It also analyzes how interactions between public fears (as the predominant factor), political coalitions, threat concepts, and cultural values, during and in some relation to dramatic international events, account for the shaping of prewar consensus. Finally, the problematic meaning of public consent for the war management and its aftermath is reviewed.

Traditional literature has emphasized how the brilliant Israeli military victory in the Six-Day War in 1967 shaped consensual reactions to the war. This chapter asserts that the story of how political order was shaped regarding the war is much more complex. It demonstrates how deep the rift was over the use of military force in the period from 1957 to 1967. The chapter shows that fear responses, a grand ruling coalition, and the formation of threat concepts and consensual values prior to the outbreak of hostilities molded the political order on the eve of the war, during its management, and in its aftermath. Some of the reasons for the future blindness of many Israeli politicians and military personnel to the destructive political outcomes of that war are also explored.

Effects of the Suez Campaign on Attitudes toward the War Issue

Four essential positions on the war issue dominated the political scene before the waiting period. The controlling party's stand was partial military activism. The other three, expressed mainly by parties opposing the government's policy, were military passivity (primarily Maki); partial military passivity (Mapam); and military activism (Herut). Only two extra-parliamentary political groups, both peripheral and tiny, expressed very dovish opinions on the war issue. One was the pacifist Matzpen, which upheld a Trotskyist ideology, the other was the socialist "Committee for Peace," which rejected pacifism but wanted numerous restrictions on the use of armed force.[1] Pre-Suez Campaign issues still exercised the public: was it moral to initiate the use of armed force? Given Middle Eastern realities, was it worthwhile for Israel to initiate wars? What should Israel's war objectives be?

Contrasting principles notwithstanding, Mapam and Gahal (Herut-Liberal bloc) joined the National Unity Government (1967), while two radical left-wing peripheral parties—Maki and Haolam Hazeh—remained in opposition throughout the hostilities. The four parties' motives in joining the coalition in 1967 can best be understood in light of the prewar controversy that surrounded the war issue.

Mapam's positions were unchanged since 1956. Israel's failure to impose peace by means of the Suez Campaign proved how vital diplomacy was in achieving peace. The solution to the conflict rested in a settlement based on resolution of the Palestinian-Arab problem; demilitarization of the Middle East; Middle Eastern neutrality in the cold war; and a comprehensive peace with the Arab states. Israel, said Mapam, must refrain from any military activity that could alter the status quo created from the withdrawal from Sinai and Gaza. Thus, from 1957 to 1967, Mapam preferred a state of neither-peace-nor-war, "shaky peace," as Yaakov Hazan put it, over war. Deterrence, rather than military operations, was stressed.[2]

Partial military passivity was also an essential precondition for Israel's independence from the Western powers. The Suez Campaign, according to Mapam, showed that Israel needed military aid to fight offensive wars. Such was in the interest of Britain, France, and the United States since the defeat of an Arab state upset its relations with the Soviet Union. The direct result of activism, argued Mapam, would be a military pact or at least regular military cooperation with Western powers. Israel would accordingly become part of the Western bloc and face the Soviet threat. Partial military passivity, on the other hand, did not involve the acquisition of huge quantities of arms, and Israel already possessed what she needed for self-defense. Military restraint also obviated the need for formal alliances since, in case of attack by the Arab states, the powers would in any case impose sanctions on the aggressor and come to the aid of Israel—the victim. Its approach alone, Mapam concluded, would facilitate the neutral foreign policy needful for Israel's survival.[3]

Mapai, the dominant party, took a different view. Its approach formed Israel's national security concept and was accepted by the National Religious Party (NRP), Agudath Israel, Poalei Agudath Israel, the Liberal party, and by Rafi and Ahduth Haavoda.[4] Mapai concluded that the brilliant military victory in 1956 had resulted from Israel initiating force and cooperating with the Western powers. The withdrawal crisis, however, proved that not even victory ensured political achievements unless suitable interpower guarantees allowed military attainments to be fully taken advantage of. Therefore, said Mapai, before launching any war, Israel should determine to what extent she would be able to realize the fruits of a military victory.[5] Accordingly, it supported a defensive strategy of avoiding war and relying on deterrence.[6]

This being so, Mapai proceeded to define the events that would serve as a *casus belli*: (a) an Arab blockade on shipping in the Straits; (b) entry of Arab forces into Sinai (demilitarized following the withdrawal in 1957); (c) an altered status quo in Jordan, due to a change of regime, the entry of military forces hostile to Israel into Jordanian territory, or a concentration of military forces on the west bank of the Jordan River; (d) terrorist attacks that jeopardized Israel's existence; and (e) diversion of the Jordan River.[7]

Of these, the first, third, and fourth predated the Suez Campaign, which followed a blockade in the Tiran Straits, recurrent fedayeen attacks, and the "defense" pact formed between Egypt and Jordan. The second and fifth, however, reflected post-Suez realities.

If any of the events defined as *casus belli* occurred, asserted Mapai, policymakers must view them as severely damaging Israel's deterrence and consider initiating a war to prevent an existential threat. Current security problems, shooting incidents, and attacks by terrorists were not perceived as real threats to the state's existence and did not justify war. The proper response to such security hazards was punitive reprisals using limited forces so as to prevent escalation.[8]

These principles differed sharply from those guiding Herut. Herut did not distinguish between "current security problems" and the danger of interstate war. Frequent shooting incidents and terrorist attacks, mainly on the Jordanian and Syrian frontiers, posed a threat to Israel's existence inasmuch as they eroded the public morale.[9] Hence, Israel must respond in full. Limited reprisals were valueless and allowed enemy units to return to base and sortie for further attacks.

Herut called upon the government to initiate either a broad-gauge military action or a war in order to occupy the territories of the enemy. Israel should then annex these territories. Herut considered this a means of preventing the return of hostile forces to areas offering strategic advantage, while at the same time liberating areas of Eretz Israel.[10]

The military passivity of Maki and Haolam Hazeh varied significantly from the Herut position. Maki was predominantly the communist party, and Haolam Hazeh was founded as a Jewish socialist party. Both asserted that the dispute could be solved only by a comprehensive agreement with the Palestinians. Recognition of the right of return of the Palestinians was seen as the desirable solution.[11] The two parties rejected the initiation of war. In moral terms, they asserted that the "Arab-Palestinian people" had a "basic right over Eretz Israel." Expediency taught that offensiveness would produce no decisive victory but would cause the Islamic peoples and the communist-bloc powers to unite against Israel. The events of 1956–57 proved the sterility of force, especially considering the temporariness of military gains. Moreover, the initiation of war meant enlisting the support of American lead imperialist nations, which sought to destroy the "toiling Arab masses," while the "toiling Jewish masses" needed ties with communist states.[12]

War was justifiable only as self-defense against a threat to Israel's existence; Israeli military activity must be designed to repulse the enemy over the state frontiers. The two parties also denounced the policy of reprisals, which neither prevented nor deterred the enemy from attacking. As a substitute, the parties recommended constructing a line of fortifications, whereby the military could seal the northern and eastern borders and prevent infiltrations.¹³

Effects of Changes in the Political-Party Structure on Political Dilemmas and the Use of Armed Force

The important changes in party structures in 1965 did not significantly affect the pattern of controversy over the war issue. The "Alignment" (composed of Mapai and Ahduth Haavoda in the Labor camp) still favored partial military activism. Yet, Ahduth Haavoda had a strong hawkish camp, headed by Yitzhak Tabenkin, which justified the use of force not only for averting existential danger but also for liberating territories of Eretz Israel. This approach was rooted in a strong sense of historical affinity with ancient Eretz Israel, of which the West Bank of the Jordan River formed a part.¹⁴

In 1965, a major change came about in the Labor camp. Ben-Gurion resigned from the leadership of Mapai, due to disputes with power groups in his party. He founded Rafi, the Israel Worker's Party, joined by Moshe Dayan and Shimon Peres. Rafi's approach to the war issue was slightly more activist than that of Mapai, headed by Levi Eshkol. But there was no fundamental difference in the positions of the two parties.

The right-wing camp, by contrast, even after Gahal (Herut-Liberal bloc) was formed, upheld the military activist approach. For Herut, the merger with the Liberals legitimized the political center and would eventually bring the electoral support it would need to form its own government. Negotiations with the Liberals skirted the use of armed force but discussed the Eretz Israel question, which remained unresolved. The Liberals rejected Herut's claim that the liberation of territories of Eretz Israel was a prime political goal.¹⁵

The controversy over permanent frontiers related to differing views of war and varying ideologies regarding liberating Greater Israel. Argument was avoidable, however, since Herut did not believe that the time was ripe for war on Jordan. And both parties, especially Herut, wanted to keep Gahal intact. Contrary to its pattern in the fifties, Herut remained reticent during the waiting period. Frequent border incidents with Syria topped the national agenda from

1965 to 1967. Gahal unanimously believed it was necessary to initiate broad-gauge military action, even war, against Syria to stop its support for the terrorists and to prevent her from infiltrating military and civilian personnel into the demilitarized zones and initiating gunfire.[16]

The founding of Gahal thus did not result in different positions, only different phraseology. Herut leaders balked at publicizing Begin's statement, at the Herut Party Center on March 23, 1967: "It is your right not merely to repulse the aggressor but also to attack him." The leadership of newly formed Gahal announced that Israel had the right to "assertive self-defense" known in international law as the right to "national self-defense."[17]

The approaches regarding military action were tested when the boundaries between the international system and the national system became even more blurred.

The War Issue in Time of Political Upheaval: Controversy during the Waiting Period (May 15, 1967–June 5, 1967)

On May 16, 1967, Egypt strengthened her armor force and infantry corps in Sinai. On May 17, Egyptian ruler Gamal Abdel Nasser addressed a demand to UN Secretary U-Thant that he evacuate the UN Emergency Force from the Egypt-Israel border. That same day, two Egyptian armor divisions were brought into eastern Sinai. Prime Minister Levi Eshkol responded with full mobilization. On May 22, 1967, Egypt denied passage to all vessels either flying the Israeli flag or carrying supplies to Israel through the Tiran Straights. On May 25, Egypt brought forward another armor division to eastern Sinai, and on June 1, 1967, entered into a "defense pact" with Jordan.

These developments, as well as Nasser's boasts of the coming destruction of Israel, electrified the political system and the military echelons, hitherto complacent in their belief that no war loomed in the next few years. The rapid march of events, over a mere two weeks, and other factors produced a period of political upheaval (crisis).[18] The response of the Western powers, primarily France and the United States, was disappointing. The political elite seemed, to various public sectors, to be avoiding needful decisions regarding the oncoming danger. The effects of this political dissent for policymakers have been described in detail mainly by Michael Brecher and Benjamin Geist.[19] I will, however, analyze the manner of reaction to the political upheaval by the Israeli public and her political system as a whole.

On learning of the shipping blockade (May 23, 1967), all parties agreed that government failure to diplomatically restore the status quo ante justified the use of armed force in order to thwart an imminent danger to the state's existence. Even Mapam, Maki, and Haolam Hazeh concurred.[20]

But all parties, including Gahal, felt a waiting period was called for, in which to try all diplomatic options (primarily, an appeal to the superpowers). Only if all else failed should the government resort to the military option.[21] As an ideological and strategic principle, Herut favored the war of offense, but the "opportune moment," the intersection of political and military conditions, had not come for a war against Egypt. Israel's foremost security problem was Syria's support for the terrorists, and so Israel should focus her military efforts on the northern frontier. Egypt, Herut theorized, did not intend to attack but was merely attempting to deter Israel from attacking Syria, and, under interpower pressure, Egypt would surely withdraw her troops from eastern Sinai. Most Herut members would have been content with the status quo on the southern border, as it was until May 1967. Firstly, because a Sinai Peninsula free of foreign forces and providing Israel with strategic depth could serve to guarantee Israel's security. Secondly, Sinai, not a part of Eretz Israel territory, did not need "liberating" by force. The Liberal Party concurred with this position.[22] Indeed, the naval blockade was seen as a severe injury, and Gahal called, during a meeting of the Knesset Foreign Affairs and Defense Committee on May 23, 1967, for a military strike. However, military delegates to that meeting asserted that the army would not be hurt by a few more days' waiting. Likewise, Elimelech Rimalt and Haim Landau, on behalf of Gahal, added their voices to the committee majority in favor of postponing the initiation of hostilities.[23]

Political debate focused on the issue of how long the government should confine itself to diplomacy to restore the previous situation on the Egypt-Israel border; many thought that military passivity was damaging to Israel's deterrent power and ability to prevail. The more a party favored military activism, the shorter the waiting time it was prepared to accept. By contrast, the more a party favored military passivity, the longer a waiting period they advocated.[24]

Public debate also flourished outside the Knesset. For the first time in Israel's history, extra-parliamentary activity was a major component of debates over public policy on the war issue. On learning of the blockade of the Tiran Straits, groups and individuals, prompted by fear for the state's survival and dissatisfaction with the government's seeming vacillation, demanded that a "national unity" government be formed and war declared.

One distinction made by theoretical literature was between extra-parliamentary groups alienated from the political establishment and whose protest aimed to destroy or significantly restructure the regime, and those organizing solely out of political dissatisfaction and wanting governmental reform. Protest groups active in the waiting period belonged to the second category. Their premise was that the Israeli democracy could win the war, provided that the most suitable political figures were appointed to leadership. Extra-parliamentary activity was the only means of exerting political influence. Individuals and groups believed that since Levi Eshkol and Golda Meir appeared indifferent to public demands for war, only extra-parliamentary activity would convince the nation's leadership of the strength of the opposition.[25] The result was a reshaping of certain features of the sociopolitical order.

One type of extra-parliamentary activity included citizens who were in anonymous groups, having no political apparatus or organization. Some of them supported an active, others only a partially active, military approach. They printed large notices on the front pages of the Israeli Hebrew-language daily press, collected petitions, and sent cables to the prime minister. Both time-consuming and costly, these actions were accordingly pursued mainly by members of the free professions and businessmen. A second type consisted of extra-parliamentary political groups; some favored a partially active and some a partially passive military approach. They organized on the basis of shared political values and included mainly women supporting Rafi and Mapai. The members of these groups belonged to a high socioeconomic class (most were residents of a prestigious district of north Tel Aviv) and operated by coordinating demonstrations and petitions. A third type was composed of four voluntary organizations that advertised their views in the Israeli Hebrew-language daily press.

The solution to the lack of political leadership appeared to these groups to lie in the appointment of leaders with military and security backgrounds (Moshe Dayan, Yigael Yadin, David Ben-Gurion, and Menachem Begin). For minister of defense, most groups wanted Dayan, whom they saw as an authoritative military leader having proved his planning and command ability as Chief of General Staff (CGS) during the Suez Campaign.[26]

The game rules of the Israeli democracy did not permit extraparliamentary activity or attempts by political parties to influence policy-making regarding security issues. Accepted practice called for discussion of military-security affairs (especially war issues) by formal and especially informal inner forums.

Eshkol and the Mapai apparatus, fearing that the crisis would heighten Rafi's public prestige, opposed the appointment of Rafi members to the government. Other parties and especially extra-parliamentary political groups, seeing these reactions, concluded that parliamentary politics were not adequate to effect a change in the attitudes of Mapai's leaders. Unconventional politics, precisely by reason of representing an unaccustomed departure, would be more effective. So a number of demonstrations were organized and petitions were signed by tens of thousands of citizens in favor of appointing Dayan minister of defense, having Rafi and Gahal join the government, and setting up an "emergency inner cabinet."[27] In Israel, such direct public involvement in matters of national security was unprecedented. With such a backdrop, the emergence of national consensus becomes especially intriguing.

Politics of Fear and Other Consensus-Forming Factors

The National Unity Government was formed on June 1, 1967. Moshe Dayan (Rafi) became minister of defense and Menachem Begin and Yosef Sapir (Gahal) ministers without portfolio. Thus, the public controversy on the war issue concluded, and the ad hoc extraparliamentary groups accordingly disbanded. Consensus during the ensuing war was the product of several principal factors, one of which was the public's anxiety responses. Fear for Israel's survival led to the creating of the grand government, which now functioned as a consensus structure, that is, a political organization promoting solidarity in the center and secondary centers of the political system.

After the withdrawal from Sinai and the Gaza Strip in 1957 and until mid-May 1967, the political system had been characterized by grade-1 anxiety responses. The various parties believed, due to the persistence of the conflict, that the Arab states aspired to destroy Israel, even though war was not expected to break out in the near future. Two exceptions to this rule were Herut and Ahduth Haavoda, which believed the likelihood of an outbreak of war to be imminent.[28] When the public first learned of the buildup of the Egyptian forces in Sinai (May 16, 1967), prevailing opinion was that Egyptian armor divisions in the Israeli border did not presage any significant change in the status quo maintained since 1957.[29]

In democratic regimes, public attitudes toward matters of national security change very slowly and gradually, if at all, since the public is far less well informed on these than on other topics. In general, the public tends to assume that a given reality conforms to its basic premises. This was also very much the case in Israel, due to the high prestige enjoyed by the political-security establishment.[30] On May 22, Eshkol reported in Knesset the further reinforcement of the Egyptian army in Sinai.[31] Many believed that Israel's survival was threatened as it had not been since 1957. The opinion crystallized that Egypt was about to initiate war in a few months or would act to stymie Israel's capacity to react militarily to Syrian moves.[32] Mapai gave vent to those fear responses. With the exception of Abba Eban and Golda Meir, most Mapai members believed the status quo in Israeli-Egyptian relations had been breached, and that Israel would almost certainly be called upon, in the near future, to demonstrate her capacity to achieve a decisive military outcome.[33] Only the very leftist parties—Maki and Haolam Hazeh, whose anxiety responses were still of the first grade—took a different view. There were, they claimed, two causes for the tension: "American imperialism," designed to stir up military tension in the Middle East in order to divert international public opinion from "imperialism's crimes" in Vietnam, and Israeli "belligerent" declarations against Syria.[34]

Global and regional developments exacerbated the sense of siege. On May 23, 1967, news of the blockade on shipping in the straits sharpened public fears.[35] The Hebrew-language Israeli press, representing a broad spectrum of political positions, cited the Holocaust as exemplifying the situation. The Jewish people in Israel, they claimed, faced a danger of annihilation unparalleled since Hitler; and any compromise regarding Israel's demand for restoration of the status quo ante would resemble Europe's consent to the partition of Czechoslovakia.[36] These fears moved the political system, even the very leftist parties, to conclude that unless Sinai were again demilitarized and freedom of shipping restored, Israel would be justified in initiating war against Egypt.

Israel endeavored to persuade the powers, and especially the United States, France, and Britain, to take steps to ensure freedom of shipping. Government spokesmen plainly stated that unless the naval blockade were lifted, Israel would have perforce to assert her "right of self-defense by virtue of Article 51 of the United Nations Charter." Days passed and no interpower assistance was forthcoming. Egypt, Syria, and Jordan continued massing troops on their respective borders with Israel. People's fears intensified.[37]

Fear responses were aired at the cabinet meeting of June 4, 1967. All ministers, even those who advocated a further waiting period, concurred that the present danger to Israel's survival had been unparalleled since 1948. Israel Barzilai and Mordechai Bentov wanted to consult with Yaakov Hazan and Meir Yaari before casting Mapam's vote in favor of initiating war, but even they admitted that the threat was both palpable and immediate.[38] The government resolution of June 4 to open war reflected public feeling that Arab threats of annihilating Israel were about to immediately materialize:

> Having heard reports of the military and political situation, the government is persuaded that the armies of Egypt, Syria, and Jordan are deployed for launching an all-frontal attack and pose a threat to the state's very existence. The government is resolved to undertake military action with the aim of liberating Israel from the noose of aggression that is tightening about her.[39]

Biosociological studies indicate that collective fear enhances social cohesiveness in a given community, with its readiness to unite in combating a perceived threat to common security. A similar conclusion is reached by studies of community response to natural disasters such as earthquakes and hurricanes, which differ, however, in the relevant context, from wars.[40] Fears inspired in Jewish society by the threat of annihilation produced broad consensus on security policy. Despite differences in principle as to the use of armed force, threat concepts now dovetailed, dissent being confined to small, peripheral political groups only.

Consensus evolved gradually. The political system concurred as to which enemy was posing a threat to Israel's existence. Whereas until May 19, 1967, Syria was perceived as the most menacing, the dynamic events now changed all that.[41] According to the May 28 government resolution, Egypt imperiled the state's existence: "The government of Israel makes known its opinion that the blockade of the Straits of Tiran to Israeli shipping is tantamount to acts of aggression against Israel."[42]

International apathy accelerated the forging of a consensus based on similar threat perceptions. The United States, Canada, Britain, and the Netherlands all issued declarations but did nothing to restore the status quo ante. There was no longer any point in playing the waiting game. On June 1, 1967, Mossad Chief Meir Amit returned from a mission to the United States where he had gathered that she would not use force to open the straits. Amit recommended waiting not more than a few days. Even the moderate foreign minister Abba Eban now concluded that the waiting period, while gaining Israel the sympathy of the Western powers, had outlived its usefulness.[43]

This reassessment by Eban, who personified moderacy in Mapai, mirrored the general mood. The siege appeared to be closing in; the deep-rooted belief of the Jewish collective psyche that the Western world was indifferent to Israel's fate colored the attitudes of most political groups. Few would deny the positions of most political elites and the armed forces in favor of a preemptive war, to avert a danger conceived as existential.[44]

At the June 4 cabinet meeting on the possible war initiative, Mapam and NRP opposed, claiming that while it appeared highly improbable, war could still be prevented. The government should delay for a few days and try to persuade the powers to adopt some international initiative. Seeing itself as possibly the only supporter of delaying the strike, the NRP withdrew its objections and voted in favor of the government resolution to open hostilities.[45]

Mapam's view was divided. The majority held that war could be averted by diplomatic means and that another ten to fourteen days should therefore be allowed in which to make the most of conciliatory options. The minority claimed that Israel had exhausted all diplomatic channels for restoring the status quo ante and now had no choice but to go to war.[46]

How Mapam ultimately voted is not known. Geist (citing no specific source) concluded in his research that Mapam supported the government. But Bentov argued that Mapam "did not support" the initiation of war and, in a personal interview granted for the purpose of this book, claimed that his party abstained. My analysis of relevant events shows that in the vote of June 4, Mapam delegates Barzilai and Bentov explained their reservations as to all wars and opted in favor of a further waiting period. They refused Eshkol's request to vote with the other cabinet ministers but indicated they would consult with the ideological leadership, Hazan and Yaari, before their position was recorded in minutes. No official reply ever came from the Mapam cabinet ministers.[47]

Most parties thought the aims of the war should be to destroy Egypt's forces in the Sinai and lift the naval blockade. Shortly before the outbreak of hostilities, as fear of the Egyptian offensive mounted, an interparty consensus emerged, claiming that the destruction of Egypt's armed forces must be the prime target and the lifting of the blockade the second.[48] Other aims such as liberating areas of Eretz Israel, imposing a peace agreement and toppling Nasser's regime were not on the national agenda. They became irrelevant in the face of a danger so ominous that Israel's very ability to cope with it seemed doubtful. Researches in the sphere of "disaster literature" and the "sociology of wars" show that when faced with imminent catastrophe, communities focus on minimal objectives of collective deployment to meet the extraordinary contingency, to the neglect of others beyond survival needs.[49]

Even the leaders of Herut, though well aware of the opportunity presented by the crisis for promoting their ideals and political interests, elected to restrain their controversial aspirations for the "liberation" of Eretz Israel. Instead, they concentrated on getting Gahal and Rafi into the Labor-Party led government; the "liberation" controversy, indeed, was liable to prevent such participation.[50]

Those weeks clearly reflected the mobilization of Jewish society in Israel. Political differences regarding armed force were bridged, and political energies were directed at the forging of a national consensus as to the projected preemptive strike. The Hebrew-language daily press also assumed that national consensus would enable Israel to profit by her qualitative edge over the Arab states. Daily press editorials accordingly posited national unity as an essential prerequisite for victory in war.[51]

Opponents of the idea, a Mapai contingent headed by Secretary Golda Meir and members of Ahduth Haavoda and Mapam, feared that the unity government would reduce their share of the rewards of power and that a Rafi-Gahal bloc would oppose that headed by Mapai. Since consensus was so important, said the opponents of the national-unity government, the cabinet composition must remain unchanged. Political wisdom, moreover, dictated avoidance of governmental reshuffles during political crises, since personnel and party changes would entail a change in state policy, and security crises, even more so, required government consistency. Consensus values were thus used to persuade competing political elites to defer from legitimizing Gahal as a partner in power and possibly making Rafi the foremost party in the Labor camp.[52]

Gahal, NRP, Rafi, and some members of Mapai countered that the crisis derived from faulty decision-making processes, with emphasis on the hesitancy of Prime Minister Eshkol. Only a national-unity government could so adeptly shape a security policy acceptable to the majority of the public, thereby producing consensus.[53] Indeed, contrary to theoretical literature, which posits that national security crises necessarily engender integration, this particular crisis appears to have stimulated and lent prominence to controversy while also precipitating a change in the fundamental characteristics of the sociopolitical order.

Aware of the need to find a solution that would enable Gahal to join the cabinet and authorize the war, Begin announced that Herut was not asking for a senior ministerial portfolio but would be content to be included in decision-making processes on military and security affairs, including the projected war. A skillful political tactician, Begin realized that any other strategy could cause Mapai to refuse to admit Gahal to any coalition. Herut also consented that the defense portfolio be awarded to either Ben-Gurion, Dayan, or Yigal Alon.[54] These tactics ultimately led to a historic change in the political status of Herut.

Spurred by fear, Mapam was also undergoing a change of political behavior. At the party's political committee meeting (May 31, 1967), Hazan recommended that Mapam consent to the inclusion of Gahal and Rafi in the government. Wanting this motion to pass unopposed he declared the following:

> I am aware of all the risks attendant on this decision. But because of the voices emanating from the front and echoing in our streets, we have no alternative, because the most precious thing we now possess is the people's faith in itself and its leadership.[55]

The result was a resolution that, while reflecting Hazan's position, also betrayed concerns that a political alliance between Rafi and Gahal would undermine Mapam's status in the government and erode the hegemony of Mapai as dominant party:

> Mapam is prepared to support the alignment's motion to include opposition party delegates in the government, if assured

that they will unite in following the government's path and that the endeavor to undermine the existing coalition will cease.[56]

Thus, consensus values helped bring the grand government to birth. Painfully apparent in this context was the organizational weakness of the ruling party. The combined efforts of the Mapai apparatus and its leading elite were inadequate in convincing the public that the political leadership could respond to the extreme emergency situation. Premier Eshkol was considered a financier, and only Labor Minister Yigal Alon of Ahdut Haavoda was deemed an authority on military strategy.[57]

The Lasswellian garrison state model shows the causes of public and party pressures for broadening the leadership basis by co-option of experts on violence. Lasswell designates the army as the primary source of threat to the existence of democracy in security crises (see Part One). But the lesson of the waiting period is that not only the military gains influence due to security crises. All security experts, including civilians, enjoy greater access of power. This holds particularly true in a fighting society where experts on violence enjoy status and prestige, even in "normal" times.

Political elites in rivalry with Mapai utilized the waiting period to promote various interests. Gahal and Rafi insisted on admittance to the government, with Dayan as defense minister. Accordingly, in early June 1967, Eshkol was faced with two alternatives for the government reshuffle: one was to appoint Alon minister of defense and Dayan major-general i/c southern command or deputy prime minister; the other was to install Dayan, the preferred candidate by reason of his military experience and his public popularity, as minister of defense. Many people expected that Dayan would put an end to the crisis, boost morale, and get a resolution through in favor of employing armed force.

The founding of the National Unity Government engendered a consensus structure. Represented in the new government were the major parties in Knesset (105 MKs), including Gahal, the main opposition party. Only a few small parties (15 MKs), accounting for 14 percent of total valid votes in the Sixth Knesset elections (1965) remained outside the government.[58]

Studies on the sociology of war show that societies in war tend to join forces for greater efficiency in combating the common enemy, to the detriment of political pluralism.[59] The forming of the National

Unity Government put an end to public debate on Eshkol's leadership. Extra-parliamentary groups suspended activity, and the press dropped its criticism of the government in favor of reporting events on the front. One all-important question occupied the national agenda: how long would the government wait before going to war? But this was no longer, as in the past, a matter for public debate. The various parties newly admitted to government aired no contrary views in public, and political groups in the opposition were prepared to wait.

The opponents of government policy had precious little room in which to maneuver in devising an alternative national agenda, especially in a political system where parties were demonstrably the principal vehicle of political communication. Debates in the political system were orchestrated exclusively by the multipopulated government. Patterns of mutual consultation and cooperation evolved in the cabinet between parties of opposing positions. Gahal and Rafi accordingly preferred intracabinet deliberations over overt criticism as a means of directly influencing policy. This was particularly significant as regards the relations of former-oppositional Gahal with the dominant party—Mapai. Collective responsibility being desirable to both parties, they restrained their arguments, for the present, from spilling over into public controversy.

Journalists tended to support prevailing values and reflect the political positions of the ruling party or its satellites. Their function, they believed, was primarily to channel information from the administration to the public, to the neglect of the feedback. The media thereby formed part of the political power structure of the Labor camp and especially Mapai, paving the way for the government's legitimizing its political and social concepts.

As the nation waited, reports emphasized the real and immediate danger to Israel's survival and the crucial importance of the public's rallying around the government policy.[60] In this sense, the media both expressed and reinforced two key consensus factors: fear responses and consensus values. While hostilities were in progress, most reporting and commentary focused on military activity, with an emphasis on what the media defined as military victories unprecedented in Israeli military history. This trend both mirrored and reconfirmed the public view that in initiating war, Israel had acted not only with justice, but with military and political foresight.[61]

Consensus during Preemptive Strike

Public identification with the military objectives became apparent as hostilities erupted and progressed. All subscribed to the notion that force must be deployed to prevent annihilation. Even military passivists deemed the war just, as having been engaged for purposes of national defense.[62] The consensus factors thus operated to produce almost absolute support for the war. In the Knesset debate of June 5, 1967, all parties supported government policy. Consensus extended also to the army, whose senior officers favored the initiation of hostilities. Also, all major public organizations, including the Histadruth Labor Federation, rallied to the consensus. Rakah (the communist party) alone dissociated itself from the general public trend. As a peripheral, basically Arab, anti-Zionist party, it criticized the initiation of the war as nonessential, since its purpose was not self-defense but furtherance of Western interests.[63]

Additional war aims during the war were the occupation of the Golan Heights and East Jerusalem. Discussion of these objectives had been confined to very partial treatment in the government and the Knesset Foreign Affairs and Defense Committee. It found no public expression.

East Jerusalem was a crucial issue. Dayan thought the city should not be captured but merely encircled; to occupy it would prolong the Arabs' will to fight. But the more hawkish Gahal and Ahduth Haavoda claimed that the city should be "liberated," seen not merely as part of the drive to frustrate the security menace but to a great extent because of its historic Jewish importance. The occupation of the Golan Heights, too, was in dispute. Eshkol and Dayan supported occupying strategic footholds that had served Syrian armor forces for shelling Israeli settlements. Ahduth Haavoda and Gahal, however, called for the occupation of the Heights in order to finally remove the constant threat against Israeli settlements along the Syrian border. Gahal was motivated by its activist approach and Ahduth Haavoda by appeals from its movement, HaKibbutz Hameuhad, to put an end to the attacks that were causing such heavy loss of life and property to settlements.[64] The future of the occupied territories was not discussed in public forums, notwithstanding fundamental differences in outlook between those (especially Herut) to whom the occupation meant liberation of territories of Eretz Israel and their opponents.

The war rapidly blossomed into a blitzkrieg. About three hundred Egyptian air force planes were destroyed in the first two hours of fighting on June 5, 1967. East Jerusalem was occupied on June 7. June 8 saw the rout of the Egyptian armor forces in Sinai followed, on June 10, by the occupation of the Golan Heights. So vividly did the reality contrast with the seeming weakness and fear of annihilation that had marked the waiting period, that secular and religious groups acclaimed the victory as a "tremendous historic achievement," "a miracle," "redemption"—and the war as a "war of salvation" and a "religious experience."[65] The term "victory" thus assumed more than the military significance of the Suez Campaign. It seemed to be endowed with mystical-religious import. The war was perceived as an event engineered by divine guidance.[66]

Even more markedly than in 1956, a tremendous elation swept the people, suddenly translated from an oppressive sense of siege and existential uncertainty to triumph, along with a pervasive urge to support the government. Criticism was condemned as severely disruptive of vital interests and as antipatriotic and even traitorous. Not only the right-wing and the political center but almost the entire socialist Jewish left, including anti-Zionist currents, embraced this view.

Another feature of the euphoria and militarism pervading the nation was the general attitude to the occupation of the territories. In the course of the fighting, the IDF occupied an area of seventy thousand square kilometers with an Arab population of about one million (some 600,000 in the West Bank, 380,000 in the Gaza Strip and northern Sinai, 8,000 in the Solomon Region, and some 7,500 on the Golan Heights). At the same time, the justness of war moves was only asked by small left-wing parties. Maki published a communiqué calling on the government and the military to not harm the Arab population of the territories, while Rakah claimed that they were suffering severe injury due to the Israeli offensive. Haolam Hazeh hastened, a mere week after the fighting ended, to propose a peace based on a full Israeli withdrawal. Uninhibited by any commitment to the Zionist ethos, they also held alien the game rules of the fighting society and challenged the conventional modes of political thinking. Their views gained scant public attention and, in general, were accorded a negative reception.[67]

Summary and Conclusions

As the principal channel for public participation in political decision-making processes, the parties were the foremost agents in molding and lending expression to the national agenda, including consensus and dissent on the war issue. The influence of extra-parliamentary political groups, while greater than in the past, was rather marginal.[68] In the waiting period, dissent was caused mainly by inter- and intraparty controversy. But agreement among parties on issues such as the founding of a grand coalition was the major generator of national consensus.

Neither in content nor in scope was the 1956 Suez Campaign consensus comparable to that of the Six-Day War in 1967. Not since 1949 had Israel subscribed to so broad a consensus in circumstantially justifying the preemptive military strike. This shift in the sociopolitical order derived from the grave effect of fear responses. Politicians and the media used the waiting period to point out the parallels between present security events and the Holocaust era, comparing Israel's situation to that of Czechoslovakia on the eve of the Munich Agreement (1938).[69] The fear of Israel's being attacked in the immediate future, and forced into a desperate struggle for survival, pervaded the public awareness.

The dominant party, Mapai, was losing some of its hegemony, and nonparty groups, particularly the army, came to exert a correspondingly greater influence on policy-making. The military subsequently acted as a pressure group in favor of opening hostilities. True, it was important in national political decision making even in the fifties, when, for example, it was largely influential in shaping the reprisals policy. In a society in wartime, the army, or any group specializing in organized violence, acquires an importance in excess of its purely military security role. But the unprecedented depth of IDF involvement in political decision-making in the waiting period was clearly shown in the meeting, on May 28, between Premier Eshkol and prominent army generals who urgently demanded that Israel initiate a war to thwart a palpable and immediate threat to her survival.[70]

The political involvement of the military went beyond the usual cooperation between policymakers and military experts. During the waiting period, the military abandoned the usual procedure whereby it made its views known to the political echelon through the defense minister or the CGS. Senior officers exerted themselves to persuade politicians to back the military's aspiration to execute war plans.

Military influence on public political participation was indirect. The General Staff's confidence in IDF's capability and their concern that a delay in initiating war would detract from the military's surprise capacity reinforced support in the various parties for the offensive. The army, however, despite the all-encompassing call-up, was unable to directly influence the public as a whole. The General Staff could put its position to the cabinet, to the Foreign Affairs and Defense Committee, and to cabinet ministers but not straight to the general public. This pattern was to change in the seventies. Thus, although the military's positions did affect various party forums, large sectors of the public were unaware of them.[71]

The consensus during hostilities was largely ascribable to four variables in the political system—fear responses, overlapping concepts of threat, consensus values, and consensus structure. Of these, by far the most important, especially in view of the relative organizational weakness of the dominant party, were fear responses.

Adherents of different political positions came together in their support for the national security doctrine, which, in the military-political circumstances in early June 1967, represented the minimal common denominator for most political groups. Where this mutual adjustment did not take place, the consensus values generated by fear responses created a secondary consensus whereby it was not to be expressed, even though government policy was thought erroneous. And the combined effect of fear responses, mutual adjustment of threat concepts, and consensus values was to generate the formation of the national-unity government. The ruling elite extended its ranks to include other political parties, while also diversifying its personnel composition. It was thereby laying the foundation for the consensus structure, namely, a broad-based government.

Also making a secondary impact were other political variables. The attributes of the war did not of themselves produce consensus, but they did operate to prevent the weakening of the consensus created shortly before the outbreak of hostilities. Another factor was the conciliatory leadership of Eshkol, who used his diplomatic flair to form the grand coalition and conduct the preemptive military strike.

The government resolved to fight, and public support for "the manner in which the government is handling problems in the present situation" rose from 75 percent before the war started to 85 percent on the date of the outbreak of hostilities, and to 88 percent while battles were in progress (altogether an increase of 17 percent).

Paralleling this trend was an improvement in the public morale, rising from 30 percent who had described their mood as "good most of the time" or "almost all the time" shortly before the war, to 47 percent who reported a good mood during the fighting. This improvement was evidently due to military attainments and its success in neutralizing the causes of the public's very serious fears (altogether an increase of 57 percent). Public opinion studies and theories of sociopolitical order call this phenomenon an "affirmative consensus," one in which the public in a democracy tends to support a certain security policy rather than "risk" causing any "damage" by evincing opposition, even where such policy runs counter to previously held positions.[72]

Public reactions were remarkably similar regardless of ethnic origin, income level, or social class in general. Support for the launching of hostilities rather than emanating from a single social class (the bourgeoisie alone, for example, as the Marxist school of thought might claim) came from the public as a whole, cutting across class distinctions.[73] Findings thus demonstrate a majority of public support for the partially activist military approach and hence for the manner in which the national-unity government responded to the threat of war.[74] Even more emphatically than in 1956, fear prompted all social classes to support the use of armed force.

With the end of the war, as in 1957, war-issue controversy patterns lapsed into latency, only to resurface, time and again, in Israel's future wars. But the manner in which the 1967 War ended, namely with Israel in occupation of Arab territories, inaugurated a new era in the annals of her political regime. This was to have a significant, long-term effect on the shaping of Israel's sociopolitical order and on consensus relative to national security and military force. The divergent approaches had not greatly changed in principle; but they had taken on a vastly different significance to that of the fifties and the sixties. From then on, they formed part of a rapidly metamorphosizing political regime and social setting. In 1967, the shift began: from the building of a democracy to adapting to its position as an occupier regime.

Now more than ever, debates as to the use of armed force were taking on an ideological-political, even a messianic, tone, even while gradually becoming an established fact of public life. And the various attitudes toward the use of armed force correspondingly came to pose a more meaningful challenge to the social order, and, hence, to exert a growing influence on the political regime's democratic essentials and the degree of legitimacy accorded it.

Part Three

Polyarchy during
Territorial Status Quo

4 Dissent and Consensus in the War of Attrition

Introduction

This chapter deals with the War of Attrition (1969–1970). While most of the studies have related to it as a transitional military stage between the war of 1967 and that of 1973, this study claims—in contradiction—that it deserves much more attention as a sociopolitical phenomenon. The chapter expounds on how extensive consensus prevailed due to a significant steering by a grand ruling coalition. Yet, some aspects of meaningful dissent were engendered, as well, for the first time in the political and social history of Israel.

The public debate marking the seventies was, could peace be established in the near future between Israel and the Arab states? What measures should the Israeli government take to promote it? And, what were the terms of the peace to which the government should aspire? Debate centered primarily on the political future of the territories occupied by Israel in 1967 (hereafter, the territories).

Because Israeli society faced political dilemmas regarding the use of force during a period of intensive border clashes, the conflict dominated the political system. Public opinion polls of the early seventies recorded a drastic increase in concern over the security situation compared to the late sixties but not over other problems, such as economic affairs. Also, an analysis of the Hebrew-language

Israeli press of the early seventies highlights the centrality of the conflict to its reporting.[1]

From July 1967 to March 1969, most security incidents involved Palestinian activity on and near the Israeli-Jordanian frontier (the Jordan Rift and the Beth She'an Valleys). Israel accordingly focused on fortification, sealing of the borders, and limited military strikes against army bases and Palestinian camps, both in reprisal for attacks and to prevent their organizing for further activities. The period from March 1969 to August 1970, during which most of the fighting took place on the banks of the Suez between the Egyptian army and the Israel Defense Forces (IDF), will be referred to as the War of Attrition.

The War of Attrition was a significant turning point in Israeli politics because it was then that certain key processes occurred. Gahal, the main right-wing party, won a public seal of legitimacy. A political protest culture evolved. Opposition positions were hammered out on matters of national security, with new sociopolitical messages beginning to be formulated. And, the political system faced the new reality of war concomitant with Israel occupation of the territories.

Control of the territories was not, nor could it be, extraneous to the political reality taking shape within the "Green Line" (Israel's pre-1967 borders). Israel had become a polyarchy—a democratic regime (within the jurisdiction of the Green Line only) but suffered very grave impairments, foremost of which was its control of a population resentful of the occupation and without political rights.[2] The Israeli democracy in uniform was coming to grips with a new reality and a constantly escalating use of force. Different attitudes toward armed force reflected this new reality.

Attitudes on the War Issue to the Outbreak of Attrition Fighting (June 1967–March 1969)

Control of the territories became a primary objective of Herut[3] and shaped its approach to foreign and security affairs. Before the 1967 War, it refused to recognize the frontier lines of the Armistice Agreement of 1949, seeking instead to change them through a war of offense. Now, however, instead of breaking the territorial status quo, Herut aspired to have its existence recognized.[4] But the Six-Day War did not change Herut's basic positions on military force. To Begin and his followers, the success of the military initiative following Gahal's inclusion in the government in 1967 legitimized military activism.[5] How, then, could military activism be held consistent with views that endorsed the status quo? The answer lies in the distinction drawn in Herut's worldview, between fundamental-ideological and operative-ideological principles.[6]

Military activism was an operative-ideological principle, a means to achieve Herut's fundamental ideological goals: the integrity of Eretz Israel (a term referring at that time to western Eretz Israel); Jewish settlement in Eretz Israel; and control of frontiers which would ensure victory in future wars.[7] Operative-ideological principles, unlike the fundamental-ideological kind, are not always relevant to political concepts. At a given time, the importance of the former may dwindle, becoming latent in that party's conception. Thus, with the IDF securely ensconced in the territories, the military activist approach was relegated to secondary position in Herut's attitudes. There were two reasons for this. First, military occupation of Judea and Samaria enabled Herut to achieve two of its fundamental-ideological goals, namely, the integrity and settlement of Eretz Israel. One of Gahal's purposes in remaining inside the labor-led government was to prevent a withdrawal from the territories. Accordingly, participation in a coalition not sharing its military-activist approach was not deemed by Herut to be inconsistent with its views. Second, the prevailing view in Herut and in Gahal was that possession of the territories provided the strategic depth for more effective defense and enabled a clear-cut defeat of the Arab armies.[8]

According to Herut, deterrence based on well-fortified borders offering geopolitical advantages would secure the status quo. At the same time, while Herut's political behavior reflected its de-emphasizing of military activism, that approach was not written off as long as border incidents and terrorist activity presented security problems. The government, asserted Herut, must maintain the status quo through limited preventative operations against Palestinian organizations and Arab armies.[9]

These attitudes prevented political friction in Gahal, since the Liberals supported the government's basic security policy but also concurred with Herut's demand that the Israeli responses be stepped up.[10] Moreover, the political constellation emerging on occupation of the territories presented Herut, despite its searing failure in the 1965 elections to the Sixth Knesset, with a historic chance for membership in the government. It could wield power, both as a party and on a personal-leadership level without, in the eyes of its members and supporters, compromising its principles on war and peace. The Labor-led National Unity Government openly favored control of the territories (although, as I shall show, on the basis of principles quite different from those of Herut). As far as Herut was concerned, reconciliation of its ideological principles with the territorial status quo had been achieved.

A wide chasm yawned between Herut as an establishment party and three small, hawkish opposition parties that more clearly expressed the activist military approach. Their definition of "Eretz Israel" included Transjordan, which, unlike Herut, they felt called upon to "liberate" militarily. One of the three, the Free Center, theorized that in view of terrorist activity on the eastern front, aided and abetted by the Jordanian administration, limited military operations could not ensure Israel's security. Party leader Shmuel Tamir stated the following in Knesset on May 25, 1968:

> If Hussein does not want peace, the time draws near when we shall have no recourse but to impose peace upon him. In the Six-Day War we halted, we did not do it. We did not cross the Jordan, we did not liberate the slopes of Naharayim. For some reason, we even left him in possession of Aqaba.[11]

The other two hawkish groups operated outside the Knesset. The activism of the "National Circles" was not appeased by the 1967 war. Israel, according to them, should initiate a war in order to liberate the East Bank of the Jordan and impose a peace on the Arab states. The government was free to refrain from using force in this manner only in return for a peace agreement with the Arab states recognizing Israeli sovereignty over all parts of Judea, Samaria, the Golan, and Sinai.[12]

While the Free Center and National Circles were guided by Jabotinski's ideology and that of the pro-revisionist undergrounds, the Canaanites stood at the very far right of the political system. The Canaanites were founded back in 1943 by Uriel Shelah (or under his pen name, Yonatan Ratosh), poet and intellectual. But not until after the Six-Day War did the group publicly, and in organized fashion, air its views on national security issues. They viewed Jewishness in ethnic, not nationalist, terms. Jews were a Hebrew people, having sovereignty over a territory that they called the "Land of Qedem," bounded by Turkey, Iran, and Saudi Arabia. To realize this sovereignty, a two-stage plan should be executed. Israel should form an alliance with her natural allies (Druze and Maronite Christians in Lebanon and Bedouin in Jordan). She should then establish peace and her independence.[13] Like other right-wing groups, the Canaanites believed territory to be of supreme importance in defining Israeli nationhood. Very great emphasis was thus attached to the use of military force.[14]

Right-wing positions on the use of armed force gradually percolated toward the center of the political system. But this process, in the early seventies, was still latent and partial. The attitudes of the Labor Party, which still dominated the political system, were thus particularly important in shaping the character of the sociopolitical order.

Labor supported retaining the territories until the conclusion of a peace agreement that provided Israel with secure, recognized boundaries. But the Jewish character of the state, they said, must be preserved, and only East Jerusalem and the Golan Heights were to be annexed. Thus, the Labor Party sought to ensure the status quo and safeguard Israel's survival via partial military activism. Deterrence would be achieved by demonstrating to the Arab states that it was not worthwhile to attack Israel, since her well-fortified borders would be difficult to breach; she could, given her strategic depth, defend herself against unprovoked attack using relatively small forces; and the IDF was prepared to make full use of its high-quality strength. As to partial military activism, the 1967 War had not altered the views of the various Labor Party factions. The military victory had merely confirmed the party's faith in its traditional line and its ability to shape the national security concept. However, the new reality allowed the army to win a future war even if Israel were attacked first.[15] The purpose of counterstrikes and preemptive attacks was threefold: firstly, to prevent terrorists from operating and to deter Arab regimes and civilian populations from abetting the terrorist groups; secondly, to restrain the Arab regimes from attrition attempts; and thirdly, to avert any imminent and palpable danger of war.[16]

Labor policy, then, was to integrate deterrence into partial military activism, on two levels. Deterrence was to be reinforced by limited military operations and if deterrence failed, Israel should initiate war. Labor recognized three situations in which Israel must use force. One was the constant breaking by the Arab states of the cease-fire, either by regular armed forces or by terrorist action. The second was an attempt by a foreign army to cross Israel's borders, and the third was an attempt to equip the Arab states with nuclear weapons.[17]

Labor's pivotal position in the political system enabled it to dictate its positions to its partners-in-government. Its attitudes were a major component of the national security concept, accepted by Agudath Israel, Poalei Agudath Israel, and the National Religious Party (NRP) in the religious camp; the Independent Liberals in the civic camp; and the State List in the Labor camp.[18]

Mapam, however, did not altogether concur with the national security concept. The aftermath of the 1967 War reinforced the ideological bond between Mapam's traditional positions regarding force and its political concept regarding peace. Shooting incidents and terrorist acts at a time when Israel's control of the territories was supposed to ensure maximum security led Mapam to conclude that military victory, while useful for averting an immediate threat of annihilation, could not, of itself, provide an intrinsic solution to the conflict. On the contrary, the military victory had engendered a destructive status quo: control of densely populated territories posed a danger to Israel's Jewish-Zionist-socialist values; and it could well precipitate a war, since the occupation intensified the Arabs' hatred.[19] Yaakov Hazan consequently stated in the Knesset (July 31, 1967):

> The issue of the West Bank is a most intricate one. Our vision too—the Mapam vision—is one of the whole Eretz Israel. But how is the whole Eretz Israel to be attained? First we must achieve peace. Assuming for the moment that we contrive to extend the country's borders, the border will have been extended but war will continue along our new borders. Is this how we are to live? . . .[20]

But however limited its value, the military victory could, Mapam claimed, facilitate a conflict resolution based on an exchange of territories for peace. It accordingly called on the government to outline a political program and begin negotiations. Until a peace was signed, said Mapam, any military attempt to impose a retreat from the cease-fire lines must be repulsed. For this position the party cited three causes: firstly, the occupation was the result of a justifiable use of force (the Six-Day War was basically a war of exigence); secondly, Israel was not an occupying regime (assuming she was not holding on to the territories with a view to annexation but merely as a bargaining card wherewith to achieve peace); and, thirdly, were the IDF to withdraw from the territories without frontier adjustments, Israel would again face an immediate threat to her existence.[21]

Mapam's outlook on war, then, had not changed. But after the 1967 War, it measured the justice of military operations not only in terms of whether they resulted from exigency or initiative but also bearing in mind the Israeli government's peace concepts and how they were to be implemented. Thus, defense of the cease-fire lines was justifiable as necessary for the success of any peace initiative. In this sense, the Zionist left was way ahead of the rest of the political system in perceiving the use of armed force in terms of the ideological values of a peace policy.

Mapam's positions somewhat coincided with those of Maki. Whereas prior to 1967 Maki had supported none but defensive means of combating terror, such as fortification of borders, it now also advocated some fairly active means to that end. Among the reasons for this were the traumas of the waiting period and the flagrant increase in terrorist activity, including international terrorism. Maki claimed that the purpose of the terrorism was to gradually erode Israel's strength, thereby giving the Arab states a breathing space in which to rehabilitate their armies and prepare for total war. While vociferously calling for a Palestinian state to be established in the territories, Maki held that the terrorist organizations were distorting the national objectives of the Palestinian people. They did not represent the territories' populations, but were Pan-Arab organizations aspiring to destroy Israel. Maki accordingly supported limited military operations in response to attacks or as a last resort for preventing them. It deemed the Karame Operation of March 21, 1968, and the IDF raid on the Beirut airport on December 29, 1968, to be essential defense measures. Haolam Hazeh (another small, left-wing Zionist party) echoed these positions but was more inclined to emphasize the need to refrain from limited military operations so as to not spoil any opportunity for negotiating with the Palestinians. These two peripheral parties were unique in that they focused on the intercommunity aspects of the conflict (Palestinian-Israeli relations), and in that, even at this very early stage of Israel's control of the territories, they posited the founding of a Palestinian state as the basis for resolving the conflict.[22]

Similarly conciliatory positions were also expressed on the extra-parliamentary plane. While the Committee for Peace was hamstrung due to differences of opinion between Zionist Mapam and non-Zionist Rakah, Siah (Hebrew acronym for New Israeli Left) and the Movement for Peace and Security were active. Both sought to change the values of Israeli society, stressing that the army must withdraw from the territories, a solution be found to the Palestinian problem, and the use of armed force prohibited, in line with the principles of partial military passivism.[23]

Mainly, then, due to Israel's control of the territories, an extraparliamentary opposition developed to Gahal and the Labor Party. While hardly affecting the national agenda, it advanced views unique in the experience of a society in wartime and would, in the future, emerge into far greater prominence. It was a most unusual departure where national security affairs were concerned.

Cracks in the Consensus: The Hinterland in the War of Attrition (March 1969–August 1970)

In March 1969, Egypt went to war with the aim of wreaking severe havoc on IDF forces on the East Bank of the Suez Canal in order to facilitate a crossing of the canal.[24] To avoid a full-scale war, Israeli policymakers aspired to confine military activity to those that were essential and sufficient to control these lines.[25] The war aims of Egypt and Israel and scope of forces participating in the hostilities were kept within strict limits. This very containment produced a relatively high level of consensus in Israel.

The attitude of each political group to the war reflected its basic view on the use of force. A prevalent opinion was that since she was acting with frustrative intent, and as long as it was vital that the cease-fire lines be maintained, Israel's was a just war.[26] The political consensus reflected public propensities. Throughout this conflict, around 75 percent of the public supported the government's policy on, inter alia, foreign affairs and security. The public was convinced, however, that no decisive military outcome or political solution was to be expected in the near future, and that the war would last a long time. Accordingly, there was no cause for the kind of national enthusiasm or sense of historic momentum that prevailed during the 1956 and 1967 wars. Public concern with the military-security situation, moreover, increased during the fighting, accompanied by growing pessimism as to the Arab states' readiness to make peace with Israel.

And, public morale dwindled but not noticeably to the detriment of public support for the governmental policy.[27]

Only two opposition parties (Haolam Hazeh and the Free Center), each returning two Knesset members, and a few, small extra-parliamentary political groups dissented. The Free Center and the Canaanites called for military operations against Egypt to be upgraded. A different stand was taken by Haolam Hazeh, Siah, the Left Alliance, and the Movement for Peace and Security. While supporting the frustrative aim of the war, they also called for the introduction of a peace initiative based on UN Resolution 242 and a solution to the Palestinian problem. According to them, aspirations nursed by Gahal and some members of the Labor Party for the annexation of the territories were preventing negotiations with the Arab states and the Palestinians, thereby needlessly prolonging the war.[28]

The structure of the party system considerably confined the public impact of these views. During seventeen months of fighting, the Knesset did not hold a single exhaustive debate on the various aspects of the war. In a regime of cabinet-parliamentary structure, in a grand coalition, such a debate could well be prevented, since the parliamentary opposition was too small and powerless. Hence, dissent was expressed primarily on the extra-parliamentary plane.

Protest was also voiced by nonpolitical, unorganized citizen groups (eighth-graders, soldiers, intellectuals, and artists). These were significant in that they placed contentious issues squarely on the national agenda. One example was the playwright Hanoch Levin who, in his play, "Queen of the Bath," attacked the militaristic values of Israeli society, protesting the establishment's indifference to casualties. High school seniors, due to be drafted within the next few months, penned a letter with a similar message, claiming that Israeli military action was an unjust war of choice, since the government was overlooking chances to negotiate.[29] Yet, relative to the ideological polarity of the different approaches, dissent was limited.

How Consensus Was Formed in the Course of a Debilitating War

Considering Israel's strategic depth and the limited scale of the belligerency, the common political belief was that the population as a whole was not in danger. As long as total war was not engaged, and the IDF either held the cease-fire lines or, pursuant to a peace agreement, withdrew to secure boundaries, no existential threat appeared to loom.[30] Public opinion rated IDF capability far higher than that of the Arab armies, so that the chances of an immediate threat to survival appeared remote. The political system was disturbed in March and April 1970 by the news that the Soviet Union (USSR) was deepening her military presence in Egypt, especially by sending fighter pilots and SA3 missile operators. Accordingly, most political groups, with the support of the greater part of the public, deemed limited war to be well conceived and justified.[31]

The time dimension was crucial to public assessment of the threat and the means for coping with it. Political groups rooting for full or partial military activism believed that if the political status quo were preserved, time would allow for a military buildup. Ultimately, they hoped, the Arab states would have no choice but to pursue peace. If so, it was quite justifiable to hold on to the cease-fire lines. All National Unity Government parties, except Mapam, shared this view.[32]

Consensus regarding the time dimension also extended to the possibility of terminating the war. All coalition parties discounted the likelihood of a diplomatic initiative leading to the termination of hostilities.[33]

While consensus prevailed on a broad spectrum of topics connected with threat concepts, dissent was not absent. Two disputed issues were the depth bombardments and the military implications of the Soviet involvement. Finding expression in these contentions were the military activism of Herut, the partial military activism of Labor and the partial military passivism of Mapam.

Commencing January 1970, the Israeli Air Force began bombing army camps, ammunition depots, radar stations, missile launchers and fuel stores situated about 80 km west of the canal. The aim was to reduce the frequency and strength of Egyptian bombardments of the canal; to destroy the Egyptian antiaircraft missile complex; and to conclude the war by bringing military and political pressure to bear on Nasser. The idea was that the Egyptian public and pressure groups within the administration would act to persuade Nasser to terminate hostilities so as to save his country further heavy damage. But when it became known how deeply the USSR was involved, these tactics changed. Security-policy shapers Meir, Dayan, Eban, and Bar-Lev thought the scope of depth bombardments should be reduced. They increased the danger of becoming embroiled in a war with the Soviet Union, and their usefulness was becoming marginal.

With such extensive aid pouring in from the Soviet Union, it was now far less likely that Egypt could be coerced into agreeing to a cease-fire. With Ahduth Haavoda and Herut dissenting, the government resolved to reduce depth bombardments to a radius of 40 km west of the canal, with the aim of preventing Egypt from rehabilitating her antiaircraft complex.[34]

The reaction of those coalition parties that opposed partial activism reflects dilemmas as to the use of military force. Until March 1970, Mapam had supported depth bombardments only. But it warned against the bombardment of civilian targets as an immoral means of bringing hostilities to a halt. Mapam feared that between the Soviet design of preventing Israeli bombardments of the Cairo region and the Israeli plan of forcing Nasser to accept a cease-fire, Israel was liable to find herself at war with the Soviet Union. Depth bombardments, said Mapam, should therefore be significantly confined to a range of not more than 20 km.[35]

While Labor and Mapam disagreed merely on the operative level, their controversy with Herut-Gahal extended also to the tactical level. Herut saw depth bombardments as a means of toppling Nasser's regime. The Soviet presence, far from mellowing this attitude, actually reinforced it. In line with its advocacy of preventive war, Herut urged depth bombardments before Soviet support could prevent Israel from achieving her war aims.[36]

The U.S. peace initiative only sparked controversy relevant to the political aspects of Israel's responding to this initiative and not to the need to end the war. In August 1970, all political groups agreed that seventeen months of fighting and a high casualty toll, and especially in view of the military escalation entailed by the Soviet involvement, a cease-fire would be most useful, and the IDF could use the time to cultivate its strength.[37] This concordance on strategic issues should be emphasized.

The similarity between the threat concepts of different political groups was sufficient to permit the forming of a consensus structure, the National Unity Government. Its members (Labor, Mapam, Gahal, NRP, and Independent Liberals) concurred on basic political and security strategy: a rejection of any withdrawal to the cease-fire lines except in the frame of a peace agreement while maintaining some strategic depth. The leaders of those parties believed that a broad-based coalitionary government would evidence the degree of national unity required for holding on to the cease-fire lines. This, in fact, was why Golda Meir wanted Gahal inside, even though, based on the results of the 1969 Seventh Knesset elections, a Labor-led government could have been formed without it. Also, as seen by Meir, Galili, and Dayan, Gahal's presence would provide a good pretext for rejecting demands by dovish Laborites (for example, Abba Eban) to initiate a peace plan based on far-reaching compromises and territorial concessions.[38]

Not even the conspicuous ideological and political polarity between coalition parties stood in the way of their mutual cooperation. Mapam was leery of any political association with Herut. Since the 1967 War, most Mapam members wanted their party to be in a bloc with Labor, Rafi, and Ahduth Haavoda. This bloc could act to preserve and cultivate socialist values and head off any danger of Herut increasing its electoral strength. But most Mapam members wanted to influence national decision making.[39] Striking a fine balance between reluctance to associate with Gahal and wanting to be in the government, Mapam declared that it would take responsibility solely for government resolutions on "foreign, security and budgetary affairs."[40] It could thus participate in crucial national decision making while simultaneously demonstrating its distaste for any direct collaboration with Gahal. Gahal, however, was eager to be in the government so as to take part in national decision making, and actively promote the process begun in the waiting period, whereby it was gaining a seal of public legitimacy as a party worthy of acceding to ruling power.[41]

Mutual interests safeguarded the consensus structure. Mapam and Gahal made no great public furor about their views on the depth bombardments and the government's reactions to the Soviet involvement. Both believed that to publicize their dispute could later be detrimental to the promotion of party interests.[42] Public controversy was accordingly expressed only through radical opposition parties and peripheral extra-parliamentary groups.

Governmental Intervention and Intolerance

Except for Haolam Hazeh, all of the parties proclaimed the need for maximal national consensus so that all resources could be fully harnessed to the needs of the military victory. This reflected their understanding that controversy was liable to divert the attention of policymakers and the general public from the nation's wartime objectives.

But the War of Attrition wore on from month to month, during which time the smooth functioning of the pluralist Knesset engendered a new difficulty: was the call for national unity not distorting the character of the democratic regime? An artificial consensus would be tantamount to amputating from the body politic the important limb of public criticism of the government.[43] In the various parties the opinion evolved that consensus was needed mainly on military and security issues but not to foreign, social, and economic affairs.[44]

The ruling party, however, had an interest in promoting a sociopolitical order characterized by a definite consensus.[45] It was helpful to Meir and other leading proponents in the Labor Party (especially Dayan and Galili) in supporting their claim that the war was justifiable under any circumstances, at all costs, and without need for a peace initiative based on territorial compromise.[46] Considering the severity of the security situation, the dominant party might well be expected to display intolerance for opposing views. Relevant research shows that external pressure intensifies the hostility of political establishments and the public majority toward nonconformists.[47] Intolerance during the war took the form of political manipulation facilitated by the way the legal system was structured in Israel.

I have already shown how the political elites formulated a series of statutory norms enabling the political establishment to control public information and neutralize its own accountability. This was based on the pretext that national security requirements dictated that certain information be kept from the public. Article 28 of The Basic Law—The government (1968) classed as privileged the debates and resolutions of the cabinet and ministerial committees on subjects of security and foreign affairs, as well as "any matters of secrecy the government shall deem vital to the state interest." Prime Minister Meir classified cabinet debates as privileged, frequently declaring these sessions to relate to security affairs. Also, military-security censorship was imposed on political topics; and vital information, for example on possible peace initiatives, was concealed from the public. Pleading confidentiality, the ruling elite could easily conceal from the public both the existence of political controversies and their subject matter, thus creating an all-pervasive, if spurious, atmosphere of national consensus.[48]

This war was the first in Israel's history to be televised. Israeli television (ITV) was established in 1968 and, during the fighting, focused mainly on the military aspects of the campaign. But its broadcasts were first edited in the studio. As distinct from its practice in the 1973 War and, more especially, the Lebanese War, ITV was not yet broadcasting live from the battlefield. Hence, the civilian sector was not visually experiencing the dreadful implications of war.[49] Also, information reaching the public on the positions of opposition political groups was partial and superficial. The national agenda was shaped by the government, a fact that found expression in media reporting. Labor Party control of ITV and the support of most Hebrew-language newspapers for official policy contributed to the forming of a consensual sociopolitical order.[50] Even so, a degree of public opposition to the government's security policy did surface. Having already delineated its scope, I shall now explore its causes.[51]

Reasons for the Emergence of a Public Opposition in Favor of Ceasing Hostilities

One reason for the growth of contention was that its authors were guided by a threat concept different from that of the majority. A number of political groups disagreed with the prevailing assessment of the time dimension in the Israeli-Arab conflict. Political groups advocating military passivism or partial military passivism conceived time as operating to Israel's detriment: its democratic values were being corrupted and Israel's control of the territories was resulting in a tyrannical use of power; failure to use the territories as a bargaining card would lead to a superpower imposed peace agreement without Israeli security guarantees; refusal on Israel's part to recognize UN Resolution 242 would be injurious to her international standing; and the Arab states' armies would improve qualitatively and quantitatively and might also obtain nuclear weapons, whose development, in combination with the Soviet involvement in the Middle East, would magnify the danger to Israel's existence.[52]

Always excepting the majority of Mapam members, all political groups favoring military passivism or partial military passivism believed that if the Israeli government were but to initiate a peace plan based on Resolution 242, proposing a solution of the Palestinian problem, the chances of making peace would be significantly increased. Seeing that the government declined such a resolution, the political groups doubted the justice of the war.[53]

The purposes of the war were also at issue, especially once the government resolved to maintain the scope of the depth bombardments. The very hawkish groups of the Free Center and the Canaanites, on the one hand, approved the defensive military objective but also demanded an absolute military victory and the imposition of a political solution on Egypt, to be achieved by destroying her military infrastructure and occupying the west bank of the Suez. On the other hand, dovish groups (e.g., Haolam Hazeh and the Movement for Peace and Security) rejected depth bombardments of any sort. Such means, they claimed, were designed to overthrow the Nasser regime and impose a political solution, and were, as such, unjustifiable as self-defense. Moreover, since the United States was supplying Israel with military aid and the USSR was directly involved in the fighting, a cease-fire alone was viewed as the proper means for preventing Israel's possible engagement in a third world war.[54]

These were the positions that sparked controversy during the fighting. All of these dovish political groups accordingly opposed the government and wanted it dissolved. The Goldman affair confirmed their opinions. Nasser had invited Nahum Goldman, chairman of the World Jewish Congress, to visit Egypt for a discussion of the conflict and its termination. The Israeli government, at the behest of Prime Minister Meir, forbade Goldman to visit Egypt. The affair betrayed, they said, the government's refusal to end the hostilities by means of non-Israeli initiated peace agreements. The government, they concluded, was "sentencing" the public to war.[55] Being mainly Zionist and capable of using the democratic procedures, these groups did not negate the legitimacy of the political regime.

The various political groups opposing the security policy were small and, other than Haolam Hazeh and the Free Center, with their four Knesset members, lacked means of parliamentary expression. They accordingly exhorted the public to resort to extra-parliamentary means of protest. No alternative channel of political communication being available to them, all these political groups both denied and hence flouted the consensus values.[56]

Dovish political groups favoring extensive restrictions on the use of force were particularly aggressive. They called upon the public to disown and smash the consensus values, for to adhere to them would mean perpetuating the war.[57] Such a stance was not only due to their stand on the war issue, their threat concepts, or their propensity, as peripheral groups, for ideological radicalism. Their behavior also stemmed from low-grade fear responses.[58] Israel's survival being presumed to be in no immediate danger, they felt that national exertions should focus not merely on combat but also on the readiness of Israeli society and the political establishment to make peace.[59]

The human costs of the fighting incited to a limited degree such protest. The toll of military and civilian dead and injured in the war was 260 and 705 respectively on the Egyptian front, 51 and 279 respectively on other fronts. Total casualties on all fronts from the end of the Six-Day War to the end of the War of Attrition was 513 dead and 1959 injured (amounting to 0.077 percent of the total Jewish and Druze population).[60] But the hostilities as such were deemed to have been imposed on Israel and were considered "no-alternative" battles. Therefore, the number of casualties was not, of itself, a principal cause of dissent, as evidenced by the fact that it was not often cited by the political groups by way of delegitimizing the military campaign.[61]

While fighting was in progress, 9 percent (on the average) were concerned "for the safety of a drafted or injured family member or a friend", compared with an average of 10.7 percent in the prewar period commencing July 1967, and 29 percent (on average) during the Six-Day War. Moreover, even in months of peak casualty toll, most of the public (averaging about 80 percent) supported government policy. These findings show that, on the whole, the public, while aware of the gravity of the military situation, was not concerned with the incidence of casualties—despite the unprecedented publicity given by the media.[62] Findings thus indicate that the civilian hinterland as a whole was able to overcome ideological differences to evince a rather high level of public spiritedness. Yet, the preparedness to bear the burden of the combat eroded.

The War of Attrition continued longer than any of Israel's previous interstate wars; hostilities endured for seventeen months with no cease-fire. The long duration of the fighting had a threefold effect on the political system. Firstly, the public grew tired of the fighting, as it showed by querying the aims of the war and when it would end. Secondly, leftist political groups grew increasingly concerned that a long drawn-out war would result in political radicalization and ultimately the ruin of Israel's democratic values. Thirdly, war-inspired political developments such as the Rogers initiative and the Goldman affair had placed the question of peace on the national agenda.[63]

The scientific literature is not unanimous on how greatly the duration of a war may influence public support for political administrations. Controversy in the course of the War of Attrition derived primarily from fundamental differences in political outlook. Yet public confidence in the government waned in view of its failure to quickly end the war and to engineer peace.

For the first time in the history of Israel's wars, this lack of confidence found expression among intellectuals, university students, and high school students shortly due for the draft. The student protest was particularly interesting, expressing as it did a change in the sociopolitical game rules of distribution of the military service burden.

There were three main reasons for this change. First, some groups believed that the military threat was not serious and, even if it existed, was not intractable and could be solved by political means. Secondly, it was widely perceived that the government was not sufficiently pursuing peace. Thirdly, with the newly acquired strategic depth, the civilian sector was less fearful of being directly involved in or harmed by hostilities.

The protest, as it related to the military service burden, was expressed in letters, penned by students, to the government. One was published by university students on April 19, 1970. It included the following:

> If the high-sounding phrase "our face is to peace" is indeed a lie—does the meaning of the term "war of self-defense" not change? And what name is to be applied to killing? My friends the cabinet ministers, this is no academic question for one called upon to take part in it one month every year; . . . excuse me, gentlemen. I no longer believe in you.[64]

Protest letters were penned in reaction to the Goldman crisis. Their authors did not refuse to serve in the army, and even signified that, if called upon, they would fight. However, they challenged the premise that compulsory service came from the lack of any alternative but to fight.[65]

Such manifestations might be collectively termed "democratization of national security." The ruling political elite had always arrogated to itself a monopoly in defining security doctrine, and the right to usurp national security issues from the realm of public debate. But the public, hitherto acquiescent, was now starting to challenge that monopoly. In chapter 3 I described how a similar process eventuated during the waiting period. But this time, it occurred while the cannon roared.

There were now more extra-parliamentary groups than Israel had customarily known. Those groups were able to break new ground for political participation, as evidenced by the demonstrations and petitions they organized and by the inclusion of members of the Independent Liberals, NRP, Labor, Maki, and Mapam in the activity of the Movement for Peace and Security. Those involved now had a vehicle for expressing their views, even if those views were an anathema to their respective parties and to the parties' interests in keeping the national-unity government intact.[66]

Summary and Conclusions

Differences as to the use of armed force proved an essential but—due to organizational, structural, cultural, and environmental causes—an inadequate precondition for generating dissent. Consensus overcame all differences. In this sense, the ruling elite, including the military-security top brass, succeeded in gaining the confidence and support of most of the public for its security policy. Even after the Israeli government resolved to accept the American initiative (August 1970), a decision supported by 79 percent of the (Jewish-Israeli) public, 86 percent desired the continuance of the political partnership between Gahal and the Alignment, while only 8 percent of those opposing the decision and 15 percent of those supporting it wanted Gahal out of the government.[67] The majority considered the unity government to be the best means for achieving the goal of holding the cease-fire lines.[68]

The economic situation conspired to support prevailing opinion. Consumer price indices were rising only moderately, and the civilian sector in general betrayed no serious symptoms of economic slump. Quite to the contrary, the war brought wealth to some of the public, while the security-military establishment was enjoying its biggest-ever arms procurement boom. Security-related expenses rose steeply to 13.9 percent of the Gross National Product (GNP) in 1970 but never came up for serious public discussion, despite the implications for Israel's economic future. Thus, for example, in 1970 there commenced an era of very large loans from the U.S. government. Compared to a modest $50 million in the fifties and sixties, the U.S. loan, forming part of American aid, stood at $345 million in 1970. By and large, the Israeli public was unaware of these figures. The relatively high quality of life prevented the war from being seen as intolerable.[69]

Yet, some limited dissent took place. Protest targeted primarily the National Unity Government, in general, and Meir and Dayan, in particular. These two leaders stood accused, even by members of their own parties (mainly Avraham Ofer and Secretary-General Lova Eliav), of being reconciled to the state of war and of suppressing possible peace initiatives due to their territorial ambitions.[70]

Once having gained strategic depth, Israel had another possible alternative: not to fight even while security risks mounted. Some political groups glimpsed this possibility and took a critical look at its government. The interaction between military and political events, and the fact that this was no blitzkrieg in the style of the 1956 and 1967 wars, reinforced the tendency toward dissent. The types of direct threats to Israel's survival did not accompany the War of Attrition and the public began to wonder about its necessity and to clamor for "peace now." A plurality of attitudes in relation to armed force was thus publicly expressed during fighting. That so diverse a range of positions could be expressed was due to the character of the political system in which there were more political groups (twenty-six) than ever before.[71]

This being so, the political elites considered it vital to band together to prevent extensive public controversy. Their control over most of the nation's resources had a most significant impact, so much that public opposition to the war was edged to the political periphery. Parliamentary opposition, moreover, wilted sadly before the daunting strength of a dominant party. Opposition to the war was consequently expressed mainly on the extra-parliamentary plane. From this vantage point, it sometimes not only negated government policy but called into question the very basic values of the political establishment.

5 The Power Illusion Smashed and National Security Affairs (Partly) Democratized

Introduction

Opposition to the national security policy became broader and more prominent in 1973. The Yom Kippur War (1973) has been eulogized due to the military blunder, and some impressive military achievements, notwithstanding. In this chapter the reader is challenged to consider which sociopolitical (including legal) mechanisms generated a national consensus in the course of the fighting. Then this chapter conveys explanations about the crucial changes in Israeli culture, and in the structure of the party system, after the war. Attention is chiefly paid to the drastic shifts within the Labor camp, including the demise of Labor's political hegemony.

Without being decided militarily, the War of Attrition ended in an Israeli victory. Egypt failed to achieve her objectives, and the political status quo remained intact. The Israeli policy of retaining the cease-fire lines encountered intransigent demands from Nasser and his successor, Anwar Sadat, for an Israeli retreat from all territories. This deadlock eliminated a peaceful resolution to the conflict and increased the likelihood of border clashes.[1] But, the outbreak of hostilities on Yom Kippur sent shockwaves through the political system and most severely affected the supporters of the no peace–no war option.

Before the 1973 War, most Israelis perceived the country as an invincible regional power. Inspired by the architects of the national security concept, they likened Israel to an impregnable fortress. The Israel Defense Forces (IDF) were expected to promptly vanquish its enemies, demonstrating clear superiority over the Arabs. Israel, with her reliance on strategic depth and confidence in "secure" borders, now had to address very grave threats to her security. The armies of Syria and Egypt advanced on the Golan Heights and across Sinai, inflicting the heaviest losses since the war of 1948. IDF troops retreated, front-line headquarters were blown up, and in sectors where enemy forces were to have been smashed by sophisticated military traps, IDF troops were sparsely deployed and lacked offensive capability.

Of the settlements on the Golan, symbols of Israel's determination to ward off security dangers by retaining her hold on that region, some had their populations evacuated and others sustained damage by Syrian missiles. The Suez Canal, which according to certain publications was to serve as an impassable belt of fire, proved surprisingly easy to cross. The belt of armor forces proved exceedingly thin. Tanks were hastily scrambled to the battlefield with insufficient equipment and ammunition. Some were demolished there and then, others shortly after engaging in battle. Heroic tales would later be told of individuals holding off the enemy armor almost single-handedly. This was their finest hour—but hardly that of their senior commanding officers. The latter, who were to become known as "the generals," would hotly debate, in the later stages of the war and after its conclusion, the measure of their rivals' guilt and the magnitude of their own successes. But, in the first days of the fighting, as the defensive holding battles commenced, they were seized with fear. The architects of the security concept believed that Israel was fighting for her life.[2] The public understood that Israel's military situation was most assailable. Frequent rumors reached the civilian hinterland about the evacuation of settlements on the Golan Heights, along with reports of heavy losses, and Israelis saw pictures of Egyptian soldiers ripping, trampling, and burning the Israeli flag; dancing with delight at the entrances to the "Bar-Lev Line" bunkers; and exulting over their bandaged and bedraggled IDF POWs shown lying on stretchers.

Most reserve forces were mobilized within the first seventy-two hours of fighting, and the economy gradually evolved into an emergency market. Public attention focused on the military victory.

But as hostilities progressed, there was no joyful sense of triumph as in the Six-Day War, and none of the enthusiasm engendered by the Suez Campaign. The illusion that the end of the War of Attrition heralded the indefinite persistence of the status quo shattered against the hard rock of reality. Eventually, as the magnitude of the military surprise became known, profound changes began transforming Israeli politics and society.[3]

The next section dwells on the centrality of the territorial status quo as a concept generated by the Labor Party in the Israeli political discourse prior to the war. Labor's leadership severely challenged any effort to oppose its conception. The following sections examine how the fundamentals of the Israeli strategic concept were proved to be erroneous and why consensus nevertheless occurred. In this context, the scope of the fear responses and how it elicited values that condemned controversy and imposed social sanctions on dissent are discussed. Yet, significant opposition was soon to be expressed even in the political center. The demise of traditional sociopolitical myths; the emergence of political extremism, including religious nationalism; the growing legitimacy of the right-wing Likud; and protest within the Labor Party against its leadership are all examined.

Territoriality and the Politics of Might (August 7, 1970–October 6, 1973)

The success of the National Unity Government (1967–70) in preserving the status quo was proof, according to Herut's outlook, of the wisdom of its own positions whereby Israel's geostrategical situation and her military strength were preventing war, rendering any peace initiative superfluous. Herut's notion was that any such initiative would hinder realization of the Whole Eretz Israel vision. It accordingly set itself to define the main issues for the Eighth Knesset elections: control of areas of Eretz Israel must be assured with, especially, possible annexation of the West Bank.[4] Three months before the Knesset elections (October 1973), Menachem Begin addressed the Herut Center (July 31, 1973), saying the following:

> For the first time, a decision on Eretz Israel can be made through a voter's ballot slip. . . . Today there is no need to fight, no need to spill blood. All we need to do is to call upon the people to vote . . .[5]

Also, Israel's strategic territorial depth was perceived as a sufficient guarantee of her basic security and an essential element thereof in its own right.[6] Military activism, on the other hand, was clearly expressed in Herut's statements on current security issues. Following the terrorist attack on Lod Airport (May 31, 1972) and the murder of the Israeli sportsmen at Munich (September 5, 1972), Herut insisted that reprisals were no longer sufficient. Major military operations, or even war, were needed to force the Arab states to expel all terrorists from their jurisdiction.[7] Haim Landau, a senior party member, firmly declared in Knesset (October 31, 1972):

> Sporadic operations do not attain our ends. . . . We hit Syria yesterday, and what we did was good. . . . And Libya is within reach. . . . And now there is no doubt that war must be engaged boldly and persistently against the Arab states directly responsible, to stamp out terror. And the address is clear—concentrations of terrorists and murderers in the Arab states and throughout Europe.[8]

Ezer Weizmann, who at that time (1972), two years after retiring from the army, was one of the architects of Herut's security concept, recommended that the air force bomb Cairo, Damascus, Tripoli, and Beirut, since they were "the proper address to send the bill for the war crimes perpetrated by the terrorists."[9] Weizmann was against selective bombing merely in the vicinity of the capitals, claiming that, as in the American bombardments of Hanoi, the Arab capitals themselves should be bombed to force them to expel the terrorists. Further, to prevent terrorists from concentrating on the Israeli-Lebanese border, Weizmann recommended occupying southern Lebanon as far as the Litani River "until the government in Beirut undertakes to impose order in its land and throw out the terrorists as Hussein did."[10]

Although Weizmann's unmistakably activist concept did not include the messianic political component that colored Begin's, it did reveal distinct elements of Clausewitz-type thinking. According to his concept, the purpose of massive use of armed force was essentially political, annulling all "external hindrance" to the vital national interest. War could therefore justifiably be initiated if Israel's control of the territories was threatened, since such control was ideologically important and crucial to state security.[11] The military activism principle dear to Gahal as a whole, and later to the

Likud, was also embraced by the Free Center, thus finding expression in the Canaanite concept, too.[12]

But the Labor leaders, architects of the national security concept, believed that in view of the results of the 1967 War and the lessons taught in 1969–70, Israel's security should be based to a greater degree than in the past on military passivism. The War of Attrition had been fought far from the Israeli hinterland. This fact confirmed the Labor Party's understanding that it was both necessary and possible to assure Israel of strategic depth, so that limited regular forces could maintain a state of readiness, while in time of war a limited engagement could be fought far from Israel's population centers. Policymakers sought to base the security concept on two elements. The enemy was to be deterred from supporting the terrorists and, more importantly, from embarking on a war against Israel. And, should this deterrence fail, there must be at least five to six days' early warning, in which to mobilize reserve forces to assist in the war deployment.[13]

Israel's dependence on the United States also affected political attitudes toward the use of force. Israel was buying up, more than ever before, American equipment and arms of better quality than the Soviets could provide, and especially Skyhawk and Phantom fighter and bomber aircraft. An artificially maintained high standard of living, while security expenditure rose steeply, made Israel all the more dependent on America for grants and loans. At the same time, U.S. political support was becoming increasingly indispensable to counterbalance Soviet backing of the Arab states. From 1970 to 1973, this dependence assumed such proportions as to significantly impact issues of war and peace, influencing Labor leaders to avoid initiating military measures liable to be opposed by the United States.[14] Accordingly, Israel only suspended its participation in the Jarring talks in response to Egypt's August 8, 1970, breaching of the cease-fire by advancing thirty-four SA missiles to within 50 km west of the canal.[15]

There was a noteworthy similarity in policymakers' responses to the possible outbreak of war in the summer of 1973. Labor leaders (especially Golda Meir, Moshe Dayan, and Israel Galili) refused to order the IDF into a state of readiness for a forthcoming attack, even though intelligence of such an eventuality arrived during that summer. Primarily, it was feared that on learning what was afoot, the United States would pressure Israel to withdraw from the territories. A like mood was reflected when on October 6, 1973, Dayan,

Meir, and the Chief of the General Staff (CGS) David Elazar debated Elazar's proposal that the air force begin a preemptive strike by bombing concentrations of Egyptian and Syrian troops, or only Syria. Dayan and Meir rejected the proposal not only because they doubted that war would really break out, and not only by reason of their boundless faith in IDF strength and the potency of the strategic depth, but also for fear that the United States might slash its support on the grounds that Israel had initiated an apparently unnecessary war.[16]

Labor attitudes toward current security, however, remained unchanged. Strategic depth was not crucial in warding off attempted terrorist actions, and the United States concurred with the government's view that terrorist clusters on Israel's borders were intolerable. Labor accordingly favored the initiation of limited military operations against Palestinian camps and headquarters as a means of preventing terrorist activity.[17] Seemingly as a result of the IDF's successes in 1967 and 1970, partial military activism had the explicit or implied support of Agudath Israel, Poalei Agudath Israel, and the National Religious Party (NRP) in the religious camp, the Independent Liberals in the civic camp, the Whole Eretz Israel Movement and the State List in the Labor camp.[18]

Mapam offered no overt opposition to Labor's leadership. To do so could jeopardize its collaboration with the dominant ruling party. Moreover, overt criticism of the Labor Party was seen as tantamount to an attack on the Alignment and an attempt to weaken the Labor camp, thus aiding the political right. Members of Mapam did, however, object to some of the basic components of Labor's policy. The party had not budged from its condemnation of the political deadlock, neither-peace-nor-war, its negation of the war of offense principle, or its advocacy of political activism for resolving the conflict. With the expanding power of the Palestine Liberation Organization (PLO), Mapam became increasingly uneasy that in the absence of any dialogue between the Israeli government and the Palestinian leadership in the territories, the PLO would gain control of political life while Israel would endeavor to stamp out terror by the use of force. Thereupon the opportunity for a political solution to the problem of the Palestinian people would be missed.[19] Mapam urged an Israeli peace initiative based on territorial compromise but one that ensured Israel secure boundaries and recognition of the Palestinian people's right to self-determination. It was considered the sole means of preventing the Arabs from attempting to militarily force Israel to withdraw from the territories and the only way to achieve a peace agreement.[20]

Mapam construed the political status quo as further proof that war was an ineffective means of achieving peace. An Israeli peace initiative should therefore be combined with partial military passivism. Thus, it opposed any military initiative against the Egyptian missiles that had been advanced to the banks of the canal in breach of the ceasefire agreement.[21] The party also denounced unrestricted military responses to terrorism.[22] The following appeared in *Al Hamishmar*:

> .... we have before us a protracted campaign, necessitating general responsibility, political wisdom, resourcefulness.... a method must be evolved that reconciles the effectiveness of the struggle with the purity of arms.[23]

Nearly approximating these positions was the Maki concept. Party leader Moshe Sneh emphasized that, if on social and economic questions Maki exhibited a Zionist-communist opposition, on the issue of war, his party took its stand with the "national defense front."[24] His use of this expression signified that Maki's advocacy of partial military passivism remained unchanged. The party clearly set forth its positions in a brief preliminary to the Seventeenth Maki Conference of February 16, 1972, "Maki views as a defensive exigency the actions of the IDF and the security forces in exterminating terrorism, paralyzing terrorist centers, [and] thwarting terrorist designs (Section 2)."[25] Free, however, of Mapam's encumbrances of coalitionary discipline, Maki publicly insisted that the government not confine its efforts to preventing terrorism by limited military action but that it promote conflict resolution by being receptive to the principle of founding a Palestinian state.[26]

The status quo was being challenged also on the extra-parliamentary plane. The Movement for Peace and Security asserted that Egypt's failure in the War of Attrition would cause her to moderate her attitudes, thereby enhancing the prospects of success of an Israeli peace initiative. The movement blamed government policy for the political deadlock that it had obtained since 1971. Like Mapam, the Movement cautioned against any attempt on Israel's part to alter, by military force, the status quo. But unlike Mapam, the Movement stressed its rejection of limited military actions, such as the air-force bombardments of Syrian army bases (November 9, 1972) which, it felt, were liable to escalate into war.[27]

While striving to have serious and comprehensive restrictions imposed on the use of armed force, it also kept up an incisive criticism against the settling of the territories. The Movement heavily stressed the damage inflicted by the occupation to the democratic values, inasmuch as the massive use of force was inherently incompatible with liberal freedoms. The settlement drive, they claimed, was hamstringing the government's options of offering peace terms based on territorial compromise, isolating Israel in world forums, and uniting the Arab states in their readiness to launch the next war.[28]

Collapse of the Mainstays of Israel's Security Concept

The champions of military passivism or partial military passivism and the advocates of military activism or partial military activism competed for political supremacy. At issue was the immediate and more remote future of the conflict. The former viewed the status quo as a passing stage, fated to be of brief duration, since the political deadlock would spur the Arab confrontation states (Egypt, Syria, and Jordan) to open war with the aim of occupying territories and thus coerce Israel into making meaningful political concessions. Hazan succinctly expressed this view in Knesset (January 24, 1973):

> The no-peace-no-war equilibrium is in constant danger [of being upset]. Unless the voice of statesmanship makes itself heard, we run an increasing risk that the roar of the cannon will.... All the threats and promises of her president [Sadat] have lapsed. This year [1973] all his notes fall due: either war or peace.[29]

The promilitary activism camp took a different view. Israel's geostrategic advantage, the superiority of her fighting forces, and the cutback in Soviet support for Egypt would deter the Arabs (for two or three years at least) from attacking.[30] Herut member Haim Landau put it this way, "Peace is achieved by maintaining an advantageous strategic position over a protracted period of time, otherwise there is no chance of peace but only of war."[31] The same view was expressed by Labor's propaganda messages in the 1973 elections purporting that Israel's security situation had never been better.[32]

Galili confidently expressed the same concept, just two days before war broke out (October 4, 1973), "in the absence of peace, we maintain the ceasefire lines on all fronts without withdrawing and remain undeterred . . . and he who would know our intentions and our territorial aspirations—let him study the map of settlements we want included in the permanent and peaceful boundaries of Israel."[33]

That concept was also reflected in plans to slash the defense budget and reduce the term of the military service; in new appointments (September 1973) to the senior military command (including the Southern Command); and in the closing down of strongholds on the Bar-Lev line, leaving the greater part of IDF armor dormant, some being shunted back to the rear lines.[34] Even the media failed to warn of the approaching tempest. In covering the Syrian and Egyptian dispatching of reinforcements to their respective fronts, they concurred with the army-intelligence assessment that the Egyptians were conducting summer maneuvers while the Syrians were anticipating possible escalation in military tensions, following the downing of thirteen Syrian MiGs by the Israeli Air Force (September 13, 1973). Also, news of Syrian preparations during the days prior to the fighting, were censored with the consent of the Editors' Committee of Israel's Daily Press.[35]

The 1973 War refuted certain premises of the Israeli security concept. Deterrence proved to be of limited value. It was based on the enemy's perception and its assessment of the value of deploying armed force. Thus, for all their geostrategic advantages, Israel's borders had not prevented the outbreak of hostilities. Israel's qualitative advantage proved inadequate in preventing enemy gains in a short space of time. Also, the manner in which war was launched, the quantity and quality of the enemy's personnel and matériel, and superpower involvement were liable to result in such erosion of the IDF's strength that its ability to achieve a decisive military outcome was prejudiced. These factors necessitated Israel's mobilizing 93 percent of her draftees and absorbing, while hostilities were in progress, a massive injection of American military aid.[36]

Shortly after the outbreak of hostilities, on October 7, 1973, the premier and the defense minister declared that the army had been deployed along the cease-fire lines in readiness for the offensive, which had been foreseen, but that the government, having considered the situation well beforehand, had resolved to forgo a preemptive strike.[37] However, the public became aware in the very first days of the fighting that neither the political nor the military establishment had responded appropriately to international circumstances and that the IDF was sustaining heavy losses. Even so, the consensus in the political system remained intact throughout most of the war, until news arrived of the cease-fire agreement (October 22, 1973). It was reflected in Knesset debates on the war (October 16, 1973) when coalition and opposition delegates alike refrained from criticizing the government, merely intimating (all but the Alignment people) that once the fighting was over the government would have to answer some hard questions.[38] The political groups believed that present exigencies dictated their refraining from public opposition.

This belief mirrored the general consensual trends. Public opinion polls reveal that most of the public believed that Israel's general situation in the military engagement was "good or very good" (62.8 percent) and declared itself satisfied with "the government's handling of the uncertainties of the situation" (86.9 percent) and of "the state's security problems" throughout the war (85.9 percent); 52 percent thought the government was right to avoid a preemptive strike, while 74 percent agreed with the decision to accept the cease-fire. The public's perception of the surprise was not accompanied by any noteworthy decline in satisfaction with government policy, compared to the period immediately preceding the eruption of hostilities. This may have been due to insufficient information and to the gradual process whereby the public learned its lessons.[39]

Only three peripheral groups deviated from the consensus: the left-wing Moked and Meri, of Haolam Hazeh, and, on the right, the Free Center. Moked and Meri believed that had the government asserted its readiness to retreat from the occupied territories, the war could have been averted. The fighting, they maintained, was not only the putrid fruit of erroneous military assessments but mainly of a wrongheaded political concept.[40] The Free Center, by contrast, highlighted current events, asserting that had the reserves been called up in time, the government could have crushed the initial attack and dictated its own peace terms.[41]

The Indispensability of Consensus under the Impact of Surprise

How was it that public opposition was scrupulously avoided (with a few exceptions) as long as hostilities continued? Fear responses provide one of the explanations. It is doubtful whether the Syrio-Egyptian offensive actually posed a threat to the state's existence. But judging by the prevailing political responses, Israel's survival was perceived to be in palpable and immediate danger. This was due to a number of factors. The all-out, coordinated military offensive on two fronts, with heavy losses; the occupation of settlements and the loss of strategic depth on the Golan Heights; the erosion of IDF strength; Frog missile attacks on settlements; the loss of territories in Sinai and Soviet involvement in the fighting, betokened a relatively protracted, total war with a heavy casualty toll. This time, Israel was forced to hold off and repulse the mass breaching of her boundaries by enemy forces, while urgently appealing for American aid.

As during the waiting period, fear was expressed by drawing parallels with the Holocaust era and the War of Independence.[42] These fears elicited descriptions of the war as, "a war over the very survival of the Jewish state" (MK and Premier Golda Meir), "a war of salvation and redemption" (MK Menachem Begin), "a war to save life and the state" (MK Yitzhak Rafael), "a war of survival" (MK Gideon Hausner), "an explicit tendency to genocide" (Yediot Ahronoth).[43] It was not until the last week of the fighting, when IDF forces stormed the main highways to Cairo and Damascus in a drive to gain the upper hand and engineer a cease-fire, that the supposedly very real threat was considered to have been averted.

Anxiety began to subside. On October 18, 1973, the CGS announced that the "war-for-survival stage" was over, and on October 20, the defense minister stated that each additional day of fighting was to the benefit of Israel, who would accordingly countenance a cease-fire only if the Arab states requested one.[44] As the cease-fire agreement neared execution on October 22, 1973, parties, politicians, and the military establishment all concurred that a victory had been won, but at the painful cost of heavy losses; there were also misgivings that Soviet military involvement might yet stoke the still flickering flames of battle.[45]

Threat concepts reflected these trends. During the seventies, the time dimension had assumed greater clarity. The Likud, Labor, and their supporters claimed that the political status quo was operating in Israel's favor. Egypt's failure to impose a withdrawal on Israel was believed, until the very outbreak of hostilities, to demonstrate that the passage of time was enabling the state to widen the quality gap between itself and the Arab states. Justification was thereby adduced for the political deadlock and Israel's retention of the territories.[46] These agreed threat concepts provided a broad basis for public consensus on national security issues. Certainly, left-wing parties, especially Mapam, had some fundamental reservations about it, but their views were not accorded prominence on the national agenda.

What did, however, draw some very barbed public criticism, especially after the combat ended, were the government's decisions not to order total mobilization and not to initiate a preemptive military strike. Inasmuch as battlefield realities contrasted so starkly with prewar pronouncements by the architects of the security concept, all political groups (except the Alignment) called for a public debate on the causes of the "blunder" as soon as the fighting terminated.[47]

Until the waiting period (1967), and to a considerable extent until the Yom Kippur War, security policy was the exclusive province of a most rarefied political elite (the premier, defense minister, and a few leading Laborites in senior cabinet positions, along with the CGS and the military-security top brass).[48] The public now demanded more control over the shaping of the security policy.

Even so, while battles were in progress, a broad-gauge consensus ostensibly prevailed. Public debate in wartime was condemned, especially if focusing on military and security issues. The logic of this view was, that in times of emergency, democratic freedoms ought not to be fully exploited because to do so could divert the public attention and the combatant forces from trying to achieve military victory and would also impinge on the morale of the troops.[49] This was the result of expediency calculations in view of the perceived danger of annihilation.

Radio, television, and the press made their contributions to the political atmosphere during the fighting. They concentrated on reporting and providing military commentary on war moves, declining criticism of the "blunder." Operating under military-security censorship, the press was also careful to not divulge information. Differences of opinion in senior officer ranks, and the manner in which the political echelon had acquitted itself, were not given media coverage. Hence, the Israel Daily Press Editors' Committee refrained from publishing Dayan's "doomsday" speech. He confided to his amazed audience that Israel was facing "the destruction of the Third Temple." A statement such as this by a man hailed as a national hero, an untarnished security genius, might have been pounced on as a significant news item. But the editors resolved to not publish it. The media, whether deliberately or inadvertently, bolstered nationalist and patriotic feeling and rejected opposition as a luxury. Prominently highlighted by the media, for example, was a massive civilian volunteer drive in aid of the war effort.[50]

Consensus values affected not the content but the modes of political participation. They forestalled public debate on disputed issues either among the coalition parties or between them and the opposition. Controversy was voiced mainly after the belligerency ended. The degree of public consent to "agree to disagree" was a function of fear responses elicited by developments in the theater of war. Such a tendency was also expressed legislatively. All parties agreed that the election campaign must be suspended, and the Central Committee for the Eighth Knesset Elections (basically an interparty political body) resolved to ban all election propaganda for the duration of the war. Greater attention was only given to the "surprise" in mid-October 1973, when it had been mostly reversed. This process was to be furthered after the cease-fire agreement took effect, and the resultant political crisis was on a scale hitherto unprecedented in Israel.

Opposition and Protest

Even before the war, the spokesmen of the dovish parties declared that Israel must initiate a peace plan.[51] Mapam, Moked, and Civil Rights Movement (CRM) reiterated these positions throughout the fighting. As MK Shmuel Mikunis said during a Knesset debate:

> In remarking on this [the Soviet Union's guilt in the outbreak of the war], we do not desist from our criticism of the government, which not only did not take advantage of the years of ceasefire on behalf of peace initiatives but actually piled up obstacles of its own making and followed a policy of "creeping annexation" of the occupied territories. . . . [The] status quo has not prevented the present pointless war. We are persuaded that had the territorial status quo been traded for a peace agreement and security arrangements, the present war would almost certainly have been avoided.[52]

Central to criticism voiced during and after the fighting was that the use of force and control of the occupied territories did not amount to a political solution to the conflict.

The political right, on the other hand, while concurring in the war's frustrative aim, had another criticism. The Likud called for further combat in order to break the enemy's will to attack in the future.[53] Shmuel Tamir, on behalf of his Likud faction—the Free Center—also called for the imposition of a peace agreement:

> In three wars we have repulsed the enemy, broken its military strength, and achieved a temporary ceasefire. Our aim in the Yom Kippur War must be to make peace. And as we have to do with a despotic regime that refuses all compromise—refuses even a ceasefire—making peace means dictating peace.[54]

Moreover, according to the political right, the IDF ought to pursue its war objectives by also deploying force against economic and civilian targets, in the hope that if these were hard hit, the populations of the Arab states would agitate for peace.[55]

The great majority of the political right was secular, while the religious right, due to come into its own in the mid-seventies, was not yet significantly affecting the sociopolitical order. Military activism, however, was embraced by Meir Kahane's several-dozen-strong extraparliamentary "Jewish Defense League." The pressure of events and survival anxiety prompted it to join the consensus in the course of the fighting. Afterwards, the league lambasted the government for refraining from eliminating the military capabilities of Syria and Egypt. The leitmotif of its concept was that Judaism imposed the duty of inheriting Eretz Israel, and force must be deployed as the sole means of founding a Jewish-Halakhic state in all its parts.[56]

These Clausewitz-style concepts were diametrically opposed, especially, to the positions of dovish groups within or left of the Labor Party. Yitzhak Ben-Aharon, an Ahduth Haavoda leader of a more dovish persuasion, stated the following (October 23, 1973):

> We are fighting for nothing but survival. Israel fights none but defensive wars. As long as . . . the Labor movement and the workers and settlers, youth and sons of Israel are the ones presently bearing the system on their shoulders, there will be no war in Israel for the sake of conquests, for vanquishing other nations, for establishing more convenient borders, but when war is imposed upon us, we risk our lives fighting it and do not regard it as the political solution.[57]

The Labor Party needed the support of those dovish groups if the consensual order were to be preserved. The political elite, headed by Meir and Dayan, faced a threat of scathing in-party opposition. Once the fighting was over, dovish groups were to express vehement protest. Yet as long as hostilities raged, they justified the manner in which armed force was being deployed. True to their preference for the restriction of force, the groups opposed attacks on civilian targets. They also consented to the government's policy of only deploying the IDF against military targets, or economic targets serving enemy armies in their belligerence, with scrupulous avoidance of any damage to civilians.[58]

The diplomatic conditions under which the war should be concluded formed the focus of public debates as the hostilities ended. On October 23, the Likud leadership published a statement vigorously rejecting any cease-fire that would involve the implementation of UN Resolution 242. Begin still believed Israel could inflict an absolute military defeat on Syria and Egypt, utterly breaking their will to fight again. The Likud's positions were shaped not by considerations of the use of armed force alone, but by its fundamental attitude toward the territories, especially the West Bank. As the Likud saw it, implementation of Resolution 242 was liable to culminate in a retreat from all the territories.[59]

To Mapam, Moked, and Meri the military victory was to be measured solely on the basis of deflective, limited military achievements and not in terms of political objectives attained in war. Military victory meant that the hostilities must cease as soon as possible, on convenient military terms approximating the status quo ante bellum. The only admissible solution to the conflict was via diplomatic settlement. The parties called for a cease-fire, claiming that the war objective (to repulse Syrian and Egyptian forces back across the borders) had been attained.[60] The religious parties, the Independent Liberals, and all political groups in the Labor Party joined in citing these grounds for cease-fire.

For the first time since 1949, the casualty count was at issue in public debates on the war. Dovish groups and Labor argued that heavy losses were another reason for Israel to rest content with achieving the frustrative objective. Likud, in the opposite corner, seeking to cast doubt on the policymakers' credibility and judgment and drum up another reason for not ending the war, blamed the heavy casualty toll on the government's tardiness in calling up the reserves.[61]

This precedent would be followed in the Lebanese War, whereby bereavement was deliberately used as a means of political persuasion and mobilization. This change is of itself indicative of how acerbic the political contention over armed force had become.

Resurfacing following debates on the cessation of hostilities and the shock of the "blunder," were political dilemmas as to permanent territorial boundaries. The Likud, anxious to stress that whereas the reserves had not been called up in time, secure borders had actually prevented Israel's destruction. Yigal Hurewitz attempted to explain his most important conclusion to the Knesset on October 23:

> After all, the borders of June 1967 gave the IDF some essential breathing space in terms of both time and territory, for which then, as now, there is no substitute. This is the most important conclusion of this war.[62]

Moked, Meri, and Mapam, on the other hand, underscored that alleged errors of judgment by decision makers stemmed from an erroneous political concept of the territories. Uri Avneri, speaking in Knesset on October 23, focused on the politically mistaken notion of "secure boundaries":

> Let us talk of that fallen idol: strategic depth. In war, it is good to have strategic depth. We therefore strenuously oppose and continue to strenuously oppose withdrawal from the territories without a peace that ensures security, ensures it in actual practice. But if the strategic depth is the very factor that prevents the peace, if we are relinquishing a chance at peace because of a wish to annex territories—then we are creating a bloody paradox, one which will condemn us to fight a war every few years.[63]

With the war over, Labor leaders repeatedly rejected opposition charges that they had blundered in not calling up the reserves and in failing to put the army in readiness. Economic requirements, they retorted, had dictated that the borders be manned by sparse forces only, since a prolonged general mobilization would have caused severe economic damage. Dayan also explained that news of the immediate danger of war only reached the political echelon a few hours before the war started.[64]

More detailed information was fed to the public as to the political and military bungling of its leaders. The political factors that had made for consensus during the war were changing. These developments, combined with the way the government responded to accountability charges, led to more intensive and extensive protest. The number of extra-parliamentary groups publicly disputing government policy increased significantly (twenty-one compared with six during the war). The protest negated the legitimacy of the government's resolutions, calling for its immediate resignation, and advocated a transformation of the collective values. Politics was characterized by "retrospective dissent" in which the war, now that it had ended, was a subject for public criticism.

The Labor leaders were held to bear parliamentary responsibility for their wrong decisions. Thus the political system for the first time reached a consensus that dissent could rightfully be expressed on national security affairs. Dayan's resignation was vociforously demanded, and as defense minister he bore ministerial responsibility for military blunders.

Factions within the Labor Party or among its supporters registered the more effective protest. Intellectuals, scientists, writers, poets, artists, and senior ex-army officers voiced their demands for the resignation of the government. They also wanted the Labor Party, in the name of democratic participation, to reopen the list of candidates to the Eighth Knesset elections (December 1973). They called for the advancement of the "doves" who favored initiating an Israeli peace plan based on significant territorial withdrawal.[65] This was the first instance of overt protest by groups within the predominant ruling party over issues of national security. The decentralization of political power was clearly being sped up.[66]

Israeli politics was still dominated by party politics. But now that the policymakers had lost credibility within their own party, protest developed all the more rapidly. The policymakers exerted themselves to put a stop to the rot that was speedily devouring their status. They leaked information, backed by explicit statements about how the cease-fire was in jeopardy and that Syria was about to resume hostilities. Implicit in this was the familiar theme of the vital need for national unity and support for the government.[67] However, still reeling from the shock of the war, increasingly outraged at the "blunder," the political system was now in a protest mood.

Time-honored myths, including Labor's unique responsibility over national security, were dismissed by a large part of the public as unfounded. With 50 percent of the reserve forces demobilized, protest groups were able to organize rapidly. The brunt of this protest was borne by young people fresh from the front who had directly experienced the worst excesses of the war.

In February 1974, demobilized soldiers formed two groups, headed respectively by Motti Ashkenazi and Assa Qadmoni. They had no definite positions regarding the war, and did not dispute the government's policy in that respect. They protested especially against and called for the resignation of Dayan, Meir, and CGS Major-General Elazar for their responsibility in not calling up the reserve forces soon enough and for not ordering a sufficient state of war readiness. They also called for Haim Bar-Lev to step down for his responsibility in putting up a line of fortifications that, while creating an illusion of power, had proved not to be worth the resources invested in it. The surprise, the protest groups argued, would never have happened had the Knesset not functioned as a "rubber stamp" for the government's decisions; as for Labor's leaders, they would not have denied responsibility for their grave mistakes were the politicians and the administration not so blandly indifferent to the common people and were it not for the degeneracy of the parties, with their deliberate disregard for their supporters' opinions.[68] Hence, the protest groups agitated for "launching a frontal attack on the system, which we want shattered and rebuilt."[69] Their goals were the formation of ministerial responsibility as a political norm, limitation of the term of office of Knesset members and ministers, increased parliamentary and extra-parliamentary criticism of national security affairs, democratization of the parties and a change in the electoral system, so as to increase political accountability.[70]

Public clamor notwithstanding, the Agranat Committee, appointed as a national commission of enquiry, being loath to probe the government's responsibility, held the military echelon to blame for the blunder. Protest groups retaliated by uniting for greater strength. Eleven minor protest groups joined forces in a single extra-parliamentary protest movement: "Our Israel." It considered demonstrations and assemblies to be the most effective means of generating changes in political game rules, and collective values. "Shinui" (Change) was founded as a two-hundred-member extra-parliamentary group. Unlike Our Israel, it aimed to become a political party and realize its goals through parliamentary activity. The founders were intellectuals who, while hardly alienated from the political system, were dissatisfied with it. In their opinion, the war had uncovered defective administrative and governmental patterns, primarily the disregard for ministerial responsibility. Its primary targets were to anchor civil rights in a written constitution, to reinforce the responsibility principle in the public administration, and to inculcate the values of "good and active citizenship in a democratic society."[71]

Lacking any definitive position on the use of military force, the protest groups clearly posited that the conflict could be solved only by peaceful means and that, as demonstrated by the war, perpetuation of the status quo could tempt the Arab states to launch a military offensive. According to Shinui, an Israeli peace plan ought to be initiated on the basis of territorial compromise "provided Israel's safety and security are assured."[72]

The emphatically hawkish Gush Emunim (Block of Faith)[73] was convinced that like the rest of Israel's wars, the 1973 clash was a result of the inevitable conflict between the Arab nation and the Zionist movement. War was conceived a functional means of "liberating" territories of Eretz Israel.[74] Two factors spurred Gush Emunim into protest action: the weakness of the dominant party and the belief that lack of preparedness and the failure to call up the reserve forces in time exhibited certain grave defects in the political system.

The policymakers' shortcomings were defined as deriving from basic defects in the secular political establishment: indifference to the future of the Jewish people, blatant disregard of the national imperative of settling and annexing territories of Eretz Israel, ideological decadence, and the preferment of personal and party over national and Zionist-religious interests. In contrast to other protest groups, Gush Emunim aspired to replace the secular establishment and political culture with a Torah-based establishment and a religious political culture. From February 1974, the Gush focused on political activity, which it termed "positive protest." The most heavily accentuated of its goals was the divine imperative of settling Eretz Israel, especially Judea and Samaria.[75]

Attesting to the unprecedented scope of public protest was the decline in the popularity ratings of the government and a rise in the number of the undecided: some 26 percent of the adult Jewish population (18 years and over) who had no specific candidate for the posts of premier and minister of defense.[76] And, accompanying this shift were calls for greater citizen involvement in national decision-making processes as a means of preventing errors of the kind perpetrated immediately before the outbreak of hostilities. The message came loud and clear especially from Our Israel and Shinui, and also from a number of parties—Independent Liberals (IL), Moked, Haolam Hazeh, and CRM—on whose behalf MK Shulamit Aloni declared:

> I do not believe you. I do not believe what you say; I do not believe in your judgment; I do not believe in your thinking and planning capability. From the moment shame takes flight, from the moment there is a failure to assume responsibility, from the moment you destroyed notions of reward and punishment, from the moment you revealed that you operate solely in accordance with personal emotional whims and that nothing short of death will pry you loose from the seats you cling to—I do not believe you; I have no faith in you. People who consider themselves indispensable—are the most dangerous of rulers.[77]

Summary and Conclusions

For the first time in the annals of the wars of Israel, the very center of the political system evinced dissatisfaction with the national security policy. Consensus prevailed in spite of it all, weakening significantly only on execution of the cease-fire agreement. The principal factors of the consensus were fear responses and threat concepts.

Fear responses reflected the immediate effects of the surprise and the breaching of the Bar-Lev Line. Political groups fearing the destruction of the Jewish-Zionist state refrained from expressing dissent. This was where consensus values came into play. It was under their influence that contentious political issues were played down.[78] But when a cease-fire was signed before the enemy forces could be soundly drubbed and when the decision makers refused to accept responsibility for their errors, the responses of the latter were seen to be widely at variance with public expectations and demands. The discrepancy was mirrored in widening dissent.

These protest groups, with their heterogeneous personal-political composition, won the sympathy of Likud, NRP, Labor, IL, Mapam, CRM, Meri, and Moked. These represented the entire political spectrum. The protest also had the support of the young political generation in most parties, including Labor and the Zionist-religious parties.

The membership of the protest groups was far younger than that of the extra-parliamentary groups spawned by the War of Attrition, and their message was distinctive. They should not be regarded as a continuation of the extra-parliamentary political groups of the early seventies. Nor were the protest groups an offspring of the political protest culture that seemingly evolved during 1969–70. They came into being as a direct result of the political convulsions that followed the 1973 War.

The elections campaign, conducted under the painful impressions that the war left, centered on two issues: was the formula, "territories in return for peace," appropriate for resolving the conflict? And, to what degree were the government and the Labor leadership responsible for the surprise? While the first issue was contentious, on the second issue, all but certain Labor Party groups agreed that the leaders had erred by their complacency, overconfidence, and their faulty conduct of decision-making processes. In the elections (December 31, 1973), support for the Alignment (Labor and Mapam) decreased by 14 percent, as against a 16 percent increase in support for the Likud.

The parties became increasingly vociferous in demanding the resignation of Dayan when, on April 3, 1974, the Agranat Committee published its report ascribing to him ministerial responsibility for military blunders. Joining the chorus this time were also Mapam and IL, on the grounds that making the CGS, David Elazar, sole scapegoat for the mistakes would be contrary to the democratic principle of ministerial responsibility. All parties also concurred that the prewar government was not fit to rule. Its ministers lacked the political wisdom needed for making important decisions. Not even the resignation of Meir's government in April 1974 was a sufficient response to prevent mounting opposition to the Labor Party.

The impact of the 1973 War on the evolution of the Israeli political system, society, economy, and culture would make itself felt over the long term. Only some of its effects are relevant to this study, for example, the 1977 Knesset elections, the defeat of Labor, and the ascendancy of Likud to power.

6 War of Initiative and Political Polarization

Introduction

The Lebanese War shall be long recalled due to the extensive public protest it witnessed. This chapter contains, indeed, an analysis of dissent during the war. Yet, I claim that the Lebanese War and the opposition to it should be understood in light of historical processes that explain how polarization had influenced Israeli politics until 1982, as well as which cultural (not only electoral and institutional) propensities had taken place, especially in the aftermath of the 1973 War. Subsequent to an illumination of the war's etiology, a detailed explication of the protest against the war and the state's reaction to it is discussed. My main argument is that extra-parliamentary protest can be understood by explaining two main issues: alterations within the party system and the war's characteristics as an intercommunal and interstate conflict. Hence, the Lebanese War clearly demonstrates the interactions between international war and internal strife and violence.

The January 17, 1985, decision to withdraw the Israeli military forces from Lebanon was an achievement for the Labor-Likud National Unity Government. The withdrawal was viewed as terminating a superfluous, protracted, and costly war that achieved little.

The opening stages of the Lebanese War (June 5, 1982), were framed as a limited military operation and were supported by most of the public, the parties and extra-parliamentary groups, and the great majority of IDF senior officers and the media. But opposition to the war gradually mounted. On June 11, 1982, a cease-fire was declared. The fighting continued, however, to the accompaniment of rising dissent. It alleged that the limited military operation was becoming an all-out offensive against the Palestine Liberation Organization (PLO) and the Syrian forces in Lebanon and not an effort to protect the settlers on the Galilee, an attempt to impose a new political and military order in the Middle East that was in line with the Likud's political concept.

By late June 1982, debate of unprecedented scope raged during the fighting, along with such unaccustomed forms of political participation as military disobedience, massive political protest, and violence. One antiwar slogan clearly reflected the public's alienation from its government:

> Do not destroy the IDF in wars for which it was never intended. Do not destroy the State, it is the only one we have. We say No to violence, No to lying and No to despair.[1]

In her previous wars Israel had sought to frustrate palpable threats to her existence or at least an immediate security danger to her basic security. The Lebanese War, however, as I shall demonstrate, represented a deviation from the national security concept established and evolved since 1949.

Three main factors led to the outbreak of the fighting and to the attendant controversy as well. One was the effect produced by the Yom Kippur War on attitudes toward issues of peace and war, reinforced by the Egypt-Israel peace treaty of March 1979. Following this, the Labor camp became increasingly opposed to the initiation of any military operation for fear of damaging Israel's relations with the United States and Egypt. The agreement, however, only reinforced Likud's and Tehiya's faith in military activism. The second factor was the impact of the 1973 War on the dispersion of political power between the various political organizations, culminating in the 1977 formation of the Likud government. The third factor was that the Palestinian problem was becoming increasingly troublesome to Israel, with an accompanying upgrading of Palestinian military activities. The combined result of it all was a growing polarization between Likud's military activism and the preference for the limited use of military force of most political groups. A detailed analysis of these processes follows.

Between Wars: Effects of the Yom Kippur War on Attitudes to the Status Quo

Regardless of Syrian and Egyptian gains in the early days of the Yom Kippur War, Mapam grimly adhered to its partial military passivism. The fact that the (Israel Defense Forces) IDF's military strength had been eroded in the course of the combat, and that the government had consented to a cease-fire before the Egyptian armies were destroyed, was proof, in the eyes of Mapam, of the limited usefulness of force. Seeing that the conflict was not amenable to definitive resolution by military means, and fearing a military buildup by the Arab states, Mapam concluded that time was working to Israel's detriment, and that she would be under ever greater difficulties in succeeding wars. The party accordingly called upon the government to initiate a peace plan. Mapam's delegates to Alignment institutions called for the erasure from the 1973 Alignment platform that called for massive settlement of the territories. The Alignment's platform was amended to that effect, not only at Mapam's behest, but as a direct result of the traumatic impact that the war had on the Labor Party.[2]

Labor, in theory, retained its traditional approach. What had changed was its willingness to apply that approach in practice. Labor applauded the government's decision of October 1973 to eschew the preemptive strike on the grounds that the U.S. administration would not have granted Israel military aid during the fighting.[3] But if Labor's military restraint was more insistent than before 1973, its political activism was correspondingly greater. Most members of the party (but not its leaders Meir and Dayan) believed the government had erred on the side of political passivism due to a mistaken belief that boundaries affording strategic advantage would prevent war. They thought that the government ought to emphasize diplomatic efforts to secure peace thereby preventing another war.

In a Knesset debate on January 22, 1974, Labor members spoke up in defense of the Egypto-Israeli disengagement agreement. Thus, for example, Minister of Justice Haim Zadok:

> Peace will not come by our gaining military supremacy. There can be no more crushing military defeat than the one we inflicted in the Six-Day War; but it did not bring peace. Peace will be achieved only through an agreement providing for mutual concessions and procuring advantages for both sides. . . . What is the alternative to such an agreement? . . . We are almost certainly in for . . . a cruel new war, which will arrive without prior warning. . . . Will the United States be at our side in that war? . . . we cannot be certain. Will the Soviet Union refrain from direct intervention? We do not know for sure. . . .[4]

The Alignment platform in the Eighth Knesset elections, published in December 1973, stressed the need for "provisional arrangements on the road to peace."[5] About two years later, the Rabin government signed an interim agreement with Egypt (September 4, 1975), in order to create conditions conducive to a purely political resolution of the conflict. Israel relinquished important territorial strongholds in return for partial political settlements. Labor leaders did not exclude the possibility of initiating military operations to avert palpable dangers to Israel's existence. But mindful of the American interest in stability, and seeing that an anti-Soviet front was solidifying in the Middle East, they feared the United States might oppose such measures, might even impose sanctions on Israel. There was, moreover, reason to doubt that a preemptive strike would be effective against an adversary equipped, since the interim agreement, with sophisticated early-warning systems.

These changes in Labor's political behavior wedged it even farther apart from Herut/Likud, which, under Begin's tutelage, proclaimed that the 1973 War had not altered the basic drive of the Arab world to destroy Israel. Partial political accords were therefore valueless, while relinquishing strategic footholds without a peace accord would tempt the Arabs all the more strongly to initiate war.[6] Referring to the disengagement agreement, Begin remarked in Knesset (January 22, 1974):

> I ask the prime minister: a few weeks ago she appeared here saying: it's not territories they want, it's Israel's very existence they seek to destroy. Since the "restoration of the Arab honor" in the Yom Kippur War, have they then mellowed, or have they become all the more insolent and audacious? . . . What has changed since then in the Prime Minister's situation assessment? But suddenly, cabinet ministers are appearing here with the announcement: they mean peace.[7]

One manifestation of the Likud's military activism was its spokesmen's reactions to a series of violent incidents on the northern border (November 1973–June 1974). They called upon the government to initiate a total war against Syria, so as to impose a political solution. As defined by Shmuel Tamir, such a war was intended: "To round off the campaign we were prevented from finishing on Yom Kippur."[8]

The Likud was also hard-pedaling its demands for accelerated settlement of the territories. The party feared that the interim agreement between Israel and Egypt might inspire the United States to impose a similar arrangement between Israel and Jordan, whereby Israel would be forced to withdraw from Judea and Samaria. Not only would this diminish Israel's strategic depth, deemed by the Likud to be an essential security asset, it would also inflict severe damage on the Whole Eretz Israel ideological vision.[9]

To sum up, in line with the trend begun during the 1969 elections, the future of the territories in general and the West Bank in particular had become the most controversial topics in Israeli politics. Bones of contention were how best to resolve the conflict, in general, and how best to approach the war question, in particular. The Likud called for political passivism (retention of the status quo through reliance on strategic depth) and military activism. Underlying this concept was a profound mistrust of the Arabs combined with the mission of territorial annexation of Judea and Samaria. The Alignment, by contrast, favored political activism (breaking of the political deadlock) and partial military activism but with a stronger-than-ever inclination toward partial military passivism.

Public reaction to the Labor party's failure in the "blunder" of 1973 was largely reflected in the May 17, 1977, elections, which led to Labor's electoral defeat and the establishment of the first Likud-led government. From then on, Israel's security would be based on Likud's military activism.

Electoral Changes and a Stronger Trend toward Political Polarity

In the Tenth Knesset elections Labor-camp parties polled 1.7 percent more votes than Likud-camp parties. The forming of the government therefore hinged on the support of the religious bloc (NRP, Agudath Israel, and Poalei Agudath Israel), which thus acceded to pivotal-parties status. The Likud, unlike the Alignment, had a political affinity for the religious parties on matters of religion and state, while NRP was politically close to Likud also regarding the annexation of Judea and Samaria. The religious camp therefore ultimately supported the Likud, thus endowing it with control over the government, coalition, and Knesset.

This process was to have important repercussions on patterns of controversy over the war issue. Israel now had, for the first time, a ruling party whose incumbency was liable to promote the most widespread public debate over national security topics. Likud's milit004Y activism was deemed unacceptable by most political groups, some 60 percent of the electorate. Patterns of contention between the ruling party and its opponents now shifted. Previously, the arena in which the ruling party contended with its major opposition lay on the political fringes (in the Suez War) or in the secondary center (in the pre-Six-Day War waiting period, the War of Attrition, and the Yom Kippur War). Now the controversy moved to the center of the political system. In some respects, this situation might be likened to that of France from 1954 to 1958, when arguments between more or less equally powerful political elites, about the French presence in Algeria, resulted in the involvement of many more political personalities and organizations than in the past.

The disengagement accords and the interim agreement moderated Israel's conflict with Egypt and Syria, reducing the danger of the outbreak of war. And the March 22, 1979, peace agreement with Egypt further eased the tensions. The "refusal states" (Arab states opposing the interim and most particularly the peace agreement) were prone to use more intensive forms of terror so as to undermine the security of the Israeli public and set the scene for war. From 1974, therefore, current-security disturbances (that is, Palestinian military activity) came in for much closer attention than basic-security issues. Three different stages are distinguishable in this context: Palestinian attacks precursive to and during the civil war in Lebanon, until the Syrian militarily intervention (1974–76); Syrian involvement and interethnic dispute in Lebanon until the Israeli-Egypt peace agreement (1976–79); and from the accord to the outbreak of the Lebanese War (1979–82).

The more preoccupied the political system became with the terror issue, the more forcibly patterns of dissent were expressed. With each succeeding stage, the different groups moved toward more polarized positions, particularly notable being the ever-increasing distance and alienation between the ruling elite and the rest of the system. This was a process in which the definition of the terror threat and the proper measures to be used against it came to be more and more bitterly disputed. The controversy marking the Lebanese War was part of this process.

The Lebanese Hazard: Public Debates on Terrorism

Most terror attacks subsequent to the 1973 War were planned and directed by Palestinian organization headquarters in Lebanon and executed by Palestinians from South Lebanese refugee camps. In reaction to the slaughter in Kiryat-Shmoneh (April 11, 1974) and the seizure of the Maalot school (May 15, 1974), Likud challenged the Alignment's distinction between current and basic security. The latter defined terrorism as a security hazard (that is, a current-security problem) but not as a danger to Israel's existence (basic-security problem). On the assumption that terrorism could not be stamped out by force, the Alignment excluded the unlimited deployment of force as not worthwhile—inasmuch as the possible risks (casualties, escalation to total war, and loss of international sympathy) were liable to exceed the potential benefit of seriously damaging the terrorist organizations. There were also moral considerations of potential harm to civilian populations, although these weighed more heavily with parties whose rejection of the use of military force was almost absolute (Mapam and Moked).[10]

The Likud, by contrast, considered that full force could be justifiably exerted. The party argued that if Israel were to initiate extensive military operations, including war, and overrun territories in south Lebanon, the terrorist problem, insofar as it emanated from Lebanon, could be solved. Limited military operations neither deterred the PLO nor prevented it from planning and organizing further attacks. In the spirit of its military activism, Likud called for a twofold change of policy toward terrorism: military force to be deployed against terrorists at all times, and not just in response to attacks; and Israel's military might to be concentrated against terror targets, broad-gauge operations designed to put a stop, instantly and for long duration, to the problem of terrorist activity launched from Lebanon. For this policy to succeed, Israel must be prepared to pay a high price on levels both political (U.S. reactions and international public opinion) and military (loss of life and materiél).[11]

Menachem Begin imparted to these security considerations a moral and ideological imperative. His conception and portrayal of the PLO was as of an entity representing no less a menace to the survival of the Jewish people than the Nazis during the Holocaust era—and out of like motivation. He argued that just as total war had been waged on the Nazis, ending in their absolute defeat, so could the use of unlimited armed force eliminate the PLO.[12] All Zionist political currents and leaders were haunted by the fate of the Jews during World War II, but none more remorselessly so than Begin.

As the civil war in Lebanon evolved into interethnic hostilities, and as, commencing March 1976, Syrian troops became involved in the fighting, Israel faced ever graver security problems on her northern border. Terrorist activity was now truly affecting Israel's relations with Syria. Labor leaders, while the Alignment was in power (1976-77), distinguished between Syria's gradual seizure of control in Lebanon and the Lebanese infighting between Christians, Muslims, Palestinians, and the terrorist organizations. Were she to occupy southern Lebanon, they reasoned, Syria was liable to invade Israel on two fronts—the Golan Heights and the Lebanese border—thus posing a real danger to the state's existence. The government accordingly drew what it referred to as "red lines": if, it warned, the Syrians were to cross the line running due east, south of Sidon, about 25 km north of and approximately paralleling the Litani River, the IDF would be forced to eject the Syrian forces from the demarcated area.[13] The future of the Christian minority and the Muslim majority, however, was not relevant to Israel's survival. This could affect current security only and did not constitute sufficient cause for Israel's initiating war.

The Alignment government accordingly took care not to fight alongside the Christian Maronites, even if their survival were threatened. Premier Yitzhak Rabin's definition of this policy was that Israel was prepared merely to help the Christians help themselves, by supplying arms, fuel, and food, but would not fight for them.[14] This was an expression of partial military activism, whereby nothing but Israel's own existential interests justified the initiation of war.

Rapidly gaining ascendancy in the opposite camp was an approach favoring the massive deployment of military force. Those shaping the security concept under the Likud (1977-84) saw no reason to distinguish between Israel's dispute with Syria and the interethnic dispute between Muslims, Christians, and Palestinians. If the Christian minority were to be wiped out or its political power destroyed, Lebanon would be overrun by Syria (and, indirectly, by the Soviet Union) and Israel's existence would be directly threatened. It followed, therefore, that an alliance between Israel and the Lebanese Christians, implying willingness on Israel's part to take up arms in their defense, would serve a most vital Israeli security interest.[15] Begin also adduced a moral argument. The Jewish people, as having been the victim of attempted genocide, must act to protect other nations from mass destruction. The Fourteenth Herut Conference (June 7, 1979) consequently adopted the following resolution:

> Israel has proved herself to be the sole surety for preventing the extermination of the Christians in Lebanon. The Jewish people, so sorely persecuted by its oppressors in the lands of its exile, will not allow a neighboring people to be destroyed.[16]

In December 1980 Begin's government gave the Christians an assurance that Israel would "send its air force into action to defend the Christians, if the Syrian Air Force attacks them."[17] Israel was now comporting herself as a power, prepared to dictate political moves in the region and forcibly prevent political changes she deemed undesirable. The government's definition of what constituted a *casus belli* expressed this attitude. Any change in the status quo finalized in Lebanon in 1977, to the detriment of Israel and the Christians, would be grounds for war against Syria.

This national security concept, however, would remain latent as long as pragmatists like Ezer Weizmann had control of security affairs. As defense minister, Weizmann balked at the heavy human and political costs that a war initiated against the terrorists would exact, and he saw no reason to initiate war against the Syrians. Foreign Minister Dayan and CGS Mordechai Gur favored partial military activism. Israel's response to the terrorist attack on the Coast Road (March 11, 1978) therefore took the form of "Operation Litani" (March 14, 1978), which, deployed on the current-security level, was only designed to reduce terrorist infiltration. It was confined to a specific radius (up to 10 km; in practice slightly more), had fairly limited objectives (creation of a terrorist-free buffer zone, or "safety belt," in southern Lebanon), and restricted firepower and human power, and all clashes against Syrian armed forces were strictly prohibited. Within such parameters, Operation Litani won broad consensus.[18]

One of the effects of Anwar Sadat's visit to Israel and the conduct of the peace negotiations was to alter some notions that Ezer Weizmann had entertained during the War of Attrition. Weizmann was forming his own ideas on the significance of the strategic changes in the Middle East as a result of the peace moves. He opposed major military operations against terrorism for fear that such operations could mortally damage the peace.[19] That attitude set him apart from Begin, Sharon, and Rafael Eitan, who were all prepared to risk war if they could prevent terrorist activity. They wanted a more grandly conceived Operation Litani. It was their hope to completely wipe out the terrorist presence, even at the cost of casualties, the suspension of negotiations with Egypt, and U.S. sanctions against Israel.[20]

Dayan resigned on October 21, 1979, Weizmann following suit on May 26, 1980. With the appointment of Eitan as CGS (April 16, 1978) and Sharon as minister of defense (August 6, 1981), the way was clear for military activism to go into effect. From then on, Israel's national security concept would be dominated by the Begin-Sharon-Eitan approach, not only on the strategic level but also on the tactical and operative levels. The new triumvirate believed that the Soviet Union's and the "refusal states'" opposition to the Camp David accords and the peace treaty with Egypt raised grave security dangers for Israel, including total war by Syria with the massive backing of the Soviet Union (USSR).[21] An even more horrendous menace, however, was perceived by Begin and Sharon. The PLO might snatch at the opportunity presented by the autonomy plan to establish a Palestinian state in Judea and Samaria. They presumed that all these dangers might be traced to Lebanon, where the PLO was building its main power base. And it was from Lebanese territory that Syria, so said Sharon, was plotting to unleash a war of annihilation on Israel.

The new defense minister regarded Lebanon as an ideal field for the deployment of military force, with the principal objectives of expelling both Palestinians and Syrians from the arena and laying down the terms of a "peace." In this way, Sharon hoped to destroy the PLO's military infrastructure, eliminating that organization as a political factor, ensure permanent Israeli control of the territories, dictate to Lebanon the terms of a political settlement, and significantly reduce the danger of war with Syria and the Soviet Union.[22]

Just one month after taking over the defense ministry, Sharon plainly presented his view at the Herut Party Center. It did not encounter even the slightest opposition:

The problem called Lebanon has three components. One is the Syrian component and we are witnessing a process of a Syrian takeover of Lebanon. . . . The second component in Lebanon is that of the terrorists. Lebanon today is the greatest world center of sabotage activity. . . . Behind all this activity stands the Soviet Union. . . . The third component in Lebanon is the Christians, the political component—how is it possible to bring Lebanon to a resolution from which there will arise a legitimate government, not a Syrian puppet government . . . that will be part of the free world, that will maintain friendly and peaceful relations with Israel? . . . The possibility of reaching a political solution depends on the Syrians not being in Lebanon. The possibility of quiet on the border between us and Lebanon depends on the terrorists not being in existence. This is the one whole complex of problems in Lebanon.[23]

Sharon was expressing a more general trend within his party. About two years earlier, at the Fourteenth Herut Conference (June 4, 1979), Begin had referred to severe instances of terrorist attacks on Jewish civilians, and said: "No more reprisals philosophy. We shall not wait for more Nahariyas. We shall not wait for a repeat Tiberias. We shall smite them whenever and wherever we choose."[24]

With Begin provisionally filling the office of defense minister (until Sharon could take over), the policy that increasingly asserted itself was that of preventive strikes against targets in Lebanon. Israel shot down two Syrian helicopters over Mount Snein (April 28, 1981); she was prepared to demolish the Syrian missiles in the Lebanese Rift Valley even before all political options had been exhausted (April 1981); and she bombed terrorist concentrations from the air (July 10, 1981).[25] But the government's most colorful escapade was the bombing of the nuclear reactor in Iraq (June 7, 1981).

The combination of circumstances arising in the late seventies and early eighties seemed to the Likud more propitious than ever before for liquidating "the dangers to Israel's existence." The state of belligerency on the southern front was at an end; memoranda of understanding had been signed with the United States (1979), and diplomatic and military collaboration between the two countries was being upgraded; the Arab states were in a struggle with one another over the peace agreement; and the Iran-Iraq War was in progress.

New Defense Minister Sharon immediately embarked on preparations for war. He coordinated with the Christian Falanges, with whom it was proposed to join forces in East Beirut, and briefed the military top brass on the full war plan, known as the "Great Pines" plan. The briefing related mainly to the plan's objectives: to militarily and politically demolish the terrorist presence in Lebanon by occupying Beirut; to force the Syrians to retreat at least to Zahla, creating an unbroken strip of territory between the IDF and the Falanges; and to install a Christian-dominated, pro-Israel government.[26]

Opposition-party members were not familiar with all the details of the military plan. But they were aware—especially the leaders of the Labor Party—of the government's aspirations to, and preparations for, total war against the Palestinians and the Syrians, including the occupation of Beirut. Public debate over the use of force started even before hostilities were launched. They mainly focused on the battle against the PLO and the proper reaction to Syria's introduction of missiles into the Lebanese Rift Valley.

The Labor Party asserted that a limited military operation in southern Lebanon would be justifiable in two situations—one, a breach of the "red lines" by Syria, combined with a failure of all diplomatic efforts to remove her forces from the area in question; and, two, the need to thwart attacks by terrorists. True to its partial military activism, Labor stressed the mistake of fighting for any Christian-Lebanese interest. Party leader Shimon Peres declared in Knesset (May 11, 1981):

> War is no trifling matter and we must not mislead others or obligate ourselves by giving blanket assurances or being swept away with vague and boundless enthusiasm.[27]

In July 1981 a cease-fire was reached between Israel and the PLO. Fearing any upset to this arrangement, which was expected to ensure calm on the northern border, Labor became increasingly disinclined to support any military operation in Lebanon.[28] Even more firmly opposed were the advocates of partial or general military passivism, who only recommended fortifying the frontier.[29]

Never before in Israel had a forthcoming war been so universally and fiercely debated as in 1981. An apparently similar controversy raged on the eve of the Suez War, with the difference, however, that almost all political groups then believed Israel to be facing a palpable threat to her survival. Mapam was at the time the only party in a secondary center to warn the government against going to battle. But in 1981 the dissent was generated at the very center and the contentions included all parties and almost all political groups.

Spilling over from the intra- and interparty plane, controversy over the approaching war spread to public personalities, intellectuals, the military, extra-parliamentary political groups, and the media. Issues that would hitherto have been treated as secrets, such as the grounds for going to war against Syria, timing of the offensive against the Syrian missiles in Lebanon, and the reasons for postponing it, were now being thrashed out in public. The Likud was clearly not in control of the political center, and in the fury of the controversy it came increasingly into friction with nonruling groups and counterelites. Some support for the government was offered by the Tehiya Party, which urged the government to hasten and launch a war for the expulsion of Syrian forces and terrorists from Lebanon.

War Breaks Out in the Guise of the "Peace for Galilee Campaign"

Never had Israeli society been divided as it was over the Lebanese War, which, to many people, appeared to have been engaged for no real cause. How, then, can the almost total consensus that accompanied the first days of the war be explained?[30]

In resolving to initiate war (June 5, 1982), the Israeli government created the impression that it was beginning a limited military operation. Section 3 of its resolution to open hostilities expressly stated that Israel sought no confrontation with Syria, unless that country's forces attacked the IDF. Section 1 of the same resolution, defining the tactical and operative objectives of the Peace for Galilee Campaign, reads, "to combat terrorists found within such range as to enable them to fire on settlements in the north of Israel." Begin interpreted the resolution for the government and Knesset as meaning that since the Russian weapons in the terrorists' possession had a 40-km range, IDF forces would fight solely with the aim of eradicating terrorists found within that range.[31]

The same assurance was given to opposition-party delegates meeting with Begin and Sharon immediately after the outbreak of hostilities. Those delegates, and particularly the Labor leaders, were aware of the Great Pines plan. Some surmised, and others knew perfectly well, that the "limited operation" was in fact a full-scale war.[32] But that did not prevent Amnon Rubinstein (Shinui) from urging his fellow party members to support the government resolution, while Labor Party Chairman Shimon Peres dubbed it "patently an act of self-defense."[33]

Announcing the supposedly limited targets of the Peace for Galilee Campaign (PGC), Begin stated in Knesset (June 8, 1982):

> We seek no clash with the Syrian army. If we can contrive to push the line 40 km back from our northern border—we shall have done our job and all fighting will cease.[34]

But even as he spoke, Israeli troops were battling the Syrian army. That very day, IDF units were paradropped south of Beirut at about 80, not 40, kilometers north of the Israeli-Lebanese border, with orders to join the Christian forces on the outskirts of the capital and seize control of the Beirut-Damascus road, vital to the Syrian interest in Lebanon. The IDF spokesman, of course, did his best to generate a "smoke screen" during the first five days of combat. But by the second day, the facts were reported in the daily press and were discussed in the Knesset Foreign Affairs and Defense Committee (June 9, 1982).[35]

When broadly debated in public about a year before the hostilities began, the war objectives had aroused bitter controversy. But during the first days of fighting, most supported the war.

Controversial War and Consensus Values

There were a number of cabinet ministers who opposed the initiation of the Lebanese War. But with the outbreak of hostilities, they kept their reservations to themselves. One of them was Dr. Yosef Burg of the NRP. Burg, like Moshe Shapiro and Zerah Werhaftig, his predecessors in the party leadership, was an advocate of partial military activism. The terror threat, in his opinion, was no justification for war and certainly not for attacking the Syrians. Other ministers—Mordechai Zippori, David Levy, Simha Erlich, and Yitzhak Berman of the Likud—lent their support in principle to military activism as a means of solving fundamental security problems. But, in view of the Syrian and Soviet involvement in Lebanon, they did not believe terrorism could be eliminated by means of war; they advocated limited military responses.

The plan submitted for government approval on June 5, 1982, spoke of a limited military operation. Zippori, Levy, and Burg gave it their support, assuming that the prime minister would prevent the Great Pines plan, rejected by the government in December 1981, from going into effect. They too believed that once the declared aims of the so-called "campaign" were achieved, a cease-fire would be declared. For the same reasons, Berman and Erlich offered no objection to the government resolution. They preferred to abstain, however, for fear that the IDF action might aggravate the civil war in Lebanon and risk provoking a military confrontation between Israel and Syria.[36]

The missile crisis; the attempted assassination of Shlomo Argov, Israel's Ambassador to Britain; and the raining of hundreds of Katyusha rockets on Israeli border settlements generated public support for a limited strike against the terrorists in Lebanon. A public majority (according to Dahaf public opinion polls—84 percent and according to a Pori survey—66 percent) favored such an operation.[37] Prevailing opinion had it that a limited military operation was appropriate to the security hazard represented by the terrorist presence close to the northern border, and that a 40-km-deep buffer zone would serve as a bulwark against attempted attacks (twenty-three Palestinian assaults had occurred since the July 1981 cease-fire between Israel and the PLO).

Even when the fighting was extended to beyond the scope of the PGC campaign, ministers opposing the whole affair kept quiet, for fear that any denunciation of the war would be construed as a rejection of their collective responsibility, whereupon they would have perforce to resign. Indeed, the entire government might be forced to resign, leaving the way open for an Alignment-led government.[38]

Not only the ministers but also opposition elements took the view that during warfare, public controversy, especially on security matters, was best avoided.[39] This thought clearly pervaded the political behavior of the Labor Party. In vain were the protests of Yossi Sarid, Abba Eban, the 77 Circle, and kibbutz-movement leaders, such as Yitzhak Ben Aharon and Yaakov Zur representing the dovish bloc. To no avail were the expostulations of two of the party's foremost experts on security affairs, Mordechai Gur and Haim Bar-Lev. Peres and Rabin, with the support of most party members, contended that public criticism of the government would demoralize the fighting forces and undermine the war effort. Thus, while Victor Shem-Tov of Mapam along with Mapai's Sarid called for a party debate on and reaction to the "scope of the destruction" in Tyre and Sidon,

Peres ruled that since the terrorists had resorted to attacks shortly before the outbreak of hostilities, the war was "just." He also stressed the importance of a "united front" during the fighting.[40] A similar position was taken by Rabin, who explained in an interview, "when shells and Katyushas fall and when there is loss of life and property, we must stand as one, on the elected government's making its decision."[41]

Even Mapam, champion of partial military passivism, and fundamentally opposed to any large-scale military operation in Lebanon, refrained from publicly denouncing the government. One of her chief leaders, Shem-Tov, put it as follows:

> Everything must be done so that Israel wins the war. . . . Obviously, the entire controversy surrounding the events that took place prior to the commencement of hostilities still exists. This controversy has not been expressed to date, because our soldiers are fighting on the front lines.[42]

Indeed, Mapam leadership condemned the war,[43] but not in public. Theoretical and empirical literature notes that extra-parliamentary groups are more inclined than other political groups to deviate from the accepted game rules of political systems.[44] But in wartime, extra-parliamentary groups too are influenced by ongoing states of emergency. In Israel, extra-parliamentary bodies firmly opposing war upheld consensus values. That was why, for example, the leadership of the Peace Now Movement resolved not to take the protest action some of its members were calling for as long as hostilities were in progress. And when the kibbutzim of the leftist-socialist Kibbutz Haartzi movement were debating what the movement's proper reaction should be, many members, particularly young people liable for the draft, claimed that for Mapam to oppose the government while the war was being fought, was tantamount to "plunging a knife in the nation's back."[45]

Similar behavior patterns characterized the parliamentary system. On June 8, 1982, when the leftist-communist Arab party Rakah tabled a no-confidence motion, the Knesset got down to its first debate on the war. Ninety-four MKs, including Labor delegates, supported the "operation," opposing votes coming from Rakah alone, while a number of other MKs expressed their rejection of the war by either abstaining or absenting themselves from the plenum.[46] Here too there was shock at the attack on Ambassador Argov and political uncertainty as to the true objectives of the PGC campaign; since the military appeared to be winning a brilliant victory, consensus values won out. People refrained from prematurely criticizing the government for fear that a successful campaign would tarnish their reputations.[47]

The cease-fire took effect on June 11, 1982, and Labor merely warned the government not to further amplify the goals of the military operation—an empty gesture, considering that it had already extended beyond its declared aims. This move, however, was an effort to prepare public opinion in case Labor opposed the government if and when the true nature of the operation and the measure of its success, or failure, became known. Labor wanted to appear as an opposition that while unswervingly loyal to the national interest, nonetheless adhered to its partial military activism in rejection of the Lebanese War.[48]

The truth was that the "Peace for Galilee Campaign" never took place. From the outset, this was war and not a limited military operation. This was the first preventive war in Israel's history to be launched against Palestinians and the first to be initiated in order to impose solutions through force. The scope of the consensus was largely contingent on the success of the government and the army in concealing their real purposes from the public.[49]

First Instances of Opposition to the War

In the first days of battle, opposition came mainly from parties on the fringes (Rakah, and the small, Jewish leftist party Sheli) and in the secondary centers of the political system (Mapam and Ratz). Those parties' attitudes to the war were determined mainly by their political approach, veering far wide of the consensus, to the Palestinian problem. The only possible solution, they asserted, was a political one, and any attempt to settle the conflict by military means was doomed to fail.[50]

Subject, however, to the discipline imposed by Peres and Rabin, Mapam merely abstained on Rakah's no-confidence motion over the war (June 8, 1982) rather than voting against it. Also Ratz's sole Knesset member, Shulamit Aloni, effectually abstained by dint of absenting herself from the Knesset debate.[51] But Rakah, free of such restraints, quickly denied the legitimacy of Israeli military action against the PLO:

> The political aims of this war are to liquidate the Palestinian people as such, to create the basis, together with harsh oppression in the occupied territories, for annexation of the (West) Bank and the (Gaza) Strip to Israel . . . to eliminate the forces of democracy in Lebanon, and put the Falanges in power . . . to rain blows upon Syria with the aim of overthrowing her regime.[52]

This time, in contrast to previous wars, Rakah was not alone, as others supported the essence of its opposition to the war.[53] Politicians in the center and secondary centers came to perceive the war as an unprofitable venture, using unjustifiable means. This happened when the arena stretched to beyond the fortieth kilometer, when casualties mounted and international public opinion condemned the bombardment of civilian population centers and especially the siege on Beirut (June 13, 1982). Shinui and Ratz went public with their opposition as did, abandoning the restraint of their leaders, a number of Laborites (Yossi Sarid, Mordechai Gur, Shlomo Hillel, and others).[54]

Meanwhile, extra-parliamentary opposition was rising. The self-imposed censorship in various parties, especially Labor, spurred some of their supporters to form an extra-parliamentary opposition of unprecedented scope and firmness.[55] June 23, 1982, saw the first antiwar demonstration organized by the Committee Against the War in Lebanon. This extra-parliamentary group, with its several hundred members, formed under Rakah's aegis and with its support. Also voicing protest was the Peace Now Movement, second-largest extra-parliamentary group after Gush Emunim. It too recognized the political existence of a Palestinian entity, accordingly rejecting any military action designed to eliminate that entity.[56]

Beirut—To Occupy or Not To Occupy?

In the meantime, the theater of war was thrusting outward. There were skirmishes with the Syrian army (June 24, 1982), the siege of Beirut was completed, and the generals were toying with the idea of breaching the city (June 27, 1982). For the first time in the history of the conflict, Israel appeared on the brink of occupying an Arab capital. To do so would involve some very fierce fighting in which thousands of civilians and hundreds of IDF soldiers were likely to be injured or killed.[57]

The view of the opposition parties—expressed primarily by Labor—was that Syria's involvement in Lebanon, while undoubtedly conducive to terrorist activity, did not amount to a threat to Israel's existence. A war with Syria, it was feared, would result in a high casualty toll and would probably precipitate total war on at least two fronts: the Golan Heights and Lebanon. The opposition, moreover, doubted that Syria could be ejected from Lebanon. Such was classified as a political objective, to be worked toward by diplomatic means.[58]

The issue most hotly debated was that of the encirclement and conquest of the Beirut. Was this necessary in terms of achieving the declared aim of "Peace for Galilee"? And, what price would IDF troops and the city's civilian population be called upon to pay? The Lebanese capital glittered enticingly, its possible occupation a tremendous achievement in the eyes of the proponents of military activism; the opponents of the war saw such an eventuality as the culmination of a willfully ill-conceived military campaign. Not only the opposition parties but even a number of cabinet ministers opposed the occupation of Beirut. NRP ministers were against the idea in principle. Two other ministers, David Levy and Mordechai Zippori of the Likud, while not opposed in principle to the takeover of a civilian strategic target, thought the operation would embroil the IDF in very bloody battles. They also stressed the harm that would be caused to Israel's image in world public opinion.[59]

In the Labor Party, the various schools of thought united in opposing the seizure of Beirut, voicing public protest against continued hostilities. They viewed the war as erroneous because it aimed to annex the West Bank to Israel, impose a political settlement on the Palestinians, and install the Maronite Christian minority in power. There was still a minority of about a hundred members in two centrist circles: "New Direction" and the "Alon Circle," who supported the total destruction of the terrorist infrastructure—an end both desirable and attainable—and the military breaching of Beirut, as a means of destroying terrorist headquarters.[60]

Attitudes in the Labor Party largely reflected the political controversy as a whole. Never before was Israel divided on the basis of different responses to the deployment of force. The Israeli public largely believed that the ruling elite had been deceptive in reporting to the opposition that the aims of the military operation were limited. This opinion was a highly influential factor in increasing the scope of the dissent. Amnon Rubinstein expressed this public mood in his speech before the Knesset (June 23, 1982):

> We have been dragged into one of the longest wars we have ever known, one of the hardest fights we have ever had. . . . Ought not the Knesset to have been informed of all this? . . . Our main job here is to see to it that the democratic processes are preserved, and not permit the Knesset to be misled.[61]

The decision makers clearly stated that they would continue to fight for the ouster of the terrorists from Beirut and from Lebanon as a whole. In an article titled "Nature of the Defensive War" (July 9, 1982) Defense Minister Sharon cited the military campaign as a defensive war, since it was aimed at liquidating the PLO and also preventing dangers to the peace process and to Israel's survival:

> We have conducted a war of initiative against terror, culminating in the campaign in Lebanon, which is designed to eradicate it totally. . . . PLO-style terrorism would in the final analysis bring upon us a total war—sooner or later—within a year or two, at a place and time not convenient to us, in a situation that could cost us an infinitely greater loss of life. . . . We therefore proceeded to a war of defense—one of the most clearly justified of our wars.[62]

According to Sharon, the occupation of Beirut was essential for military victory. Above all, the victory would prevent the founding of a Palestinian state and ensure Israeli control of the territories. Sharon's article succinctly expressed the position that a preventive war could solve strategic problems, and that the use of force was both permissible and desirable.

On another occasion, Sharon outlined the military and political objectives of the war:

> From a military point of view, the PLO can be completely neutralized. From a political point of view—almost completely. The PLO can also operate out of Cairo, Baghdad, or Jordan. But that cannot be compared to a situation in which it has had control of a stretch of land contiguous with Israel's border, where it has maintained a quasi-state. This the PLO will no longer be able to do.[63]

In reply to a journalist's question concerning the aims of the fighting, the defense minister said: "Peace for Israel and peace for the Israeli people. The well-being of Lebanon has an impact on Israel's well-being."[64] CGS Eitan went on to describe another of the combat's political aims:

> Our war here is a war over Eretz Israel, not over Beirut and not for the Christians. . . . We want the terrorists out of here. That is the aim. If we can manage that, the struggle over Eretz Israel will look different. . . . We have come for the struggle over Eretz Israel.[65]

Begin, as always, added an ideological touch. In a lecture at the National Security College (August 1982) the prime minister clarified the historic justification for the PGC. Citing Israel's wars and the world wars, Begin stated that a military strike initiated when no exigency existed made victory possible at the cost of a small number of casualties. He hence deduced the advantageousness of the preventive war:

> It is by no means imperative that war be waged only out of want of alternative. There exists no moral precept whereby a nation must or may fight only when it has its back to the sea. Such a war is liable to precipitate a disaster, if not a holocaust, on the entire nation, causing it terrible loss of life.[66]

Dissent also prevailed among the fighting forces. As a "democracy in uniform," most of Israel's Jewish citizens serve in the armed forces. As a result, the IDF largely reflects the spectrum of political positions in Jewish-Israeli society. Hence, the widespread public dissent over the Lebanese War found an echo in the military. Hostilities wore on, claiming more and more victims; the notion gradually took hold throughout the military that this war was intended for realizing party-political rather than national purposes. Soldiers, especially those at the front, became increasingly dubious as to whether this war was in fact vital to Israel's survival.

The IDF fought most of its battles in or near densely populated areas, such as Sidon and Beirut. Flatly contravening all that the soldiers had been taught about the "purity of arms," the military was raining heavy fire from land, sea, and air on those towns. The troops grew weary of the protracted (nearly three years) stay in very hostile surroundings; of frequent military encounters; of having to act as police details to separate local warring factions; and of the casualty toll. They became increasingly skeptical as to the justice of the war, and more firmly set against it.[67]

Dissent among the military was reinforced when it encircled Beirut, by means of heavy bombardments and by cutting off water and electricity supplies. But it was the proposed breaching of the city that aroused the most vehement protest. Soldiers stated their misgivings as to the casualties they expected to suffer, remarking that the occupation of Beirut would do more to serve the Christians than to realize any vital Israeli interest.[68] Regular servicemen gave vent to their doubts in company talks that were described by Deputy CGS Major-General Moshe Levi as "very distressing," and officers argued against total war in various IDF forums, such as senior staff and command meetings.[69]

The opposition brewing in the military found its first public expression in a letter penned by three officers to the prime minister (July 13, 1982) in which they argued that the breaching of Beirut was unnecessary and that its anticipated cost in IDF casualties would be high. The officers stated that by making their letter public they hoped to prevent the operation from taking place. As a form of political participation, this was unheard of. But these same views were echoed by OC Armor Brigade Eli Geva, whose notice of resignation (July 25, 1982) amounted to conscientious disobedience intended to dissuade the political and the military echelons from occupying Beirut. The same kind of political behavior was exhibited by Brigadier-General Amram Mitzna, who on September 23, 1982, announced his resignation as OC Staff and Command School.[70]

While few reacted publicly, there were many who chose a subtler form of protest. Soldiers stopped volunteering for policing missions and current security activity; they performed their military duties less efficiently than before; they took care not to volunteer for officer training or chose not to extend their regular duty. Some merely asked their friends on the home front to protest and oppose the war. Others waited to be discharged from national or reserve service in order to express their views in protest groups.[71]

The protestors were not pacifists, but they maintained that political dialogue with the Palestinians was the sole means of achieving peace. War was only a last-resort means of ensuring survival. In their views, attacks on civilians represented the dehumanizing element of wars conducted with the aim of occupying territories rather than thwarting an existential danger.[72] Peace Now preached a peace initiative, including dialogue with both PLO-affiliated and other

Palestinian delegates. Most of its several thousand members, repudiating the Israeli consensus, deemed the Palestinian national movement legitimate. The Labor Party could accordingly not serve them as a vehicle for political expression.[73]

Studies of extra-parliamentary opposition, for example, that by Kaase and Barnes, state that dissatisfaction with the ability of a party to serve as a channel of communication will result in extra-party activity, and the forming of protest groups.[74] The protestors concluded that the various political parties were tied by the parliamentary game rules and were consequently unable to register unequivocal public opposition to the war.[75] Their aim was to have the fighting stopped, to get Defense Minister Sharon to resign, and to set in motion an investigation of the decision-making processes that led to the war and its principal developments.[76]

Consensus values started to crumble more noticeably throughout July 1982. Over 100,000 people rallied to the Peace Now demonstration of July 3, 1982, proving how widespread public support was for the protestors' messages. Public debate was strongly highlighted by the media. Most of the media advocated the dissent, leading protestors to hope that the government would accede to their demands.[77] Some other protest groups arose in addition to Peace Now and the Committee Against the War in Lebanon. One of them was "Yesh Gvul" (There Is a Limit), which numbered several hundred demobilized soldiers. As they perceived it, the only way to end the hostilities was by an extraordinary act of protest that would shock the political system: they would refuse to serve in Lebanon.

Military disobedience was justified according to the social contract on which democracy was based. The soldier's duty to obey the state's orders and to fight an enforced war was bound up with his being part of the life of the community and derived from the social contract. On the other hand, the state had no right to mobilize its citizens for a war of aggression, when there was no danger to its existence. If it did so, the soldier was entitled to disobey a normative imperative (such as order, law) on the strength of which he could be sent to war.[78] Since many of its members defined themselves as Zionists, they recognized the legitimacy of the regime and the government. Thus they were willing to suffer the lawful penalties imposed for draft-dodging. Commencing July 1982, some 150 Yesh Gvul members refused conscription orders. Some 900 others signed declarations stating that if called up, they would refuse to serve in Lebanon.[79]

Most parties (excepting Rakah) and extra-parliamentary groups denounced this refusal. They pointed out that in Israel protest could be addressed through conventional political participation and that there was, therefore, no reason to resort to disobedience. The same view was held by the "Soldiers against Silence" group, founded in July 1982 by about 2,000 demobilized soldiers and officers opposing the occupation of Beirut. It called for full information to be disclosed to the public as to the circumstances under which the war was engaged, its targets, and how decisions were made during the fighting.[80]

The Sabra and Shatila Slaughter

The slaughter at the Sabra and Shatila refugee camps, and the fact that it was perpetrated under IDF control, caused a major public uproar. Many (51 percent according to one survey, 30 percent according to another) held Israel directly or indirectly responsible for what happened.[81] For Labor leaders, this was a perfect opportunity for pointing out the government's shortsightedness. For the first time since the fighting began, Labor members wholeheartedly abandoned consensus values. Chairman Shimon Peres echoed the message of the protest groups. The aim of the war was political: to annihilate the PLO as a political factor, to appoint a moderate Palestinian leadership in the territories, and to annex the West Bank.[82]

All protest groups, with opposition parties following suit, demanded an investigation into the slaughter. The government, (ministers Zvulun Hammer and Yitzhak Berman dissenting) flatly refused, thereby instigating further dissent. During the seven days following the slaughter, until the Kahan national inquiry commission was set up, more than 300,000 persons taking part in fifteen demonstrations called for such a commission to be established, for the government (and especially Defense Minister Sharon) to resign, for the war to be ended, and for the military to be rapidly withdrawn from Lebanon, pending suitable security arrangements. Rallying the largest number of protestors was the so-called Four Hundred Thousand Demonstration organized (September 25, 1982) in Tel Aviv by the Alignment and Peace Now. At that time, some 40 percent of the public defined the war as unnecessary and called for its termination.[83]

Not only was dissent of this order unprecedented in Israel, it was unparalleled in many Western democracies. The Four Hundred

Thousand Demonstration attracted a turnout of not less than 5 percent of the Israeli public. As such, it outstripped attendance at demonstrations against other wars in Israel or elsewhere in the Western sphere, including those staged against the Vietnam War in the United States or the Algerian War in France.

The government appointed a state commission of inquiry, enabling the public scrutiny of the refugee-camp slaughter to be handed over to a quasi-judicial tribunal. Evacuation of the PLO from Beirut also ended at about that time (September 1, 1982), symbolizing to many people the conclusion of the essential chapters of the war. Debate over the Lebanese issue would from now on center on whether, and how, IDF troops should pull out. Controversy might accordingly have been expected to simmer down. But the withdrawal was postponed, the casualty toll continued to mount, and the dissent raged on.

Protest groups and opposition parties pointed to the hundreds of dead, thousands of wounded, and the $2.5 billion that the war had cost without achieving its principal targets. The Palestinian organizations had not been wiped out, terrorism continued out of Lebanon, Israel and Lebanon had not reached a stable settlement, severe damage had been done to Israel's relations with Egypt, interethnic strife in Lebanon was worse than before, and the Syrians had greatly bolstered their status.[84]

The Likud and other war supporters responded that neither the war nor its objectives were the cause of the controversy. The opposition parties were simply using the prolonged duration of the war to promote their own particular interests, injure the Likud, and engineer a change of government.[85] Their members and the media were denounced as "poisoners of wells," as "backstabbers of the nation," "a fifth column," "poison," and so forth.[86] For the first time in Israel's history, controversy over the use of force gave rise to charges of disloyalty against a party posing the central opposition to the political establishment.[87]

The Kahan Inquiry Commission report, published in February 1983, established that the policymakers had been negligent in the exercise of their discretion, thereby reinforcing the view that the political elite did not deserve the public's confidence. From then until the withdrawal was completed, protest in a wide variety of forms was a matter of course. There were newspaper ads, activists' assemblies, sit-ins outside the offices of the prime minister and minister of defense, and heavily attended demonstrations marking significant dates, such as that of the outbreak of the war. One of the prominent issues to be protested was the casualty toll.

Casualty Toll as a Cause of Dissent

The war claimed 657 dead and 3,887 wounded Israeli soldiers.[88] In each of Israel's previous wars, with the exception of the Suez Campaign, the casualty count had been higher. But these earlier wars had been fought to thwart a palpable threat to some vital basic security interest. The Lebanese War, however, aimed merely to eliminate the terror nuisance, which could not endanger the State's survival. A comparison between Israel's losses in the Lebanese War and the number of victims claimed by Palestinian military activities against Israel shows the war to have been relatively costly, claiming more lives than all IDF antiterrorist operations since 1949 combined. This was more, in fact, than the total count of victims claimed by terrorism (civilians, tourists, and soldiers) since the Suez Campaign. The number of fatal casualties in the war was 3.7 times the number of terrorist victims during the seven years preceding it, and the number of wounded amounted to 3.05 times the total persons injured as a result of terrorist activity in the same period.[89] From July 1981, when the cease-fire agreement took effect, until the beginning of the war, only one individual was hurt in terrorist attacks.[90]

Proponents of partial military activism claimed that a limited operation (up to 40 kms only) would have resulted in an immeasurably smaller number of victims. This was the first of Israel's wars in which the casualty count was cited as grounds for such conspicuous political opposition to the further conduct of hostilities.[91] This was poignantly illustrated by the posters used at sit-ins outside the home of Prime Minister Begin, which chalked up the number of war dead over the words "What Are They Dying For?"

The war lasted three years in all; it was Israel's longest, twice as long as the War of Attrition and more than twice as long as the War of Independence. The public was now asking, what was the use of a war against terrorism in which terrorism had not been eliminated, or against Syria, who had proceeded to reinforce her military presence in Lebanon? And, what was the use of rendering assistance to undisciplined Christian forces that were not competent to rule effectively in Lebanon?

Most affected were the combatant forces themselves, who frequently came face to face with civilian battles, brutal murders, looting, the slaughter of defenseless refugees and the crucifixion and rape of women by Christian Falanges, Shi'ite terrorism inspired by religious fanaticism, deserted towns and desolate villages, ruined houses, streets strewn with corpses, the inhabitants reduced to despair. Some populations were extremely hostile, whether grimly and fatalistically awaiting approaching death or looking to a bleakly hopeless future.

IDF soldiers faced cruel dilemmas: to injure civilians of dubious innocence or to risk their own skins? To kill, possibly without cause, or be killed? Some resolved the glaring contradiction between what they had been taught and what they were required to do by magnifying the negative image of the Arab as devoid of human characteristics; their political views accordingly became more radical. Growing political radicalism in Israel was a reaction to the high casualty toll of the fighting. This is shown by the relatively high number of votes polled by the radical right-wing parties Kach and Tehiya in the army in the 1984 Eleventh Knesset elections: 2.5 percent of soldiers taking part in the elections voted for Kach (compared to 1.5 percent of the general electorate) and 11.1 percent for Tehiya (compared to 4.5 percent of the general electorate and 6.6 percent of soldiers' votes in the 1981 Knesset elections). One of every seven soldiers voted for the very hawkish Tehiya or Kach.

Consensus of Opposition:
The Majority Condemn the War

Support for the fighting recorded a constant decline. Never more than 84 percent even in the first months of the war (according to other findings—66 percent), it was down by the fourth month to 67 percent (other findings—45 percent), plunging to a low of 37 percent by the third year (other findings—20 percent). As it wore on, the public began learning that while the PLO was in fact being politically and militarily weakened, the war was costing more than it was worth.[92] Opposition to the security policy was reflected, inter alia, in a 25 percent decline in the popularity of Premier Begin and Defense Minister Sharon; a 43 percent drop in those who assessed the government's performance as good to very good; a 39 percent decline in the number of those who viewed the Likud as "the party best suited to run the country"; and a 45 percent erosion of electoral support for the Likud. Already in June 1983, after one year of war, 50 percent of Likud supporters opposed the war (as against 89 percent of Alignment supporters).[93]

The mass media helped generate the dissent. Its involvement in the Lebanese War was unprecedented. Party organs expressed their parties' condemnation of the war, and the media in general mirrored the debate on both the home and fighting fronts. The protest was expressed by different media sources, many of them nonparty-affiliated, representing diametrically opposed political positions. *Maariv* and *Yediot Ahronoth*, for example, were hardly less critical of the government than *Haaretz*. Opposition was not confined to politically dovish reporters; others, with a more activist political outlook also objected to the war.[94] As for Israel television, its programs, as usual, had to obtain prior approval before being broadcast. This procedure sometimes involved bitter wrangling among the members of the board of directors with regard to the various programs reflecting dissent.[95]

The character of the Israeli media had changed since the sixties and the seventies, and this change affected the forcefulness of its criticism. There were many more "fighting journalists" who tended to differ with the prevailing norms and to criticize the political establishment. They did so by using satire and other, unconventional styles. The press was significant in that military correspondents were prepared, during the fighting, to serve up military-security information that revealed the truth of the war, thus allowing for the dissent.[96]

The war's supporters sometimes complained that the controversy on the home front was causing a limiting of the war's objectives. This argument emanated mainly from the ruling elite, who were attempting to prove that the protest was an inconsequential trifle compared with the widespread popular support they presumably enjoyed. Gradually forming were antiprotest groups aimed at countering the dissent. In June 1982, these groups published petitions against the staging of demonstrations. In mid-July, as dissent mounted, some two hundred academics and about one hundred senior reservist officers organized themselves into a group called "Peace and Security." The public debate, according to this group, was not legitimate, and, under the rules of representational democracy, the government retained the right to initiate force in such scope, at such time, and against such adversary as it deemed appropriate. Demonstrations during war, they said, were injurious to the underpinnings of the democratic regime.[97]

Yet, protest prevailed.[98] More and more nonruling groups joined the dissent. Before the fighting erupted, the political system boasted two extra-parliamentary groups that held well-defined views on the war issue (Gush Emunim and Peace Now). By the time the war ended in 1985 there were twelve such groups in regular operation, as well as a few unorganized ones. Adding their political voice to the general uproar were voluntary bodies such as the kibbutz movements and youth organizations, groups of citizens directly affected by the war as well as various elites.

Since the Likud government was identified with a specific political bloc, the political system had no democratic apparatus to prevent the aggravation of the controversy. Tehiya's joining the government on July 23, 1982, with a view to strengthening it and enabling the fighting to continue, proved that hawkish positions were preventing the government from helping to tone down political rivalries. It in no way tried to reconcile these differences and thereby prevent contentions from escalating into violent outbursts. Regardless of cost, the war continued. And not until the National Unity Government came to power in 1984 did the withdrawal commence. Intolerance toward protest groups was encouraged by various cabinet ministers. Thus, Defense Minister Sharon's denunciation of oppositionaries as "poisoners of wells" was pounced upon by the war's supporters as tacit license to injure their political adversaries.[99]

On February 8, 1983, following publication of the Kahan Commission Report, Peace Now staged a demonstration calling for Sharon's resignation. An explosive grenade lobbed into the crowd killed one of the demonstrators, Emil Grunzweig. The shock waves generated by this murder put a stop to the smear campaign against political rivals. The murder, it was feared, was liable to precipitate further radical acts of political violence. Knesset members and extra-parliamentary groups reached the conclusion that if the destruction of the democratic regime was to be forestalled, all must pull together for national conciliation.

Gush Emunim and Peace Now discussed game rules for extra-parliamentary controversy. And on February 15, 1983, the Knesset conducted one of the few debates ever held in Israel on its democratic political culture. Knesset members of all factions stressed the need to uphold law and order and to respect the right of every citizen to express his and her views without fear of injury.[100] Obscenities and mudslinging continued to pepper verbal exchanges in and out of the Knesset. But the war's opponents could now demonstrate without being physically attacked by antiprotest groups.

Security problems in Lebanon, especially Shi'ite terrorism, grew more acute, support by international public opinion was being rapidly eroded, and the casualty toll continued to grow. In the third year of the war, 86 percent were in favor of withdrawal "now" (of these, 26 percent wanted an unconditional withdrawal, while 60 percent thought certain conditions should be ensured). About 94 percent supported the government resolution of January 17, 1985, calling for stage-by-stage withdrawal to the international border. The great majority of Likud voters were also convinced that it was no longer profitable for the war to continue or for the IDF to remain in Lebanon.[101] The planners of the war and its supporters, including OC Syrian Front, Avigdor (Yanosh) Ben-Gal, Yehoshua Sagi (who served as OC Intelligence Branch during the war), Energy Minister Yitzhak Moda'i, and Housing and Construction Minister David Levy, admitted in early 1985 that the campaign had been a very costly failure.

It was in this atmosphere that the National Unity Government resolved to pull out of Lebanon. The two large ruling parties, Likud and Labor, made their wishes known; the government itself was structured on the basis of a mutual-veto mechanism; Rabin, who opposed some of the war's objectives, was now minister of defense. The die was cast, and Likud members had to consent to the withdrawal even though all their leaders, with the exception of David Levy, wanted the IDF to remain in place until Syria withdrew her forces.[102]

Summary and Conclusions

The Lebanese War conformed to a Clausewitz-type pattern.[103] The architects of the security concept, spearheaded by Begin, Sharon, and Eitan, initiated the fighting in what appeared to them to be optimal environmental conditions, with the aim of resolving the terrorist problems. It was a preventive war, conceived for the purpose of altering the status quo, redirecting processes that were deemed negative, and creating a new international order. What they learned from previous wars was that Israel must inflict a preemptive strike, extracting maximum benefit at minimal cost. They were particularly mindful of what they considered Golda Meir's error in not preempting the Yom Kippur War. The Begin-Sharon-Eitan triumvirate thus failed to distinguish between the preemptive strike, which may well have been appropriate immediately prior to the outbreak of the 1973 war, and the preventive strike.

The Lebanese War was far from being Sharon's one-man show. On the contrary, it was supported by all of the Likud leadership and the great majority of party members. These facts do not support the claim that Begin was deceived and misled by Sharon. Previous chapters have shown Begin as generally in favor of wars of initiative, heedless of any subtle distinctions between current and basic security. As one of the leaders who had blueprinted the military activism approach in the fifties, he was a supporter of the Lebanese War before it ever broke out. His somewhat autocratic leadership did not allow him to concern himself with operative details, and he had reservations about a number of objectives, such as fighting against Syria and the occupation of west Beirut. But he favored a war of offense designed to annihilate the PLO, thereby assisting, as he conceived it, in the solution of the Palestinian problem.[104] Along with the other standard bearers of military activism—Moshe Arens, Ariel Sharon, Yitzhak Shamir, Yochanan Bader, Geulah Cohen, Yuval Neeman, Rafael Eitan, and others—he upheld the propriety of its logic. This strategy went into effect in spite of being publicly disputed and even though the war's progenitors were aware of Likud's weaknesses as a ruling party.

In the Knesset elections of 1981, Likud polled 6 percent less support than the Alignment had received in the 1973 Knesset elections that followed the military blunder. It had to confront a highly resourceful opposition, wielding significant influence in the political center. Confrontations between the Likud government and various counterelites (the media, academics, public administration, and the Histadruth Labor Federation) were indicative of the political force behind the opposition. Even so, the ruling elite preferred to underscore the potential advantages of its controversial, preventive war.

In military, political, social, and economic terms, the fighting exacted a heavy toll. Dissent might be considered as one of its highest costs, because dissent engendered long-term instability, ramming an implacable wedge between mutually antithetical social groups. The war's initiation, its scope, its objectives, and its manner of conduct ran counter to the outlook of most political groups. Large sectors of the public made light of the PLO threat, and the threat emanating from Lebanon did not, in their opinion, warrant the war. The main causes of dissent were neither social nor economic, but political. No economic emergency regime was declared by the government, and the Israeli citizenry was not called upon to participate in the economic burden of the hostilities.

The difficulties demonstrably experienced by the governments of Rabin (1974–77) and Begin (1977–83) in managing affairs of state, sorely tried the public's faith in the establishment's ability to solve Israel's essential problems. Consequently, extra-parliamentary activity was sought by greater numbers of citizens than ever before.[105] The political parties were losing status, while extra-parliamentary groups proliferated and attained greater political weight, thereby also gaining the organizational and financial backing of both opposition and coalition parties. Mapam, Ratz, and Labor were not the only parties to support protest groups. Gush Emunim and the Whole Eretz Israel Movement had the support of the Tehiya and the Likud.[106] Without being a cause of dissent per se, this process accelerated and expanded the controversy and diversified its content. For two and a half years (June 1982–January 1985) protest groups held hundreds of demonstrations and assemblies. Protest was not directed solely against government policy. It also sometimes challenged the rules and values whereby the democratic regime was operating.

A radicalization process was part of the dissent. While the Lebanese War cannot be scientifically proved to have been the direct cause of this trend, the belligerent atmosphere could hardly fail to have its effect. Support for radical parties favoring the forceful imposition of a solution to the Israeli-Arab-Palestinian conflict rose between the Tenth and the Eleventh Knesset elections (1981–84). The Tehiya reaped an electoral increase of 74 percent, while Kach quadrupled its previous total, recording a higher rate of increase than any other Jewish party in the 1984 elections.

At the opposite pole, the anti-Zionist and non-Zionist left also benefitted from the war. Seeing that Zionist opposition parties were not overtly opposing the fighting, citizens defining themselves as Zionists felt motivated to support Rakah's antiwar activities. During the hostilities, Jewish activists flocked in unprecedented numbers to Rakah. Not only that, but a number of Rakah leaders supported protest groups representing citizens of the Zionist camp (The Committee Against the War in Lebanon, Yesh Gvul). Rakah made great strides toward total legitimacy: in contrast to previous situations, it now also reflected the opinions of a number of Jewish groups and

Zionist Knesset members. Never before had the party been so well tolerated.[107]

Despite the extensive protest, the Lebanese War wrought no substantive changes in the various approaches to the war issue. Instead, parties and extra-parliamentary political groups interpreted the outcome of the war through their prewar perspectives, thus reinforcing their previous positions. Prewar dissent had focused on modes of combating terrorism, and so did postwar dissent. Likud and Tehiya believed that as a result of the fighting, the PLO had emerged a much weaker political player and military adversary and that this achievement justified the policy of preventive strikes.

But other parties and extra-parliamentary groups favoring limited force (particularly the Labor Party) claimed that the war only pushed the terrorists away from the border and brought a relative measure of security to the Galilee, a goal that could have been achieved by a limited military campaign. The rest of the war objectives, they claimed, had not been achieved at all. Terrorism not only persisted, it had become more violent, and a dangerous new type of terror—Shi'ite terror—had emerged. The Christians had largely lost their influence in Lebanon; peace between Lebanon and Israel had not been gained; Syria had fortified her standing in Lebanon, making the PLO and the Christians all the more dependent on her; and the Palestinian problem now figured larger than ever in international awareness. These groups accordingly reasserted their unequivocal opposition to all wars of choice.[108]

7 Israeli Society and Politics during the Gulf War

Introduction

History provides us with a diversity of human experiences illuminative for students of politics and society. While the Lebanese War was the first due purely to Israeli military offense, the Gulf War was the first in which Israel was only involved passively, not as a belligerent but rather as a victim. It is claimed in this chapter that the Gulf War intensified state involvement in society. The militaristic characteristics of the Israeli society came to light despite the military passivity. Hence, the experience of the Israeli society in the course of the Gulf War is another indicator of the blurred boundaries between the international system and domestic politics, as well as a manifestation of the militaristic propensities in a society in wartime.

Scientific literature commonly asserts that democratic societies and regimes, when confronted by perceived dangers to their national security, tend to convert into their military equivalents. Such countries, the theory goes, generally become warlike in character, inclined not merely to react but actually to initiate military operations.[1] An examination of Israel during the Gulf War (1991), however, produces distinctly different conclusions.

The Gulf War brought into sharp relief the interactions arising between a country's internal politics and its international relations, on the one hand, and between wars and relations of society and state on the other. Thus, for example, while most of the Israeli public found no fault with its government's military nonresponse to Iraqi missile attacks on its cities, it did, however, show itself to be a fighting community.

Although within the Green Line (pre-1967 borders) certain features of democracy were suspended for the duration, the democratic regime did not collapse. Moreover, even though its foundations were greatly reinforced by the Gulf War, Israel's fighting society was not, on the whole, insistent that armed force be deployed against Iraq, and the country maintained an essentially passivist stance. In other words, the manner in which Israel comported herself resulted from the interplay of many more factors than the professional literature to date would have predicted. Conventional wisdom would conclude that political regimes, and their responses to severe crisis situations, can be fairly neatly divided into two distinct, nonoverlapping types: aggressive and militaristic societies with an ingrained tendency toward initiating wars and military operations; and civilian, democratic societies defending themselves, under duress, against external national threats. Such a typology should be rejected as inaccurate due to the nature of the Israeli society in wartime.

Prior to War—Israel and the Intifada

Political dilemmas over the use of armed force in the Intifada, from its inception in December 1987, offered very little hint as to what might occur. The Likud and Labor parties had the greatest difficulty in formulating appropriate responses to the intricate and dynamic emerging realities. Both deplored permitting an independent Palestinian state to arise in the territories. But Israel should, they formulated, consider entering into U.S.-initiated diplomatic negotiations, rather than hold elections in the territories. So similar were the two parties on this issue that the extremes of the political spectrum reacted by moving toward diametrically opposite positions.

Groups to the left of Labor brought powerful pressure to engage in direct talks with the Palestine Liberation Organization (PLO), based on recognition of Palestinian rights to full political self-determination. Groups to the right of Likud, by contrast, stridently demanded that Jewish territorial settlement intensify, preliminary to immediate annexation. Both camps believed the Intifada was the result of the failure of the political elites to solve the problem of the territories. And each camp confirmed its positions, since the Intifada showed that time was working against Israel. The right feared an imposed political solution, and the left worried that the government might resort to strong-arm tactics, such as outright annexation or the expulsion of the Palestinians.

These attitudes reflected the growing polarization of Israeli society, in general, and between and within the two major political elites, in particular. Likud and Labor differed on the tone of negotiations with the Palestinians and even squabbled over an acceptably composed Arab-Palestinian delegation to such talks. Labor favored a territorial compromise in the frame of a Jordanian-Palestinian confederation. Likud, by contrast, envisioned an autonomous Palestinian entity wholly subject to Israeli rule. The two elites concurred, however, over using massive armed force against the Palestinian uprising to avoid facing a "critical mass" that would lead to a Palestinian state. The Labor Party, with its Ben-Gurionist tradition, doubted the Palestinian problem could be completely solved through armed force. Meanwhile, the Likud was beginning to wake up to the need to reckon with the U.S. administration.

Within the parties, too, were various shades of opinion. Ariel Sharon headed a sizable faction of Likud members calling for far stronger military measures to quell the Palestinian uprising, thus destroying any Palestinian chances for full self-determination. Expel the Palestinians from the territories, they said, and punish them. The "Great Eretz Israel Front," comprising the Tzomet, Moledet, and Tehiya parties, and also supporters of Gush Emunim and the National Religious Party (NRP) agreed. Unexpectedly, the Intifada was uniting the secular right wing with the religious right wing in a cross-party alignment based on community of interests on the territorial question. Inside Labor, however, "dovish" groups and younger party members, supported by Mapam, Ratz, and those from "Peace Now," urged instead a political initiative to establish a Palestinian state.

While the major parties remained, on the whole, entrenched in their positions on subduing the Intifada by force, the public, usually militant against terrorism, began to shift its mood, pondering if a political solution was possible. More wanted territorial compromise (about 32 percent) or even a Palestinian state (approximately 18 percent). And, fewer people (only about 5 percent) argued for formal annexation of the territories to Israel, while some 10 percent thought the Palestinians in the territories should be forcibly deported to Arab states.²

There were two principal reasons for this trend toward moderation. Firstly, the Israeli public grew tired of the status quo. In overwhelming contrast to attitudes when the Intifada erupted, a decisive majority (95 percent) saw ahead nothing but further violence and possibly even an untenable defense burden. Secondly, most citizens concluded that Israel should disengage herself entirely from the territories, engineering a complete separation between the Palestinians in the territories and the Jews living within the Green Line. The more bitterly these two groups clashed, and the higher the casualty toll mounted, the more coexistence seemed impossible. This reversal of public trends, therefore, was triggered neither by a proclivity for pure dovish principles nor by some abstract idealist passion for peace. It derived from a need to pave genuine roads toward the resolution of an especially grim security problem.

At the same time, Israeli attitudes continued to be polarized over the use of force in the territories and against terrorism generally. In that respect, extreme differences of public opinion reflected those between and within the political elites. For example, 32 percent of Labor supporters were in favor of deploying considerable, even massive, armed force to quash the Intifada. A greater number, 49 percent, felt that the best means to that end would be a very selective use of force to be applied only if all else failed. In Likud, by contrast, as many as 63 percent deemed the use of appreciable or even heavy force to be the proper response for quelling the Palestinian uprising. Attitudes on the extreme right and left were far more emphatic. Of the far right, 67 percent favored the use of overwhelming force to suppress the Intifada. Of the far left, on the other hand, 85 percent approved the severely restricted use of armed force or a policy of total military passivism, inasmuch as they felt the most appropriate Israeli response to the Intifada was to establish a Palestinian state.³

The Forming of Consensus

The political pattern was drastically altered when Iraq invaded Kuwait in August 1990. Iraq's ruthless leader, Saddam Hussein, also threatened Israel's population centers; he was rumored to possess ICBMs armed with chemical and possibly even biological warheads and to be attempting to develop nuclear weaponry. Apprehension of the vulnerability of the Israeli home front to attack mounted to an all-time high. It was also feared that an "eastern front" might be formed, encompassing Iraq, Syria, other Arab "refusal" states, and the PLO. As the predicted date for a U.S. attack on Iraq approached, the Israeli press reported IDF estimates that Iraq was capable of hitting Israeli urban centers with as many as fifty Scud missiles. Although this would not result in mass annihilation, it was a sufficiently alarming prospect.

Unprecedented measures were accordingly taken to protect the civilian population. Protective kits were distributed in anticipation of possible biochemical attacks. A nationwide civil-defense instruction campaign was launched. "Sealed" rooms were prepared in all households, and emergency headquarters were set up. Israel's society gradually transformed itself into a quasi-military community.

"Disaster-research" literature has suggested that, in adverse situations, societies tend to develop consensual propensities and that the content of their political discourse changes dramatically.[4] Indeed, Israel's discourse is security-oriented at all times. Yet the repercussions of the Gulf War were somewhat different from those occasioned by the Intifada, an interethnic conflict, which to some degree emphasized the ideological motif of the public discourse. The Intifada forced Israeli society into a measure of soul-searching unprecedented since 1948 as to its national identity, the Palestinian problem, and permanent borders. No clearly demarcated boundary separated the warring communities nor their mutual relations in the Palestinian-Jewish struggle. By contrast, the anxiety that gripped the nation on the eve of the Gulf War underscored the military dimension of the public discourse.

In discussing the military aspects of the war, most politicians agreed that Israel might need to resort to arms. The old adage "The friend of my enemy is also my enemy" came to mind upon contemplating the PLO's overt solidarity with Saddam Hussein and the support expressed by the Palestinians for Iraq's invasion of Kuwait. Israel's operative consensus changed, and political game rules were rethought. Many politicians on the Zionist left who, prior to Iraq's aggression, had begun to believe the PLO was genuinely moderating its stance and renouncing former aspirations of destroying Israel, reevaluated those assessments. If the Zionist left had envisaged the possibility of Israeli-PLO-Palestinian coexistence, these hopes now seemed dashed. Statements by leftist leaders reflected their change of attitude. Avraham Burg, for example, a prominent Labor "dove" who had previously spearheaded mass demonstrations against the Likud government's policy, declared as follows:

> Up against an enemy like Saddam, even the rosiest dreams of peace must fragment. In embracing him, Arafat has done worse damage to all attempts at rapprochement between us than all Shamir's passive indifference. . . . The mortal blows struck by those two and the events of the past weeks have utterly deadened any prospect of peace out of love of humankind or brotherhood between nations. . . . The time has come to separate the one nation from the other, for we cannot live together.[5]

Similar remarks were made by Ratz MK Yossi Sarid, another of Israel's leading "doves." He stated the following:

> One needs a gas mask for protection against the revolting, poisonous odor wafting from the PLO's attitude to Saddam Hussein. . . . If it is permissible to support Saddam Hussein who, without batting an eyelid, has murdered tens of thousands of his political opponents and gassed Kurdish men, women, and children, maybe it is not so terrible to support the policies of Shamir, Sharon, and Rabin. . . . Were my support for a Palestinian state solely due to my belief that the Palestinians, too, deserve a state of their own—I would now renounce such support. But I continue to endorse their right to self-determination and to a state, because it is my own right to disburden myself of the Israeli occupation of the territories, and of the damage that the occupation inflicts. . . .[6]

All dovish groups within the Zionist consensus concurred that it was pointless to underscore coexistence, and all that could now be sought was a separation between the two nations, based on mutual recognition and self-determination. The all-pervasive, deep concerns prodded the Jewish sector to behave uniformly even while entertaining different political views. The Likud elite emphasized that Israel, when confronted by security challenges, must exclude any preparedness for withdrawing from the territories. The Likud was considerably aided in this by the media coverage, both in Israel and worldwide, of the PLO's unqualified support for Iraq.

The fundamental argument put forward by students of war, such as Lewis Coser and Georg Simmel, whereby interstate wars produce consensus, was thus found to apply also to situations of severe security crisis.[7] However, whereas Simmel stressed the importance of external threats in producing consensus and Coser ascribed greater significance to the manner in which different groups and individuals interpret such threat, the Israeli case clearly demonstrated the extent to which a government's active intervention in citizens' daily lives can play a decisive role in fashioning political order.

Governmental Intervention in Society

The first Scud missiles began hitting population centers on January 18, 1991, especially in the Tel Aviv area, and state interference was notched up higher again. A special state of emergency was declared, and civilian life became subordinated to the army and the security establishment. A partial explanation for the process can be found in the Lasswellian model whereby, in time of grave security crises, key functions of the civilian sector are taken over by the military experts. In contrast to that model, however, sociopolitical changes in Israel did not represent any form of surrender by the political echelon to the demands of the military, but rather derived from the political wish to obtain the military's assistance (involving also martial legislation) so as to further tighten government control over the public. Such control was deemed essential by both the ruling elite and the army, to ensure attainment of the country's defense aims. In consequence, the political system began to strongly feature symptoms of what Clinton Rossiter has called "constitutional dictatorship."[8]

Economic life largely adapted itself to emergency legislation, and all aspects of social and cultural life were directly affected by the state of belligerence. Working hours, for example, were restricted, and public assembly after dusk was banned, making it possible for the government to maintain control over the population's movements with a minimum of disruption. In doing so, the government bypassed the Knesset and disregarded a High Court ruling limiting the government from using emergency regulations to improve its efficiency excepting those means to spur the rapid enactment of Knesset legislation. Instead of amending the Civil Defense Law to enable the Knesset to exercise reasonable public control over its emergency legislation, the government empowered the minister of defense to institute emergency regulations. The minister declared a special civil-defense situation, arrogating to himself the authority to restrict freedom of movement and to oblige all citizens to remain at home or in a public shelter.

Most members of the public were not overly concerned with the finer constitutional points of this legislation. Anxiety for personal survival and the all-sweeping consensus were enough to keep them from protesting even if they had their suspicions. This behavior further confirmed Noam Chomsky's claims that ruling elites will typically exploit the fears of the populace, and Jurgen Habermas' observation that the "rule of law" provides a lever for increasing control over society by state mechanisms. Again in evidence here was the phenomenon described by the social historian Martin Shaw, whereby wars operate to extend the scope of state intervention at the expense of the civilian society.[9]

Within the bounds of that political discourse, those publicly disputing the national security policy risked inviting opprobrium for disloyalty. In time of war, political establishments show an increased tendency to deal violently with potential or actual demonstrators.[10] Israeli Arabs were sternly warned by Police Minister Roni Milo not to exhibit active political support for Iraq (as, for example, by means of demonstrations) and not to interfere in any way with Israel's security deployment in the face of the military threat. Thus, the perceptions entertained by Israel's Jewish political administration became increasingly divorced from her actual demographic reality, featuring both a Jewish-Israeli and a Palestinian-Israeli entity.[11]

Jewish-Israeli national boundaries were all too clearly delimited when civil-defense kits started being distributed to civilians. Israeli Arabs finally received them after appealing to the High Court; the Palestinians of the territories never received them at all. A frantic appeal to the High Court a few days before the fighting started ultimately secured kits for East Jerusalem and Arab villages in "Greater Jerusalem."[12] Boundaries of nationality were defined in terms of religion, the demarcation becoming all the more conspicuous with the arousal of general suspicion that Arabs in Israel and the territories, closely identifying with Iraq, might exploit the warfare for perpetrating acts of sabotage. But what actually happened was that, after a short time, Israeli-Arab leaders repudiated the Iraqi invasion, declaring their loyalty to the state and their obedience to all decisions issued by its governmental institutions.

Nevertheless, the consensus and fears engendered by the war made the Jewish society more intolerant than ever. Both the government and the army issued statements to the effect that in the event of an attack Israel's urban areas would be liable to suffer the severest damage, and all rural areas must therefore take second priority in the distribution of gas masks. But in view of the general intolerance toward Israeli Arabs, this was clearly begging the question: since most of the Arab population is rural whereas the Jewish population is predominantly urban, would not such a pro-urban policy be primarily injurious to the Arabs?

Fears over the war were used to further restrain the Intifada by targeting its leaders. Particularly noteworthy was the administrative arrest imposed by the minister of defense on Palestinian leader Seri Nusseiba, allegedly collaborating with Iraq by delivering fax messages concerning Israel's defensive deployment against Iraqi missile attacks. The executive refused to disclose its evidence to substantiate the charges on the grounds that disclosure would result in serious damage to state security. Eventually, to avoid revealing its real reasons for arresting Nusseiba, the government agreed, at a Jerusalem District Court hearing, to shorten Nusseiba's detention from six to three months.

The spirit of intolerance pervading the government was also clearly expressed by its decision on February 5, 1991, to coopt Moledet, thereby legitimizing its transfer notions. By so doing, Likud aroused grave suspicions among both Zionist and non-Zionist parties that its policy might henceforth include the forcible deportation of Palestinians from the territories, possibly of Israeli Arabs as well. As a result, for the first time since the war began, the Knesset plenum staged stormy debates, and both the government and Premier Shamir came in for scathing criticism. Likud was acting in light of past experience: nine years earlier, in 1982, it had similarly exploited the public's exclusive preoccupation with national security issues (the Lebanese War) to rope the Tehiya Party into the government. This time, in view of Moledet's advocacy of transfer policy, the political responses were even more severe.[13]

The political elite placed itself virtually beyond the reach of public criticism. Only a handful of cabinet ministers—chiefly members of the ministerial committee on security affairs—were informed of national security decisions. Even so, the premier and defense minister made most important decisions alone, without seriously consulting with or even reporting to any of their colleagues in the government. This kind of decision-making process is typical for Israel, particularly in time of war and extraordinary security crises. In the Gulf War, as in previous wars, it was proposed that new, special decision-making forums be formed. One proposal envisaged the reinstatement of the "national-unity government." But personal rivalries—especially between Shamir and Peres—as well as the recent trauma occasioned by the fall of the national-unity government in March 1990 quickly dashed that prospect.

The experience of the Gulf War demonstrates how strongly a ruling elite is inclined to bolster its power by holding both its decisions and its indecisions unaccountable to the public. During the fighting, the government evaded reports to the Knesset, and the premier withheld information from its committees. The Knesset Foreign Affairs and Defense Committee, was made powerless by its exclusion from information more valuable than that purveyed by the mass media. The media themselves were under tighter military control, especially by the IDF spokesman and the military censor. Israel's two radio stations were merged for the duration, ruling out even that limited degree of pluralism offered by the electronic media in less hectic times. The Israeli society found it quite natural that the military should take over the war reporting, while also instructing the public on how to behave. Public opinion surveys indicate the strength of the consensus: some 90 percent concurred with the merger of the radio stations.[14] Astoundingly, the public waived its right to more diversified reporting. The explanation lies in Israel's overvaluation of state symbols in time of war and national security crises.

For six weeks the home front found itself subjected, with no real air defense, to a cruel regimen of ballistic missile attacks. Yet the administration suppressed almost every impulse to question the government's wisdom to take shelter in "sealed" rooms, which in fact offered scant protection in the event of a direct or nearby hit. Even during the hostilities, rumors began to circulate alleging the defective condition of many gas masks, but these were quickly and effectively squashed. The army issued vigorous, even overweening denials of any defect, asserting that the population had been provided with very effective protection against a chemical or biological attack. Under the cloak of censorship, the public was given only very selective information, while the communiqués issued by the army spokesman usually provided, at best, mere fragments of the whole picture. Army generals were banned from granting all interviews, even commentary, clearly indicating to the extent to which the government was prepared to control information. The very distribution of civil-defense kits helped firm the consensus by reinforcing public fears and fostering the notion that the government was responding effectively. Even political parties as dovish as Ratz, which had previously spearheaded active opposition to government policy, supported its military passivism, applauding Prime Minister Shamir's leadership.

Convincing evidence that many civil-defense kits were either wholly or partly defective finally surfaced after the war. Reports published by the State Comptroller's Office soon after the fighting ended showed that many such kits would have been incapable of furnishing even a minimal degree of protection in the event of a chemical or biological attack. This further buttresses my contention that, whereas theoretical literature claims consensus to be a positive political phenomenon, serious damage may result from like-minded thinking.

The Public Discourse during the Gulf War

The public generally comported itself during the war with commendable obedience and discipline. In most of Israel's previous wars, with a large proportion of the population mobilized for military service, it was difficult for extra-parliamentary opposition to organize. But where the call-up is restricted in scale (as during the Lebanese War), protest groups are more easily mustered. In the Gulf War, mobilization was of a civilian type. Most of the military-reserve pool was not drafted but employed under supervision of state authorities. Thus, about 200,000 workers became part of the "economy in time of emergency" services. Public support for the government's military passivism further reinforced discipline and obedience. About 80 percent felt that Israel "ought to stay in calm control and not react for the moment."[15]

Although the civilian population sustained direct missile attacks, casualties were light and the government contrived, throughout, to convey the impression that its handling of the crisis was resolute and effective. Most of the public, unaware that the military restraint was the result of American pressure, did not query what had become of the repeated assurances of the defense authorities and the prime minister that Israel would respond militarily and not confine herself to self-defense.

The IDF, however, was familiar with the truth, and some senior officers called for action against Iraq. But due to the subordination of the military to the political echelon, differences with the government over that issue did not burgeon into public debate. Also, heavy anxiety and consensus values reinforced the military's obedience to the government. The fact that the war left Israel relatively unscathed enhanced the general opinion that her democracy had proven itself. At the same time, the already weakened faith in Israel's all-conquering ability to vanquish any aggressor single-handedly gave way to a more realistic appraisal. The unabashedly nationalistic Shamir government chose to break the rule whereby Israel trusted her military strength alone. For the first time since the war of 1956, foreign forces were called upon to defend Israel's airspace and population, and this was met by popular acceptance, by the active support of all political groups, and by a general absence of protest.

Common threat concepts were thus changing. Many more people began to accept that Israel's military power was far from limitless. Thousands of citizens flew Israeli flags and affixed "We Are All Patriots" stickers to their vehicles, evidencing more of a sense of solidarity than in times of abeyance. But that solidarity derived from a particularly acute case of national nerves: about 40 percent of the public testified to having fallen prey, "often" or "sometimes" during the war, to attacks of anxiety. Toward the end of January 1991, 36 percent confessed that they might not be able to cope with the war's stresses if Scud missiles continued to fall on Israeli population centers.[16] Naturally enough, tension was highest in areas hit by missiles, the Tel Aviv region, and Haifa. Never before in the chronicles of Israel's wars did the public's endurance capacity so clearly indicate signs of strain. Some left the country either permanently or temporarily. Others abandoned their homes, at least during the fateful night hours. But for all that, most supported the government's position.

The Gulf War was the first occasion since 1949 in which the civilian hinterland of Israel was actively involved in hostilities. Euphoria over victories as experienced up to 1967, perplexities in the face of Israel's "goliath-like" strength after that time, the self-identity dilemmas occasioned by the ever more intrusive Palestinian-Israeli conflict, all gave way to a primal, traditional sense of common ethnic origin, of community, of a Jewish society fighting for its life. These were not militarization processes in the narrow Lasswellian sense, but rather a shortening of political distances, the boundary lines between the society and its ruling apparatuses being redrawn.

Usually, an Israeli's "patriotism" was measured in terms of whether he or she either mobilized or volunteered for war work. In the Gulf War, by contrast, the criterion was survivorship, assimilation into the collective mind-set of being reconciled to military passivism, staying put throughout the missile attacks on the home front. Slogans such as "We'll come through this, too" appeared on outdoor posters and were repeatedly played over the radio, faithfully reflecting both the nature of the encounter and the recognition that no alternative currently offered itself. Much of the population was subject, for about a month and a half, to a virtual nocturnal curfew, which brought cultural life and entertainment almost to a standstill, reinforcing the atmosphere of reluctant acquiescence to an externally imposed malaise.

This was why even left-wing political groups tended to restrain themselves when very stiff curfews were imposed on the Palestinians in the territories. Peace Now and smaller groups of intellectuals called upon peace organizations throughout the world to support Israel through the crisis. Any forcible occupation, they said, must be opposed, and once the crisis was over, they would redouble their efforts to solve the conflict through Palestinian self-determination. But first, they stressed, Saddam Hussein's "genocide regime" must be crushed. In the Zionist left-wing eyes Israel had been transformed, for a while, from executioner to victim. State symbols were thus again greatly enhanced by war at the expense of democratic values. In Israel's case, the regime's Jewish elements were reinforced, while the Palestinian problem was dislodged from the nation's wartime agenda, since any attempt to solve it would have been considered at odds with the "national logic."

The war was an interstate rather than an interethnic conflict. It strengthened the public's tendencies to rally to a national Jewish identity. Iraq, as an external threat, helped crystallize that identity and distracted the public's attention from the need to peacefully resolve the Israeli-Palestinian conflict. The Palestinians were yet again conveniently branded by the political elites and most of the public as a satanic adversary. In the course of the fighting, a few manifestoes were published in the territories and a few hesitant voices were raised against the Iraqi aggression, betraying a fear that it might prove damaging to Palestinian interests. Certain Palestinians of the territories accused Iraq of engaging in the forced transfer of

Palestinians out of Kuwait. But these few sporadic gestures of protest left the Israeli political system singularly unimpressed.

Instances of national economic mismanagement escaped criticism due to the extraordinary state of emergency. For example, about 300,000 wage earners were forced to absent themselves from work for the first four days (January 18–21, 1991) following the initial Scud attacks. Yet the government not only proposed no compensation but actually toyed with the idea of deducting days from the workers' annual vacations. In addition, entire sectors of the economy, such as education, employing tens of thousands of workers, were effectively paralyzed for most of the war. Yet no measures were taken to provide alternative employment. It was not until about three weeks after the war began that the treasury, the Histadruth Labor Federation, and the employers' associations decided to cooperate in an attempt to steer the economy through the crisis. Some wage earners, particularly working mothers who had no option but to remain at home to look after their children, began to feel the strain. But this elicited no extra-parliamentary protest, and was raised for discussion by only a handful of Knesset members and a small number of Histadruth functionaries. In that respect, too, the Gulf War differed from its predecessors. This time, even on the functional level of adaptation to the environment, the system was plagued by frequent instances of malfunction. Yet due to the interplay of society and state, as well as the nature of the consensus, no major public debate was aroused by these issues, either during or after the fighting.

After the Storm

The Gulf War ended and life reverted to "normal." The state loosened its control of the broadcasting networks, the economy went back to "business as usual," and the people resumed their former lifestyles. The game rules of the democratic regime had not really been put to the test, due to the relative efficacy of the political regime during the war.

Generally, the war prompted an inclination for the Israeli-Jewish public to be more skeptical of its chances of establishing an unshakable presence in the Middle East by armed force.[17] Yet, the basic concepts of the political elites as to the use of force remained unchanged. Thus, once public debate over the issue of strategic depth resumed, the various parties, far from rethinking their former positions, promoted them more vigorously than ever.

According to Likud, the Iraqi blitzkrieg of Kuwait and Saddam's use of ballistic missiles amply illustrated what would likely happen if a pro-Iraqi Palestinian state were to arise alongside Israel. Labor retorted that the war clearly proved how vital the stability and strategic depth of Jordan was to Israel's security. Labor Chairman Peres argued that the "Jordanian option" should therefore now be revived. By this he meant it was time to try once more, with the participation of a Palestinian delegation, to solve the Arab conflict on the basis of a territorial compromise with Jordan. Political "doves" in Labor and parties to its left claimed that strategic depth was a mere myth and that in an era of advanced military technology, there was no strategic advantage to be gained by holding on to the West Bank. On the contrary, to maintain the territorial status quo was to bait the Arabs into launching yet another war. The best security that Israel could gain would be that achieved by a stable peace, answering the Palestinian right to political self-determination. Parties right of Likud, by contrast, claimed that the PLO's unqualified solidarity with Iraq proved the urgent need to annex the territories.

8 The Inter-Communal Conflict of the Intifada and the Israeli Regime (1987–93)

Introduction

Until now, you have learned primarily about the sociopolitical aspects of interstate wars (and the Lebanese War, which had meaningful intercommunal facets). This chapter, which deals with the intercommunal and interethnic Israeli-Palestinian conflict, refers to the erosion and changes that the Intifada inflicted on the social fabric and political setting in Israel. Dealing with attitudinal, behavioral, and institutional dimensions, I argue that the Intifada increased the institutional weaknesses of the Israeli state and also engendered some attitudinal moderation toward the resolution of the Israeli-Palestinian conflict.

While most of the public paid attention to the interstate dimension of the conflict, the Palestinians in the West Bank and Gaza Strip began a revolt against the Israeli occupation. Thus, from the end of 1987 until 1993 (with the important exception of the Gulf War), the Israeli political system emphasized and was influenced by the violent intercommunal struggle between Palestinians in the territories and Israeli-Jews, either in Israel proper (within its 1949 borders) or in the territories.

What were the effects of this harsh intercommunal dispute on the scope and content of the Israeli political order? This chapter deals primarily with the following issues: (1) Attitudes and contentions regarding military force and political options as means to resolve the Arab-Palestinian-Israeli conflict at large or, particularly, the Intifada and the Palestinian problem. (2) Military-civilian relationships and "the rule of law" in Israel and in the territories facing the Palestinian uprising. (3) The Intifada's effects on the Israeli public and state-society relations.

Military Force and Political Options

The Israeli public and its elite were surprised by the eruption of the Intifada in December 1987.[1] Most felt that efforts should be directed against the Arab countries, especially Syria, and after the Gulf War, greater attention was given to Iraq and to the Gulf states. The Palestinian problem, however, was considered to be a reflection of the prolonged interstate Arab-Israeli conflict. Thus, the "national unity-government" had to grapple with an unpredictable event. For the first time since the cease-fire agreements were concluded in 1949, the main political controversies were over the execution of military force against Palestinians under direct Israeli military and administrative control. The "War on Palestine"[2] was within the military, political, social, and economic boundaries of the same state. These special features significantly influenced the nature of the political order in Israel. The Intifada was not an international war, in the usual connotation of this term. Yet, it also could not be considered a civil war. The Palestinians did not challenge Israel within its 1949 borders but directed their efforts against the Israeli occupation in the territories. Most of the Palestinian factions in the West Bank and Gaza Strip demanded a halt to Israeli settlements and a prompt Israeli withdrawal from the territories. Therefore, the Intifada did not endanger Israel's existence. It did, however, undermine basic, traditional Israeli political attitudes.

The approaches described in this book regarding military force affected the partisan attitudes toward the Intifada. On the one hand, non-Zionist parties to the left of the Labor Party, which maintained the political approach of total passivity, demanded the cessation of all Israeli military action aimed at quelling the uprising and pressed for immediate Israeli withdrawal from all the territories. These parties, especially the Arab-Jewish Progressive List, also encouraged extensive military disobedience in order to change the formal Israeli Intifada policy of military suppression. This was a clear rejection of the Likud-Labor coalition's policy.

On the other hand, the Zionist parties to the left of Labor supported the use of force on a very limited scale, as a legitimate and defensive means against Palestinian attempts to attack Israeli soldiers. They opposed, however, all moves made to punish Palestinian civilians or to prevent them from expressing their aspirations for political independence. Those parties—Mapam, Ratz, and Shinui—regarded formal, direct, and permanent negotiations with the Palestine Liberation Organization (PLO), and the eventual establishment of an independent Palestinian state in the territories, as the only realistic option if the hopeless impasse were to be broken. That impasse, in their view, had produced a situation in which Israel was losing its democratic character, while the Palestinians were being deprived of their basic human rights.

By contrast, parties in favor of using force in the context of the conflict (Labor and parties to the right of it) tended to refrain from addressing the moral aspects of the new reality. They justified the execution of military force, even though principally used against civilians, on the grounds of its utility in vanquishing the Intifada. The consensus achieved between them (especially between Likud and Labor) was founded largely on their common rejection of an independent Palestinian state between Israel and the Jordan River. The Intifada, indeed, was conceived by them as an unjust attempt to impose upon Israel the abandonment of its traditional principles and to negotiate with the PLO, directly and openly, over the prompt establishment of a Palestinian state.[3]

All the same, a fundamental difference existed between those in favor of realpolitik and compromise and those who supported power politics and coercion. The latter, exemplified by the Likud, saw the Intifada predominantly as a military problem capable of and deserving military methods. By contrast, the former, especially the Labor Party, tended to emphasize that "the Intifada is a political problem with military aspects rather than a military problem with political aspects."[4] In keeping with this point of view, shared by all Labor Party members, Labor constantly opposed the Likud's policy, as fashioned by Prime Minister Shamir. It repeatedly demanded that efforts be made to reach a political solution based on territorial compromises. Labor spokesmen, most prominently Peres and Rabin, announced publicly that although efficient military measures might reduce the scale of the insurrection, such measures would never resolve the Intifada and could not result in peace.

In consequence, the then-defense minister, Rabin, announced his plan (January 20, 1989) for a political solution based on free elections in the territories and a significant Israeli withdrawal. That plan met with strong opposition from the Likud and parties to the right of it, who believed that Israel could and had to impose its sovereignty over the territories or at least ensure its permanent control, even by using considerable military force.[5]

In 1990, I interviewed a representative sample of Israeli members of the Knesset (MKs) and asked them:[6] "What, in your opinion, is the desirable solution to the question of the territories and to the Palestinian problem?" The findings reveal a basic contention between the two major parties regarding the diplomatic options. While a majority among the Likud members supported the idea of autonomy for the Palestinians in the West Bank and Gaza Strip as a permanent solution, most of the Labor members supported territorial compromise as the permanent solution.[7]

Yet, both parties considered Palestinian autonomy as the preferable interim solution. Such an option would grant the Palestinians some independent authorities to manage their domestic lives, while Israel preserved its powers in the spheres of (primarily) national security and foreign affairs. Thus, both parties tended to perceive autonomy as a transitional stage, notwithstanding the Likud's view of it as a permanent solution. While Likud perceived the autonomy to be the best means to ensure Israel's control of the Gaza Strip and especially the West Bank, Labor hoped that autonomy would generate a certain degree of mutual confidence between Palestinians and Israeli Jews. Both parties considered the continuation of the violent Intifada as a threat to their respective aspirations. Labor and Likud alike claimed that a perceived Palestinian victory would lead to the solidification of the old Palestinian claims to forcibly expel the Israelis from all the territories, including East Jerusalem, and to occupy virtually all of Israel itself.

The Israeli policy reflected the common fear of the Palestinians' insistence on their "Right of Return," namely, the self-declared right of the Palestinian nation to settle in Israel proper, without any restrictions. Thus, the proponents of both parties advocated, in principle, the forceful suppression of what they declared the Palestinian rebellion. In the period between 1987 and 1993, the partisan contentions were not altered drastically, but signs of limited tactical moderation were detected. Under consistent American pressure, the Likud agreed to the participation of Palestinians, de facto members of the PLO, in the talks with Israel. Facing the fact that no political party, with the exception of the extreme right, conceived of the Intifada as a war, the strife between different approaches became very public.

In the previously discussed theoretical terms of this book, the internal political conflicts in the course of the Intifada were a result of different perceptions of threats and various degrees of fears. The contentions regarding the proper way to deal with the Intifada were one of the factors that led to the breakdown of the National Unity Government in 1990.

The Army, the Political Elites, and the Rule of Law

The Intifada was fought between civilians and the organized Israeli army. For the first time since the war of 1948–49, Israel employed extensive coercive military power against people, most under the age of sixteen, armed only with stones, knives, and Molotov cocktails. The long battle with a civilian population led to unprecedented dilemmas and exacerbated relations between the government and the military. The longer the Intifada endured, the sharper the public controversy became over the use of excessive military force against the Palestinians in the occupied territories. The suddenness and sheer intensity with which the Intifada erupted, the bloody riots that accompanied it, the heavy casualties that it brought, and the unpleasant discovery that it could not be rapidly subdued shocked the Israeli government and army to the core.

In the early stages of the uprising, the government failed to take the proper steps to restore order. The directives that it issued to the army were so ambiguous that military commanders in the territories found themselves operating without clearly defined goals. This often led army personnel to react impetuously and to use exaggerated force, which also reflected their frustration in failing to quell the violent riots and the determination of the hostile population. Thus, frequent instances of blatant military brutality were recorded.

A particularly prominent instance came to light in the trial of four soldiers from the combat force of the "Givati Brigade." The accused were charged with beating to death a Palestinian from

Jibaliya, in the Gaza Strip. Acquitted on manslaughter, they were nevertheless found guilty of grievous assault and of obeying an illegal command. The four were sentenced, in September 1989, to a few months in jail, demoted in rank, and transferred from their unit. Later, in October 1989, they were pardoned by Commanding Officer, Southern Command, General Matan Vilna'i. In justifying his decision, Vilna'i stressed that he had taken due consideration of the fact that the men had committed their crime while serving in circumstances in which their lives were in daily danger. His writ of pardon nevertheless confirmed the gravity with which he viewed their act, for the writ fully certified their demotion and dishonorable removal from a prestigious brigade.[8]

Altogether, grave disparities became evident between the government expectations for the military to produce quick and efficient solutions to the uprising, on the one hand, and the army's methods and speed in containing the riots, on the other. All of these factors emerged during the sensational prosecutions of officers and ranks accused and, in some cases, convicted of unlawfully harassing and beating unarmed Palestinian civilians.

One of the most important trials was that of Colonel Yehuda Meir, a senior commander on the West Bank, who was charged with ordering his troops, in January 1988, to carry out the brutal beating of twenty innocent residents of the Palestinian villages Beita and Hawarra. Meir claimed that the alleged ruthless maltreatment of Palestinians was in accordance with the policies advocated by then-Minister of Defense Rabin. The military court ruled (April 1991), however, that the orders given to Colonel Meir by the OC Central Command, as well as those dispensed by the minister of defense, were lawful and that he had deviated from the authority granted to him, had issued illegal commands to his subordinates, and must therefore be found guilty of the offense of causing grievous bodily harm.[9]

Colonel Meir's trial expressed instances of grossly unbecoming behavior by officers and soldiers. This, as well as the sentences from a number of trials, eroded and stained the prestige of the army. In reaction, the military authorities accused the political establishment of shirking its responsibilities and abandoning the army, to both the grave problems created by the Intifada and to the severe criticism leveled by the public and the courts. But these were not the army's only difficulties. The professional military's relative autonomy had been eroded since the Yom Kippur War, but never were the army, and its operations, subjected to such public political pressures as during the Intifada.

On the one hand, the right-wing parties, supported by claims of Jewish settlers that their lives in the territories were being persistently terrorized, pressed hard for the implementation of tougher measures against the Palestinians. Their demands intensified in 1992–93 following an increase in murderous attacks committed against Jews in the territories. Indeed, in some instances settlers took the law into their own hands. These acts occasionally resulted in the killing of Palestinians. On the other hand, the parties on the left, with the encouragement of various Israeli peace groups, claimed that the army was using intolerable force against the Palestinians. The verbal clashes between these two opposing views aggravated the difficulties faced by the military high command, already confronted by the unusual phenomenon of its senior officers facing MKs bearing protests and politically motivated demands. The army was being drawn into political controversy in a manner that could endanger its professionalism and even conceivably erode its loyalty to the government.

The military rule in the territories was also reflected in the Israeli laws and regulations that were imposed in the occupied regions. There were 481 Palestinians deported; hundreds of homes were sealed or blown up by the army; and over 25,000 administrative arrests were made without judicial supervision.[10] Despite the authority of the Israeli Supreme Court in the territories, its judicial policy was to abdicate on political issues and not to intervene in the decisions or activities of the security forces.

Yet, the state of affairs in the territories was so difficult that the Supreme Court was compelled to establish minimal protection of the Palestinians. It ruled that neither the deportation of Palestinian agitators nor the blowing up of their homes would henceforth be tolerated except when the security forces considered these to be the only means of preventing hostile acts against the troops. The Court also ruled that detainees have the right to have their families and lawyers informed of their arrests and places of detention.[11] These decisions, with all their limited force, were exceptions to the general tendency to respect the policy of the Israeli government in the occupied territories.

The most prominent example of the degree to which the Supreme Court inclined to legitimize the government's actions in the territories took place in 1992. Following a series of murderous attacks on Israeli Jews by Hamas activists, the government expelled 415 Hamas activists into Lebanese no-man's-land. By doing so, it ignored Article 49 of the Fourth Geneva Convention, which prohibits expulsions. It also ignored the Israeli law that necessitates that appeals be heard before a deportation can take place. In fact, the security authorities acted under heavy public pressure to stop the killings. Hence, the Palestinians were deprived of basic human rights. They were expelled before their personal involvement in the terrorist acts were proved. The Supreme Court, however, upheld the government's decision of January 1993, claiming that the murderous character of the Hamas terrorist activities justified the deportation.[12]

The political and military struggle over the future of the territories also had an impact on the rule of law within the annexed territories. Emergency laws restricting individual rights were frequently used, especially in East Jerusalem. Two notable examples were the imposition of censorship of political articles appearing in Arabic newspapers in East Jerusalem and the placement of prominent, suspected PLO members in "administrative detention," thus effectively denying them of their liberties without court intervention.

An instance of this practice involved the order issued on December 6, 1989, against Faysal al-Husayni, a resident of East Jerusalem, which limited his freedom to travel from there to other places in the occupied territories. The order was for a period of six months and stated that al-Husayni, a major Palestinian leader, would be arrested if he transgressed any of its provisions.[13] The army explained the order by claiming that it was "necessary for the protection of the public's security." It appeared, however, that the step was taken for the purely political reason of limiting the political freedom of a suspected PLO activist.

Within the boundaries of the pre-1967 "Green Line," by contrast, the legal system was more liberal. Yet, the period under review witnessed considerable controversy over the exercise of the amendment to the Prevention of Terror Order promulgated in August 1986, which made it illegal for Israelis to meet with representatives of the PLO; the maximum penalty for transgression was three years in jail. A notable case in which that amendment was enforced was that of Abie Nathan, an Israeli citizen known for his many unconventional pro-peace efforts. Nathan was sentenced twice because of his meetings with the PLO's Yasir Arafat. Reactions to these cases were extremely vigorous. While Israel's right-wing parties lauded the court for Nathan's convictions (one in 1990 and one in 1991) and punishment, the left claimed that the order constituted anti-democratic legislation.[14]

The legal system became increasingly obliged to contend with politically motivated instances of noncompliance with the law. Breaches were committed in the territories by Jewish settlers who opened fire on Palestinians and by soldiers who refused to serve in the territories because they opposed the Israeli occupation.[15] When attempts were made to enforce the law, political pressures were brought to bear on the courts. When settlers were charged with offenses, the right responded; when soldiers were charged with draft dodging, the left protested.[16] Thus, the intercommunal conflict eroded the relative professional autonomy of the Israeli legal system.

The General Public in the Course of the Intifada

Since its inception at the end of 1987 and until the conclusion of the Oslo agreement (September 13, 1993), the Intifada inflicted a high casualty toll among Palestinians and Israelis alike: 1,163 Palestinians and 160 Israeli-Jews lost their lives.[17]

More Israelis than ever before felt that the political and territorial status quo could no longer be tolerated. Only 5 percent of the Israeli-Jews presumed in 1990 that the status quo was beneficial for Israel, and in 1991 4.7 percent held the same opinion; in 1992 and 1993, only 2.5 percent considered the status quo preferable.[18] Many Israelis believed that changes had to be made in favor of achieving desirable ends. The Intifada created a physical threat close to home, hence a psychological burden on many Israeli civilians. This new situation of deepening insecurity in daily life explains the growing desire for solutions and the rejection of the status quo.

Therefore, despite the polarization among the Jewish-Israeli public regarding the future of the territories, the softening trend was stronger than the hardening propensity. In 1990, 37.6 percent supported dovish solutions to the intercommunal conflict (that is, a Palestinian state or territorial compromise), and 28.5 percent in 1991; 29.4 percent in 1992, and 39.2 percent in 1993 had the same opinion. This represented a sharp rise in the dovish trend in comparison to trends of the seventies and the eighties.[19] This tendency was not limited to long-term issues, but applied to short-term ones as well. Thus, in comparison to the seventies and eighties, more people supported dovish options as possible interim solutions: 25 percent in 1990, 27 percent in 1991, 32.1 percent in 1992, and 29.9 percent in 1993.[20]

The growing support expressed the feelings of many Israelis that the war against the Intifada could not be won militarily. Whereas winning wars sometimes tends to reduce anxieties and promote harder attitudes, losing can encourage softer attitudes. American public opinion underwent a softening process following the military fiasco in Vietnam, as did French public opinion during the latter stages of and after the Algerian War. The Israeli army was not defeated by the rebelling Palestinians and even achieved some military gains. Yet, the inability to quell the uprising was perceived by the public as a reflection of basic weakness. This image of weakness was part of a trend since the war of 1973, a trend that was strengthened during the war in Lebanon, the Gulf War, and more so by the Intifada.

Indeed, the Intifada stimulated dissent among the political and military elites and among the general public. It revealed different perceptions of threat, a lack of political structures that could have facilitated national consensus, and a significant decline in the impact of consensus values. Compared to the war of 1956, the structure of the party system during the Intifada could not prevent public opposition. Furthermore, the citizenry did not experience the same degree of fear of destruction as it did during the war of 1967.

The Intifada was not only over the occupied territories but was also generated and managed within the territories. Thus, and more than ever, the controversies in Israel about the future of the Gaza Strip and especially the West Bank inflamed political dissent during the hostilities. The fragmentation of the party system, analyzed earlier in this book, enabled the articulation of conflicting opinions regarding military force and the future of the territories.

This fragmentation made it difficult for the state to preserve internal order. The mass media was an additional factor in molding public opinion. The Intifada spurred greater investigative coverage than before, with the media reflecting the doubts and criticism of Israelis about how to handle the crisis. The events were dynamic, yet the Israeli censors were sluggish in approving reports. The mass media, then, used foreign, even Palestinian sources of information and evaded the supervision of the censor. The fact that issues regarding the use of force became associated with the issue of the territories also contributed to the mass media's tendency to protest against the political establishment, especially against the Likud-led coalition.

The prolonging of this conflict facilitated public adaptation to the violent engagement, and in turn the Intifada lost its image as a severe international military crisis. While the prevalent political language until 1989 defined it as a security crisis, the discourse changed after it was somewhat confined in 1989. Gradually, the political language denoted the crisis as endogenous to the Israeli political setting. Subsequently, the mass media perceived it as more legitimate to refer to the Intifada as a "political crisis," in contrast to a "war," thus criticizing the government's inability to solve the problem.

The dissent and the weakening of the state's apparatus eventually led to the rise of the Labor Party to power in 1992. Controversies over the use of force were not the main cause of the Likud's electoral defeat. Yet, the public held that a significant element of the Likud's weakness was the failure of its extensive use of force to quell the uprising and increase the level of daily security in Israel. The Labor-led government's policy toward the Intifada was based on that party's traditional approach regarding force. The uprising was perceived as a primarily political problem. Hence, the government, with the endorsement of parties advocating partial passivism, could pave the way for the Oslo Agreement. Rabin and Peres fostered a process of historical reconciliation and separation between Israelis and Palestinians as an alternative to the inability to resolve the Palestinian problem by military force.[21]

Conclusions

For the first time since 1949, Israelis faced internal struggles over the issue of how to cope with a revolt supported by a majority of the Palestinians. The military found itself engaged in police functions, aimed mainly to subdue a national revolt in the occupied territories. Consequently, more groups and individuals than ever before presumed that only compromise could solve the conflict. No political structure could control the conflicting powers and processes in order to bring about a national consensus in Israel. From this perspective, the Intifada was the continuation of the Lebanese War. However, while the intercommunal aspect was less clear from 1982 to 1985, it became much more prominent after 1987. Groups, organizations, and individuals who protested against the war in Lebanon became more active during the Intifada.

The theoretical model explored in this book claims that internal order in democracies is molded and regulated by the effects of international events as those events are perceived and reflected in the internal settings. The mechanisms in internal politics that have shaped political order have also been defined. In other words, the basic observation is that there are no clear or permanent boundaries between the international system and internal politics. Indeed, the basic tenets of the political order in Israel were stiffly challenged during the Intifada. Where should the permanent territorial borders of the Jewish state be drawn? What should the relationship with the Palestinians be? What are the meaning and scope of Israeli nationality? What limitations should be imposed on the execution of military force? The Jewish political regime could not suggest innovative and civilian solutions for these basic dilemmas and could not maintain national consensus.

Part Four

Book Findings in Comparative and Theoretical Perspective: From a Wartime Society to a Civilian Society

9 The Long-Term Effects of Wars and the Emergency Situation

Introduction

This chapter addresses the cumulative ramifications of the Arab-Palestinian-Israeli conflict on Israeli politics. It further emphasizes the arguments from a theoretical and comparative perspective.

In the following sections, I interpret the empirical and theoretical findings of this study by further utilizing the literature of conflict studies and comparative politics. Sections 1 and 2 emphasize the dual nature of the protracted emergency situation as an external and internal phenomenon. As of 1995, Israel has been under perceived siege, yet it has not become a garrison state. In this conjunction, sections 3 and 4 pinpoint issues of obedience and attitudes regarding military force. I argue to the prevalence of militaristic (cultural, legal, and institutional) characteristics. Political forces of moderation have existed, however. Sections 5 and 6 reinforce my argument that two variables should be included in any effort to understand the effects of the protracted conflict: war fatigue and the struggle between modernization and Jewish nationalism.

Subsequent to the review of findings about the protracted emergency situation, this chapter deals with war as a unique event. Sections 7 and 8 illuminate the book's theoretical model, which includes, first, the very blurred boundaries between the state and the international environment; second, the dynamic relations between the state's apparatus and social forces; and, third, the mechanisms by which political order might be shaped. The most important components of these mechanisms are fears (as political resources), ruling coalitions (primarily as consensual structures), values of protest and essentially values of consensus, and the content and assortment of threat concepts. Section 9 clarifies the degree to which the distinction between elites and the public is relevant for further understanding of this book's findings. Sections 10, 11, and 12 suggest, based on this study, theoretical ways to comprehend, define, and measure consensus and dissent. The last section summarizes my argument for why dissent might be very helpful for political settings, while consensus might be easily manipulated against any political change.

The Emergency Situation as a Factor Both Extraneous and Indigenous to the Political System

Never has Israel brought her enemies to total surrender. All her wars have ended, not in agreed or enforced peace settlements (as in the European case, for example) but in armistice agreements and ceasefires. This has led to a long-lasting status quo of neither peace nor war. Democracy thus took root under the cloud of a continual menace. In this ongoing state of emergency, the conflict's international elements (mainly the Arab states' attitudes toward Israel and superpower involvement) meshed with its interethnic elements (Jewish-Israeli-Palestinian relations). Understandably, Israel's public discourse bore the imprint of this conflict just as her very existence became its inherent motif.

On Israel's accession to statehood, in natural sequence to the Yishuv era, and also partly due to the influence of British tradition on the Zionist movement leaders, democracy, as defined by the ruling elite, was installed as the obvious regime befitting a state having pretensions to justice, morality, and a sense of uniqueness.[1] As the years went by, Israeli public life clearly reflected the smooth, functional efficiency of the democratic regime. Despite her six wars (not counting the Intifada and the Gulf War) and thousands of security incidents, the up-building of the nation proceeded apace. Even though the national defense budget steadily grew (especially after the Yom Kippur War) to as much as one third of the Gross National

Product (GNP),[2] the political regime still budgeted for the absorption of immigration, settlement, and social needs.

Never has Israel been militarily defeated. And in all but the Lebanese War and the Intifada, she achieved most of her war objectives. It is hardly surprising, therefore, that most of the Israeli public is confident of the military capacity of the state. This national ethos is blatantly doubted by the far right, especially by Gush Emunim; even though the Gush has not proposed the negation of democracy as a primary value, it has suggested that democracy is an obstacle to the annexation of Judea and Samaria. The Gush has advocated lawbreaking as a tactic of political activity in the frame of democracy.[3] Certain groups of extremist West Bank settlers have pushed the Gush line to even further limits, disputing its alignment within the National Religious Party (NRP), Tehiya, and Likud, and expressly calling for the democratic game rules to be broken, if necessary through violence, so as to facilitate massive use of force against Arabs and Palestinians. Their precursors in challenging the legitimacy of the democracy were, in the fifties, the "Sulam" group, and, in the seventies, "Dov" and other groups. The essence of this antidemocratic spirit was found in Kach, and some affiliated factions, which aspired to an Halakhic-Jewish theocracy. The army, according to this concept, is divinely ordained, and the deployment of the most extensive force, including for the expulsion of Palestinians, a Jewish religious imperative.

State under Siege, but not a Garrison State

Accepted practice in wartime, even in democracies, countenances the curtailment of freedom of expression and the avoidance of public debate, if only for limited periods. The underlying premise of this "public truce" is that if the plurality of positions on the use of force is aired in public, the nation's staying power may be undermined to the point of risking defeat. This does not apply to a war deemed by groups and individuals to be unjustified. In light of democratic values, objection may be expressed to a war that appears not only erroneous on the operative level but totally unwarranted in political, military, and moral terms. Thus, for example, tens of millions of Americans publicly opposed the Vietnam War, and a majority of French people (90 percent) gradually came to support a total withdrawal from Algeria. Radical right-wing groups in the United States and France, for their part, called for the war's opponents to be deprived of their freedom of speech. Similar manifestations were recorded in Israel during the Lebanese War.[4]

Consensus values, and the manner in which they are manipulated by the ruling elite, are the price of democracy's survival in ongoing emergency situations. The stability of democracy in wartime is assured by the public's consent to the system's basic values but also rests on public consensual propensities. The centrality of the state in the political culture makes the public amenable to persuasion of the need for consensus, even at the price of not expressing itself.

The notion pervading Israel, even after 1967, was that military defeat in war meant annihilation.[5] This further bolstered the predominance of security considerations in shaping public policy. Both the successive governments of Labor and Likud and the military had to cope with the difficulties of a small state needing to focus its best efforts on security. Demographic constraints precluded, in Israel, the distance maintained in most European wars of the professional army and the civilian hinterland, keeping the latter totally divorced from the war effort. Israel's all-encompassing compulsory draft and long periods of reserve duty even in times of abeyance (subject to exceptions approved by security service laws and political practice) distinguish her from the Western democracies.

Posing a certain contrast to the Lasswellian model, whereby every democratic regime becomes, in a protracted state of emergency, a militarily authoritarian regime ("garrison state"), civilian echelons in Israel evolved mutual relations with the security establishment in general, without direct or immediate injury to the existing regime.[6] This was due to the very broad assent of Jewish-Zionist democratic society as to values, concepts, and interests, ascribing tremendous priority to armed force.

This is not to say that the army as an organization of experts on matters of violence did not exert great influence. The army and the security establishment form a large part of the political establishment, where their influence as pressure groups is enormous. Where the army and the security establishment recognize the democratic regime as legitimate, obedience will ensue on the strategic level, even though the efficacy the democratic regime can show in dealing with long-lasting security crises is an important precondition for the persistence and prevalence of that obedience. One criterion that will be applied by the military-security establishment in measuring such efficacy will be the degree to which the political elite respond to its pressures. In Israel, it responds most satisfactorily, due to Israel's attributes as a society in wartime. That susceptibility, however, does not necessarily lead to the destruction of basic democratic principles, such as freedom of expression and organization.

Another prime factor that prevents the society in wartime from becoming a militaristic society with an authoritarian regime is that the army is subordinate to the political elite and is used for political purposes. An outstanding example in Israel is the deployment of military force to create domestic consensus and raise the popularity of the ruling party, especially when Knesset elections are in the offing.[7] Thus a fighting society, operating primarily within the framework of democracy, is exposed to military processes, though not from direct subordination of the political echelons to the military elite but from emphasizing the ultimate importance of national security.

The Lasswellian model does not posit a distinction between militaristic society and society in wartime. Brazil, for example, is a militaristic society since, in the nineties, her army functions as a veto group that determines the nature of the regime, even though democracy has been established. Israel, on the other hand, is a society in wartime in which processes of militarization take place within the frame of a democratic political system.

Militarization, while certainly detracting from the democratic nature of the political regime, as is shown later, does not directly and immediately bring about its destruction. Militarization has both a short-term and a long-term impact. In the short term, it fortifies public endurance to carry the burden of an ongoing emergency situation, so that consensus can be built even in wartime. In the long term, militarization blunts the sensitivity of elites and the general public to individual and minority rights, eroding the importance of democratic behavior norms.

Political-Constitutional Perspective: Military Disobedience

Service in the Israel Defense Forces (IDF) had come to symbolize the Israeli citizen's membership in the Jewish-Zionist community. Refusals of the draft were conceived by the majority of the public to merit severe condemnation. Until the outbreak of the Lebanese War in 1982, there were seldom refusals on political grounds connected with national security.[8] Up to and throughout the Six-Day War, almost all instances of refusal had a specific pacifist or conscientious basis in opposition to violence. The infrequent refusals after 1967 stemmed from the debate over the future of the territories and were confined to the peripheral political left.

Refusal during the Lebanese War, by contrast, was a means of protest, openly adopted by a few hundred individuals, some of them officers, some who had served in combat status, and not all of whom were identified with marginal political groups. But though many people identified with the refusers' claims that this war was demonstrably useless and immoral, they were denounced, also by opponents of the war (such as members of Peace Now), on the grounds that such disobedience was liable to undermine Israel's strength.

The Supreme Court, too, condemned draft-dodging. Unlike the United States, Britain, and Germany, the Israeli judiciary system does not recognize the right to refuse the draft, be it for political or for patently conscientious reasons. In 1983, Yaakov Shein was called up for one month's military service in southern Lebanon. Shein refused, saying that, according to his "conscientious outlook," "the IDF presence in southern Lebanon is unlawful and inconsistent with basic notions of justification of belligerent acts." He was put on disciplinary trial and given thirty-five days' detention. He was later sentenced to twenty-eight days more for refusing another reserve service call-up order. On receiving a third order for reserve duty, he appealed to the Supreme Court, but his appeal was dismissed.[9] In giving its reasons for the dismissal, the Court lent expression to Israel's character as a community in wartime, preferring the collective security interest over individual freedoms:[10]

> The whole great complex affair of law on the one hand and conscience on the other, of the duty and need to maintain military service in order to defend the sovereignty of the state and the well-being of its inhabitants on the one hand and refusal to go to war for reasons of personal conscience on the other, must be reviewed in light of the particular circumstances of time and place; but the difficult security situation of Israel does not resemble the difficult security situation of other states, securely ensconced within their borders. This material difference is also a major and important consideration in elucidating the issue before us.[11]

The concept of a democracy in wartime is also significant in other important respects. The emergency regulations, the option of administrative arrest, the absence of a clear statutory framework whereby the executive can supervise the General Security Service, military censorship, the lack of definite criteria for disqualifying radical groups from taking part in Knesset elections and discriminatory practice against Israeli Arabs are all deemed acceptable by a majority of the public, as being part of Israel's defensive stance against her enemies. The judiciary system, too, permits a part of the public to be disenfranchised of its rights, and moreover demarcates the bounds of the permissible and the inadmissible in public debate.

The definition coined by Supreme Court Justice Yoel Zussman (1965), and since adopted by the Court, of Israel as a "self-defending democracy" reflected this concept. Said Justice Zussman, in upholding the disqualification of a radical Arab list, Al-Ard, from running for the Knesset elections, even without express legal provision:

> Just as an individual is not bound to agree to being killed, neither is a state obliged to consent to being annihilated and erased from the map. . . . The German Constitutional Court . . . spoke of a "fighting democracy," which does not open its doors to acts of sabotage in the guise of legitimate parliamentary activity. For myself, as far as Israel is concerned, I am prepared to confine myself to "self-defending democracy," and tools for defending the existence of the state are at hand, even if we have not found them set forth in detail in the Elections Law.[12]

In 1985, the Basic Law–The Knesset was amended by the addition of Section 7A, whereby a party could be deprived, on certain conditions, of its right to take part in the Knesset elections. Enacted in a similar spirit is Section 21(2) of the West German Constitution (1949) allowing the Federal Constitutional Court to outlaw a party (including its right to take part in elections) if it seeks "to undermine or avoid the basic liberal-democratic order or endanger the existence of West Germany." The Israeli statute, however, differs in several respects from the West German.

What matters in the present context is that the import of Section 7A is far more sweeping and its applicability far wider. Enacted due to the electoral success of the racist Kach party, after obtaining a Supreme Court injunction against its disqualification, Section 7A was designed to close a loophole in the Israeli legal system.[13] Its purpose was to fashion a sociopolitical order based on Jewish-Zionist nationality and to bend the democratic game rules to that aim. The first clause of Section 7A reads:

> No list of candidates shall take part in the Knesset elections if its aims or acts express or imply any one of the following:
> (1) Negation of the existence of the state of Israel as the state of the Jewish people.

This clause, enabling Arab parties to be placed outside the scope of parliamentary game rules, thereby prevents, as it were, opposition to the crucial tenets of the Jewish-Zionist political order. This is a hard, problematic clause, since it imposes a harsh restriction on civil freedoms and rights. Yet it gained the judicial blessing of the Supreme Court. This proves that the judiciary elite is not immune to the influence of the political attributes and components of the fighting community.[14]

The Supreme Court, however, at the same time ruled that the Central Knesset Elections Committee was entitled to invoke this clause only under certain conditions, those surrounding Israel's security situation. In 1989, the Supreme Court ruled on an appeal against the decision of the elections committee to the Twelfth Knesset (1988) not to disqualify the Progressive List, basically an Arab list, also having Jewish members. The committee decided, on a margin of one vote only (20 versus 19), not to accede to the disqualification petition, thereby rejecting the application of Likud and Tehiya. The Court justified the committee's decision and ruled that the basic right to express deviant opinions was not to be denied except when there existed a "near certainty" of "clear and present danger to the existence of the state."[15] The legal precedent thus established a judicial criterion known as the "near certainty" test. This test was also applied, for example, as a means of striking a balance between military censorship and freedom of expression.[16]

The judiciary elite, then, has established a balance, even in cases where "deviant" positions are expressed, enabling democratic procedure to be upheld in the frame of a fighting community. This is not to say that the judiciary elite has completely prevented injury to the liberal democratic essences. This is also due, inter alia, to the fact that the Supreme Court was operating in the frame of judicial interpretation, without the power to nullify Knesset laws on material democratic grounds. Nor should it be forgotten that the self-interest of the Supreme Court precludes its acting in such a way as to overstrain relations with the legislative branch, if only because the latter may react with legislation injurious to the Supreme Court.

Between Pacifism and Imperialism

Alongside an almost total consensus as to the importance of security considerations, Israelis have subscribed to a wide diversity of positions on topics of war and peace, and on whether or not the Israeli-Arab-Palestinian conflict can be resolved. When peace was debated, the key question was the future of the territories (especially the West Bank); but when war and the use of armed force came up for discussion, there were any number of moot points: the necessity, nature, objectives, moves, and termination of a war and also the making of decisions during its progress.

My research shows that the principles of dissent on the subject of military force, and especially war, remain basically unchanged since 1949. The political distance between the different approaches narrowed, however, after the Six-Day War, since the Likud was to concentrate, from then on, on perpetuating Israeli control of the territories, relegating to second place the initiation of war. But with the Yom Kippur War, the peace agreement with Egypt, the gradual aggravation of the Lebanese problem, and the Intifada the trend reversed, political distance increasing once more. Most Labor Party members came out more strongly in support of diplomatic efforts and against military initiatives, whereas most Likud members favored military activism or at least preferred the status quo to any drastic political change.

The controversy among the advocates of different approaches reflects basic dilemmas on the question of how life is to be lived under the perceived menace of the outbreak of war. As I have shown earlier, a political regime that has to deal with wars may be forced to compromise on how far basic democratic values will be realized. The proponents of military activism would like military-security considerations to take even greater precedence over democratic liberal values. That is the only way, they feel, to ensure that greater resources will be allocated to preparing the army for war and thickening settlement in the territories. But other schools of thought, especially the proponents of military passivism and partial military passivism, tend to ascribe greater importance to the cultivation of democratic values, even at the expense of security considerations.

Diversity of opinion in Israel is not an absolute. No powerful political organization militates for pacifism, and no very extensive support is available for imperialistic concepts, a fairly unique state of affairs. Some European states, notably Britain and France prior to World War II, and also the United States commencing from 1900, had renowned philosophers, intellectuals, world-famous statesmen, and major political parties in whose eyes interference in the affairs of other countries was a legitimate means of gaining control over economic, military, and political sources of power. These imperialistic concepts had the support of the greater part of the public in those countries.

The Second World War, while serving to moderate these views, did not do away with them completely. Even during the fifties, many French people sought to recoup superpower status for their country, and Charles de Gaulle's election to the presidency in 1958 was significantly due to his having promised a "Greater France" and continued French rule of Algeria. In a similar spirit, 40 percent of the British public supported the Suez Campaign in 1956, in the expectancy of their country's rising once again to world-power status.[17]

Many Americans were eager, after World War II, for greater U.S. intervention in remote continents. As the Korean War, bitterly controversial during its last two years, came to an end, 71 percent of the American public signified their wish to see the United States figuring "actively" in world affairs. A similar trend was to prevail later on: upon conclusion of the Vietnam War, 40 to 65 percent of the American public favored some degree of military involvement throughout the world, while only 8 percent came out flatly and unreservedly in support of isolationism. The approval of most of the American public for operations in Grenada (October 1983), Libya (March 1985), the siege of the Persian Gulf (August 1990), as well as the launching of the Gulf War (January 1991), showed that in spite of the "Vietnam trauma" the United States could muster a good show of public support for global involvement. Such a policy is approved for four main purposes: to safeguard "international order," to ensure the stability of the "free" world, to secure U.S. economic interests, and to block the advance of ideologies conceived as dangerous to American capitalism.[18]

The uniqueness of Israelis is explained by the character of the Jewish society in Israel and Israel's status as a small state, laboring at once under demographic, geographic, economic, political, and military constraints. Jewish society in Israel is basically one of migrants, most of whom fled there to escape some danger to their lives or on being uprooted from their places of domicile. A large segment of the Israeli-Jewish population or their parents survived traumas, such as pogroms in Eastern Europe, the Holocaust, Stalinist and post-Stalinist terrorism, or anti-Jewish violent riots in North Africa. In the Middle East, they had to face a politically hostile environment. Accordingly, day-to-day survival became the paramount aspiration.[19]

For the very same reasons, and also due to her dependence on foreign powers, Israel evolved a sense of weakness. All schools of thought subscribed to this view. All were aware of Israel's limited strength, of her being a small state. But those favoring military activism were inclined to decry the significance of this weakness. Rather, they claimed, existing military might should be used to dictate political arrangements, even at the risk of displeasing the superpowers. The roots of this concept can also be traced to Jabotinskian logic: all struggles are absolute; the only alternative to defeat is victory, and compromise is unrealistic.

The partial-military-activism school on the other hand took the view, largely formed by Ben-Gurion, that although Israel was certainly equal to coping with the Arab states (and hence also with the Palestinians), she must recognize the cost of the use of force and the limits of her strength in relation to her neighbors. All this was especially pertinent in view of the superpowers' involvement and their probable active interference in military conflicts. Israel must therefore maintain a deterrence but use force only in emergency; and she must not use her army to try to impose politically strategic solutions.

The concept of relative weakness derives to a certain extent from the ideological underpinnings of the Zionist movement. This was in essence an ethnocentric, humanist movement. Its main interest was to ensure the survival of the Jewish people. And this aspiration displaced any thoughts of ruling over another nation or exploiting it for national needs. The same notions informed security concepts and were the source of the David-Goliath syndrome. Many people in Israel, aware of their country's qualitative military advantage over the Arab states and tired of the persistence of the conflict, nonetheless preferred to make use of the slingshot only against a threat to survival. The broad-based rejection of all imperialistic trends created much opposition to any war of offense (such as the

Lebanese War) that seemingly sought to dictate political settlements to another nation.

Sharon, as defense minister during the Lebanese War, developed a concept of securing Israeli national interests around and beyond the outskirts of the near Middle East: "The sphere of Israel's strategic and security interest should be extended beyond the states of the Middle East and the Red Sea, so as to include, in the eighties, states such as Turkey, Iran, and Pakistan, and regions such as the Persian Gulf and Africa, and especially north and central Africa."[20] To be sure, this was not the classic European- or American-style imperialism envisaging occupation for the purpose of economic control and exploitation. But it represented a salient departure from the Israeli security concept that prevailed hitherto; it was far more aggressive.

The Israeli national security concept had traditionally distinguished between vital interests that must be defended by military means for the state's survival (freedom of shipping, for example), and meritorious interests, which, although they would serve to improve the security situation, were not essential for survival, so that the use of force in their defense was not justified (for instance, the nonpresence of foreign forces in northern Lebanon). As far as the range of Israel's security interests was concerned, Sharon's positions outstripped even those of Herut. Herut did not intend to extend the bounds of Israel's security and direct interests beyond Eretz Israel or contiguous areas.

Sharon's attempt to apply, in the Lebanese War, his version of forcefulness elicited the outright opposition of numerous groups. This shows that despite militarization processes, public consent to all wars is by no means certain. Moreover, crucial practices in Israel (such as the wearing down of public endurance), especially since the seventies, have diminished the assurance of public consent to wars.

War Fatigue

War is hard to get used to, even in a society living under constant threat. While the public adapts to an enduring state of emergency, war stands out as an extraordinary event.[21] Adjusting Israeli society to emergency situations meant setting up legal, security, and economic apparatuses that would ensure a rather efficient operation of the home front in wartime.[22] But never did the Israelis become completely accustomed to war. My findings indicate that, in wartime, public fears for collective and individual survival have increased. At the same time there have been outbursts of enthusiasm and patriotism (usually in short-term wars) or a sharp downturn in the national mood (usually in protracted wars). However, Israeli society, also notably sensitive on the subject of war victims, can hardly be said to have become adjusted to war.

Both the War of Attrition and the Yom Kippur War had the approval of the public consensus, but both lasted long enough to prove just how unaccustomed the public really was to war. Expectations that hostilities would soon cease were crushed; motivation to fight decreased as the casualty toll mounted and reserve-service periods grew longer. The home front's sense of identity with the fighting forces waned, and social solidarity tended to erode.

The demands made by war on small states such as Israel are tremendous. For a combative effort, Israel is forced to mobilize up to more than 90 percent (and in any case not less than 50 percent) of her conscriptable human power. So each war, especially a long one, heavily burdens the collective and the individual. The stress on the citizen (and especially the reservist) is not only psychological but economic as well.[23]

The need to shoulder this load has two political effects. Firstly, the collective subordination to compulsory draft enables the political regime and the administration to ensure the population's compliance with the political game rules. In this way, the state is provided with a means of controlling its subjects. The military security discourse, dictated by the ruling elite, predominates. In a fighting society, the political elite can easily repudiate protests of economic or social import, and strike them off the national agenda, all on the grounds that they are irrelevant and harmful in light of the challenges posed by "national security."[24] Secondly, citizens bearing the military burden may be moved to protest against the manner in which military force is deployed despite a willingness in principle to obey the political regime. Unenforced wars (the Suez Campaign and, more emphatically, the Lebanese War) aroused doubts in some quarters as to the justice of the combat and whether the national and personal price exacted was worthwhile. Torn by such doubts, citizens were less able to identify with the national security policy and less willing to harness themselves to the realization of "national interests."

My study established that partly due to public fatigue in the course of wars (especially, the Wars of Attrition, Lebanon) people were less willing to resign themselves to the casualty toll. Motivation to fight was also damaged. Fatigue caused dissent and intensified demands for an immediate end to the fighting. Protest on national security topics resulted also from the erosion and weariness that set in due to Israel's succession of wars in general. The earliest manifestations of this process came after the Six-Day War. With the occupation of territories in 1967, there appeared to be a greater chance that a peaceful alternative might be found, whereupon the public began to question the inherent inevitability of wars. Acquiring strategic depth also boosted confidence in Israel's might and her ability to defeat the Arab states. During the Attrition and Yom Kippur Wars, a consensus evolved whereby concluding the military campaign itself was no longer enough. Some groups (especially Likud and entities to its right) sought to dictate a peace in line with the military-activist approach. Others (Labor and entities to its left) wanted Israel to use the opportunity presented by the cease-fire to launch diplomatic negotiations and achieve a fair political settlement. Thus, while the right aspired to destroy the Arab will to fight, the center and left looked for definite political achievements and not necessarily absolute military victory.

On comparing the events of the War of Attrition with those of the Yom Kippur War, we find an increase in fatigue commencing from the early seventies. On the whole, political attitudes toward the enemy in the War of Attrition were more moderate. Even the military-activism camp by and large refrained from insisting that an absolute and immediate military solution be forced. During the Yom Kippur War, by contrast, many politicians, even including the partial military-activism set, no longer content to merely repulse the enemy, called for a decisive victory. The military passivism and partial military passivism camps countered by calling for an Israeli peace initiative and the resolution of the Palestinian problem in particular. In 1969 and 1970, only marginal groups came forward with demands of this kind. Upon termination of the Yom Kippur War and immediately thereafter, more voices were raised challenging the myth that "War is the inevitable outcome of Arab hostility."

Further to the 1979 peace agreement with Egypt, with war still liable to break out in spite of it and terrorism still rampant, some political groups set up a more insistent demand for the conflict to be settled once and for all by radical means. It was their way of expressing fatigue with the status quo. The "dovish-dovish" groups, as Yehoshefat Harkabi defined them,[25] called for political settlements to be furthered by an Israeli peace initiative encouraging the establishment of a Palestinian state in the territories.[26] Hawkish groups, on the other hand, were for solving strategic problems by military might.

The key party in this hawkish camp, Likud, rose to ruling power in 1977, and its leaders initiated the Lebanese War. Its initiation was in itself an expression of fatigue. Fatigue motivated the use of the most radical coercive means with a view to putting an end to the protracted conflict. But the attempt to overstep the bounds of military force that had been customarily employed against terrorism created dissent. The longer the war lasted, and the more clearly it was perceived to be deviating from the declared aims of the Peace for Galilee Campaign (PGC), the more the Israeli public came to doubt, allowing latent fatigue to surface to the point of open and direct opposition to the war. The possible outbreak of war is of course a constant facet of Israeli public awareness. But the public is also tired of war and of the unremitting emergency situation with its attendant large measure of uncertainty. This fatigue helps create dissent in relation to wars and is another motive in the development of extreme power-based concepts.

Modernization and Jewish Nationalism

Modernization means three political forms relevant to this study: first, the fragmentation of political power foci; second, the shift from democracy under the hegemony of a dominant party to democracy ruled by a nonaxial party; and third, greater readiness evinced by increasing numbers of citizens involved in direct political action.

As a rule, when consensus prevails, modernism based on liberal values may make for a high degree of political stability. Not so, however, in states such as Israel, where political awareness is prominent, society fictionalized, the political center torn by severe public controversy, and a militaristic tendency prevails; in such a state, modernism will aggravate dissent.[27] When the democratic game rules are insufficiently defined, when awareness of liberal values is scant, when nationality is defined on the basis of religion, when parties proliferate and competition is rife, the very process of modernization itself can foster political destabilization.

Commencing in the sixties, Mapai's status as the dominant party began to falter. Milestones in its gradual loss of influence were quarrels in the Mapai leadership between Ben-Gurion and Eshkol (1963), the founding of Rafi (1965), and inadequate response to public demands for war to be initiated during the waiting period (1967). On top of this, the distinctive party line on peace became blurred during the National Unity Government (1967–70); then there was the Yom Kippur War blunder (1973); the weakening of the political alliance between Labor and the religious Zionist camp, and also economic mismanagement. Herut, by contrast, gradually established its public legitimacy through its alliance with the Liberals, as an opposition party both worthy and capable of governing. This process, too, had a number of salient points, which were the founding of Gahal (1965) and Gahal's inclusion in the government (1967), involving its voluntary waiver of cabinet portfolios, so that while sharing the credit for the brilliant 1967 military victory, it got none of the blame for the 1973 War.

Political dilemmas as to the future of the territories accelerated polarization and weakened the center of the political system. Likud's preparedness to sign the peace agreement with Egypt, and the ensuing evacuation of Yamit, increased the political support for right-wing Tehiya, Gush Emunim, and Kach, which promoted annexing the West Bank and voiding the Egypto-Israeli peace accord. On the other hand, as Labor avoided advancing a peace initiative, dovish groups (Shinui, Ratz, Sheli, the Progressive List, Lova Eliav's list, Peace Now) urged the government to initiate territorial compromise on the West Bank or total retreat from those territories.[28]

Further to this process, evolving gradually from the early seventies, there emerged, as Likud came to power, a bipolar status quo. Its two main features were the absence of an axial ruling party capable, like Mapai in its dominance period (1949–73), of settling controversy before it spilled over to create public rifts and the emergence of radical right-wing political groups, who increased their power as right-wing Likud moved closer to the political center.

The growing influence of nonruling groups on the national agenda was a further expression of these processes. Public distrust of the ruling elite reached the point that people awoke out of their apathy. A main cause of dissatisfaction was the absence of any clear solution to the Arab-Palestinian-Israeli conflict. Nonruling groups called for radical and absolute solutions to the problem of the territories, while Labor (Alignment) and Likud proposed more partial solutions, which would allow them to remain at the political center and reinforce their public standing. Making their entrances respectively on the right and left wings of this political setting came, in 1974, Gush Emunim and, in 1978, Peace Now. Both these movements controlled dozens of satellite protest groups.

With the advance of Israeli technology, the mass media both proliferated and gained sophistication.[29] Nonruling groups were thereby better able to address their demands and criticisms directly to the executive. After 1973, the media themselves became, more than ever before, a rather investigative pressure group. The multidirectional political communication that began to form in Israel in the late seventies detracted from the administration's sense of omnipotence, giving the public a greater ability to intervene in decision-making processes. The clamor resulting from the Lebanese War was due, inter alia, to the broad range of communication options now enjoyed by the protestors, helping them to convey their messages. In contrast to the media's tendency, in Israel and elsewhere, to identify in times of national security crisis with government policy, a significant reversal was recorded during the Lebanese War.[30] During that period, certain seasoned newspapermen, experts on security affairs (such as Zeev Schieff, Ehud Yaari, and Eitan Haber), expressed opposition.[31]

Israeli rule of the West Bank created political dilemmas involving social rifts—which in turn contributed to political radicalization and violence. Two rifts are particularly relevant. The ethnic tension between Israelis of Western or Eastern European origin ("Ashkenazis") and those from Middle East countries ("Sephardis"). The other divides the religious from the secular. After 1967 these rifts were strongly linked to the growing controversies over settlements in the territories and security. Religious citizens, especially Sephardis, tended toward political hawkishness and were more supportive than the secularists, especially Ashkenazis or Israeli-born, of the drive to rule the West Bank and to use brute force toward the Arabs as a means of solving the conflict. To the extent that the future of the territories topped the national agenda, social rifts became political rifts and ethnic and religious differences were expressed with unprecedented political fervor.[32]

Domestic political events during the Lebanese War and the Intifada deepened these rifts. Attitudes toward force ranging from the active to the passive were associated with political, ethnic, and religious affiliations. Those favoring eminently dovish positions, who aspired to an Israeli peace initiative and who would willingly grant legitimacy to any Palestinian concern, including those expressed by the Palestine Liberation Organization (PLO), considered military actions (excepting, on occasion, retaliatory actions), as inciting hostility, and, hence, as clearly counterproductive to political reconciliation. Others, sometimes called "dawks," favored partial dovish positions, were prepared for limited compromise, rejected the legitimacy of a Palestinian state and believed that force was justifiable for thwarting a palpable danger but not as a means of imposing peace. The hawks, meanwhile, acclaimed the status quo, opposed compromise, advocated Israeli rule of the territories, and ruled out any possibility of setting up a Palestinian sovereign entity. In their opinion, the use of extensive force was a proper means of preventing any change in the post-1967 status quo.

Sephardis and native-born Israelis of Sephardi parentage tend to support military activism, while Ashkenazis and their native-born Israeli descendants tend to favor approaches that might justify the use of only limited force. A similar parallel exists on the religious-secular axis. The religious evince a greater tendency than the secular to favor an overall hawkish approach, and hence also military activism.One of the hallmarks of the growing fundamentalism of certain religious groups was a mounting tendency, during the eighties, toward nationalism. Nationalism draws greater support for strong-arm approaches toward Arabs and Palestinians, and hence also toward an offensive war or a "divinely-ordained war." This attitude emerged in the Lebanese War. Many religious party members, especially those of Morasha, Agudath Israel, and Poalei Agudath Israel, strong factions within the NRP, and also the religious members of Tehiya wholeheartedly supported the war.[33]

On the other hand, with modernization under way, among specific segments of the Israeli public, each succeeding war bred more dissent than its predecessors. With the exception of Suez, each of Israel's wars lay the foundations for dissent in the next war. The Suez Campaign served to reinforce the myth of IDF invincibility, thereby contributing to the consensus of the end of the waiting period in favor of inflicting a preemptive strike. The occupation of territories in 1967 accentuated ideological-political and military-security dilemmas as to how to resolve the conflict. The War of Attrition generated doubts as to the inevitability of Israel's wars with the Arab states. The Yom Kippur War accelerated the process of cynicism toward the elite while the Lebanese War and the Intifada compounded doubts of the real need for deploying armed force, while also further undermining confidence in the nation's policymakers.

Wars as Disturbances in Democratic Political Systems

Public dissent attended the Wars of Attrition, Yom Kippur, and Lebanon and the interethnic conflict of the Intifada. The Suez Campaign aroused dissent, though not publicly expressed during the fighting. These refute the almost axiomatic premise that extreme military-security emergencies "extraneous" to the political system necessarily create political consensus and social integration in that system.[34]

Firstly, not every war creates a sense of shared fate or a feeling that harm to the state means harm to the group and to a particular individual. Secondly, the goal of military victory does not always create cooperation, in disregard of opposing views. Thirdly, no proof has been found for the theory that war necessarily brings consensus by providing an outlet for aggression: aggressive impulses are sometimes seen to engender controversy. Fourthly, even though in time of war democracy inclines toward monism and uniformity of political behavior, pluralism of attitudes still persists both on the individual and on the group planes.

Contrary to the assumption of functionalism and structural functionalism, society and politics do not necessarily incline toward consensual order. The premise of the aforesaid paradigms is that every function or nonfunction is meant to contribute, and so does contribute, to consensus. These approaches have been found inappropriate to an exhaustive study of state, society, and war. On the other hand, according to the conflict approach (especially as deriving from neo-Marxist sources), the group-interest approach and the elitist approach, the forming of a national consensus is by no means a natural and obvious phenomenon but depends, especially when the order has a conflict-type infrastructure, on the nature of mutual relations between groups and organizations in the political system.[35] This attests to the complexity of the subject of this book and the need to avoid being shackled by commitment to only one all-inclusive scientific approach.

Accordingly, I shall further outline my conclusions relevant to Israel, in comparison with Western democracies. Unlike Western settings during hostilities, for example, Britain in World War II and France in the Algerian War,[36] Israel has no special code of laws valid in wartime, as distinct from the legal codex in times of abeyance. Because of its structural adaptation to the ongoing state of emergency, Israel adjusts more easily than other democracies to war status. A series of laws—emergency laws; security-service laws; civil-defense laws; penal laws; and fiscal demands on the public that are perennially in force even in times of nonbelligerency—have made it easier for Israel to function in war situations, even in the face of howling dissent.[37]

Ideally, this reality is the kind to be desired under existing circumstances. But in practice, the society in wartime proves to pay a very high price to the detriment of democratic tenets (such as uncensored freedom of expression). The Supreme Court is itself affected by the public discourse, and its contribution to the forming of a liberal democracy is therefore only partial. This is even more clearly indicated by the tendency of the Court to refrain from interfering in the acts or omissions of the military in the territories.[38]

The degree to which Israeli society has partially adapted to the ongoing state of emergency is also apparent in the economic sphere. Baruch Kimmerling found that although Israel's economic system adjusts quickly and efficiently to states of war, conditions lead to economic overcentralization. Alex Mintz examined the extent of influence of Israel's military-oriented industries. They smooth the passage of economy from states of abeyance to states of war. But through them, the security establishment exerts an excessive influence on the political elite.[39]

Yonathan Shapiro found that what sustained democracy during ongoing emergency situations was the reproduction of the Yishuv's political pattern, central to which was a dominant party. But the nature of the democracy it preserved was procedural rather than liberal. Dan Horowitz, Moshe Lissak, and Yoram Peri found that the relations between the army and the elected political elites, based on militarization of the civilian sphere and civilization of the army, ease transition from states of abeyance to states of war without palpable or exceptional danger to the democratic regime.[40]

Yet, war interferes with the political and institutional functioning. In all of Israel's wars, the political order of priorities has changed: topics heading the national agenda prior to the outbreak of hostilities were replaced by the new goal of victory. Political structures and behavior patterns therefore had to perform differently. Voluntary organizations, parties, and extra-parliamentary political groups dealt only with war issues.

The Basic Law: The Knesset does not allow for the suspension of the Knesset due to war, nor do the emergency regulations provide for doing so. But in short wars, Knesset may barely have time to assemble before the fighting is over, as happened in the Suez Campaign. This can limit the public's control of security policy. Even when the Knesset Secretariat manages to convene the House plenum, other legislation bears the scars: attention is directed exclusively to the war and its impact. Similarly, in wartime the media refrain from raising issues unrelated to the conduct of hostilities, concentrating primarily on reporting, sometimes with commentary, on war developments and their implications. Yet in long lasting engagements like the War of Attrition or the Lebanese Wars, the political system gradually resumes "normal" functioning, and the Knesset meets to review current domestic problems.

Values and Consensus Structures

The general public in Western democracies tends to presume that dissent in time of war is injurious to the morale of the fighting forces, the preparedness to enlist for the war effort, and the judgment of the policymakers. Thus, for example, during the Korean War, 40 percent of the war's supporters in the United States believed that "communists and disloyal persons in the State Department have caused serious damage to the national interest." They articulated the McCarthyite atmosphere that anyone opposing the war was liable to be branded a communist. During the Vietnam War, 48 percent of the war's opponents were reluctant to give public expression to their objections, believing "we must support our fighting men."[41]

Feelings and concepts as to a common fate, a temporary preparedness to forgo some of the attributes of democracy, militaristic feelings, and the manipulations of the ruling elite—all combine to create consensus values. The individual in wartime tends to assimilate into the collective and waive his right to criticize the administration, unquestionably accepting, for a while, the raison d'ètat. This implies that the attainment of victory must come before all else, even at the price of democratic values.

Israel, as a society in wartime, is even more susceptible to the influence of consensus values than Western democracies. Some of Israel's wars have been fought only several hundred kilometers away, sometimes not even more than a few dozen kilometers from her population centers. The enemy has generally enjoyed quantitative superiority while stating its intent to destroy Israel's Jewish population. Accordingly, most of the public has viewed some of their wars as life and death struggles. Not so the wars fought by the superpowers of Europe and the United States since World War II. Those wars were fought thousands of kilometers from home, and although they were usually perceived as vital to national interests, they were not thought to be fateful for the population's survival.[42]

One historic interval that may be likened to Israel's situation during the waiting period was Britain's position in the summer and fall of 1940. The British armed forces stood dwarfed by the mighty Wehrmacht, and a deep anxiety seized the British public. In both the British and the Israeli situations, national unity was deemed a precondition for repulsing the danger and gaining victory.[43] But Israel, as stated, has had to face very real fears not only in the waiting period. There was a basic fear of the Arab world; there was fear of dangers liable to materialize in the nearer future, say, within months, as following the Egypto-Czech arms deal (1955); and there was fear of annihilation, liable to happen within days or weeks at most, such as in the first stages of the Yom Kippur War.

Fear responses figured significantly in the making of consensus and dissent. They affected the ability and willingness of individuals and groups to construct threat concepts and put their trust in the aims of the nation's wars and the manner of their conduct.

Consensus was obviously more all-encompassing when military objectives matched the common denominator shared by advocates of force. What was this minimal common denominator? In the absence of widespread public support for pacifist concepts in Israel, a broad consensus has emerged in times of imposed wars (Six-Day and Yom Kippur wars). When individuals and groups concur in the principal objective—victory in a war of exigency—controversy on other issues is often pushed aside, even when other issues, such as the government's acts and omissions in the course of the fighting are war-related. This does not hold true of wars conceived as being a direct outcome of ideological political goals, and hence nonessential (Suez, the War of Attrition, and, most especially, Lebanon and the Intifada). Nevertheless, the Lebanese War and the Intifada stand apart from Suez and the War of Attrition. In the last two, consensus prevailed at the center and secondary centers of the political system, while in the first two even the very center was riddled with controversy. An important reason for this difference was the combination of contradictory approaches (to the issue of military force) and the structure of the political map.

Lacking a consensus structure, the parties opposing the war had no political interest in refraining from dissent. This was what happened at the end of the Yom Kippur War (when the Likud objected to the acceptance of UN Resolution 338), in the Lebanese War (when Labor and its supporters finally learned the true aims of the fighting), and in the course of the Intifada, following the breakdown of the national-unity government. In other wars, however, mutual government interests prevented dissent from reaching full-scale development. While Mapam objected to the Suez Campaign, and Gahal opposed some moves in the War of Attrition, both parties shared collective governmental responsibility and consent to the security policy.

A major factor in this behavior was the wish to achieve party goals. Such elitist-rulership considerations, as accumulating political power and having a say in the allocation of national resources, weigh quite heavily with politicians even in wartime. However important, war issues are not the only causes determining how politicians will react to a given emergency situation. It is also important to them that their party be in a position to influence policy-shaping, even in a government that is waging a war wholly at odds with their outlook. As long as political groups have a vested interest in the existence of a consensus structure (as during the War of Attrition), any number of dilemmas regarding the conduct of the war can be resolved within the government.

A good example is the forming of the National Unity Government during the Lebanese War (September 1984), which reduced dissent at the center. Labor Party leaders, on the one hand, retracted their declared intention of calling for a commission of inquiry to examine the events of the war; and Prime Minister Shimon Peres appealed for a renewal of the "consensus." The Likud, on the other hand, refrained from overtly criticizing what it deemed the lack of adequate military initiative in the sphere of security.[44]

The use of wartime consensus structures is by no means unique to Israel. In Britain, with its tri-party system, national-unity governments were formed in both world wars so as to reduce possible friction between Conservatives, Labor, and Liberals.[45] In France, in June 1958, at the height of the political crisis over the Algerian War, de Gaulle formed a national-unity government, delegating him limitless powers for bringing the crisis to an end. Opposition to his policy was gradually displaced to the political fringes, where it was confined mainly to the Organisation Armée Secrete (OAS), the military underground.[46]

These instances illustrate the distinctive character of the consensus structure, compared with other types of interparty cooperation that are not stable enough to be classified as a "structure."[47] Political cooperation, once consensually institutionalized, reduces the risk of public dissent. In principle, the more akin the opposition ("dissenting party") is on issues of armed force to the ruling party, and the stronger the ideological unity within the government regarding issues accepted by the opposition, the greater the interest of the dissenting party to be part of the government in spite of its stance on the war or the manner of its conduct. Thus, for example, in the Suez Campaign and the withdrawal from the Gaza Strip in 1957, Mapam acted contrary to its views, since it regarded those issues as secondary compared to the social and economic issues on which it concurred with Mapai.

Political Parties, Political Activity, and the Public

This book has dealt mainly with parties and especially their leadership. The literature of social sciences frequently poses the question of to what extent positions and responses of political parties and elites are bound up with those of the public.[48] Up to and during the Six-Day War, the Jewish public in Israel tended to support and identify with party positions and responses to war. There were three reasons for this: (1) it seemed axiomatic that wars (Suez and the Six-Day War) must necessarily end in victory; (2) the social and ideological unity featured by most party organizations often mirrored the social characteristics of their supporters; and (3) to the public the parties represented a principal means of political communication with the policymakers.

After 1969, however, individuals and groups stepped out of party frameworks to undertake direct political activity. This devaluation of party identification was due to various causes, three of which are relevant to this study. Firstly, people came to doubt the necessity of wars and were disappointed with the failure of the elites to put an end to the conflict. Secondly, the military rule in the territories, especially on the West Bank, intensified the rift between hawks and doves, while the various party frameworks proved inadequate to express the entire range of positions on the issue. And, thirdly, the political parties were no longer the only channels of political communication.

Israeli political parties lean more strongly toward consensus than the general public; in this, Israel resembles Western democracies. As Herbert McClosky shows in his research,[49] the reasons for this are mainly the party interest of sharing national rewards; greater awareness of parties and political elites of consensus values, which frequently serve their aspirations to determine policy without the constraint of public pressures; and the desire to preserve "social order." In other words, the parties do not fully reflect public moods. But contrary to McClosky's findings, I am not inclined to believe that the tendency toward consensus by party members, as distinct from the general public, is necessarily due to the general public's obliviousness to democratic values. Extra-parliamentary political activity, after all, springs from public awareness of the values and rights of democracy.

Unlike dissent in the United States over the Vietnam War, dissent in Israel regarding the use of armed force has not proceeded directly from social or economic but from political causes. This, in some senses, is quite surprising on the face of it. Wars have led to a gradual increase in the defense budget's share of the GNP, thereby reducing the potential allocation of resources to the solution of social problems. A persistent emergency situation has detracted from the attention accorded to social problems, not only by diverting the attention mainly to security affairs but sometimes by actually providing the nation's leaders with an excuse not to attend to social issues. The sociologist Shlomo Swirski goes so far as to assert that the Ashkenazi establishment has even initiated wars so as to distract the oriental communities from criticizing the discrimination against them.[50] Wars have also significantly affected the sexual stratification of Israeli society, according preference to men over women in fields of political activity.[51]

Why, then, has there been no wide social protest against wars? The explanation lies in Israel's status as a political regime and a society in wartime. Wars are conceived by most Israelis not as having been engendered by the particularist interests of the ruling elite but as resulting from an external political and military reality. The ongoing state of emergency then enables the elites to proclaim the need for national consensus. The rather even distribution and scope of the draft burden (not counting exemptions given to certain groups and individuals) preclude complaints that only the lower classes suffer damage. Military service, moreover, provides the lower strata with a sort of psychological, social, and political compensation, instilling pride and a sense of power. Indeed, low socioeconomic status, Middle Eastern origin, and political hawkishness are found to coincide.[52] It is true that in the Lebanese War a number of small groups of Middle East extraction, holding dovish views, did protest on the grounds that the IDF presence in Lebanon was being financed at the expense of resources that should have been allocated to neighborhood renewal and sweeping social integration. But even here the main cause of dissent was political (opposition to what they considered a needless war), with the social message merely an additional argument in favor of terminating hostilities.

Mindful of the causes of dissent and consensus on the macro-political level as set forth in this book, it is possible to affirm that on the micro-political level, the approach of a particular political group toward a specific war is influenced by four political variables: (a) fundamental positions regarding force, (b) religiosity-secularism, (c) parliamentarianism—extra-parliamentarianism, and (d) remoteness from social and political power foci. Hence an extra-parliamentary (nonparty), secular, political fringe group with a military-passivist approach tends to oppose all wars, except those imposed on Israel by enemy armies. By contrast, an extra-parliamentary (nonparty), religious political fringe group with a military-activist approach will tend to support all wars and refrain from dissent (except in special instances, such as severe mismanagement of the war).

The Facets of Consensus

Consensus during war has manifested itself on two levels, one being that of government-public relations. Consensus means support for the government. This is where the influences exerted by the political elite are particularly important, in view of the tendency of elites to exploit the emergency situation for internal ends. The second level is that of intergroup relations. Here, consensus means concurrence between political organizations and various groups to cooperate during the fighting to the extent needed for military victory, while downplaying existing controversies.

In all instances, consensus has derived from the aggregation of conscious or unconscious agreements, based either on correct information or on misinformation, and political manipulations by state institutions and, especially, by the political elites. Consensus has also taken the form of indifference, lack of response to the war, and in unchallenged acceptance of government resolutions. Often consensus has been expressed through conventional political activity, such as voting and parliamentary support. In a few instances, participation in unconventional political activity occurs, such as demonstrations of support for the government.

Consensus during war has reinforced the legitimacy of the state and government policy, especially over the use of armed force, thereby contributing to political stability, while legitimacy and stability have made it easier for the administration to mobilize manpower and other resources. Consensus, however, has been harmful to pluralism and to the forming of a liberal democracy. Consensus is not in itself an expression of a democratic or liberal culture, for by reinforcing unifying trends, it leaves all opposition to war exposed, more than in the past, to manifestations of intolerance.

Consensus also hinders processes of change, since any such endeavor is seen as endangering unity and arousing differences of opinion that are liable to threaten political stability, thereby damaging, as it was perceived, prospects of victory. It emerges, then, that consensus relieves possible sources of short-term instability, but in the long term promotes centers of sociopolitical disorder. Poignantly illustrating this paradox is the fact that during the Yom Kippur War, the Black Panthers, who protested against the social deprivation of Middle Eastern Jews, were edged off the national agenda; yet the problem of ethnic relations may well in the future become a source of social and political upheaval.[53]

How to Assess Consensus

Based on this study I conclude that consensus in war is to be defined as a situation incorporating at least the following components: (a) subordination to the democratic regime and its institutions and acceptance of at least some of the values and symbols of the political system, (b) acknowledgment of the legitimacy of the elected government and compliance with state laws and democratic procedures, (c) acceptance of some collective norms of political behavior, especially avoiding public contentions over military and security issues in times of severe emergency, and (d) agreement as to political and military action options on the strategic level. For present purposes, it is immaterial whether subordination and acceptance are conscious or unconscious, whether based on true information or on false information and manipulations.

Apart from the changes needing to be made in components (c) and (d) depending on the subject to which they relate, the foregoing definition will also fit consensus created in democratic regimes on topics not necessarily relating to military force. The definition is accordingly offered as a theoretical formula covering the essentials of the consensus phenomenon in democratic regimes. Consensus thus has important implications for political systems, whether deriving from false awareness, as defined by Marxists and neo-Marxists, or from the true awareness of individuals and groups, as defined by the pluralist and behavioral schools. The definition relates to the properties of minimal consensus, although it may include additional features: (e) recognition of the need for cooperation with the government for the conduct of the war and attainment of victory; (f) cooperation between the parties, including the ruling party, advocating different approaches on the war issue, even to the point of forming a consensus structure; (g) agreement as to possibilities of political and military action at all relevant levels; (h) identification with the government's policy on war, crossing over divisions of social class, political party, and organization; (i) avoidance of public argument on any public issue (not only on military and security issues) until the end of the war; and (j) sociopolitical cohesiveness.

These components may be used for diagnosing not only the existence of consensus but also its scope. Hitherto, scientists were in the habit of defining consensus and its scope in quantitative or logical and mathematical terms. Charles M. Grigg and James W. Prothro, for example, claimed that only the consent of at least 75 percent of the public to a given policy could be seen as consensus.[54] But, consensus is not necessarily amenable to only quantitative or logical definition. Moreover, the assertion that the agreement of less than 75 percent of a given public does not amount to consensus has neither empirical nor normative foundation. Nor indeed is there any empirical or normative justification for the assertion that in a system in which concurrence is formed in those percentages, nothing but consensus prevails. Like dissent, consensus is not an absolute but a relative phenomenon. The researcher's job is therefore to demarcate the scope and properties of each. In light of this book's findings, it is recommended that consensus in a given society be classified in accordance with the criteria listed earlier (the terms "positive" or "negative," do not indicate value preferences).

1. *Minimal (basic) consensus*:[55] components *A+B*. This has formed in all of Israel's wars (the only exceptions in the Lebanese

War and the Intifada being recorded by members of Yesh Gvul and others who supported military disobedience). Minimal consensus is essential for the basic stability of a democratic regime, regardless of whether it is imposed by elites, making manipulative use of or withholding information, or whether it results from pluralistic dynamism. Considerable influence in Israel is exerted by the elites and the manner in which they exploit the emergency situation. Without those two components of consensus, a democratic regime cannot exist, certainly not for any length of time, and there is likely to be a shift to an authoritarian or totalitarian regime. In default of component B only, the stability of the regime will suffer damage, and processes of delegitimization will ensue, to the point of civil disobedience and coups d'ètat.

2. *Negative consensus: components A+B+C*.[56] It is based entirely on second-degree agreement—agreement to refrain from controversy. This consensus appeared in the first month of the Lebanese War, when opposition party members learned of the war's true military objectives, and yet most of them refrained from expressing dissent, because overt opposition might, they feared, interfere with the attainment of victory.

3. *Minimal positive consensus: components A+B+C+D*.[57] Interesting historical precedents for consensus of this kind are found in the United States throughout most of the Korean War, and in Israel in the Suez Campaign, and again in the first days, up to June 11, 1982, of the Lebanese War. While negative consensus ensures system stability in the course of a given war, minimal positive consensus is characterized by interparty cooperation, and helps build infrastructure for the full-scale mobilization of the nation's resources.

4. *Positive consensus (minimal positive consensus + components E or E+F)*. Positive consensus prevailed in the Attrition and Yom Kippur wars. Another illuminative example is France, during the Algerian War, after de Gaulle formed his government. Positive consensus occurs primarily in cooperation between political elites at the center and secondary centers of the system, sometimes in an official framework (such as the "national-unity" government in the War of Attrition). Also capable of being defined as positive consensus is preparedness for cooperation in official frameworks (for example, the Likud's proposals to form a "national-unity" government during the Yom Kippur War).[58]

5. *Most positive consensus (positive consensus + components G-J)*. Two historic precedents for consensus of this kind are Britain in

World War II and Israel in the Six-Day War. It is typical of this kind of consensus that it encompasses all aspects of the hostilities, from commencement through progress to termination. A very strong sense of threat produces identification with the government and readiness to refrain, for the duration of the fighting, from debate on any public topic whatsoever.

By classifying the various components of the consensus we are able to measure its strength. The more positive the consensus, the more it reinforces the tendency of individuals and groups to cooperate and obey the government. Consensus, in other words, is as powerful as it is positive. On the other hand, the total of all organizations in the political system, and the proportion of the public that supports the war or some of its aspects, can serve to indicate the scope of consensus (and hence also the scope of dissent). But quantitative measurement alone is not enough. It ignores the influence of a given group in the political system. Thus, for example, the influence on the national agenda of a party opposing the war may well be greater than the combined influence of a number of parties supporting the war. I therefore recommend, based on this study, other criteria as indices of the scope of consensus.

Both qualitative and quantitative dimensions may be attributed to the scope of consensus (hereafter, the scope ranges from a minimum of 1 to a maximum of 4). For methodological purposes I have used the definitions of center versus periphery, without adopting the value-based or factual paradigmatic contexts of these definitions, as sometimes presented in literature to date.[59]

1. *Consensus of ruling party—periphery.* A ruling party belonging to one flank of the political system does not enjoy the support of the center nor of most political groups in the secondary centers, but it is supported primarily by marginal groups (flank-affiliated only). This happened during the Lebanese War when consensus gradually became confined to the peripheral right-wing, hawkish flank of the political system. A similar situation occurred in France toward the end of the Algerian War (1958–62): support for continued French rule gradually became the sole province of groups on the right political periphery.

2. *Consensus of ruling party—secondary centers—periphery.* A ruling party at the center is supported not by the foremost opposition party but by satellite political groups at the secondary centers and on the fringes of the system. This was the situation in the United States after 1968 in the course of the Vietnam War, in Britain

during the Suez Campaign (October-November 1956), during certain periods in France in the course of the Algerian War (1954-58), and in Israel in the first two months of the Lebanese War (June-July 1982).

3. *Consensus of ruling party—center—secondary centers*. This typifies a political system disputed only by marginal political groups. It happened during the Suez Campaign and the War of Attrition and at certain times in the United States during the first stages (1964-68) of the Vietnam War, when dissent was mainly articulated by groups of pacifists and social movements opposing the rules of the democracy in their country.[60]

4. *Consensus of ruling party—center—secondary centers—periphery*. A state of affairs characterizing "agreed wars" in which expressions of dissent are absent or very few and far between. Examples are Israel in the Six-Day War and Britain in World War II. Normally, this situation occurs especially in societies under severe danger (real and perceived) for survival.

How to Assess Dissent

The criteria serving to determine the scope of consensus can also be used to define the scope of dissent.

1. *The periphery dissent with the ruling party*. This emerges in wars that reflect a traditional national security concept. The war is denounced only by marginal groups, since they seek solutions the majority deem radical (immediate end to the fighting or deployment of absolute force so as to impose political solutions). A significant example is Israel in the course of the Suez Campaign.

2. *The fringes and the secondary centers dissent with the ruling party*. Dissent of this kind is typical of the political system ruled by a dominant party or in which the ruling party is not dominant but controls the system axis. In this situation, the ruling party prevents dissent from spilling over into the system center (as, for example, when the War of Attrition was coming to an end).

3. *The periphery, secondary centers, and center dissent with the ruling party*. In this state of affairs, the war is disputed also by influential groups located at the political center. As a result, the entire system—center, secondary centers, and political flanks—is divided between the war's supporters and its opponents. This deepens various social and political rifts, even when not directly war-

related. The system destabilizes, the government experiences increasing difficulty in exercising its rule, and processes of delegitimization set in, with political game rules progressively trampled on. This phenomenon was recorded both in the United States at the height of its involvement (1968–72) in the Vietnam War and in Israel during most of the Lebanese War (1982–85).

The opponents of war form part of the "political society." They air their views publicly in the expectancy of finding acceptance and causing a change in the existing situation, as for example a shift in war objectives or the termination of hostilities. As long as they believe that the accepted political game rules enable them to express themselves freely and exert an influence, they will try to engineer the change through routine, conventional political activity, such as speeches in Knesset or advertisements in the press. But as soon as they determine that present vehicles are inadequate in communicating with target audiences (as immediately following the Yom Kippur War or during the Lebanese War), they will turn to unconventional political means.

In extreme situations, the adversaries of war try resorting to violence as a means of realizing their political goals. But the opponents of Israel's wars—like their counterparts in the United States—have used this ploy only in extraordinary situations, since they actually oppose any use of force. The few instances where violence has been used has usually been due to attempts by police forces to disperse demonstrations. There have also been instances, here and there, of violent clashes between a war's antagonists and its supporters.

Internal Conflicts, Rulership Mechanisms, and Social Changes

By intensifying conflictual-behavior elements, controversies produce change, thereby helping to shape a more democratic society. The dissent engendered by the Yom Kippur War ultimately led to a replacement of the ruling party in 1977 and was a most important factor in altering the party map in Israel. The Lebanese War reinforced the stalemate between the major parties, Labor and Likud, while also increasing the strength of small parties representing more particularist interests. Dissent heightened public awareness of the option of direct political activity, loosening dependence on party apparatuses, ruling elites, and the bureaucracy and breeding a higher degree of political tolerance. For example, controversies made groups of the war's objectors more ready to accord legitimate status to non-Zionist groups (most of them Arab-Jewish groups, such as Rakah). Due to such disputes, the boundaries of political legitimacy expand to soften political intolerance toward rejected groups.

Contentions have affected the political system in other aspects. They have opened up lines of communication for groups that in times of severe emergency and consensual wars were assigned secondary importance. For example, intellectuals and women received more political voice in the War of Attrition, the aftermath of the Yom Kippur War, the Lebanese War, and the Intifada. By virtue of controversy, attention has also been drawn to problems previously swept aside, as, for example, the arguments over the ethnic gap during the Lebanese War.

The Israeli governments essayed various methods of preventing controversy, as described in previous chapters: manipulative use has been made of the regime's power so as to create consensus (the Suez Campaign and the Lebanese War); the government monopoly of the national media has been utilized for circumscribing freedom of expression and spreading disinformation (the Suez Campaign, the War of Attrition, the Yom Kippur and Lebanese wars); war objectives have been ideologized (the Lebanese War); the army has been harnessed to the attainment of political goals (especially the Lebanese War); and the theme song of threatened annihilation has been played over and over again.

In connection with this final point, the architects of the security policy have notably stressed the defensive role of the IDF as compared with the enemy's active aggression, aimed at destroying Israel. Thus, the Suez Campaign was meant to foil activities "tending to deprive" the inhabitants of Israel "of peaceful living." The Lebanese War was undertaken "so as to get the northern settlements out of the range of (enemy) fire."[61] But most regularly trotted out was the myth of the siege, sometimes expressed in so many words as the "noose" in the Six-Day War, sometimes implied by comparison with the Holocaust (the Yom Kippur and Lebanese wars) and sometimes inferred as part of an Arab "stage-by-stage" plan for destroying Israel (Suez, the War of Attrition, and the Intifada).

What the public was generally offered, in lieu of information, was the annihilation myth, wherewith the leaders hoped to achieve consensus and head off social and political changes. Until the end of the Six-Day War, this myth was securely anchored in the public consciousness; but once the territories were occupied, it became a less effective means of generating consensus.

10 Final Conclusions: Establishing a Civilian Society

Like tribes in remote corners of the world, societies in wartime tend to resist sweeping changes. The ruling elite, like tribal elders, incline to warn of danger to the collective security if the status quo is not maintained. The military, and especially its senior officers, presumes that if any changes are in order, they should be minimal and measured in military security terms only. The general public is prone to anxieties and threat concepts learned from past wars rather than anticipated developments, tending to externalize previous traumas. And, those who preach far-reaching reforms are delegitimatized, with the support of the legal system, educators, and intellectuals.

If Israel remains with strong characteristics of militarization processes, her democracy could break down. Exceedingly polarized, Israeli society and its political discourse focus too narrowly on the use of armed force. Future wars, if and when they break out, will be far more dangerous than their predecessors to the civilian hinterland. The Iraqi Scud missile attacks on Israel during the Gulf War (1991) show that in an age of sophisticated weapons, the importance of strategic depth shrivels. Until 1995 Syria was building up a long-range ballistic weapons system, Arab armies were increasingly becoming equipped with biological and chemical weaponry, and a number of Arab states were endeavoring to develop and deploy nuclear arms. In wartime, such or similar capabilities would bring a much heavier burden on the civilian hinterland. Yet, more indications of war fatigue are noted and will likely increase with each additional war and with each successive incident of massive terror.

In view of these trends and since differences between home and battle fronts may well blur to the point of extinction, consensus on the subject of war becomes infinitely more crucial for the civilian population and its ability to cope with catastrophes and high levels of anxiety over individual and collective survival.[1] The significance of the social component in the national security concept, in strengthening public support for military operations, heightens as the level of risk in that operation rises and the fighting lengthens. The failure of a major controversial military operation is liable to shake the foundations of democracy. Even a military gain may cause political destabilization, due to its high economic and human costs. Experiences in the United States, France, and Britain teach that armed force ought not to be deployed except when there is no alternative and when the character of the operation conforms to the common denominator of approaches to the use of armed force.

Israeli security policy should accordingly be guided by the following principles: (a) Israel will only initiate war to thwart an immediate or palpable threat to her existence; (b) in the current security sphere, Israel should follow a policy of limited preemptive strikes to frustrate terrorist action and should launch reprisals as necessary. It is recommended that *casus belli* should consist solely of interests of utmost importance to Israel—such as a blockade on the freedom of navigation, massive entry of hostile military forces into Jordan, the development of a war of attrition with Syria, flagrant violations of peace agreements (or future peace agreements) by the entry of substantial military forces into demilitarized zones, the introduction of threat-posing nuclear weapons into the region, or an Arab armed attack on Israel;[2] (c) Israel will refrain from attacking population centers and will focus rather on military or strategically important targets, such as fuel dumps and airfields.

Israeli politics and society, and that of Western democracies, cannot be properly understood without comprehending the influence of wars and emergency situations on the political regime and the substantial damage that military conflicts may inflict on democratic tenets. This book has analyzed two key phenomena of political order—consensus and dissent—which indicate the range of responses a political system can expect in such situations. In this context the book has portrayed the antinomy between democracy and wars. It has shown that despite the functional adaptability of the regime to warfare conditions, wars ravage democratic fundamentals. To sum up, I shall list a number of particularly problematic points in the optimum transition of Israel from a society in wartime to a civilian society:

1. *Military discourse.* Ruling elites, political parties, and extra-parliamentary groups have all emphasized military security affairs. Accordingly, Israel does not have politically meaningful social movements that focus on social issues (for example, ethnicity, social equality). As a result, the nation's leaders cannot easily find alternative solutions to problems. The future of the territories, for example, is discussed chiefly in terms of security criteria. The degree of likely damage to national security becomes the yardstick for determining what is and what is not permissible. This is conspicuously reflected in the clear preference accorded to defense in state budget planning and also in the operation of the Israeli judiciary system and in many of the Supreme Court's decisions. Transition to civilian society will require change to downplay this priority.

2. *Secrecy.* The political system operates under a heavy cloak of secrecy on matters defined as "national security." This secrecy is frequently imposed by the ruling elite on patently political affairs as well. As a result, the citizen stands largely helpless in exercising supervision over his government. Media development in Israel has somewhat narrowed the scope of secrecy, but it is still used extensively. Shifting to a civilian society will mean drastically reducing or even totally eliminating such censorship, except on certain specialized issues, such as those connected with nuclear policy.

3. *Totalization of the conflict.* Most proponents of the use of armed force, and many Likud and Labor supporters, assume that the conflict is unresolvable unless the Arab-Palestinian side withdraws all its basic demands (such as the right of return, sovereignty over East Jerusalem, and an independent Palestinian state in the West Bank and Gaza Strip). Changing to a civilian society depends on Israelis recognizing that the nature of interstate and interethnic conflict is relative and that peace must come from compromise, from mutual concessions between rightful, if at once contradictory, positions of competing and equally hostile national movements.

The Israeli-Palestinian interim agreement of September 1993 was a positive sign of change. Five points should be emphasized as notable facets of change (the implementation of that agreement is, however, complex and problematic): (*a*) this was the first formal agreement between Palestinians and Israelis regarding the resolution of the conflict, and here using direct channels of communication; (b) this was the first time that each side has mutually acknowledged the political legitimacy of the other; (c) this was the first time that all controversial issues have been defined as diplomatically debatable, including those of East Jerusalem and the holy places; (d) this was the first time that Palestinians and Israelis have formally renounced military violence as a means of political bargaining; and (e) this was the first time that the conflict between Palestinians and Israelis was not about myths of equity but about a realistic and durable partition of the land.

4. *Conservatism.* Israeli society is conservative in its thinking patterns on civic issues. It hesitates, for example, to annul irrelevant legislation (such as some of the emergency regulations) and is reluctant to enact a liberal written constitution. A manifestation of ultraconservatism is the tendency of religious groups to construe Judaism in extremist terms as a combative, territorialist religion, ascribing supreme political importance to the use of armed force.[3] Transition to a civilian society is contingent on cultivating courageous civic-thinking habits, drawing on the richly diverse aspects of Judaism rather than those that ostensibly justify coercion.

5. *Social stratification.* Political control and the manipulation of national security needs for domestic political purposes divide Israeli society, based on the distinction between combatants and noncombatants, while political behavior is overinfluenced by national security considerations. This results in the social deprivation of the Israeli working class, the Israeli Arabs, and women. The social structure befitting a civilian society should be based on egalitarian political, economic, and social foundations.

6. *Military-state relations.* The Israeli army, always a major institution in Israeli politics, dominates many spheres of life above and beyond military security issues. For example, compulsory military service has proved an efficient system of social mobilization and political education, in turn generating loyalty to the state. Indeed, military experience, to give another example, has been a very important asset for political promotion.

The Israeli military has often been used by the ruling elite for its political purposes. The Israeli invasion of Lebanon (1982) is a clear expression of this phenomenon. The military was instructed to carry out partisan and ideologically political motives. Nevertheless, the effect of the military on the general culture and on decision-making processes cannot be undercut. Culturally, Israel is a nation in arms. Institutionally, only very few decisions in Israeli foreign affairs or national security have been forged without direct consultations with the army and the defense ministry. A civilian society should narrow the effects of military discourse and empower independent civilian apparatus of supervision over the military security establishment.

7. *Siege mentality and isolationism.* The fighting society, living under relatively high anxiety, tends to presume that the outside world misunderstands it or is even hostile to its basic national interests. By taking this view, the society can justify its isolationism. The political regime is conceived by most of the public to be a "self-defending democracy," and external pressures are perceived as possible blows to basic national security needs. Transition to a civilian society will require Israel to pay more attention to the strictures of other countries and international organizations, and not just the United States, upon whom she is structurally dependent.[4]

I do not claim that an overall peace in the Middle East is a remote goal. It is not. But peace is a multifaceted notion. A formal peace, or peace on the level of elites, might be attainable. A formal peace may also be imposed from the outside, for example, by the United States. And, such a peace may promote the attainment of real peace. But, the two kinds should not be confused. Real peace means coexistence, yet a society with strong military characteristics is incapable of abiding by such a concept. Coexistence, of course, also depends on the Arabs and the Palestinians, but their readiness alone to make real peace with Israel is not enough. Without change in Israeli society and politics, coexistence will not prevail. Until the definite transition is made to a civilian society, Israel may be regarded, at best, as a partial nonfailure.

Notes

Chapter One

1. J. R. Frears, *Politics and Elections in the French Fifth Republic* (New York: St. Martin's Press, 1977), 192–237. The changes in France were the transition to the Fifth Republic by means of a constitution vesting the president with the very broadest executive authority. In regard to the influence of the Vietnam War on the United States's foreign and defense policy, under the provisions of resolutions enacted by Congress (November 1973), it is incumbent upon the president, by the War Powers Act, to report to Congress any involvement of the United States in an armed conflict where the president does not declare war. See *U.S. Code Annotated*, title 50, sec. 1541–1548. For a discussion see: J. H. Ely, *War and Responsibility: Constitutional Lessons of Vietnam and Its Aftermath* (Princeton: Princeton University Press, 1993).

2. A typical example of research literature focusing on the sources of wars, rather than studying domestic politics is *War*, L. Bramson and G. W. Goethals, eds. (New York: Basic Books, 1968). For examples of good studies that combine the research of international relations with internal politics, regarding war and peace, see Z. Maoz and B. M. Russett, "Normative and Structural Causes of Democratic Peace, 1946–1986," *American Political Science Review* 87, no. 3 (1993): 624–38; B. M. Russett, *Controlling the Sword* (Cambridge: Cambridge University Press, 1990); B. M. Russett and T. W. Graham, "Public Opinion and National Security Policy: Relationships and Impacts," *Handbook of War Studies*, ed. M. I. Midlarsky (Boston: Unwin Hyman, 1989) 239–57. For a critical analysis of studies that deal with peace and war, see J. S. Levy, "Domestic Politics and War," *Journal of Interdisciplinary History* 18, no. 4 (spring 1988): 653–73; A. George, *Presidential Decision Making in Foreign Policy: The Effective Use of Information and Advice* (Boulder: Westview Press, 1991). For a good review of war in international relations, see M. I. Midlarsky, *On War: Political Violence in the International System* (New York: The Free Press, 1975).

3. Britain and France in World War I (1914–19) and World War II (1939–45), France in the wars of Indochina (1946–54) and Algeria (1954–62),

Britain and France during the Suez Campaign (1956), Britain during the Falkland War (1982), the United States in the course of World Wars I and II, the Korean War (1950–1953), and the Vietnam War (1964–73). Of all of these, the only instance of immediate public domestic controversy occurred in Britain with the outbreak of the Suez Campaign, from the political center. See V. W. Kerkheide, *Anthony Eden and the Suez Crisis of 1956* (Cleveland: Ph.D. diss., Case Western Reserve University, 1972), 188–339; J. E. Mueller, *War, Presidents, and Public Opinion* (New York: John Wiley, 1973), 42–168; N. Wahl, *The Fifth Republic* (New York: Random House, 1959); D. Thomson, *Europe Since Napoleon* (New York: Penguin, 1978), 522–67 J. Joll, *Europe Since 1870* (New York: Penguin, 1983), 179–257.

    4. K. Burk, *War and the State* (London: Allen and Unwin, 1982); S. Rosen, "War Power and the Willingness to Suffer," *Peace, War, Power and Numbers*, ed. B. M. Russett (Beverly Hills: Sage Publications, 1972); W. N. Medlicott, *Contemporary England* (London: Longman, 1978), 415–68. For comparisons with Middle East politics, see A. Dowty, et al., eds., *The Arab-Israeli Conflict: Perspectives* (New York: Praeger, 1984); Y. Evron, *The Middle East: Nations, Superpowers, and Wars* (New York: Praeger, 1973); Y. Evron, *War and Intervention in Lebanon* (Baltimore: Johns Hopkins University Press, 1987); R. O. Freedman, ed., *The Middle East after the Israeli Invasion of Lebanon* (Syracuse: Syracuse University Press, 1986); I. Lustick, *For the Land and the Lord: Jewish Fundamentalism in Israel* (New York: Council on Foreign Relations, 1988); I. Peleg, *Begin's Foreign Policy 1977–1983: Israel's Move to the Right* (New York: Greenwood Press, 1987); B. Kimmerling and J. S. Migdal, *Palestinians: The Making of a People* (New York: The Free Press, 1993); A. Hewedy, *Militarization and Security in the Middle East: Its Impact on Development and Democracy* (New York: St. Martin's Press, 1989).

    5. I refer to Britain and France in the course of World War I, France during the Indochinese and Algerian wars, and the United States during the Korean and Vietnamese wars. See note 3.

    6. Thomson, *Europe since Napoleon*, 373–75.

    7. Joll, *Europe since 1870*, 202–29; Kerkheide, *Anthony Eden and Suez Crisis*, 188–350; Mueller, *War, Presidents and Public Opinion*, 23–175; Wahl, *The Fifth Republic*; R. A. Diamond, ed., *France under de Gaulle* (New York: Facts on File, 1970), 28–48. *Sondage Revue Française de L'Opinion Publique 1957–1963*, no. 2 (1959): 27–38; *Sondage Revue Française*, no. 3 (1960): 39–62.

    8. See note 7.

    9. Meaning of the term pre-paradigm: a situation in which researchers of the same discipline or subdiscipline fail to agree regarding basic notions

and methodology. For a comprehensive definition of the term, see T. S. Kuhn, *The Structure of Scientific Revolutions* (Chicago: University of Chicago Press, 1962).

10. Erich Fromm, *The Sane Society*, trans. Z. Weissman et al. (Jerusalem: Rubinstein Publishers, 1975), 11, 12, 68.

11. E. H. Sutherland and D. R. Cressey, *Principles of Criminology* 7th. ed. (Philadelphia: Lippincott, 1966), 24, 254–57; L. A. Coser, *The Functions of Social Conflict* (New York: The Free Press, 1956), 144. At the same time, Coser recognized the fact that war can sometimes cause disintegration in the social system; Coser, *Social Conflict*, 92–95; and also Lipsitz, "The Study of Consensus," *International Encyclopaedia of the Social Sciences*, ed. D. L. Sills, vol. 3 (1968), p. 269; G. Simmel, *Conflict* (Glencoe: The Free Press, 1955); E. Durkheim, *Suicide* (New York: The Free Press, 1951); K. R. Popper, *The Open Society and Its Enemies*, 5th ed. (Princeton: Princeton University Press, 1971), 43, 198. Also see for analysis of problems concerning political order in times of wars: I. Lustick, *Unsettled States, Disputed Lands: Britain and Ireland, France and Algeria, Israel and the West Bank–Gaza* (Ithaca: Cornell University Press, 1993); J. S. Migdal, *Strong Societies and Weak States* (Princeton: Princeton University Press, 1988).

12. P. A. Sorokin, *Man and Society in Calamity*, 2nd ed. (Westport: 1973), 88, 133–44, 274–75.

13. M. Stohl, *War and Domestic Political Violence* (Beverly Hills: Sage Publications, 1976), 82–95. See also an instructive paper on this issue reaching the same conclusion in regard to the Vietnam War: R. Brooks, "Domestic Violence and Wars: A Historical Interpretation," *Violence in America* ed. D. H. Graham and T. R. Gurr (New York: Signet, 1969), 503–21.

14. H. D. Lasswell, "The Garrison State," *American Journal of Sociology* 46 (1941): 455–68.

15. C. W. Mills, *The Power Elite* (New York: Oxford University Press, 1956); for an analysis of the notion of the military-industrial complex, see A. Mintz, "The Military-Industrial Complex: The American Concept and the Israeli Reality," *State, Government and International Relations*, no. 26 (1987): 15–31.

16. R. Miliband, *Class Power and State Power* (London: Verso, 1983) 259–78; M. Shaw, *War, State and Society* (London: Macmillan Press, 1984); A. Giddens, *The Nation-State and Violence* (Cambridge: Polity Press, 1985).

17. Levy, "Domestic Politics and War," 653–73.

18. T. Skocpol, *States and Social Revolutions: A Comparative Analysis of France, Russia, and China* (Cambridge and New York: Cambridge

University Press, 1979); M. N. Barnett, "High Politics Is Low Politics," *World Politics* 42 (1990): 529–62; M. N. Barnett, *Confronting the Costs of War* (Princeton: Princeton University Press, 1992).

19. Coser, *Social Conflict*, 92–95; L. Kriesberg, *Social Conflicts* (Englewood Cliffs: Prentice-Hall, 1982); A. A. Stein, "Conflict and Cohesion," *Journal of Conflict Resolution* 20 (1976): 143–66.

20. J. S. Levy, "The Diversionary Theory of War: A Critique," *Handbook of War Studies*, ed. M. I. Midlarsky (Boston: Unwin Hyman, 1989), 259–88.

21. See, for example, R. E. Lane, *Political Man* (New York: The Free Press, 1972).

22. S. Verba, "Public Opinion and the War in Vietnam," *American Political Science Review* 56 (1967): 317–33; A. Etzioni, *Demonstration Democracy* (New York: Gordon and Brench, 1970); D. Yankelovich, *The Changing Values on Campus* (New York: Washington Square Press, 1972); D. Yankelovich, *The New Morality* (New York: McGraw-Hill, 1974).

23. S. H. Barnes and M. Kaase, eds., *Political Action* (Beverly Hills: Sage Publications, 1979), 160–63, 188, 444, 487; H. D. Wright, *The Dissent of the Governed* (New York: Academic Press, 1976), 257–301; E. N. Muller, *Aggressive Political Participation* (Princeton: Princeton University Press, 1979); A. Carter, *Direct Action and Liberal Democracy: Violence and Civil Disobedience* (New York: Harper & Row, 1972); T. R. Gurr, *Why Men Rebel* (Princeton: Princeton University Press, 1970); J. H. Skolnick, *The Politics of Protest* (New York: Simon and Schuster, 1969).

24. See above, notes 13–15, 17–23; and also J. Habermas, *Observations on the Spiritual Situation of the Age* (Cambridge: MIT Press, 1984), 1–28, 67–121; J. H. Skolnick, *The Politics of Protest*.

25. A. Arian and A. Antonovsky, *Hopes and Fears of Israelis* (Jerusalem: Jerusalem University Press, 1972), 149–65.

26. For an example of this concept, see research of Benjamin Akzin in which the political system in Israel is designated a system of political parties: B. Akzin, "The Role of Parties in Israel," *Integration and Development in Israel*, ed. S. N. Eisenstadt, R. Ben Yosef, and C. Adler (Jerusalem: Jerusalem University Press, 1970), 9–46.

27. D. Horowitz, "The Permanent and the Fluid in the Israeli Security Concept," *War of Alternative*, ed. A. Yariv (in Hebrew) (Tel Aviv: Jaffe Center for Strategic Studies, 1985), 57–77; M. Lissak, "The Social Price of the Wars of Israel," *The Price of Power*, ed. Z. Offer and A. Kovar (in Hebrew) (Tel Aviv: Maarakhot, 1984), 27–32; S. Feldman and H. Rechnitz-Kijner, *Deception, Consensus and War: Israel in Lebanon* (Tel Aviv: Jaffe Center for Strategic Studies,

1984); Yishai Menuhin and Dinah Menuhin, eds., *The Borderline of Obedience* (in Hebrew) (Tel Aviv: Yesh Gvul Publishers, 1985); I. Peleg and O. Seliktar, eds., *The Emergence of Binational Israel* (Boulder: Westview Press, 1989); D. Peretz, *Intifada: The Palestinian Uprising* (Boulder: Westview Press, 1990); R. O. Freedman, ed., *The Intifada: Its Impact on Israel, the Arab World, and the Superpowers* (Miami: Florida International University Press, 1991). (See especially the articles by K. W. Stein, R. Freedman, and A. Arian.)

28. Exceptions to this rule are a few good studies, of which I cite the following: Z. Segal, "Military Censorship: Powers, Judiciary Criticism of Its Actions and Draft for an Alternative Arrangement," *Iyunei Mishpat* 15, no. 2 (July 1990): 311–42; Lustick, *For the Land and the Lord*; Peleg, *Begin's Foreign Policy*; Y. Shapiro, *To Rule Hast Thou Chosen Us* (in Hebrew) (Tel Aviv: Am Oved, 1989); Y. Shavit, *The Mythology of the Right* (in Hebrew) (Tel Aviv: Bet-Berl, 1986); Z. Raanan, *Gush Emunim* (in Hebrew) (Tel Aviv: Sifriat Poalim, 1980); A. Sprinzak, *Illegalism in Israeli Society* (in Hebrew) (Tel Aviv: Sifriat Poalim, 1986); D. Horowitz and M. Lissak, *Distress in Utopia* (in Hebrew) (Tel Aviv: Am Oved, 1990), 240–71; G. Doron, *Rational Politics in Israel* (in Hebrew) (Tel Aviv: Ramot, 1988); A. Arian and M. Shamir, "The Primarily Political Functions of Left-Right Continuum," *The Elections in Israel, 1981*, ed. A. Arian (Tel Aviv: Ramot, 1983); E. Inbar and G. Goldberg, "Is Israel's Political Elite Becoming More Hawkish?" *International Journal* 44 (summer 1990): 631–60; M. Keren, *The Pen and the Sword* (Boulder: Westview Press, 1989); E. Inbar, *War and Peace in Israeli Politics: Labor Party Positions on National Security* (Boulder: Lynne Rienner, 1991); O. Seliktar, *New Zionism and the New Foreign Policy System of Israel* (Carbondale: Southern Illinois University Press, 1986); D. Vital, *The Survival of Small States* (in Hebrew) (Tel Aviv: Am Oved, 1973); U. Bialer, *Between East and West: Israel's Foreign Policy Orientation 1948–1956* (Cambridge: Cambridge University Press, 1990). See also a series of publications by E. Yuchtman-Yaar and Y. Peres on public attitudes on matters of national security in the *Israeli Democracy* periodical.

29. Of the various attitudes in different religious groups regarding Israel's legitimacy, see A. Ravitzky, "The Future and the Possibilities," *Israel toward the Twenty-First Century*, ed. A. Har-Evan (in Hebrew) (Jerusalem: Van Leer, 1984), 135–99.

30. A survey by the Van Leer Institute (1983) of political attitudes among Jewish youth indicates that about 30 percent want an authoritarian regime. It may be assumed that support for radical solutions is greater among the youth than among adults. See also public opinion polls of Professors E. Yuchtman-Yaar and Y. Peres, dated 1989 and 1990, in the periodical *Israeli Democracy*. For Israel as a "formal democracy," see Y. Shapiro, *Democracy in Israel* (in Hebrew) (Ramat-Gan: Massada, 1977). For a profound analysis of the Israeli political culture, see M. J. Aronoff, *Israeli Visions and Divisions:*

Cultural Change and Political Conflict (New Brunswick: Transaction Books, 1989); Y. Peres and E. Yuchtman-Yaar, *Trends in Israeli Democracy* (Boulder and London: Lynne Rienner, 1992).

31. Y. Shavit, *Restraint or Response 1936–1939* (in Hebrew) (Ramat-Gan: Bar-Ilan University Press, 1983); N. Yellin-Mor, *Israel Freedom Fighters* (in Hebrew) (Jerusalem: Shakmona, 1974), 57–70, 175–81, 233–47, 259–302. For a critical review, see B. Morris, *The Birth of the Palestinian Refugee Problem, 1947–1949* (Cambridge: Cambridge University Press, 1987); A. Shlaim, *Collision across the Jordan* (New York: Columbia University Press, 1988); B. Morris, *1948 and After* (Oxford: Oxford University Press, 1990); I. Pappe, *The Making of the Arab-Israeli Conflict, 1947–1951* (London and New York: Tauris, 1992); D. J. Gerner, *One Land, Two Peoples: The Conflict over Palestine* (Boulder: Westview Press, 1991), 11–48; K. W. Stein, *The Land Question in Palestine 1917–1939* (Chapel Hill: University of North Carolina Press, 1984); K. W. Stein, "One Hundred Years of Social Change: The Creation of the Palestinian Refugee Problem," *New Perspectives on Israeli History*, ed. L. J. Silberstein, 57–81; D. Peretz, "Early State Policy toward the Arab Population, 1948–1955," *New Perspectives*, 82–102.

32. Arguments related mostly to operative topics as, for example, the occupation of the Latrun Police Station, see Arieh Yitzhaki, *Latrun—The Campaign over the Road to Jerusalem* (in Hebrew) (Jerusalem: Kanah, 1982); there were also disputes between Ben-Gurion and the General Staff over Ben Gurion's refusal to cast the entire weight of military strength into the field, so as to allow a convenient starting point for negotiations: Z. Lanir, "Political Goals and Military Objectives of the Wars of Israel," *War of Alternative*, 117–56.

33. Ben-Gurion's speech to the Provisional State Council (June 17, 1948), *Protocols of the Provisional State Council*, vol. 1, pp. 331–32; and see also *Diaries of David Ben-Gurion*, July 11, 1948.

34. Speech by David Ben-Gurion during Knesset deliberations (April 21, 1949), *Divrei Haknesset*, vol. 1, pp. 307–8.

35. *Deliberations of the Provisional State Council* (September 27, 1948), vol. 1, pp. 27–29.

36. See note 35, p. 27.

Chapter Two

1. In the Third Knesset elections (1955), Herut polled 12.6 percent of the votes, nearly a 100 percent electoral increase compared to the Second

Knesset elections of 1951, when it polled 6.6 percent of votes. Herut's position as an opposition party was notably strengthened as Mapai's electoral power declined, from 37.3 percent to 32.2 percent of total votes (or 14 percent), and as compared to a loss in the combined electoral strength of the socialist lists (Mapai, Ahduth Haavoda, and Mapam). Mapam (the socialist party of the Hashomer Hatzair movement and HaKibbutz Haartzi) polled 7.3 percent of all votes to the Third Knesset and was represented in the seventh government (gaining a Knesset vote of confidence on November 3, 1955) by Mordechai Bentov (minister of development) and Israel Barzilai (minister of health).

2. Moshe Sneh, "The Israeli Tragedy," *Kol Haam*, November 23, 1956, p. 2; and also chapter 3, paragraph 5, of the summary of the Thirteenth Maki Conference, *Kol Haam*, September 19, 1956, p. 3.

3. Mordechai Bentov, interview by author, January 12, 1984; Yaakov Hazan, interview by author, May 3, 1984.

4. See the *Diaries of David Ben-Gurion*, July 31, 1955, p. 16, BGA. As to the attitudes of the other parties, see Knesset Debates (October 18, 1955; November 3, 1955), *Divrei Haknesset*, vol. 21, pp. 107–98; 247–8; 262–3.

5. A. Drori, ed., *Book of the Fourth National Conference of the Herut Movement* (Tel Aviv: Herut Movement Secretariat, 1957), 54–63; Begin's speeches during Knesset Debates (June 18, 1956) *Divrei Haknesset*, vol. 21, pp. 2044–45.

6. For an example of the use of this term, see Begin's speech in Knesset (October 15, 1956) *Divrei Haknesset*, vol. 21, p. 67.

7. Ibid., p. 70.

8. Editorial, *Herut*, October 22, 1956, p. 1. See also Begin's speech in Knesset (October 18, 1956) *Divrei Haknesset*, vol. 21, p. 91.

9. Editorial, *Herut*, October 25, 1956, p. 1.

10. Section 12 of the resolutions of the Fourth Herut Conference, *Herut*, October 12, 1956, p. 2.

11. Ibid.

12. Speeches by Begin and Bader at the Herut Center (March 4, 1956), *Minutes of Herut Center*, container 9/1, pp. 1–11, HA; Begin's speech to the Herut Center (October 11, 1956), *Minutes of Herut Center*, 9/1, p. 8, HA.

13. Speeches by Haim Landau, Bader, Begin at Herut Center (March 4, 1956), see note 12, pp. 2–11; Arieh Ben-Eliezer's speech in Knesset (November 3, 1955) *Divrei Haknesset*, vol. 21, pp. 265–67.

14. Begin's speech at the Fourth Herut Conference, *Herut*, October 2, 1956, p. 1.

15. The deterioration of the domestic situation in Jordan and the danger that Iraqi troops would alter the status quo in the Middle East greatly concerned Herut. Party leaders therefore formed the opinion, as early as March 1956, that a war of initiative should be launched on two fronts (Egypt and Jordan), although Menachem Begin believed a military operation against Jordan would not necessarily cause Egypt to intervene in the war; see Begin's speech to Herut Center, March 4, 1956, *Minutes of Herut Center*, 9/1, pp. 4–5, HA.

16. Editorial, *Herut*, October 28, 1956, p. 1.

17. Yochanan Bader, interview by the author, December 22, 1983. See also Ben-Gurion's report of his meetings with various prominent persons, *Diaries of Ben-Gurion, 1956*, September 1, 1956–October 26, 1956, pp. 62–253, BGA; and also Y. Shapiro, *To Rule Hast Thou Chosen Us* (in Hebrew) (Tel Aviv: Am Oved, 1989), 125.

18. For a summary of Mapam's concepts on social and economic affairs, see Meir Yaari, *Struggling for Liberated Toil* (in Hebrew) (Tel Aviv: Am Oved, 1972).

19. Bentov interview, 1984; see also Yaakov Hazan's statement to the Mapam Youth Brigade that war should be launched only in exigency, that is, when designed to thwart an immediate danger to the state, *Al Hamishmar*, October 7, 1956, p. 1.

20. Meir Yaari's speech at the council of Kibbutz Haartzi in Mizra (March 29, 1956) 8.20.5 (2), p. 22, HHA.

21. See notes 26, 29 below; also Yaakov Hazan, interview by author, May 3, 1984.

22. Statement of Israel Barzilai at Mapam public assembly (October 13, 1956), *Al Hamishmar*, October 14, 1956, pp. 1, 4.

23. Speech by Hazan at the Mapam Political Committee session, (October 30, 1956), 90.66 (2), HHA.

24. Speech by Yaakov Hazan at the Mapam Center (August 15, 1956), 68, 90 (1) *Handbook* 8, HHA (original pages unnumbered).

25. Meir Yaari, *Struggling for Liberated Toil*, 125–26; and item 1, Mapam Political Committee resolutions summing up the Suez Campaign, November 1956.

26. Yaakov Hazan in a speech to the Knesset (October 16, 1956) *Divrei Haknesset*, vol. 21, p. 86.

27. Ibid., p. 87.

28. Report by Barzilai to the political committee of Mapam (October 4, 1956), (original pages unnumbered), 90.66 (2), HHA.

29. Yaari's speech to Mapam Political Committee, ibid., pp. 125–26.

30. Moshe Dayan, *Suez Campaign Diary* (in Hebrew) (Tel Aviv: Am Hasefer, 1965), 17–20; see also *Diaries of Ben-Gurion*, days July 31, 1955 (Ben-Gurion outlines the security policy he wants established as a condition for forming a government under his premiership); August 7, 1956 (reports a talk with Begin in which the latter calls for a war initiative, since, in his view, an opportune moment has arrived); September 9, 1956 (Ben-Gurion outlines a possible war plan against Egypt and Jordan); and also, September 25, 1956 (Ben-Gurion first obtains the consent of Levi Eshkol, Golda Meir, Kadish Luz, and Bekhor Shitrit to the contemplated initiation of the Suez Campaign) and, September 28, 1956 (Ben-Gurion states that in his opinion there is no doubt that Nasser is about to attack Israel)—*Diaries of Ben-Gurion*, 1955, p. 162, and 1956, pp. 25–235, BGA.

31. *Diaries of Ben-Gurion*, July 31, 1955, October 24, 1955, BGA.

32. Dayan, *Suez Campaign Diary*, 57–58.

33. Knesset Debates (June 18, 1956), *Divrei Haknesset*, vol. 21, p. 207; *Diaries of Ben-Gurion*, 1955, July 30, p. 159, BGA. Moshe Sharett, *Personal Diary* (Tel Aviv: Maariv, 1978), 1552–1638.

34. See Ben-Gurion's speech to Mapai Center (January 31, 1957) meetings of Mapai Center, 23/57, vol. 1, p. 3, LA; *Diaries of Ben-Gurion*, 1956, pp. 109–10, 113–14, BGA.

35. Editorial, *Al Hamishmar*, October 21, 1956, p. 1. Mapam Political Committee debates (October 30, 1956), 90.66 (2), HHA.

36. See note 35.

37. Speeches by Begin, Landau, and Bader to the Herut Center (March 4, 1956) container 9/1, 2, HA.

38. Ibid.

39. See *Diaries of Ben-Gurion*, 1956, entries from September 25, 1956, pp. 109–10, BGA; Zerah Werhaftig, interview by author, April 12, 1984.

40. Ibid.

41. See Bentov and Hazan, interviews by author; also Yaari's speech to the Mapam Political Committee (October 30, 1956).

42. See note 41. Due to his prior assumption that Mapam would oppose the war, Ben-Gurion took care, throughout the war preparations, to not inform the Mapam delegates that a campaign was contemplated. See *Diaries of Ben-Gurion*, 1956, report of meeting with Israel Barzilai (October 26, 1956), 253, BGA; Bader, interview, and Elimelech Rimalt, interview by author, March 25, 1984.

43. Editorial, *Al Hamishmar*, October 30, 1956, p. 1.

44. Yaakov Riftin speech and the resolutions of the Mapam Political Committee (October 30, 1956), 90.66 (2), HHA.

45. See statement by Israel Barzilai and Meir Yaari calling upon the women of Israel to volunteer for the Health Service, *Al Hamishmar*, November 1, 1956, p. 1.

46. Editorial, *Herut*, November 11, 1956, p. 1; Begin's speech at Knesset debates (November 7, 1956), *Divrei Haknesset*, vol. 21, pp. 202–3.

47. See speeches of Yaari, Hazan, and Riftin in Mapam Political Committee (June 14, 1956), 90.66 (2), HHA.

48. Resolutions of the political committee (June 14, 1956) minutes of the meeting, ibid.

49. Meir Yaari's speech to the political committee (October 30, 1956), minutes of committee meeting, 90.66 (2), HHA.

50. Bentov, interview. See also Kovlanov, Yaari, and Vishinski at Mapam Political Committee meeting (February 25, 1957), 90.66 (2), HHA.

51. See note 44, Mapam Political Committee meeting (November 2, 1956), 90.66 (2), HHA.

52. See Hazan's speech at Knesset debates on Sharett's resignation: Hazan's speech (June 18, 1956) *Divrei Haknesset*, vol. 21, p. 2061, and also Rimalt, Hazan, Werhaftig, Bentov, and Bader interviews. See also speeches of Prime Minister Ben-Gurion, Peretz Bernstein (General Zionists), and Herzel Berger (Mapai) in Knesset (November 7, 1956) *Divrei Haknesset*, vol. 21, pp. 199, 203, 205.

53. *Davar*, October 30, 1956, p. 1; also Uri Avneri, "We Are All Army," *Haolam Hazeh*, December 12, 1956, p. 3. Bodies promoting volunteerism included, for example, the Civil Servants Organization and the Women's Organizations Council and the Board of Directors of the Jewish Agency in Jerusalem, *Al Hamishmar*, November 3, 1956, p. 4.

54. Paragraph 1 of the resolutions of the Mapam Political Committee (November 22, 1956), HHA.

55. There are no public opinion polls relative to this period, but all parties except Maki and Mapam were in favor of Israel's cooperating with the Western powers.

56. Kovlanov's speech to the Mapam Political Committee (November 22, 1956), HHA.

57. Yaari's speech to the Mapam Political Committee (October 30, 1956), HHA.

58. Knesset debate on Suez Campaign (November 7, 1956) *Divrei Haknesset*, vol. 21, p. 199.

59. Dan Kamai, "At a Fateful Hour," *Herut*, October 30, 1956, p. 2; editorial, *Herut*, November 4, 1956, p. 1.

60. Yaari in his summing up of the Mapam Political Committee meeting (October 30, 1956).

61. *Kol Haam*, October 30, 1956, p. 1.

62. Israel Hertz, "Front and Hinterland," *Al Hamishmar*, p. 2.

63. Editorial, *Davar*, November 8, 1956, p. 1.

64. Ben-Gurion's statement, and also statement by Golda Meir that Israel would take "an independent line of defense" by deploying regular armed forces, *Davar*, October 21, 1956, p. 1.

65. Peretz Bernstein's and Elimelech Rimalt's speeches at Knesset debate (October 16, 1956) *Divrei Haknesset*, vol. 21, pp. 78–81, 101–3.

66. Speech of Yitzhak Meir Levin at Knesset session of October 16, 1956, ibid., 91–92.

67. See note 66, speech of Yizhar Harari at Knesset session October 16, 1956, 97–9; also Moshe Kol, interview by author, December 30, 1984.

68. Speech of Idov Cohen at Knesset debate (November 7, 1956) *Divrei Haknesset*, vol. 21, pp. 213–15. Also Rimalt, interview.

69. Editorial, *Hazofeh*, October 5, 1956, p. 1; see also resolution of 12th Hapoel Hamizrahi Conference (March 1956) calling for action to "stamp out" fedayeen groups; see N. Aminoah, ed., *Twelfth Conference of Hapoel Hamizrahi in Eretz Israel* (Tel Aviv, 1957), 145.

70. Speech of Yitzhak Rafael at Knesset debates (October 16, 1956) *Divrei Haknesset*, vol. 21, pp. 81–84.

71. Werhaftig, interview.

72. Resolution of HaKibbutz Hameuhad Council at Ashdot Yaakov (November 11–12, 1955), submitted to the 18th Kibbutz Conference, July 1960, p. 26, AHA.

73. Remarks by Israel Galili, a party leader, during the Histadruth discussions on state security (March 20, 1956), report of the Histadruth Labor Federation 8th Conference, p. 299.

74. Resolution of HaKibbutz Hameuhad Council (June 29–July 1, 1956), AHA.

75. See statement by Yigal Allon in favor of initiating a military operation with a view to averting severe threats, *Haaretz*, July 1, 1956, p. 2; also speech by Israel Galili in Knesset debates (October 16, 1956), 84.

76. Speech by Begin at session of Herut Center (March 4, 1956) container 9/1, file 1, p. 2, HA.

77. Speech by Israel Galili (October 16, 1956) *Divrei Haknesset*, vol. 21, pp. 83–85.

78. Yaari's speech at the political committee of Mapam (June 14, 1956), 90.66 (2), HHA. Yaari also thought Israel's survival was in danger but denied the claim that the danger was an immediate one, thus not justifying the initiation of a war.

79. Yaari's draft summation of the deliberations of the political committee of Mapam (November 22, 1956), ibid.

80. See deliberations and resolutions of the Mapam Political Committee (November 22, 1956), 90.66 (2) (original pages unnumbered), HHA.

81. Ibid., paragraph 2.

82. Debates of the various parties in Knesset following the reprisals in Qalqilya (October 15–17, 1956) *Divrei Haknesset*, vol. 21.

83. Data collated from "Suez Campaign," extension handbook of the Information Department of the prime minister's office and also from the

Central Bureau of Statistics, as to the size and composition of the population of Israel in 1956; see also Rimalt interview and Knesset debates (November 7, 1956).

84. See speeches by Meir Argov (chairman of the Foreign Affairs and Defense Committee of the Knesset) and of Giora Josephtal (secretary of Mapai Center), *Al Hamishmar*, November 11, 1956, p. 4.

85. Paragraph 3 of the resolutions of the Mapam Political Committee (November 22, 1956), HHA; editorial, *Herut*, November 2, 1956, p. 1.

86. Kamai, "At a Fateful Hour," *Herut*, October 30, 1956, p. 2.

87. See Pinhas Tuvin, "Government of Israel—Whither?" *Kol Haam*, September 18, 1956, p. 2; also *Kol Haam*, October 15, 1956, p. 1; *Kol Haam*, October 19, 1956, p. 1; *Kol Haam*, October 28, 1956, p. 1.

88. Editorial, *Kol Haam*, October 30, 1956, p. 1; editorial, *Kol Haam*, November 1, 1956, p. 1; Esther Vilenska, "A Number of Comments to the Leaders of Mapam on Equality and Peace," *Kol Haam*, September 14, 1956, p. 2.

89. *Kol Haam*, November 4, 1956, p. 1; also Moshe Sneh, "The Israeli Communist Party—Defender of the Peace and Future of the Homeland," *Kol Haam*, November 2, 1956.

90. Moshe Sneh, "The Israeli Communist Party," *Kol Haam*, November 2, 1956, p. 2.

91. See paragraph 2 of the resolutions of the Mapam Political Committee, in the summation of the Suez Campaign (November 1956), 90.67 (2), HHA.

92. See remarks of Mapam senior members during political committee debates on November 22, 1956, and March 25, 1957, 90.66 (2), HHA.

93. Yaari's speech to the Mapam Political Committee (November 22, 1956), HHA; Barzilai's speech to the Mapam Political Committee (March 25, 1957), 90.67 (2), HHA.

94. Y. Amit, "In View of the Dangers," *Al Hamishmar*, November 29, 1956, p. 2.

95. Paragraph 3 of the resolutions of the political committee in summation of the Suez Campaign (November 1956), 90.67 (2), HHA.

96. Speeches by Bentov and Barzilai at the Mapam Political Committee session of March 25, 1957, 90.67 (2), HHA. Also, the phrase "wrongful war in justifying circumstances" is taken from Yaari's summing-up at the Mapam Political Committee session of November 26, 1956, HHA.

97. Begin's speech at Herut Center (December 6, 1956), *Minutes of Herut Center*, 9/1, p. 8, HA.

98. Begin's speech in Knesset (November 7, 1956) *Divrei Haknesset*, vol. 21, 201; also see pp. 202–3.

99. Editorial, *Herut*, November 11, 1956, p. 1.

100. Editorial, *Herut*, October 30, 1956, p. 1; editorial, *Herut*, December 24, 1956, p. 1.

101. Y. Peri, *Between Battles and Ballots* (London: Cambridge University Press, 1983), 159–61; Moshe Dayan, *Milestones* (in Hebrew) (Tel Aviv: Yediot Ahronoth, 1976), 267–71.

102. See debate at Mapai Center (December 20, 1956) *Minutes of Party Center Session*, 23/56, vol. 1, LA. See also Mapai Center debates, January 3, 1957, *Minutes of Party Center Session* (January 3, 1957), 23/57, vol. 1, LA.

103. See Yaari's speech at the Mapam Political Committee session (November 22, 1956), HHA.

104. Begin's speech to Herut Center (November 15, 1956), and also Herut Center debates (December 6, 1956), (December 27, 1956), *Minutes of Herut Center*, 9/2, HA.

105. Percentages computed on basis of electoral support for the various parties, as it emerged from the results of the Third Knesset elections (1955).

Chapter Three

1. I have already elaborated on the positions of Mapam and the Committee for Peace in the previous chapter; as to Matzpen's positions, see N. Yuval-Davis, *Matzpen—The Socialist Organization of Israel* (in Hebrew) (Jerusalem: Hebrew University, 1977), 40–45.

2. M. Chizik, "Struggle for an Alternative Path and Problems of the United Front," *Hedim*, 52 (1959): 3–17; Israel Barzilai's speech in Knesset (April 10, 1962) *Divrei Haknesset*, vol. 33, pp. 1857–58.

3. Meir Yaari, "List of Headings Toward the Third Mapam Conference," *Al Hamishmar*, December 6, 1957, p. 2.

4. See Haknesset debates (January 24, 1967) *Divrei Haknesset*, vol. 49, pp. 997–98 (speech by Moshe Una NRP); p. 1000 (Shimon Peres, Rafi); pp. 1003–4 (Gideon Hausner, Independent Liberals); pp. 1004–6 (Yitzhak Meir Levin, Agudath Israel); p. 1008 (Yaakov Katz, Poalei Agudath Israel).

5. Meir Yaari, "List of Headings Toward the Third Mapam Conference," *Al Hamishmar*, December 6, 1957, p. 2, notes 6, 7 below.

6. Prime Minister Eshkol's statement on the security situation (October 17, 1966) *Divrei Haknesset*, vol. 49, pp. 2–5; Shimon Peres, *David's Sling* (in Hebrew) (Jerusalem: Wiedenfeld & Nicholson, 1970) 184.

7. Prime minister's statement on the security situation (October 17, 1966) *Divrei Haknesset*, vol. 49, pp. 2–5; declaration by CGS Yitzhak Rabin, *Lamerhav* May 14, 1967, p. 3.

8. Prime minister's statement (April 10, 1962) on the UN response to the action in Nuqeib, *Divrei Haknesset*, vol. 33, pp. 1850–52.

9. Speech by Arieh Ben-Eliezer (October 18, 1966) *Divrei Haknesset*, vol. 47, pp. 39–42; speech by Haim Landau in Knesset (January 24, 1967) *Divrei Haknesset*, vol. 49, pp. 994–95.

10. Menachem Begin, "Warnings, Concentrations, and Threats," *Hayom*, May 19, 1967, p. 3; Menachem Begin "Blood in the Sea of Galilee," *Herut*, March 23, 1962, p. 2.

11. Uri Avneri's speech in Knesset (January 24, 1967) vol. 49, pp. 1008–9; also, speech by Shmuel Mikunis, (January 24, 1967) vol. 49, pp. 1013–14.

12. Speech in Knesset by Esther Vilenska on UN reaction to Nuqeib operation (April 10, 1962) *Divrei Haknesset*, vol. 33, pp. 1859–60; speeches by Uri Avneri and Shmuel Mikunis (October 18, 1966) *Divrei Haknesset*, vol. 49, pp. 34–37.

13. Moshe Sneh, *End of the Beginning* (in Hebrew) (Tel Aviv: Kibbutz Hameuchad Publishers, 1982), 117; clause 4 of the Haolam Hazeh's summarizing motion of Knesset debates (January 24, 1967) *Divrei Haknesset*, vol. 49, p. 1020.

14. Speech by Moshe Carmel at Ahduth Haavoda Center (October 10, 1965) Dept. 10/13, container 16, file C, AHA; Yigal Alon's declaration (May 13, 1967) *Lamerhav*, May 14, 1967, p. 2.

15. Menachem Begin's speech at Herut Center (March 30, 1967), *Herut Center Minutes*, HA. Yochanan Bader, interview by author, December 22, 1983.

16. Speech by Yosef Serlin in Knesset (January 24, 1967) *Divrei Haknesset*, vol. 49, pp. 1014–16; Herut summarizing motion on Knesset debates on the security situation (January 24, 1967) *Divrei Haknesset*, vol. 49, p. 1020.

17. Menachem Begin's speech at Herut Center (March 23, 1967) *Herut Center Minutes* (original unpaginated), HA.

18. Moshe Carmel, interview by author, April 22, 1985. B. Geist, "The Six-Day War" (Ph.D. diss., Hebrew University, Jerusalem, 1974), 490.

19. See Geist, "The Six-Day War," 81–397; M. Brecher, *Decisions in Israel's Foreign Policy* (London: Oxford University Press, 1974), 327–61, 417.

20. See summarizing motions on Knesset debates (May 23, 1967) *Divrei Haknesset*, vol. 49, pp. 2268–69; "On the Brink" *Haolam Hazeh*, May 31, 1967, p. 3.

21. Knesset debate on the political and security situation (May 22, 1967) *Divrei Haknesset*, vol. 49, pp. 2225–44; and Knesset debate (May 23, 1967) *Divrei Haknesset*, vol. 49, pp. 2267–69.

22. Begin, "Warnings, Concentrations and Threats," p. 3; resolution of Herut directorate (May 21, 1967), *Minutes: Meetings of Herut Directorate—Resolutions* (original unpaginated), HA.

23. Editorial, *Herut*, May 29, 1967, p. 1; editorial, *Herut*, May 26, 1967, p. 1.

24. Bader and Carmel, interviews; Elimelech Rimalt, interview by author, March 25, 1984; and also, Nathan Peled, interview by author, June 18, 1985; Zerah Werhaftig, interview by author, April 12, 1984.

25. For theoretical background, see T. R. Gurr, *Why Men Rebel* (Princeton: Princeton University Press, 1970). *Haaretz*, May 30, 1967, p. 1 (advertisement by citizens calling for the founding of a national-unity government); similar advertisement in *Haaretz*, May 26, 1967, p. 1. S. Nakdimon, *Toward Zero Hour* (in Hebrew) (Tel Aviv: Ramdor, 1968), 242–43.

26. Nakdimon, *Toward Zero Hour*, 242–43.

27. See Tevet, *Moshe Dayan*, 566–67; Nakdimon, *Toward Zero Hour*.

28. Z. Schieff, "The Egyptians Threaten from the South," *Haaretz*, May 19, 1967, p. 2 (here Schieff expressed the opinion that there was still scant likelihood of the outbreak of war); *Davar*, May 18, 1967, p. 1. The Herut newspaper also believed the Egyptian moves might be purely for show, while nonetheless expressing fear of the danger of the outbreak of war: *Herut*, May 17, 1967, p. 1. There is notably no public opinion poll data on this issue relative to the period.

29. See *Minutes of Herut Directorate Meetings (1966–1967)* (date of meeting not specified), speech of Arieh Ben-Eliezer, 47–49, HA; Zeev Zur, interview by author, December 31, 1984.

30. For bases of public opinion in Israel on national security topics, see A. Arian, I. Talmud, and T. Hermann, *National Security and Public Opinion in Israel* (Boulder: Westview Press, 1988).

31. Prime minister's statement in Knesset (May 22, 1967), vol. 49; also see Brecher, *Decisions*, 372.

32. *Davar*, May 19, 1967, p. 1; Zur and Carmel, interviews.

33. Zur and Carmel, interviews.

34. Speech in Knesset by Shmuel Mikunis (May 22, 1967) *Divrei Haknesset*, vol. 49, pp. 2243–44; also speech at same Knesset session by Avneri, pp. 2241–43.

35. Geist, "The Six-Day War," 145.

36. S. Schnitzer, "The Test," *Maariv*, May 26, 1967, Friday supplement, p. 3; H. Justus, "Confrontation at Zero Hour," *Maariv*, May 26, 1967, p. 3; E. Livneh, "Return of the Hitler Threat," *Haaretz*, May 31, 1967, p. 2; Z. Schieff, "The Sandglass," *Haaretz*, May 29, 1967, p. 2; editorial, *Lamerhav*, May 28, 1967, p. 2; H. Zemer, "On the Brink of No Choice," *Davar*, May 26, 1967, p. 3; editorial, *Al Hamishmar*, May 28, 1967, p. 1; editorial, *Hazofeh*, May 25, 1967.

37. Abba Eban's speech at a press conference (June 5, 1967), *Davar*, June 6, 1967, p. 2; *Davar*, May 24, 1967, p. 3.

38. Mordechai Bentov, interview by author, January 12, 1984; Werhaftig, interview.

39. This resolution was officially published by the government of Israel on the fifth anniversary of the war: *Haaretz*, June 5, 1972, p. 1.

40. A. H. Barton, *Communities in Disaster* (New York: Anchor Books, 1969) 63–332; G. H. Grosser, ed., *The Threat of Impending Disaster* (Cambridge: MIT Press, 1971), 1–105.

41. Knesset debates (May 23, 1967), vol. 49; statement by Levi Eshkol (May 29, 1967) *Divrei Haknesset*, vol. 49, pp. 2283–85; and also statement by Golda Meir, *Davar*, May 25, 1967, p. 2.

42. *Haaretz*, May 29, 1967, p. 2.

43. Abba Eban, *Life Story* (in Hebrew) (Tel Aviv: Maariv, 1978), vol. 2, pp. 335–408.

44. "Survey Series on Public Domestication," *Zrakor*, Issue 13, Institute for Applied Social Research (Jerusalem, August 1967), 6–10.

45. Werhaftig, interview.

46. Speeches by Yaakov Riftin at Mapam Political Committee (May 18, 1967); (May 31, 1967); Y. Riftin, *Guardianship* (in Hebrew) (Tel Aviv: Sifriat Poalim and Kibbutz Ein Shemer, 1978), 276–77.

47. See Geist, "The Six-Day War," 389; M. Bentov, *Days Tell* (in Hebrew) (Tel Aviv: Sifriat Poalim, 1984), 155–58.

48. *Mapam Political Committee Debates* (May 31, 1967), (June 19, 1967) 2 (66) 90, HHA; Herut Center meeting (June 15, 1967) *Minutes of Herut Center Meetings* (original unpaginated), HA.

49. Barton, *Communities in Disaster*; Grosser, *Impending Disaster*.

50. Bader, interview; Shapiro, *To Rule*, 166–71.

51. *Haaretz*, June 1, 1967, p. 1 (citizens' advertisement calling for "national unity" and a national-unity government); Herut Center debates (June 2, 1967) HA; Werhaftig, interview; Shmuel Mikunis's speech in Knesset (June 5, 1967) *Divrei Haknesset*, vol. 49, p. 2318; Uri Avneri, "We Trust in the Unity of the State of Israel," *Haolam Hazeh*, June 6, June 7, 1967, pp. 6–7; editorial, *Maariv*, May 28, 1967, p. 1; editorial, *Lamerhav*, June 2, 1967, p. 2; Sneh, *End of the Beginning*, 116–17.

52. Editorial, *Al Hamishmar*, May 30, 1967, p. 1.

53. *Haaretz*, May 25, 1967, p. 2.

54. Speech by Arieh Ben-Eliezer at Herut Center (June 2, 1967), HA.

55. Debates on the resolutions of the Mapam Political Committee (May 31, 1967) 2 (66) 90, HHA.

56. Ibid.

57. Arieh Ben-Eliezer's speech at Herut Center (June 2, 1967), HA; Rimalt, interview; Bader, Werhaftig, interviews.

58. See note 57.

59. P. A. Sorokin, *Man and Society in Calamity* (New York: E. P. Dutton, 1942), 11–26; B. Bahnson, "Emotional Reactions to Internally and Externally Derived Threat of Annihilation," in Grosser, *Impending Disaster*, 251–80.

60. Editorial, *Al Hamishmar*, May 28, 1967, p. 1; *Herut*, June 5, 1967, p. 1; Shmuel Segev, "The Egyptian Concentrations in Sinai," *Maariv*, May 18, 1967, p. 9; editorial, *Lamerhav*, June 4, 1967, p. 2.

61. Editorial, *Al Hamishmar*, June 6, 1967, p. 1; Uri Avneri, "Why Did This Round Break Out?" *Haolam Hazeh*, June 7, 1967, p. 9; Zeev Schieff, "The Three Days of Battle," *Haaretz*, June 9, 1967, p. 3; see also *Davar*, June 8, 1967, p. 1 (Dayan's statement at a press conference whereby, as early as the third day of the war, military victory had been won).

62. Bader and Werhaftig, interviews; *Mapam Political Committee Debates* (May 31, 1967) 2 (66) 90, HHA; Uri Avneri, "On the Brink," *Haolam Hazeh*, May 31, 1967, p. 3; Sneh, *End of the Beginning*.

63. Knesset debates (June 5, 1967) *Divrei Haknesset*, vol. 49, pp. 2316–17 (Meir Vilner's speech).

64. Zur, Rimalt, Bader, and Carmel, interviews; and Moshe Kol, interview by author, December 30, 1984; Moshe Dayan *Milestones* (in Hebrew) (Tel Aviv: Yediot Ahronoth, 1976), 440–50. Geist, "The Six-Day War," 454–55.

65. See various expressions of joy in victory: Uri Avneri, "Peace Plan," *Haolam Hazeh*, June 14, 1967, p. 4 ("A Historic Event"); Meir Yaari stated, "This victory verged on the miraculous"; see Yaari's speech at Mapam Political Committee (June 19, 1967) 2 (66) 90, HHA; Herut Center called the campaign "a war of salvation"; see section 2 of Herut Center resolutions (June 15, 1967) *Minutes of Herut Center Meetings, 1967–1970*, HA (original unpaginated).

66. Rabbi Haim Halevi, *Niv Hamidrashiya*, 5728, p. 55.

67. Meir Vilner's speech in Knesset (June 5, 1967) *Divrei Haknesset*, vol. 49, pp. 2316–17; for Maki's statement and its warnings not to harm the population of the territories, see Sneh, *End of the Beginning*, 117–18. The first party to propose a peace settlement was Haolam Hazeh (June 14, 1967); see Uri Avneri, "Peace Plan," *Haolam Hazeh*, June 14, 1967, p. 4.

68. Brecher, *Decisions*, 410.

69. Livneh, "Hitler Threat," 2; statement by Israel Galili that Israel was not Czechoslovakia or Munich, *Davar*, June 4, 1967, p. 2; statement by Mordechai Bentov that Nasserism was Nazi in character and a "neo-Hitlerism in Arab guise," *Haaretz*, June 4, 1967, p. 2.

70. Geist, "The Six-Day War," 291–92.

71. The press did not publish the army's position. The last interview given by the CGS before the war began was on May 14, 1967, to *Lamerhav*. See *Lamerhav*, May 14, 1967, p. 3.

72. See V. O. Key, *Public Opinion and American Democracy* (New York: Alfred Knopf, 1961), 27–76.

73. Data collated from a report of the Institute for Applied Social Research: see "Public Opinion on Daily Affairs," *Zrakor*, Issue 22, Institute for Applied Social Research (Jerusalem: October 1969) (including appendices); and also "Series of Surveys on Public Problems," *Zrakor*, Issue 13, Institute for Applied Social Research (Jerusalem: August 1967), 6–10.

74. See note 73.

Chapter Four

1. See S. Peled, "Stability and Changes in the Structure of Israeli Public Positions from the End of the Six-Day War to December 1970," (Ph.D. diss., Hebrew University, Jerusalem, 1976), 152, 283, B. Kimmerling, "Prominence of the Israeli-Arab Conflict as a Social Indicator, 1949–1960," *State, Government and International Relations* (1974): 100–26.

2. For a definition of the term polyarchy, see R. A. Dahl, *Democracy and Its Critics* (New Haven: Yale University Press, 1989), 225–64.

3. Herut distinguished between annexation directed at the whole Eretz Israel vision, and possession directed at security objectives. See speech by Arieh Ben-Eliezer, Herut Center (June 15, 1967) *Minutes of Herut Center*, HA; speech by Ben-Eliezer (March 25, 1968) *Divrei Haknesset*, vol. 51, pp. 1593–94.

4. See note 3: speeches by Ben-Eliezer and Landau.

5. Yochanan Bader, interview by author, December 22, 1983.

6. For the distinction between ideological-operative and ideological-fundamental principles, see M. Seliger, *Ideology and Politics* (New York: The Free Press, 1976).

7. Article 5 of the Herut Center Resolutions (June 15, 1967), HA; and also speech by Landau in note 4.

8. Speeches by Yaakov Meridor and Arieh Ben-Eliezer at Herut Center meeting (June 15, 1967), HA; and Landau's speech, note 3 above; and Begin on ITV, January 7, 1969, *Davar*, January 8, 1969, p. 2.

9. Haim Landau's motion to the agenda (October 29, 1968), *Divrei Haknesset*, vol. 53, pp. 104–5; Landau in Knesset debate (February 19, 1969) on the government's announcement of the terrorist attack on an airplane in Zurich, *Divrei Haknesset*, vol. 54, p. 1660.

10. Yosef Serlin's speech in Knesset (November 11, 1968), *Divrei Haknesset*, vol. 53, pp. 214–17; Yosef Sapir at Liberal Party Council (July 25, 1968), *Haaretz*, July 25, 1968, p. 2.

11. Shmuel Tamir's speech in Knesset (March 25, 1968) on the Karame Operation, *Divrei Haknesset*, vol. 51, p. 1600.

12. Dr. Israel Eldad, interview by author, August 15, 1985.

13. U. Ornan, "The War and the Peace," *From Victory to Downfall*, ed. Y. Ratosh (in Hebrew) (Tel Aviv: Hadar, 1976), 81. Also Ratosh, *From Victory*, 31–39, 367–70.

14. Ratosh, ed., *From Victory to Downfall*, 54–57, 131–40, 169–77, 326–27, 334.

15. Center meeting (October 23, 1968), file 23/68, vol. 2, LA; also Abba Eban at party center (May 15, 1969), file 23/69, vol. 1, pp. 3–27, LA; Golda Meir's speech at party center (June 5, 1969), file 23/69, vol. 2, p. 56, LA. Particularly stressed by the party was the need to retain control of the Golan Heights as a means of preventing attacks on Israeli settlements and also for an Israeli military presence at Sharm Es-Sheikh, to ensure freedom of shipping. See also the debate on the party's security- and foreign-affairs platform, including territories (September 11, 1969), file 23/69, vol. 3, LA. Speech by Levi Eshkol (March 25, 1968), *Divrei Haknesset*, vol. 51, p. 1613.

16. Moshe Dayan to Kol Israel (Israel Radio) (March 24, 1968), *Davar*, March 25, 1968; and Dayan to students in Haifa (March 20, 1969), *Haaretz*, March 21, 1969, pp. 1, 2.

17. These grounds were implied in statements by Premier Eshkol and Defense Minister Dayan and not denied publicly by other decision makers, and hence may be regarded as implicit casus belli; Dayan in Knesset (October 29, 1968), *Divrei Haknesset*, vol. 53, pp. 107–8; Moshe Dayan, *A New Map, Different Relations* (in Hebrew) (Tel Aviv: Sifriat Maariv, 1969), 92–93; Eshkol in Knesset (March 25, 1968), *Divrei Haknesset*, vol. 51, p. 1613.

18. See speeches by Yitzhak Rafael (NRP), Yizhar Harari (Independent Liberals), and Avraham Verdiger (Poalei Agudath Israel) in a Knesset debate on the Karame Operation (March 25, 1968) in note 11, 1594–95, 1601–2, and for draft summarizing resolution by the Labor Party, see note 11, p. 1613. According to the Seventh Knesset elections, 67.2 percent of the Jewish population is seen to have supported Labor positions on the war issue. According to the Institute for Applied Social Research, the support of the Jewish public for the government's security policy (primarily for Labor positions) was 70–80 percent. The Whole Eretz Israel Movement also favored holding on to the cease-fire lines and hence also supported the war objectives. See its statements (May 14, 1969) *Haaretz*, May 15, 1969, p. 3. The movement leadership and most of its members belonged to the Labor Party and supported Labor positions on the war issue, see Zvi Shiloah, *A Great Land for a Great Nation* (in Hebrew) (Tel Aviv: Otpaz Ltd., 1970), 227.

19. Yaakov Amit, "To Live and to Win Peace," *Al Hamishmar*, July 14, 1967, p. 2. Mordechai Bentov, interview by author, January 12, 1984. Israel Mehlmann, "There Is an Alternative," *New Outlook* 13, no. 1 (January 1970): 28–42.

20. *Divrei Haknesset*, vol. 49, p. 2779.

21. Speeches by Meir Yaari and Yaakov Hazan at Mapam Center (July 6, 1967), *Al Hamishmar*, July 7, 1967, pp. 1, 2. Mapam called for safe borders (an Israeli presence at Sharm Es-Sheikh, the demilitarization of Sinai, Israeli control of the Golan Heights, frontier amendments in the West Bank to ensure IDF control of a number of vital ridges, the demilitarization of the other areas of the West Bank, and annexation of Gaza to Israel). Mapam also called for Jerusalem to be united under Israeli sovereignty, with an independent administration for the Arabs and autonomy for members of all religions in administering their holy places.

22. Shmuel Mikunis, *In These Tempestuous Times* (in Hebrew) (Tel Aviv: Maki Central Committee Publishing House, 1969), 463; Moshe Sneh, "Hair's-breadth," *Kol Haam*, November 8, 1968, pp. 2, 3.

23. When in January 1968 a majority (65 percent) of Mapam members resolved in favor of forming the Alignment, some members seceded to form Siah, headed by Ran Cohen and Yosef Amitai, and the Left Alliance, headed by Yaakov Riftin and Elazar Peri, with a combined membership of 150. They aimed to wield an extra-parliamentary influence on Labor and especially on Mapam. See Yossi Amitai, "Position and Question: Why?" *Siah*, August 1969, 1st edition (original unpaginated). Siah aspired to apply socialist principles and make peace based on Israel's gradual withdrawal from all the territories (excepting ridges on the Golan Heights seen as vital to the defense of Israel). Ran Cohen, "Israel—Security and Frontiers," *Siah*, August 1969, pp. 15–19, and Arik Ben-Shachar, "Peace," *Siah* (original unpaginated). The Movement for Peace and Security founded in early 1968 as an extra-parliamentary pressure group had a few dozen activists, most of them intellectuals from the Hebrew University, Jerusalem. Heading the movement were Dr. Gad Yatziv and Professor Yehoshua Arieli. See Gad Yatziv, interview by author, May 30, 1985; and *Minutes of Session of the Movement*, July 1, 1968. Thanks are due to Mr. Latif Dori, movement activist, for affording me access to his private archives. Matzpen repudiated Zionist values, seeking to overthrow the existing political establishment by means of world revolution resulting from world-class struggle. Matzpen manifesto, *Matzpen*, no. 54, June–July 1970, pp. 10, 12. The Left Alliance and Matzpen opposed cooperation with any foreign power, including the Soviet Union: see Yaakov Riftin, "Politcal Deterioration as Injurious to Vital Interests," *Dapei Brit Hasmol*, April 1970, pp. 2–3; "To Foil the Conspiracy," *Matzpen* 55, August–September 1970 (original unpaginated).

24. Nasser's statement on conclusion of the deliberations of Egypt's ruling party (March 30, 1969), *Haaretz*, March 31, 1969, p. 1.

25. Moshe Dayan in a lecture to students (May 28, 1969), *Haaretz*, May 29, 1969, pp. 1, 2; speeches by Golda Meir (June 5, 1969) and Abba Eban (June 15, 1969) at Mapai Center, *Mapai Center Sessions*, file 23/69, vol. 1, pp. 3–18, LA.

26. For various party positions, see the statement by Premier Meir on the new government's being presented to Knesset (December 15, 1969), *Divrei Haknesset*, vol. 56, p. 198; Yaakov Hazan, "The Political Campaign and the Military Campaign-Combined Tools," *Al Hamishmar*, May 10, 1970, p. 2; Ezer Weizmann at the Tenth National Herut Conference (November 10, 1970) pp. C6–C19, *Herut Movement—Minutes*, HA; Gideon Hausner in Knesset (December 15, 1969), *Divrei Haknesset*, vol. 56, pp. 209–10; Avraham Verdiger (Poalei Agudath Israel) in Knesset (November 16, 1970), *Divrei Haknesset*, vol. 59, pp. 167–68.

27. See P. Alon and D. Freulich, "Positions on Topics of Policy and Security and the Public Morale," current survey, The Institute for Applied Social Research (May 1970) table no. 4; P. Alon and D. Freulich, "Report Following Government Resolution Regarding the American Initiative," telephone survey, The Institute for Applied Social Research (August 1970) p. 18. During the war, until the Goldman affair, only 1.3 percent on average thought the Arab states would be prepared for peace, and 7.6 percent that they might perhaps be prepared for peace. After the Goldman affair, 2 percent thought the Arab states would be prepared for peace, and 21 percent that they might be prepared for peace. See Alon and Freulich, The Institute for Applied Social Research (May 1970), table no. 6; and survey following the Goldman affair, The Institute for Applied Social Research (April 6, 1970) table no. 1.

28. Latif Dori, interview by author, June 7, 1985; Uri Avneri, "Mothers," *Haolam Hazeh*, no. 1653, May 7, 1969, p. 11.

29. Finding political expression were the high school seniors groups who authored the "seniors'" letters, university students, and intellectuals and artists' groups who likewise organized on a basis of personal acquaintanceship and shared ideas.

30. This opinion was clearly expressed by Yigal Alon that Israel was "invincible," since her frontiers were well fortified, *Haaretz*, June 3, 1969, p. 2, and by Dayan that it was not a war of no-alternative, but a battle for establishing secure borders for Israel, July 28, 1970, *Haaretz*, July 29, 1970, p. 1. See also Ezer Weizmann's speech to the Tenth Herut National Conference (November 10, 1970), *Conference Resolutions and Deliberations*, pp. C6–C19, HA. Also see Hazan, "The Strength To Resist and the Courage To Decide," *Al Hamishmar*, May 29, 1970, p. 2.

31. Speech by Dayan, April 10, 1969, *Haaretz*, April 11, 1969, pp. 1, 2; Abba Eban at Mapai Center (May 15, 1969), *Mapai Center Session*, file 23/69, LA; speeches by Eshkol, June 7, 1969, *Haaretz*, June 18, 1969, p. 2; debate on Alignment platform clauses on security issues, *Mapai Center Sessions* (September 19, 1969) file 23/69, vol. 3, LA; for Maki position, see Mikunis, "Those Who Isolate Israel from Within," *Kol Haam*, August 15, 1969, p. 2.

32. Dayan at the Staff and Command School, *Haaretz*, August 8, 1969, p. 10; speeches by Arieh Ben-Eliezer and Menachem Begin at Ninth Herut Conference (May 28, 1968), *Report on Resolutions of Herut Conferences*, pp. 17/–18/3, 19/3–22/3, HA; Knesset debates on composition and program of new government (March 1969), *Divrei Haknesset*, vol. 54, pp. 1967–68, 1971–72.

33. Arie (Lova) Eliav, interview by author, June 14, 1985; Nathan Peled, interview by author, June 18, 1985; speeches by Begin and Ben-Eliezer, see note 32.

34. See *Haaretz*, March 24, 1970, p. 1 (report of security sources); statement by Dayan before students in Tel Aviv (April 6, 1970), *Haaretz*, April 7, 1970, pp. 1, 3; Haim Herzog, *The People Shall Rise Up Like a Lion* (in Hebrew) (Jerusalem: Edanim Publishers, 1983), 173–76.

35. See Mapam Political Committee debates (February 4, 1970), especially speeches by Yaari and Barzilai, 66A (4) HHA; Hazan, "The Political Campaign and the Military Campaign," *Al Hamishmar*, May 10, 1970, p. 2.

36. Ezer Weizmann's speech at the Tenth Herut National Conference, pp. C6–C19, HA, and Ezer Weizmann, *Thine the Heavens, Thine the Earth* (in Hebrew) (Tel Aviv: Maariv, 1975), 322.

37. See Knesset debates on Israeli response to U.S. initiative (August 4, 1970), *Divrei Haknesset*, vol. 58, pp. 2755–98; and especially excerpt from Begin's speech, p. 2765. At Labor Center meetings, Golda Meir and Haim Herzog noted the military importance of cease-fire. Meir claimed it would prevent escalation due to Soviet involvement. Their position was disputed by Ahdut Haavoda members who opposed cease-fire for fear it would intensify international pressure for an IDF retreat from the banks of the canal. See *Mapai Center Sessions* (August 16, 1970), file 23/70, vol. 2, pp. 1–27, 33–38, 55–57, LA.

38. Eban at Labor Party Center (May 15, 1969), vol. 1, pp. 3–27, LA. Debates at Labor Party Center (September 11, 1969), file 23/69, vol. 3, LA; and also Mapai Center debates on coalitionary negotiations with Gahal (December 8, 1969), 23/69, vol. 3, LA.

39. Speech by Hazan, Knesset debates (December 15, 1969), *Divrei Haknesset*, vol. 56, pp. 207–8; Yaari's speech at Mapam Political Committee (December 6, 1969), no. 30 (4) A66.90, HHA.

40. Mapam Center deliberations on option of joining national-unity government (December 8, 1969), *Mapam Center*, no. 18, (2) 68.90, HHA.

41. Knesset debates (December 15, 1969), *Divrei Haknesset*, vol. 56, pp. 203–5, 213–16.

42. Ibid., pp. 200–2, 208–9, 214, 219, 226, 229–30. See Knesset debates (December 15, 1969) notably expressing the parties' tendency to emphasize similar and agreed subjects over topics of dissent. This being so, minorities of both Mapam and Herut called on their parties to resign from the government. See Bader's speech at Tenth Herut Conference, HA, pp. 16/6–18/8.

43. See Knesset debates on the program of the new government (December 15, 1969), vol. 56, pp. 200, 204, 207–9, 213, 215, 222, 226.

44. Hazan in Knesset (December 15, 1969), vol. 54, pp. 207–9; Golda Meir's speech at Mapai Center (September 11, 1969), inveighing even against debate on the peace issue, as long as there was no real possibility of peace, file 23/69, vol. 3, p. 42, LA. See also Knesset debates on the American peace initiative (August 4, 1970), *Divrei Haknesset*, vol. 58, pp. 2752–53, 2769, 2770, 2772.

45. See Knesset debates (December 15, 1969), pp. 207–9.

46. Eliav, interview; Y. Beilin, *The Price of Unity* (in Hebrew) (Tel Aviv: Revivim, 1985), 13–34.

47. M. Shamir and J. Sullivan, "Political Tolerance in Israel," *Magamot*, vol. 29, no. 2 (1985): 145–69.

48. For Golda Meir's relations with the Editors' Committee, see Z. Lavi, "The Editors' Committee—Myth and Reality," *Journalists' Yearbook—1987* (in Hebrew) (Tel Aviv, 1987), 63–77.

49. The electronic media were less inclined than the press to express clear political positions, since all their reports were in news editions. See ITV Archives, Romema, Jerusalem, card-index file "War of Attrition."

50. This conclusion derives from content analysis of Israeli Hebrew-language daily press. For example, in March 1969 (when war broke out), *Haaretz* made twenty-five references to the war, of which only five were critiques or commentary on government policy. This trend persisted throughout the war, in all newspapers, except for small-circulation newspapers of peripheral groups, such as Matzpen.

51. In the following subsection, the parties and extra-parliamentary political groups publicly opposing the war will be referred to in short as political groups.

52. For the attitude of the Movement for Peace and Security, see *Haaretz*, September 1, 1971. Gad Yatziv, interview by author, March 23, 1985, and Dori, interview by author, May 5, 1986; position of Maki, speech by Shmuel Mikunis, *Haaretz*, February 26, 1970, p. 2; Mapam's position, Mordechai Oren, "We Shall Pursue a Policy of Initiating Peace," *Al Hamishmar*, April 26, 1970, p. 2; position of Haolam Hazeh, Uri Avneri in Knesset (May 5, 1969), *Divrei Haknesset*, vol. 54, pp. 2349–50.

53. Movement for Peace and Security Leaflet no. 1; Yigal Laviv, "Give Peace a Chance," *Dapei Brit Hasmol*, October 1969, p. 3; Uri Avneri, "War with the Russians," *Haolam Hazeh*, no. 1714, July 8, 1970, pp. 14, 19.

54. Matzpen Manifesto, *Matzpen*, no. 54, p. 12; Gershon Rabinowitz, "In View of a Bleak Horizon and Facing Gloomy Criticisms," *Dapei Brit Hasmol*, February 1970, p. 5; Yonatan Peled, "The U.S.A., the U.S.S.R., the Middle East and All That," *Siah*, no. 12, March 1972, pp. 16–17.

55. Demonstration by the Movement for Peace and Security (April 8, 1970), *Haaretz*, April 9, 1970, p. 3.

56. Yossi Amitai, "The Case of the Fool," *Siah*, no. 5, August 1970, pp. 11, 16; Uri Avneri, "Mothers," *Haolam Hazeh*, no. 1653, May 7, 1969, p. 11.

57. Avneri, "Mothers."

58. See also, for example, *Naashush*, no. 4, 1970 (original unpaginated).

59. This subject was particularly emphasized by the Movement for Peace and Security. See Yatziv and Dori, interviews.

60. Computation based on reports of the IDF spokesman as published in *Haaretz*. These reports were verified by comparison with M. Naor's book *The War after the War* (in Hebrew) (Tel Aviv: Publishing House of the Ministry of Defense, 1970), and data were also collated in I. Raviv, "Israel's Security in the Third Year since the Six-Day War," *Maarakhot*, no. 204, January 1970, p. 11.

61. Hazan at Mapam Center (September 11, 1969), no. 18 (2) 68–90, HHA; Mikunis, "Dangerous Paralysis," *Kol Haam*, February 26, 1970, p. 2; Dayan at high school student assembly (July 28, 1970), *Haaretz*, July 29, 1970, p. 1; Begin in Knesset debate on American peace plan (August 4, 1970), *Divrei Haknesset*, vol. 58, p. 2765.

62. The Institute for Applied Social Research (May 1970), table 2; see note 27.

63. See Leaflet no. 2 of the Movement for Peace and Security, pp. 16–17 (open letter by Yehoshua Arieli to Haim Guri), Latif Dori Archive.

64. Letter from Yoram Sadeh to the government of Israel, *Haaretz*, April 19, 1970, p. 10.

65. Yatziv and Dori, interviews; Movement for Peace and Security manifesto calling for a demonstration against the government's policy in blocking peace initiatives, *Haaretz*, April 7, 1970, p. 2.

66. This fact was clearly expressed in relation to Mapam members, some of whom took part in the activity of the Movement for Peace and Security against the government in which Mapam was a member. Mapam leadership was divided on how to proceed in these matters. Bentov claimed members so desiring should be permitted this activity. Hazan was opposed. But finally Bentov's position prevailed, since the leadership saw the movement as a positive means of arousing public opinion in favor of a governmental initiative. See leaflet by Mapam Secretary-General Naftali Feder (April 1972), Latif Dori Archive.

67. A. Pesah and D. Freulich, "Report Following Government Resolution Published on July 31, 1970, Regarding the American Peace Initiative," telephone survey, August 2–3, 1970, The Institute for Applied Social Research, pp. 8–17.

68. No aggregate data are available, but inference can be drawn from the fact that retention of the cease-fire lines was the Israeli government's most emphatically declared political principle, and the basis for political cooperation between Gahal and Labor.

69. A. Razin, "For the Honey and the Sting," *The Price of Power*, ed. Z. Ofer and A. Kovar (in Hebrew) (Tel Aviv: Ministry of Defense, 1984), 48.

70. See report on demonstrations against government policy, *Haaretz*, April 9, 1970, p. 3; Eliav, interview.

71. Reference is to eighteen political groups that ran for the Seventh Knesset elections (excepting the "Abe Nathan to the Knesset List," "Young Israel," and "The Sephardi Movement" which made no impact at all on the political system) and, in addition, the Whole Eretz Israel Movement, the Committee for the Prevention of Retreat, the Canaanites, the Left Alliance, Siah, the Committee for Peace, the Sharshevski Group, and Matzpen.

Chapter Five

1. Abba Eban, *Life Story* (in Hebrew) vol. 2 (Tel Aviv: Maariv, 1978), 481–89; Gideon Rafael, *Privy to the Secrets of Nations* (in Hebrew) (Jerusalem: Edanim, 1981), 210, 228–42, 251–55. Yitzhak Rabin, *Service Log* (in Hebrew) vol. 2 (Tel Aviv: Maariv, 1979), 326–71; Yossi Beilin, *The Price*

of Unity (in Hebrew) (Tel Aviv: Revivim, 1985), 116–58. For challenges to these premises, see Mordechai Gazit, *The Peace Process* (in Hebrew) (Tel Aviv: Hakibbutz Hameuchad Publishers, 1984).

2. Regarding Moshe Dayan's appearance before the Israel Daily Press Editors Committee (October 9, 1973), see H. Bartov, *Dado* (in Hebrew) Part 2 (Tel Aviv: Maariv, 1978), 135–36.

3. For a description of war moves, see Haim Hertzog, *The People Shall Rise Up as a Great Lion* (in Hebrew) (Jerusalem: Edanim, 1981), 180–265.

4. Menachem Begin and Haim Landau at the Herut Center (January 14, 1973), *Herut Center Minutes* p. 5, HA. The term campaign over Eretz Israel was coined by Herut spokesmen themselves. See Begin and Arie Naor at Herut Center (May 30, 1973), pp. 7–8, *Herut Center Minutes* 18–19, HA.

5. Begin at Herut Center (July 31, 1973) *Herut Center Minutes* (1972–73), p. 26, HA.

6. Minutes of Herut directorate (February–October 1973) and Herut Center (December 1972–October 1973), HA; Ezer Weizmann, "Preserving Our Achievements," *Eretz Israel*, September 1972, p. 9.

7. Menachem Begin, "Leftism, Nationalism, National Awareness," *The Herut Movement* (in Hebrew) (Herut Movement Publications, 1973), 27–29.

8. Knesset debates on the release of the Munich murderers (October 31, 1972) *Divrei Haknesset*, vol. 65, p. 223.

9. Weizmann, *Preserving Our Achievements*.

10. Ibid.

11. Ezer Weizmann, "Free of Complexes," *Yediot Ahronoth*, March 29, 1972, p. 9.

12. The Likud was formed in order to foster cooperation between parties that sought to annex the West Bank and to increase Herut's chances of forming a government. The approach of the Likud, as that of its dominant faction Herut, was one of military activism. See Begin at Herut Center (July 31, 1973), *Herut Center Minutes*, p. 1, HA.

13. See Israel Galili, David Hachoen, Beni Marshak, and Moshe Carmel at Labor Party Center (February 11, 1971) file 23/71, vol. 1, pp. 8–43, LA; premier's reply to Uri Avneri's query regarding secure boundaries: *Divrei Haknesset*, vol. 60, p. 2455. That most Labor Party members aspired to retain Israeli control of the territories was reflected in the confirmation accorded by the Labor secretariat (September 3, 1973) to the formula

approved by Labor cabinet ministers (The Galili Document) whereby the government was to institute an increased settlement drive in the territories and reinforce existing settlements. See premier's statement and Carmel's speech in the Knesset (November 16, 1970) *Divrei Haknesset*, vol. 59, pp. 146, 153–55.

14. About willingness not to strike first blow, see Moshe Dayan, *Milestones* (in Hebrew) (Tel Aviv: Yediot Ahronoth, 1976), 571. Concerning Israeli dependence on the United States, Rabin, *Service Log*, 325–81; Eban, *Life Story*, 460–65.

15. For details of Egyptian breaches, see M. Dayan's reply to query by Shmuel Tamir (January 6, 1971) *Divrei Haknesset*, vol. 59, p. 857. For the responses of the architects of the national security concept, see Dayan *Milestones*, 425–55; Rabin, *Service Log*, vol. 1, pp. 302–11.

16. Eban, *Life Story*, 501–2; Golda Meir, *My Life* (in Hebrew) (Tel Aviv: Maariv, 1975), 309–10, 313; Dayan, *Milestones*, 576; Bartov, *Dado*, 10–25. Golda Meir also informed U.S. ambassador Kenneth Keating (October 6, 1973) that Israel would not strike a preemptive blow but would sustain the enemy offensive and then proceed to a counteroffensive: Bartov, *Dado*, 495.

17. Meir in Knesset (November 16, 1970), vol. 61, p. 146; Meir's speech and Labor's summarizing draft (June 5, 1972) on murder at Lod Airport, *Divrei Haknesset*, vol. 64, pp. 2676–79.

18. Knesset debate on premier's statement regarding political situation (February 9, 1971) *Divrei Haknesset*, vol. 59, pp. 1310–16. And also see Knesset debates (June 9, 1971) *Divrei Haknesset*, vol. 61, pp. 2681–83; 2685–89.

19. Yaakov Hazan in Knesset (January 24, 1973) *Divrei Haknesset*, vol. 66, pp. 1376–77; M. Bentov at Mapam Political Committee (July 26, 1973) 8 (154) 90, p. 16, HHA.

20. Mapam Political Committee debates (January 12, 1972), especially Meir Yaari 1 (154) 90, p. 33, HHA; Mapam Political Committee (October 18, 1972) 3 (154) 90, HHA.

21. Yaakov Hazan, "Our Campaign for Peace—Nature and Target," *Al Hamishmar*, August 14, 1970, p. 2; Hazan at Mapam Center, March 15, 1973, 3 (139) 90, pp. 54–64, HHA.

22. Haika Grossman in Knesset (September 12, 1972) in debate on government report of murder at Munich Olympiad, *Divrei Haknesset*, vol. 64, p. 3737. See also Mordechai Bentov, interview by author, January 12, 1984.

23. Editorial, *Al Hamishmar*, October 3, 1972, p. 1. The editorial was aimed also at the Dov Group and the Jewish Defense League, which called on the Jewish public to resort to counter-terror and attack Israeli Arabs and Palestinians in the territories in reprisal for terror.

24. *Kol Haam*, January 19, 1972, pp. 6–7; and also see S. Mikunis in Knesset (March 16, 1972) *Divrei Haknesset*, vol. 63, p. 1856.

25. *Kol Haam*, February 16, 1972, pp. 14–15; see also Maki opposition to a military response to the advance of the Egyptian missiles in August 1970; Sneh in Knesset (November 16, 1970) *Divrei Haknesset*, vol. 59, pp. 172–74.

26. S. Mikunis in Knesset on the release of the Munich murderers (October 31, 1972) *Divrei Haknesset*, vol. 65, pp. 233–34.

27. D. Bar-Nir, "Who Is Responsible for the Non-Peace?" *Shalom Ubitahon*, no. 1, January 1973, p. 4; Latif Dori movement manifesto, "A Clear Yes to the Jarring Initiative" (September 1970), Latif Dori Archives.

28. Bulletin of Peace and Security, no. 2, July 1973 (articles by Akiva Simon, Meir Pa'il, Gershon Rabinovitz, and Esther Vilenska).

29. Hazan in Knesset (January 24, 1973) *Divrei Haknesset*, vol. 66, p. 1376; Nathan Peled at Mapam Political Committee, July 26, 1973, pp. 3–11, 8 (154) 90, HHA.

30. M. Begin, "The Right and the Force," *Maariv*, May 11, 1973; M. Begin, "Likud Birth Pangs," *Maariv*, August 31, 1973.

31. Haim Landau at Herut Center (January 14, 1973) *Herut Center Minutes* (1973), p. 10, HA.

32. Most Labor election ads stressed the leadership's reliability and expertise in the economic, social, political, and security spheres.

33. *Davar*, October 5, 1973, p. 2.

34. Eden, *On the Banks of Suez*, 43–48; 62–68.

35. See, for example, *Haaretz*, October 3, 1973, p. 1; and discussion: "Freedom of the Press Versus State Security," *Monthly Review* 2 (1990): 3–16.

36. In regard to the scope of call-up in Yom Kippur War and its implications for the Israeli economy, see B. Kimmerling, *The Interrupted System* (New Brunswick: Transaction Books, 1985), 3–4, 45–81.

37. *Haaretz*, October 7, 1973, pp. 1–2; similar statement made by M. Dayan at press conference (October 14, 1973) *Haaretz*, October 15, 1973, pp. 1–2.

38. Knesset debate on government statement concerning the situation (October 16, 1973) *Divrei Haknesset*, vol. 68, pp. 4477–93.

39. Survey, "Public Morale in the First Ten Days of the Yom Kippur War," Institute for Applied Social Research, Jerusalem (October 17, 1973), pp. 13–15; Survey, "Public Morale on the Eleventh Day of the Yom Kippur War," Jerusalem (October 19, 1973), pp. 7, 12; Survey, "Public Morale Before and After the Cease-fire," Jerusalem (October 26, 1973), pp. 7, 10–11; public attitudes throughout the war were calculated based on arithmetic averages.

40. Shmuel Mikunis in Knesset (October 16, 1973) *Divrei Haknesset*, vol. 68, pp. 4490–92; *Kol Ham*, October 22, 1973, p. 4.

41. Shmuel Tamir in Knesset (October 23, 1973) *Divrei Haknesset*, vol. 68, p. 4530.

42. Knesset debates (October 16, 1973) *Divrei Haknesset*, vol. 68, pp. 4477–92.

43. See note 42, Knesset debates, pp. 4474–92; and see editorial, *Haaretz*, October 7, 1973, p. 9.

44. Bartov, *Dado*, 266–67; *Haaretz*, October 21, 1973, pp. 1, 3.

45. See Knesset debates (October 23, 1973) *Divrei Haknesset*, vol. 68, pp. 4510–41.

46. See notes 33–34.

47. Menachem Begin, "From Noon of the Day of Atonement," *Maariv*, October 12, 1973, p. 10.

48. Members of the political elite participating in the shaping of the security concept during Golda Meir's premiership were Golda Meir, Moshe Dayan, and Israel Galili.

49. Knesset debates (October 16, 1973) *Divrei Haknesset*, vol. 68, pp. 4476–93; see also summarizing draft of all house factions (except Rakah) calling (paragraph 4) on the entire nation "to stand united behind the army," *Divrei Haknesset*, vol. 68, p. 4495; and the Knesset debates (October 23, 1973) *Divrei Haknesset*, vol. 68, pp. 4512–39.

50. ITV Archives, card-index file: Yom Kippur War. See especially reports 11988/73, 12000/73, 12109/73, 12196/73, 12305/73, 12355/73, 12392/73, 12679/73, 12854/73.

51. Manifestoes of the Movement for Peace and Security (January 26, 1971), (October 22, 1972), (November 29, 1972), Latif Dori Archives; political speeches of Uri Avneri and Yaakov Hazan (June 9, 1971) *Divrei Haknesset*, vol. 61, pp. 2689, 2697.

52. S. Mikunis in Knesset (October 16, 1973) *Divrei Haknesset*, vol. 68, pp. 4491–92.

53. M. Begin in Knesset, ibid., p. 4478.

54. See note 52, Tamir in Knesset, pp. 4489–90.

55. Haim Landau, "Aims of the Campaign," *Yediot Ahronoth*, October 12, 1973, pp. 1, 10.

56. Manifesto of the Jewish Defense League, "Victory to the Arabs," *Yediot Ahronoth*, October 26, 1973, p. 20.

57. Yitzhak Ben-Aharon in Knesset (October 23, 1973) *Divrei Haknesset*, vol. 68, p. 4522.

58. Dayan, *Milestones*, pp. 609, 631, 639; Bartov, *Dado*, p. 121. Following government approval given on October 9, 1973, for bombing military targets in Damascus, the air force on that date proceeded to a bombardment in which a number of civilian targets, such as houses and hospitals, were hit; see *Haaretz*, October 10, 1973, pp. 1, 2.

59. Knesset debates (October 23, 1973) *Divrei Haknesset*, vol. 68, pp. 4510–12, 4529–30, 4538–41; M. Begin, "Not the Wars of the Jews But Discussions between Jews," *Maariv*, November 9, 1973, p. 20.

60. Knesset debates (October 23, 1973) *Divrei Haknesset*, vol. 68, pp. 4516–17, 4532–33, 4535–36.

61. See note 60, Shmuel Tamir in Knesset, p. 4530.

62. See note 60, Hurewitz in Knesset, p. 4521.

63. See note 60, Avneri in Knesset, pp. 4532–33.

64. Labor Center debates (November 28, 1973), *Minutes of Labor Center Session*, 23/73, vol. 2, pp. 13–20, 34–36, 41, 46, 55, LA.

65. Ibid.

66. Ibid. Also, Arie Lova Eliav, interview by author, May 14, 1986.

67. See Dayan's statement that if Golda Meir were to appoint him defense minister in her government he would accept since this was an emergency situation: *Haaretz*, January 15, 1974, p. 1; Golda Meir at Mapai Center, December 5, 1973.

68. A January 1974 Dahaf survey showed that 40.6 percent of the public concurred with Sharon's criticism of the conduct of the war: *Haaretz*, February 1, 1974, p. 2; Pori surveys showed that in February 1974 only 21.5 percent wanted Golda Meir as prime minister (as against 65.2 percent before the outbreak of the war): *Haaretz*, February 14, 1974, p. 1.

69. Mordechai (Motti) Ashkenazi at a demonstration organized by him, *Haaretz*, March 25, 1974, p. 3.

70. Ad by M. Ashkenazi, *Haaretz*, February 17, 1974, p. 8; for coverage of various demonstrations, see *Haaretz*, February 18, 1974, p. 3; February 22, 1974, p. 3; March 13, 1974, p. 4.

71. Amnon Rubinstein, *A Certain Degree of Political Experience* (in Hebrew) (Jerusalem: Edanim, 1982), 34–35 and the appendix.

72. Ibid.

73. Z. Raanan, *Gush Emunim* (in Hebrew) (Tel Aviv: Sifriat Poalim, 1980), 36–38.

74. Ibid., 196–97.

75. E. Don-Yehiya, "Jewish Messianism, Religious Zionism and Israeli Politics: The Impact and Origin of Gush Emunim," *Middle Eastern Studies*, 23, no. 2 (1987): 215–34.

76. See Pori survey, *Haaretz*, March 22, 1974, p. 1; *Haaretz*, December 25, 1973, p. 14.

77. Shulamit Aloni in Knesset (March 10, 1974) *Divrei Haknesset*, vol. 69, p. 611.

78. I computed the ratings of satisfied persons, as stated, throughout the entire war. See Institute of Applied Social Research, "The Cease-Fire and Peace Problems as Seen by the Israeli Public (October 21–23, 1973)" (Jerusalem, 1973) appendices 3, 7. The percentage of those satisfied was 88 percent (on average, throughout the entire war), as noted.

Chapter Six

1. Avraham Burg's speech at the "Demonstration of the Four Hundred Thousand" (September 25, 1982) *Maariv*, September 26, 1982, p. 4.

2. Speech by Victor Shem-Tov at Mapam Political Committee (November 12, 1973) 14 (154) 90, p. 3, HHA; speeches by Nathan Peled and Naftali Ben-Moshe at Mapam Political Committee (October 28, 1973), 13 (154) 90, pp. 7, 33, HHA.

3. *Labor Center Sessions* (January 31, 1974–February 24, 1974), 23/74, vol. 3, LA, especially speech by Haim Bar-Lev, pp. 21–23. For U.S. administration warnings to Israel after the Yom Kippur War not to initiate a preventive offensive and their effects on the Israeli security concept, see E.

Inbar, *Israeli Strategic Thought in the Post-1973 Period* (Jerusalem: Israel Research Institute of Contemporary Society, 1982), 3.

4. Knesset debates on government announcement of disengagement agreement with Egypt, *Divrei Haknesset*, vol. 69, p. 53.

5. See Alignment Eighth Knesset electoral platform and also Labor Center Sessions, note 3.

6. Knesset debates on government resolution to sign disengagement agreement with Syria (May 30, 1974) *Divrei Haknesset*, vol. 70, pp. 1463–64 (Elimelech Rimalt), 1467–70 (Menachem Begin), 1478–79 (Shmuel Tamir); Knesset debate on government announcement of interim agreement with Egypt (September 3, 1975) *Divrei Haknesset*, vol. 74, p. 4134 (Likud draft summation).

7. *Divrei Haknesset* (January 22, 1974), vol. 69, p. 48.

8. For explanations of the terms tactical war of attrition, strategic war of attrition, and war of initiative, see D. Horowitz, "Constant and Variable in the Israeli Security Concept," *War of Alternative* (in Hebrew) (Tel Aviv: Jaffe Center for Strategic Studies, 1985), 93–100. For Shmuel Tamir's comments, see motion to the agenda to discuss the war of attrition in the north (April 29, 1974) *Divrei Haknesset*, vol. 70, p. 1167.

9. Moshe Nissim and Ariel Sharon in Knesset debates on attempt to establish settlement in Sebastia (July 31,1974) *Divrei Haknesset*, vol. 71, pp. 2550, 2565–68.

10. See Meir Pail (Moked) in Knesset (May 20, 1974) regarding the government announcement of terrorist attack on Maalot, *Divrei Haknesset*, vol. 70, pp. 1335–36.

11. See Sharon in Knesset debate (April 17, 1974) on terrorist attack on Kiryat Shmoneh, *Divrei Haknesset*, vol. 70, pp. 1157–58; Begin, Sharon, and Tamir in Knesset debate (May 20, 1974) on terrorist attack on Maalot, *Divrei Haknesset*, vol. 70, pp. 1310–13, 1320, 1339.

12. Begin in Knesset (May 20, 1974) *Divrei Haknesset*, vol. 70, pp. 1310–11.

13. See Yitzhak Rabin, "Lebanon, the Storm and the Quiet," *Yediot Ahronoth* (Saturday Supplement), September 30, 1977, p. 1.

14. Yitzhak Rabin, *Service Log*, vol. 2 (Tel Aviv: Maariv, 1979), 503. Z. Schieff and E. Yaari, *The Garden-Path War* (in Hebrew) (Jerusalem, Tel Aviv: Schocken, 1984), 46–51; S. Schiffer, *P.G.C. Snowball, Secrets of the Lebanese War* (in Hebrew) (Tel Aviv: Edanim, Yediot Ahronoth, 1984), 22–23.

15. Sharon at Herut Center (September 21, 1981) *Herut Center Minutes* (1979–81), pp. 18–20, HA; Yosef Rom at Herut Center (August 30, 1978) *Herut Center Minutes* (1978), pp. 4–5, HA; Eitan Livni, interview by author, May 4, 1986.

16. Conference Minutes, p. 2, HA.

17. Ezer Weizmann, *The Battle for the Peace* (in Hebrew) (Tel Aviv: Edanim, 1981), 249–57; also lecture by Mordechai Gur on Operation Litani, "Dapei Elazar," (in Hebrew), p. 49.

18. See Weizmann, in note 17.

19. Weizmann, *The Battle for the Peace*, 250–56; Rafael Eitan, *Story of a Soldier* (in Hebrew) (Tel Aviv: Maariv, 1985), 161–62.

20. See speech by Sharon, note 15, pp. 18–19; Sharon at Herut Center (August 24, 1980) *Herut Center Minutes* (1980), p. 27, HA; Begin at Herut Center (November 19, 1981) *Herut Center Minutes* (1981), pp. 20–21, HA; also "Speech That Was Never Delivered," a speech that was to have been delivered by the then Minister of Defense Sharon, before a symposium of the Jaffe Center for Strategic Studies (December 19, 1981); text of speech appears in *War of Alternative*, ed. A. Yariv (Tel Aviv: Jaffe Center for Strategic Studies, 1985), 157–59.

21. See Sharon's speech, note 15, p. 20; A. Naor, *Government in War* (in Hebrew) (Jerusalem: Hebrew University, 1986), 29–31; Z. Schieff and E. Yaari, *The Garden-Path War*, 38.

22. Sharon's speech, note 15, p. 20.

23. Sharon's speech, ibid.

24. Speech at Herut Conference, *Minutes of National Conference*, HA.

25. For that strategy, see D. Horowitz, "Military Thinking and Civilian-Military Relations," *Israeli Society and Its Defense Establishment* ed. M. Lissak (London: Frank Cass, 1984), 83–102; A. Yaniv, *Dilemmas of Security* (New York: Oxford University Press, 1987).

26. Schieff and Yaari, *The Garden-Path War*, 94–111.

27. *Divrei Haknesset*, vol. 91 (2) p. 2634.

28. See Labor Party Bureau Resolution (January 1982) "Migvan," 72 (August 1982): 47–49; Rabin's statement that Israel should not presume to solve problems of terrorism by extensive use of armed force nor should any military operation be initiated unless a war of attrition developed on the northern frontier, *Al Hamishmar*, June 3, 1982, p. 3.

29. Victor Shem-Tov, interview by author, June 12, 1986.

30. See Knesset debates on the fighting (June 8, 1982) *Divrei Haknesset*, vol. 94, pp. 2735–47.

31. See Israel Government Communiqué (June 6, 1982), from the *Israel Government Yearbook* (1983), p. 17; Begin in Knesset (June 8, 1982), *Divrei HaKnesset*, Vol. 94, p. 2747.

32. Shem-Tov, interview. Shem-Tov was present at those meetings with Likud leaders Sharon and Begin; Shulamit Aloni, interview by author, May 12, 1986. Yitzhak Rabin, interview in *Migvan* 72 (August 1982): 3–4.

33. For Rubinstein's position see interview with Aloni, who had discussed the matter with Rubinstein; for Peres's statement, see *Davar*, June 7, 1982, p. 2.

34. *Divrei Haknesset* (June 8, 1982) vol. 94, p. 2747.

35. See *Maariv*, June 7, 1982, p. 2; televised confrontation between MK Ehud Olmert and Gad Yaakobi (February 5, 1984) on "New Evening." Concerning "fog of war" in the first five days of the fighting, see the then-IDF Brigadier General Yaakov Even, interview on radio program "Strategic Depth" (April 2, 1984).

36. Schieff and Yaari, *The Garden-Path War*, 97–98, 105–6, 117–18; S. Schiffer, *Secrets of the Lebanese War*, 92–94; Naor, *Government in War*, 47–52; Yitzhak Berman, interview by author, May 2, 1986.

37. See *Haaretz*, November 18, 1982.

38. Berman, interview, see note 36.

39. The few exceptions to this rule, such as Aloni and Sarid, openly expressed opposition to the war. See *Divrei Haknesset* (June 8, 1982), vol. 94, p. 2736 (interjection by Shulamit Aloni).

40. *Maariv*, June 15, 1982 (report on Knesset Foreign Affairs and Defense Committee session of June 14, 1982), p. 2; *Maariv*, June 20, 1982 (report on Alignment Political Forum session of June 19, 1982), p. 2; also, see Shimon Peres in Knesset (June 8, 1982) *Divrei Haknesset*, vol. 94, p. 2738; Shem-Tov, interview.

41. *Al Hamishmar*, June 7, 1982, p. 2. Also see Rabin's Statement, *Maariv*, June 11, 1982, p. 20.

42. Interview in *Al Hamishmar*, June 8, 1982, p. 2.

43. *Al Hamishmar*, June 11, 1982, p. 2 (Clause 4 of Resolutions).

44. A. Etzioni, *Demonstration Democracy* (New York: Gordon and Breach, 1970); R. M. Fogelson, *Violence and Protest* (New York: Doubleday, 1971).

45. About the developments in Peace Now Movement, see L. Galili, "What Is Happening in Peace Now," *Haaretz*, July 8, 1982; Mordechai Baron, *Peace Now—Portrait of a Movement* (in Hebrew) (Tel Aviv: Hakibbutz Hameuhad, 1985), 54–56.

46. See *Divrei Haknesset* (June 8, 1982), vol. 94, pp. 2735–47.

47. See Berman, Shem-Tov, and Aloni, interviews; also see Tamar Eshel, "Not Opposing a Just War," *Migvan* 72 (August 1982): 29–32 (especially p. 32).

48. See, for example, Yitzhak Rabin, *The War in Lebanon* (in Hebrew) (Tel Aviv: Am Oved, 1983), 37–38. On date of speech (June 11, 1982), IDF forces were several dozen kilometers beyond the 40 km. See also *Alignment Faction Sessions* (June 8, 1982), in *Hadashot*, special edition "Third Anniversary of the Lebanese War," June 7, 1985, pp. 21–23. These minutes were not denied by party spokesmen. Peres is quoted as saying that support should not be given to the "communists" in their motion of nonconfidence in the government (June 8, 1982).

49. See S. Feldman and H. Rechnitz-Kijner, *Deception, Consensus and War: Israel in Lebanon* (in Hebrew) (Tel Aviv: Jaffe Center for Strategic Studies, 1984).

50. *Divrei Haknesset* (June 8, 1982) vol. 94, pp. 2735–47; Aloni and Shem-Tov, interviews; see also Mapam Convention's resolution denouncing the Lebanese War, *Al Hamishmar*, June 11, 1982, p. 2 (Clause 4 of the Resolutions).

51. See Aloni, interview.

52. Meir Vilner in Knesset (June 8, 1982) *Divrei Haknesset*, vol. 94, pp. 2735–36.

53. Aloni, for example, declared during the debate that she was one of those who were prepared to listen to Rakah's criticism of the war, see note 50, p. 2736. In general, the speeches of Tewfiq Toubi and Meir Vilner did not elicit much reaction during the debates.

54. See *Maariv*, June 15, 1982, p. 2; *Maariv*, June 20, 1982, p. 2; Knesset debates (June 23, 1982) *Divrei Haknesset*, vol. 94, pp. 2889–93.

55. See M. Bar-On, *Peace Now*, 54–57; Shem-Tov, interview. For an example of the disillusionment of Labor-camp members with the responses of the Labor Party leadership shown in the forming of the Ometz group,

see *Maariv*, July 21, 1982, p. 3. Shimon Peres, on the other hand, plainly stated, at the beginning of the war, his objection to demonstrations: *Haaretz*, July 11, 1982. See also Zali Reshef, interview in *Yediot Ahronoth*, 7-Day Supplement, April 11, 1985, pp. 8–9.

56. See statement by Peace Now, warning against escalation toward war in Lebanon, *Haaretz*, June 5, 1982; query by Peace Now, "What Are They Dying For?" *Haaretz*, June 16, 1982; Movement caution to Deputy Prime Minister Simha Erlich, to refrain from occupying Beirut, *Haaretz*, June 23, 1982.

57. See, for instance, the Alignment arguments in Knesset of whether west Beirut should be occupied, *Maariv*, June 30, 1982, p. 3. Of this issue from standpoint of the then CGS Rafael Eitan, see R. Eitan, *Story of a Soldier*, 266–301.

58. See interview with Rabin, *Migvan* 72 (August 1982): 2–9; Peres in Knesset (June 8, 1982) *Divrei Haknesset*, vol. 94, p. 2739; and Rubinstein in Knesset (June 23,1982), *Divrei Haknesset*, Vol. 94, pp. 2890–91.

59. Berman, interview; also Schieff and Yaari, *The Garden-Path War*, 225–26, 261–62.

60. Alignment draft summation in Knesset re "Peace for Galilee Campaign" (September 8, 1982) *Divrei Haknesset*, vol. 94, pp. 3637–38; Y. Rabin, *The War in Lebanon*, 48. Also report on positions of Alon Circle in Labor, see *Maariv*, July 5, 1982, p. 3.

61. Speech in Knesset (June 23, 1982) *Divrei Haknesset*, vol. 94, p. 2891.

62. *Maariv*, July 9, 1982, p. 21.

63. Quoting Sharon at Knesset Foreign Affairs and Defense Committee, *Maariv*, June 28, 1982, p. 2.

64. As per TV program "This Week—Diary of Events," *Maariv*, June 27, 1982, p. 4.

65. *Maariv*, July 2, 1982 (weekend edition), p. 5. In regard to political aims of the war, see also statement by Foreign Minister Yitzhak Shamir, *Haaretz*, July 30, 1982, p. 1, indicating that, concerning terrorism, the aim of the war was to get the terrorists out of Beirut by armed force and to liquidate the PLO. See also report on Foreign Affairs and Defense Committee, *Haaretz*, June 25, 1982, p. 2. Sharon enumerating war aims for the committee: (a) minimal objective—purge of an area of 45 km of terrorists; and two additional aims: (b) ejection of all foreign forces from Lebanon; (c) laying of groundwork for a sovereign, stable, independent regime in Lebanon, which

would want a peace agreement with Israel. See also, statement by Sharon at Knesset Foreign Affairs and Defense Committee, *Maariv*, June 28, 1982, p. 2.

66. *Maariv*, August 20, 1982, p. 20.

67. See I. Shiloni, *Three Circles of Lebanon* (in Hebrew) (Tel Aviv: Yosef Sherbrak, 1986). See also testimony of Ran Cohen on debates in the army, *Maariv*, July 23, 1982, p. 23. Report on statements by Eli Geva about his resignation from post of OC Brigade, *Maariv*, July 26, 1982, p. 1; report on Soldiers Against Silence and their objection to the breaching of Beirut, *Maariv*, August 10, 1982, p. 9; reports on demonstrations by soldiers (demobbed or on leave) and on debates in the army, *Maariv*, August 13, 1982, p. 20; report on resignation of Brigadier-General Amram Mitzna from command of Staff and Command School, *Maariv*, September 24, 1982, p. 3; report on debates in the army and opposition to the war, Y. Erez, "Lebanese Sand Table," *Maariv*, September 24, 1982, p. 14.

68. *Maariv*, August 10, 1982; *Maariv*, September 24, 1982.

69. Deputy CGS Moshe Levi, interview in *Maariv*, July 9, 1982, p. 2.

70. *Maariv*, July 14, 1982, p. 1; *Maariv*, September 24, 1982, p. 1.

71. See note 67, especially reports of Shiloni and Erez.

72. See *Maariv*, August 10, 1982, p. 9; report on protest of demobbed soldiers via Yesh Gvul, see *Maariv*, July 14, 1982, p. 3; report on Soldiers Against Silence, *Maariv*, July 23, 1982, p. 3.

73. See *Minutes of Peace Now Secretariat*, September 5, 1983, Movement Archives; also Naftali Raz, "From Protest Movement to Initiatory Movement," Movement Archives.

74. S. H. Barnes and M. Kaase, eds. *Political Action* (Beverly Hills: Sage Publications, 1979).

75. See notes 72 and 73; *Minutes of Peace Now Secretariat* (1982–84).

76. Aloni, Shem-Tov, and Dori, interviews.

77. For report on demonstration, see *Maariv*, July 4, 1982, p. 3. Re the tactical approach: at Peace Now Secretariat meetings, members stated that demonstrations were an effective means of getting messages across, and many, such as Zali Reshef, opposed cooperation with other political bodies for fear of compromising the distinctiveness of their movement, see *Minutes of Peace Now Secretariat* (1982–84), Movement Archives.

78. Analysis based on various articles in I. Menuhin, ed., *Limit to Obedience* (in Hebrew) (Tel Aviv: Yesh Gvul, 1986), and on statements by

group spokesmen: *Maariv*, July 14, 1982, p. 3; September 7, 1982, p. 9; *Haaretz*, May 8, 1983, July 11, 1983, July 24, 1983.

79. *Haaretz*, November 29, 1983; "Glance at the News," ITV, December 16, 1983.

80. For report on Soldiers Against Silence, see *Maariv*, July 12, 1982, p. 3.

81. According to Dahaf survey, 51 percent. See *Monitin*, no. 50 (October 1982): 89; other findings (about 30 percent) per Pori: *Haaretz*, January 3, 1982.

82. *Maariv*, September 29, 1982, p. 2 (report on Alignment Directorate Meeting); Shimon Peres in Knesset (September 22, 1982) *Divrei Haknesset*, vol. 94, pp. 3685–86.

83. According to Pori survey, *Haaretz*, November 18, 1982. According to Dahaf survey, 19–29 percent negated the war at this stage—see *Monitin*, no. 51 (November 1982). But the Dahaf survey did not distinguish between absolute negation of the war and negation of some of its objectives. Rate of opposition to the war was thus probably higher than shown by Dahaf findings.

84. See Knesset debates (June 23, 1982) *Divrei Haknesset*, vol. 94, pp. 2889–91 (Shinui), 2903–6 (Rakah); Knesset debates (January 3, 1983) *Divrei Haknesset*, vol. 95, pp. 834–35 (Mapam) and also Knesset debates (October 31, 1983), pp. 87–89 (Alignment).

85. See Knesset speech by Haim Druckman (June 29, 1982), denouncing the "high-minded" who opposed a "defensive war than which none could be more amply justified," *Divrei Haknesset*, vol. 94, p. 2948, and Sharon in Knesset (September 22, 1982) claiming that the terrorists were deriving encouragement from demonstrations in Israel, pp. 3698–99; *Maariv*, September 30, 1982, p. 3, report on debates of Knesset Foreign Affairs and Defense Committee; Yochanan Bader, "Demonstrations or New Elections," *Maariv*, September 30, 1982, p. 5.

86. *Maariv*, June 29, 1982, p. 2 (Sharon); *Maariv*, June 29, 1982, p. 4 (Council of Judea and Samaria); *Maariv*, July 16, 1982, p. 22 (Yitzhak Shamir); *Maariv*, August 1, 1982, p. 3 (Begin); *Maariv*, August 29, 1982 (Roni Milo).

87. See note 86, declarations by Begin, Shamir, and Sharon, and also statement by Sharon on ITV that the war was for peace between Lebanon and Israel, and that the well-being of Lebanon was also the well-being of Israel, *Maariv*, June 27, 1982, p. 4. And, also A. Arian, *Public Opinion in Israel and the Lebanese War* (in Hebrew) (Tel Aviv: Jaffe Center for Strategic Studies, 1985).

88. Based on figures of the IDF spokesman; see also IDF spokesman's statement on June 10, 1985, on conclusion of withdrawal from Lebanon, as published in "Monthly Review" on the fortieth anniversary of Israel's independence; see also U. Benziman, *Haaretz,* "Third Anniversary of the Lebanese War," June 1, 1985, p. 3.

89. D. Horowitz, E. Sivan, Y. Porat, et al., eds. *The Superfluous War—Questions and Answers on the War in Lebanon* (in Hebrew) (Tel Aviv: Sha'al, 1983), 14–15.

90. For report on breach of cease-fire by Palestinians, see Y. Erez, "The Northern Borders: The Clock Hands Stopped a Minute before Twelve," *Maariv,* May 14, 1982, p. 13; also, *Maariv,* May 9, 1982, p. 3.

91. *Divrei HaKnesset,* vol. 94, pp. 2889–91; 2903–6.

92. This conclusion is indicated by the following: in early February 1984, 67.6 percent believed the PLO had been militarily weakened by the war and 47.5 percent that it had been politically weakened by the war. Despite this, only 31.3 percent (Pori) considered war beyond 40 km justified, see *Haaretz,* February 10, 1984; *Haaretz,* February 3, 1984.

93. Data collated from Pori and Dahaf. See *Haaretz,* November 22, 1982, January 4, 1983, February 13, 1983, and June 14, 1983—concerning public opinion as to whether the Likud was suitable to form a government; *Haaretz,* August 4, 1982, November 8, 1982, December 21, 1982, February 8, 1983, May 8, 1983, June 26, 1983, November 9, 1983, February 13, 1984—as to degree of popularity of the various persons. *Haaretz,* August 5, 1982, November 22, 1982, January 4, 1983, February 13, 1983—about the assessment of government performance. See also findings on assortment of attitudes to the Lebanese War in the Likud and in the Labor Party, *Monitin,* no. 58 (June 1983) (findings of Dahaf).

94. See, for example, S. Rosenfeld, "Attrition at the Gates of Beirut," *Maariv,* July 30, 1982, p. 14.

95. Especially sensational was a February 1984 ITV broadcast showing paratroopers singing protest songs against Defense Minister Sharon before the TV cameras.

96. Re "Israeli fighting press," see D. Goren, *Communication and Reality* (in Hebrew) (Jerusalem: Keter, 1986), 163.

97. See *Haaretz,* July 22, 1982, p. 2; *Haaretz,* July 21, 1982, p. 1; Y. Kotler, "Peace by the Marksman's Weapons—Between 'Peace' and 'Security,'" *Maariv,* August 13, 1982, p. 17.

98. Clearly in evidence was the influence of ethnic and religious factors. The leaders of all protest groups, other than Mizrah Leshalom (The

Orient for Peace) were Ashkenazis (of Western or Eastern European origin), as were the vast majority of their activists, members, and supporters. One of the purposes of Mizrah Leshalom was to change all of that. Similarly, most religious citizens supported the war, as against the preponderance of secularists among its detractors. See A. Arian, *Public Opinion in Israel and the Lebanese War*.

99. Re Tehiya positions in favor of the Lebanese War, see Yuval Neeman, *Open-Eyed Policy* (in Hebrew) (Ramat-Gan: Revivim, 1984), 109–11; speech by Geulah Cohen in Knesset (June 23, 1982) *Divrei Haknesset*, vol. 94, p. 2897. For defamation of opponents of the war, see notes 85, 86.

100. See Knesset debates (February 15, 1983) *Divrei Haknesset*, vol. 96, pp. 1340–1420, and especially pp. 1418–20 (draft summation).

101. See Pori findings, *Haaretz*, December 27, 1984, September 19, 1984, February 6, 1985. This is compatible with the opposition of a considerable proportion of Likud voters to war beyond 40 km.

102. See Eitan Livni, interview; and also *Maariv*, January 11, 1985, p. 11; *Maariv*, January 14, 1985, p. 1.

103. For use of this term in connection with the Lebanese War, see Z. Lanier, "Political Goals and Military Targets in Israel's Wars," *War of Alternative*, 117–56.

104. Shem-Tov, in interview by the author, attested to the content of Begin's talks with him and with Peres and Rabin; also Berman, interview; see also Begin's article in support of "War of Alternative," *Maariv*, August 20, 1982, p. 20. Begin was present at all his party's debates detailing the Great Pines plan and did not object to it.

105. See testimony of protest movement activist Bar-On, *Peace Now*, 22–125.

106. *Herut Directorate Sessions*, April 16, 1974, July 28, 1974 (speeches by Haim Landau and Eitan Livni).

107. Only in a very few instances were Rakah members subjected, in Knesset debates, to cries of "shame" because of their position on the Lebanese War. Regarding most topics pertinent to the war—its political goals, its moves, and the number of casualties—Rakah was ahead of other political groups, who echoed its own positions only at a later stage. See also interview with MK Vilner, *Yediot Ahronoth*, July 15, 1984, p. 3. Vilner attests that in the course of the Lebanese War, an unprecedented number of Jewish activists joined his party.

108. See Rabin's statement, *Maariv*, August 30, 1985, p. 2; Mordechai Gur's answers to viewers' questions on TV program "There Is a Question,"

September 6, 1985; Rabin's speech at Tel Aviv University, *Kol Israel*, May 22, 1986. Rabin stated in this forum that "all attempts to impose a political solution by the use of armed force have failed." Rabin's statements on TV program "Meet the Press" (NBC) as published in *Maariv*, December 30, 1985, pp. 1, 9.

Chapter Seven

1. H. D. Lasswell, "The Garrison State," *American Journal of Sociology* 46 (1941): 455–68.

2. G. Goldberg, G. Barzilai, and E. Inbar, *The Impact of Intercommunal Conflict: The Intifada and Israeli Public Opinion* (Jerusalem: The Leonard Davis Institute, 1991).

3. Ibid., 38–45.

4. A. H. Barton, *Communities in Disaster* (New York: Anchor Books, 1969), 63–322.

5. Avraham Burg, "To Be a Carnivorous Dove," *Davar*, September 18, 1990, p. 7.

6. Yossi Sarid, "Let Them Come Look for Me," *Haaretz*, August 17, 1990, p. 13.

7. L. A. Coser, *The Functions of Social Conflict* (New York: The Free Press, 1956); G. Simmel, *Conflict* (Glencoe: The Free Press, 1955).

8. C. Rossiter, *Constitutional Dictatorship* (New York: Harper & Row, 1963).

9. M. Shaw, *War, State and Society* (London: Macmillan Press, 1984).

10. M. Stohl, *War and Domestic Political Violence* (Beverly Hills: Sage Publications, 1976).

11. For an expanded treatment of this topic, see G. Barzilai and Y. Shain, "Israeli Democracy at a Crossroads: A Crisis of Non-Governability," *Government and Opposition*, vol. 26 (3) (July 1991): 345–67.

12. HCJ 168/91, Miladi Murcus v. the Minister of Defense et al., *Piskei Din*, vol. 45 (1): 467.

13. See Knesset debates over MK Rehavam Zeevi joining the government, February 5, 1991, *Divrei Haknesset*, vol. 120, pp. 2030–55.

14. S. Levi, "Support for the Government: As during the Six-Day War," *Maariv*, February 1, 1991, p. 7. The author reports on the surveys run by the

Institute for Applied Social Research, Jerusalem; see also the report on a telephone survey run by the same institute: *Haaretz*, January 28, 1991, p. 3a.

15. Ibid. Also see Z. Segal and G. Barzilai, "An Administration Bereft of Goodwill," *Haaretz*, February 14, 1991, p. 2b.

16. See note 14.

17. See report by Roni Shaked on the survey conducted by the Institute for Applied Social Research, Jerusalem, dated June 1991: *Yediot Ahronoth*, June 7, 1991, p. 4; for analysis of dispositions of the public and the elites, see G. Barzilai, G. Goldberg, and E. Inbar, "Israeli Leadership and Public Attitudes toward Federal Solutions for the Arab-Israeli Conflict before and after Desert Storm" *Publius* 21 (summer 1991): 191–209; G. Barzilai and I. Peleg, "Israel and Future Borders: Assessment of a Dynamic Process," *Journal of Peace Research* 31, no. 1 (1994): 59–73.

Chapter Eight

1. See E. Yaari and Z. Schieff, *Intifada: The Palestinian Uprising* (New York: Simon & Schuster, 1990).

2. This notion appears in D. J. Gerner, *One Land, Two Peoples: The Conflict over Palestine* (Boulder: Westview Press, 1991). For additional analysis of this encounter, see R. O. Freedman, ed., *The Intifada: Its Impact on Israel, the Arab World, and the Superpowers* (Miami: Florida International University Press, 1991); see especially the articles by A. Arian, R. O. Freedman, and K. W. Stein; J. S. Migdal and B. Kimmerling, *Palestinians: The Making of People* (New York: The Free Press, 1993); I. Peleg and O. Seliktar, eds., *The Emergence of Binational Israel: The Second Republic in the Making* (Boulder: Westview Press, 1989); D. Peretz, *Intifada: The Palestinian Uprising* (Boulder: Westview Press, 1990).

3. For details, see G. Barzilai, "Israel," *Middle East Contemporary Survey*, 13 (1989): 419–45

4. For this declaration of Shimon Peres, see Israeli TV, February 8, 1989.

5. See G. Barzilai, "A Jewish Democracy at War: Attitudes of Secular Jewish Political Parties in Israel toward the Question of War (1949–88)," *Comparative Strategy* 9 (1990): 179–94.

6. I would like to acknowledge Professors E. Inbar and G. Goldberg for their fruitful participation in this research project. For the various distributions of the findings, see G. Barzilai, G. Goldberg, and E. Inbar, "Israeli

Leadership and Public Attitudes toward Federal Solutions for the Arab-Israeli Conflict before and after Desert Storm," *Publius* 21 (Summer 1991): 191–209.

7. Ibid.

8. *Maariv*, October 2, 1989. The full protocols of the trial have not been publicly published.

9. *Haaretz*, Friday Bulletin, April 12, 1997; the annual report of the Israeli Information Center for Human Rights in the Occupied Territories (1989), p. 100. The full protocols of the trial have not been publicly published.

10. The data is based on the monthly and annual reports of B'Tselem, The Israel Information Center for Human Rights in the Occupied Territories.

11. HCJ 358/88 The Civil Rights Association v. The Commander of the Central Area, *Piskei Din*, vol. 43 (2): 529. The decision was made in 1989. Also see the *New York Times*, August 12, 1989; *Maariv*, December 6, 1989.

12 See: HCJ 5973/92 The Civil Rights Association V. The Ministry of Defense (28.1.1993).

13. *Jerusalem Post*, December 7, 1989.

14. See, for example, *Maariv*, October 22, 1989.

15. See G. Barzilai and Y. Shain, "Israeli Democracy at the Crossroads: A Crisis of Non-Governability," *Government and Opposition* 26, no. 3 (1991): 345–67. For an analysis of the origins of Jewish fundamentalism, see I. Lustick, *For the Land and the Lord: Jewish Fundamentalism in Israel* (New York: Council on Foreign Relations, 1988).

16. Barzilai and Shain, "Israeli Democracy."

17. Reports of B'Tselem, the Israeli Information Center for Human Rights in the Occupied Territories.

18. See G. Goldberg, G. Barzilai, and E. Inbar, *The Impact of Intercommunal Conflict: The Intifada and Israeli Public Opinion* (Jerusalem: Leonard Davis Institute, 1991); Barzilai, Goldberg, and Inbar, "Israeli Leadership"; A. Arian and R. Ventura, *Israeli Public Opinion and the Intifada: Changes in Security Attitudes 1987–1988* (Tel Aviv: Jaffe Center for Strategic Studies, 1989); M. Shamir and A. Arian, "The Intifada and Israeli Voters: Policy Preferences and Performance Evaluations," *Elections in Israel—1988*, ed. A. Arian and M. Shamir (Boulder: Westview Press, 1990). The data for 1992 and 1993 are based on my public opinion polls with E. Inbar.

19. Goldberg, Barzilai, and Inbar, *The Impact of Inter-communal Conflict*; Barzilai, Goldberg, and Inbar, "Israeli Leadership and Public Attitudes"; Arian and Ventura, *Israeli Public Opinion*; Shamir and Arian, "The Intifada and Israeli Voters." The data for 1992 and 1993 are based on my public opinion polls with E. Inbar.

20. See note 18.

21. G. Barzilai and I. Peleg, "Israel and Future Borders: Assessment of a Dynamic Process,"; G. Barzilai, "Territory, State and Power: The 1992 Elections," in E. Karsh and G. Mahler (eds.) *Israel at a Crossroads: the Challenge of Peace* (London: British Academic Press, New York: St. Martin's Press, 1994), 137–50; A. Arian, M. Shamir, "Two Reversals: Why 1992 was not 1977," in A. Arian and M. Shamir, *The Elections in Israel 1992* (Albany: State University of New York Press, 1995) 17–53.

Chapter Nine

1. See, for example, speech by Israeli President Chaim Weizmann at inaugural session of constituent assembly (February 14, 1949) *Divrei Haknesset*, vol. 1, pp. 5–7; D. Horowitz, M. Lissak, *From Yishuv to State* (in Hebrew) (Tel Aviv: Am Oved, 1977), 272–316. Nevertheless it was, as defined by Shapiro, a procedural democracy: Y. Shapiro, *Democracy in Israel* (in Hebrew) (Ramat-Gan: Massada, 1977), 18–46.

2. Z. Ofer, A. Kovar, eds., *The Price of Power* (in Hebrew) (Tel Aviv: Maarakhot, 1984), 33–73; R. Teitlebaum, *Society, Security and All That Lies Between* (in Hebrew) (Tel Aviv: The Peace Center, Forum for Social Justice and Peace, 1989).

3. E. Sprinzak, *Every Man Whatsoever Is Right in His Own Eyes—Illegality in Israeli Society* (in Hebrew) (Tel Aviv: Sifriat Poalim, 1986), 121–45.

4. Yochanan Bader, "The Peace of Galilee and the Unity of the Nation," *Maariv*, June 24, 1982, p. 5; Ariel Sharon, interview on ITV: "This Week—Diary of Events," report in *Maariv*, June 27, 1982, p. 4.

5. B. Kimmerling, *The Interrupted System—Israeli Civilians in War and Routine Times* (New Brunswick: Transaction Books, 1985).

6. D. Horowitz, "Is Israel a Garrison State?" *The Jerusalem Quarterly* 4 (summer 1977): 58–75.

7. G. Barzilai and B. Russett, "The Political Economy of Israeli Military Action," *Elections in Israel—1988*, ed. A. Arian and M. Shamir (Boulder: Westview Press, 1988), 13–35.

8. For an analysis of various aspects of refusalism in Israel, see L. Sheleff, *Conscientious Refusalism Out of Civil Loyalty* (in Hebrew) (Tel Aviv: Ramot, 1989); G. Doron, "Conscientious Refusalism as a Regulator of Policy," *International Problems: Society and State* 28 (1989): 26–35.

9. HCJ 734/83, Shein v. Minister of Defense, *Piskei Din* 38 (3): 393.

10. Ibid.

11. Ibid., 403 (Verdict of Justice Menachem Alon).

12. Elections Appeal (E.A.) 1/65 Yerdor vs. Sixth Knesset Central Elections Committee, *Piskei Din* 19 (3): 365, 390.

13. See Amendment no. 9 to the Basic Law: The Knesset (adopted in Knesset on July 31, 1985).

14. As distinct from the situation in the United States and Germany, HCJ was not empowered to nullify laws passed by Knesset on the grounds that they are contrary to basic democratic tenets. Here there prevailed the principle of the sovereignty of the Knesset, even though, in practice, HCJ sometimes construed individual rights in Israel very broadly.

15. E.A. 2/88 Yehoram Ben Shalom et al. vs. Twelfth Knesset Central Elections Committee and Progressive Peace List, *Piskei Din* 43 (4): 221 (especially: 246–47).

16. HCJ 73/53, 87/53 "Kol Haam" and "Al Itihad" vs. Minister of the Interior, *Piskei Din* 7 (2): 871; HCJ 680/88 Schnitzer vs. Chief Military Censor, *Piskei Din* 42 (4): 617.

17. N. Wahl, *The Fifth Republic* (New York: Random House, 1959), 16–22, 84–86; see Kerkheide, "Anthony Eden and the Suez Crisis of 1956" (Ph.D. diss., Case Western Reserve University, 1972), 305–38.

18. See tabulation of public opinion polls' results: R. Chandler, *Public Opinion* (New York: Bowker, 1972), 180, 182; R. S. Erikson and N. R. Luttbeg, *American Public Opinion* (New York: John Wiley, 1973), 52, 175–79; J. Mueller, *War, Presidents and Public Opinion* (New York: John Wiley, 1973) 152.

19. See Y. Shavit, *Restraint or Response 1936–1939* (in Hebrew) (Ramat-Gan: Bar Ilan University Press, 1983).

20. "Ariel Sharon's Speech" ("The Speech That Was Never Delivered"), December 19, 1981, *War of Alternative*, ed. A. Yariv (in Hebrew) (Tel Aviv: Jaffe Center for Strategic Studies, 1985), 160.

21. P. A. Sorokin, *Man and Society in Calamity* (New York: E. P. Dutton, 1942), 11–26; B. Bahnson, "Emotional Reactions to Internally and Exter-

nally Derived Threat of Annihilation," *The Threat of Impending Disaster*, ed. G. H. Grosser et al. (Cambridge: MIT Press, 1964), 251–80.

22. Kimmerling, *The Interrupted System*, 45–81.

23. Military reserve service in Israel applies to men up to age 54, causing economic damage on the collective level while millions of work hours are lost per year. Economic damage is also sustained on the individual level, particularly by the self-employed, who are hard put to run small businesses while also serving long stints of reserve duty. See Kimmerling, *Interrupted System*, 45–81, 90–91; debate on the impact of the economic-psychological burden on emigration from Israel, see Y. Cohen, "The Israeli-Arab Conflict and Emigration," *Magamot* 32, no. 4 (January 1990): 433–47.

24. See J. Habermas, ed., *Observations on the Spiritual Situation of the Age* (Cambridge: M.I.T. Press, 1985), 1–28; M. D. Feld, *The Structure of Violence: Armed Forces as Social Systems* (Beverly Hills: Sage Publications, 1977), 13–30.

25. B. Neuberger, ed., "Three Israeli Approaches," *Diplomacy in the Shadow of Confrontation* (in Hebrew) (Tel Aviv: Open University, 1984), 207–11.

26. Proposed solutions included a wide range of possibilities, from a Palestinian-Jordanian confederation to an independent Palestinian state.

27. D. Apter, *The Politics of Modernization* (Chicago: Chicago University Press, 1965), 1–80, 422–63.

28. Shinui and Ratz were positioned not in the flanks but in the secondary centers of the system. Their attitudes, however, especially those of Ratz, were often opposed to Israeli government policy on foreign affairs and security.

29. See lecture by Dr. Y. Reuveni at the annual conference of the Israel Political Science Association (Hebrew University, 1984); and also Y. Cohen, "Journalists and Soldiers: A Clash of Interests," *I.D.F. Journal* 3, no. 2 (1985): 63–76.

30. See D. Goren, *Communication and Reality*, 170–72; S. Verba, "Public Opinion and the War in Vietnam," *American Political Science Review* 61, no. 2 (1967): 317–33.

31. For a thorough discussion of this point, see Part three, chapter 6.

32. Regarding the link between hawkishness and ethnic extraction, see M. Shamir and A. Arian, "Ethnic Voting in the 1981 Elections," *State, Government and International Relations*, vols. 19–20 (1982): 88–104; A. Arian,

M. Shamir, and R. Ventura, "Public Opinion and Political Change: Israel and the Intifada," *Comparative Politics* 24, no. 3 (1992): 317–34.

33. See speech by Menachem Porush, Agudath Israel (September 8, 1982) *Divrei Haknesset* vol. 94, p. 3629; Shmuel Alpert, Agudath Israel, and Hanan Porat, Tehiya (June 29, 1982) *Divrei Haknesset*, vol. 94, p. 2951-61. Re link between religion and nationalism, see Y. Liebman, "The Religious Component in Israeli Nationalism," *Gesher* 2/113 (winter 1984): 63–78.

34. See Part one, chapter 1.

35. Compare L. A. Coser, *The Functions of Social Conflict*; and also M. Gluckmann, *Custom and Conflict in Africa* (Oxford: Basil Blackwall, 1956); T. T. Skocpol, *States and Social Revolutions* (Cambridge: Cambridge University Press, 1979), 3–43.

36. See E. S. C. Wade and A. W. Bradley, *Constitutional and Administrative Law* (London: Longman, 1985), 547–74; R. A. Diamond, ed., *France under de Gaulle* (New York: Facts on File, 1970), 32–48.

37. Thus, for example, the Basic Law: The Army (1976) (Section 4), the Defense Service Law-1959 (Combined Version) (Sec. 26 et al.), and The Military Justice Law-1955—all provide penalties for military disobedience. See HCJ 734/83 Yaakov Shein vs. Minister of Defense and CGS.

38. See Z. Segal, "The Military Censorship: Its Powers, Judiciary Control of Its Acts and Proposal for an Alternative Arrangement," *Iyunei Mishpat* 15, no. 2 (July 1990): 311–42. R. Shamir, "The Political Role of the High Court of Justice" (in Hebrew) (master's thesis, Tel Aviv University, 1989); Comp. M. Shamgar, "The Observance of International Law in the Administered Territories," *Israel Yearbook of Human Rights*, vol. 1, pp. 262–78.

39. Kimmerling, *The Interrupted System*; A. Minz, "The Industrial-Military Complex: American Concept and Israeli Reality," *State, Government and International Relations* 26 (spring 1987): 15–31.

40. Y. Shapiro, *Democracy in Israel* (in Hebrew) (Ramat-Gan: Massada, 1977), 112–44; Y. Shapiro, *An Elite without Successors* (in Hebrew) (Tel Aviv: Sifriat Poalim, 1984), 15–65, 107–57; D. Horowitz and M. Lissak, *Distress in Utopia* (in Hebrew) (Tel Aviv: Am Oved, 1990), 240–71; Y. Peri, *Between Battles and Ballots* (Cambridge: Cambridge University Press, 1983).

41. See Goren, *Communication and Reality*, 196–97; and also Mueller, *War, Presidents and Public Opinion*, 49, 162.

42. See Brodie, *War and Politics* (New York: Macmillan, 1973); N. Sheehan, *The Pentagon Papers* (New York: Finer, 1971), 145–54; H. Dooley, "The Suez Crisis, 1956; A Case Study in Contemporary History," part 2 (Ph.D. diss., University of Notre Dame, 1976), 545–614.

43. Re the consensus in Britain, see R. R. Titmuss, *History of the Second World War: Problems of Social Policy* (London: Longmans, Green, 1950), 322–51.

44. Except for a number of statements by Ariel Sharon, minister of commerce and industry in the National Unity Government, and of MK Yaakov Meridor, see radiophonic debates on "Yesh Inyan" program, October 10, 1985.

45. J. Turner, "Cabinet, Committees and Secretariats: The Higher Direction of War," *War and the State*, ed. K. Burk (London: Unwin, 1982), 57–83; W. N. Medlicott, *Contemporary England 1914–1964* (London: Longman, 1967), 427–38.

46. See R. A. Diamond, *France under de Gaulle*, 15, 28, 32, 34, 36, 39, 42–48.

47. A "structure" is a permanent (as distinct from an impermanent) pattern of cooperation. For a definition of the term, see D. Mitchell and M. Lissak, *Dvir Lexicon of Sociology* (in Hebrew) (Jerusalem: Dvir, 1984), 73–75.

48. See B. M. Russett and T. W. Graham, "Public Opinion and National Security Policy," *Handbook of War Studies*, ed. M. Midlarsky (Boston: Unwin Hyman, 1989).

49. H. McClosky, "Consensus and Ideology in American Politics," *American Political Science Review* 58, no. 2 (1964): 361–82.

50. S. Swirski, *Israel—The Oriental Majority* (London: Zed Books, 1989). For a different analysis of the ethnic rift in Israel, see Y. Peres, *Ethnic Community Relations in Israel* (in Hebrew) (Tel Aviv: Sifriat Poalim, 1977); H. Herzog, *Political Ethnicity* (in Hebrew) (Tel Aviv: Hakibbutz Hameuchad Publishers, 1986); E. Ben-Rafael, *The Emergence of Ethnicity—Cultural Groups and Social Conflicts in Israel* (London: Greenwood Press, 1982).

51. See Y. Atzmon, "Women in Israeli Politics," *State, Government and International Relations* 33 (winter 1990): 5–18.

52. G. Shafir and Y. Peled, "As Prickles in Your Eyes: Socioeconomic Features of Rabbi Kahane's Voting Sources," *State, Government and International Relations* 25 (spring 1986): 115–30; Y. Peled, "Ethnic Exclusionism in the Periphery: The Case of Oriental Jews in Israel's Development Towns," *Ethnic and Racial Studies* 13, no. 3 (1990): 345–67.

53. Peres, *Ethnic Community Relations in Israel*, 174–75.

54. E. Shils and L. Lipsitz, "Consensus," *International Encyclopedia of the Social Sciences*, ed. D. L. Sills (New York: The Free Press, 1968), 260–71; G. J. Graham, "Consensus," *Social Science Concepts*, ed. G. Sartori (Beverly

Hills: Sage Publications, 1984), 89–124; J. W. Prothro and C. W. Grigg, "Fundamental Principles of Democracy: Bases of Agreement and Disagreement," *Journal of Politics* 22, no. 2 (1960): 276–94; McClosky, "Consensus and Ideology."

55. For the derivation of this term, see V. O. Key, *Public Opinion and American Democracy* (New York: Knopf, 1958), 50–53.

56. Similar terminology appears in Key, *Public Opinion*, 40–50. He refers to "negative consensus" as a consensus implicit in apathy, while I have used it to denote second-rate consensus. Both approaches imply an identical political outcome: avoidance of dissent.

57. See Mueller, *War, Presidents and Public Opinion*, 159–67.

58. See R. A. Diamond, *France under de Gaulle*, 15–48.

59. The original paradigmatic context is presented by Mitchell and Lissak, *Dvir Lexicon of Sociology*, 73–75; for a theoretical analysis, see E. Shils, *Center and Periphery: Essays in Macrosociology* (Chicago: University of Chicago Press, 1975).

60. See G. Barzilai, "Democratic Regimes during War and Postwar Periods: Israel from a Comparative Outlook," *International Problems: Society and Politics* 54, nos. 1–2 (1990): 20–36.

61. Quotations from resolutions of Israeli governments.

Chapter Ten

1. Regarding the importance of consensus in bearing bereavement and maintaining morale, see R. M. Titmuss, *History of the Second World War: Problems of Social Policy* (London: Longmans, Green, 1950) re the British public in World War II; also Y. Dror, *Major Israeli Strategy* (in Hebrew) (Jerusalem: Leonard Davis Institute and Akadamon, 1989) re the Israel public in the War of Independence and the Six-Day War.

2. See D. Horowitz, "The Permanent and the Fluid in the Israeli Security Concept," *War of Alternative*, 57–115; A. Levita, *Israel's Military Doctrine: Defensive and Offensive* (in Hebrew) (Tel Aviv: Hakibbutz Hameuchad Publishers, 1988); re nuclear policy, see Y. Evron, *Israel's Nuclear Dilemma* (in Hebrew) (Tel Aviv: Yad Tabenkin-Ramat Efal, 1987); E. Inbar, *Israeli Strategic Thought in the Post-1973 Period* (Jerusalem: Israel Research Institute of Contemporary Society, 1982); A. S. Klieman, *Israel and the World after 40 Years* (New York: Pergamon, 1990).

3. See E. Inbar, "War in the Jewish Tradition," *State, Government and International Relations* 26 (spring 1987): 1–14.

4. Daniel Bartal has found that Israel's national isolationism largely contributes to coercive tendencies: D. Bartal "Siege Mentality" (in Hebrew), lecture at conference at University of Tel Aviv, summer 1989; see also D. Bartal, "Siege Mentality in Israel," a lecture at the convention of the International Society of Political Psychology (Tel Aviv, Israel, June 1989).

Bibliography

Abbreviation of Archives

AHA   Ahduth Haavoda Archive
BGA   Ben-Gurion Archive
HA   Herut/Likud Archive
LA   Labor/Mapai Archive
HHA   Mapam Archive

Private Archives

Peace Now Movement Archive
Latif Dori Archive

Mass Media Archives

ITV Archive
The National Press Archive at the Hebrew University, Jerusalem
Press Archive at Tel Aviv University

Books, Edited Volumes, and Scientific Articles

Akzin, B., "The Role of Parties in Israel," *Integration and Development in Israel*, eds. Eisenstadt, S. N., Ben Yosef, R., and Adler, C. (Jerusalem: Jerusalem University Press, 1970).

Apter, D., *The Politics of Modernization* (Chicago: Chicago University Press, 1965).

Arian, A., *Public Opinion in Israel and the Lebanese War* (in Hebrew) (Tel Aviv: Jaffe Center for Strategic Studies, 1985).

Arian, A., and A. Antonovsky, *Hopes and Fears of Israelis* (Jerusalem: Jerusalem University Press, 1972).

Arian, A. and M. Shamir, "The Primarily Political Functions of Left-Right Continuum," *The Elections in Israel, 1981*, ed. A. Arian (Tel Aviv: Ramot, 1983).

———, "Two Reversals: Why 1992 was not 1977," in A. Arian and M. Shamir, *The Elections in Israel 1992* (Albany: State University of New York Press, 1995).

Arian, A., M. Shamir, and R. Ventura, "Public Opinion and Political Change: Israel and the Intifada," *Comparative Politics* 24, no. 3 (1992): 317–34.

Arian, A., I. Talmud, and T. Hermann, *National Security and Public Opinion in Israel* (Boulder: Westview Press, 1988).

Arian, A., and R. Ventura, *Israeli Public Opinion and the Intifada: Changes in Security Attitudes 1987–1988* (Tel Aviv: Jaffe Center for Strategic Studies, 1989).

Aronoff, M. J., *Israeli Visions and Divisions: Cultural Change and Political Conflict* (New Brunswick: Transaction Books, 1989).

Atzmon, Y., "Women in Israeli Politics," *State, Government and International Relations* 33 (winter 1990): 5–18.

Bahnson, B., "Emotional Reactions to Internally and Externally Derived Threat of Annihilation," *The Threat of Impending Disaster*, ed. Grosser, G. H. et al. (Cambridge: MIT Press, 1964).

Barnes, S. H., and M. Kaase, eds., *Political Action* (Beverly Hills: Sage Publications, 1979).

Barnett, M. N., "High Politics Is Low Politics," *World Politics* 42 (1990): 529–62.

———, *Confronting the Costs of War* (Princeton: Princeton University Press, 1992).

Bar-Nir, D., "Who Is Responsible for the Non-Peace?" *Shalom Ubitahon*, no. 1, January 1973.

Bar-on, M., *Peace Now—Portrait of a Movement* (in Hebrew) (Tel Aviv: Hakibbutz Hameuhad, 1985).

Bartal, D., Siege Mentality in Israel, a lecture at the convention of the International Society of Political Psychology (Tel Aviv, Israel, June 1989).

Barton, A. H., *Communities in Disaster* (New York: Anchor Books, 1969).

Bartov, H., *Dado* (in Hebrew) Parts 1,2 (Tel Aviv: Maariv, 1978).

Barzilai, G., "Israel," *Middle East Contemporary Survey*, 13 (1989): 419-45.

——, "A Jewish Democracy at War: Attitudes of Secular Jewish Political Parties in Israel toward the Question of War (1949-1988)," *Comparative Strategy* 9 (1990): 179-94.

——, "Democratic Regimes during War and Postwar Periods: Israel from a Comparative Outlook," *International Problems: Society and Politics* 54, nos. 1-2 (1990): 20-36.

——, "Territory, State and Power: The 1992 Elections," in Karsh, E. and Mahler, G., eds. *Israel at a Crossroads: the Challenge of Peace* (London: British Academic Press, New York: St. Martin's Press, 1994).

Barzilai, G., G. Goldberg, and E. Inbar, "Israeli Leadership and Public Attitudes toward Federal Solutions for the Arab-Israeli Conflict before and after Desert Storm" *Publius* 21 (summer 1991): 191-209.

Barzilai, G., and I. Peleg, "Israel and Future Borders: Assessment of a Dynamic Process," *Journal of Peace Research* 31, no. 1 (1994): 59-73.

Barzilai, G., and B. Russett, "The Political Economy of Israeli Military Action," *Elections in Israel—1988*, ed. A. Arian and M. Shamir (Boulder: Westview Press, 1988).

Barzilai, G., and Y. Shain, "Israeli Democracy at the Crossroads: A Crisis of Non-Governability," *Government and Opposition* 26, no. 3 (1991): 345-67.

Beilin, Y., *The Price of Unity* (in Hebrew) (Tel Aviv: Revivim, 1985).

Ben-Rafael, E., *The Emergence of Ethnicity—Cultural Groups and Social Conflicts in Israel* (London: Greenwood Press, 1982).

Ben-Zvi, A., *The United States and Israel* (New York: Columbia University Press, 1993).

Bialer, U., *Between East and West: Israel's Foreign Policy Orientation 1948-1956* (Cambridge: Cambridge University Press, 1990).

Bramson, L., and G. W. Goethals, eds., *War* (New York: Basic Books, 1968).

Brecher, M., *Decisions in Israel's Foreign Policy* (Oxford: Oxford University Press, 1974).

Brodie, R., *War and Politics* (New York: Macmillan, 1973).

Brooks, R., "Domestic Violence and Wars: A Historical Interpretation," *Violence in America*, eds. Graham, D. H. and Gurr, T. R. (New York: Signet, 1969).

Burk, K., *War and the State* (London: Allen and Unwin, 1982).

Carter, A., *Direct Action and Liberal Democracy: Violence and Civil Disobedience* (New York: Harper & Row, 1972).

Chandler, R., *Public Opinion* (New York: Bowker, 1972).

Cohen, Y., "The Israeli-Arab Conflict and Emigration," *Magamot* 32, no. 4 (January 1990): 433–47.

Coser, L. A., *The Functions of Social Conflict* (New York: The Free Press, 1956).

Dahl, R., *Democracy and Its Critics* (New Haven: Yale University Press, 1989).

Dayan, M., *Suez Campaign Diary* (in Hebrew) (Tel Aviv: Am Hasefer, 1965).

——, *A New Map, Different Relations* (in Hebrew) (Tel Aviv: Sifriat Maariv, 1969).

——, *Milestones* (in Hebrew) (Tel Aviv: Yediot Ahronoth, 1976).

Diamond, R. A., ed., *France under de Gaulle* (New York: Facts on File, 1970).

Don-Yehiya, E., "Jewish Messianism, Religious Zionism and Israeli Politics: The Impact and Origin of Gush Emunim," *Middle Eastern Studies*, 23, no. 2 (1987): 215–34.

Dooley, H., "The Suez Crisis, 1956; A Case Study in Contemporary History," part 2 (Ph.D. diss., University of Notre Dame, 1976), 545–614.

Doron, G., *Rational Politics in Israel* (in Hebrew) (Tel Aviv: Ramot, 1988).

——, "Conscientious Refusalism as a Regulator of Policy," *International Problems: Society and State* 28 (1989): 26–35.

Dowty, A., et al., eds., *The Arab-Israeli Conflict: Perspectives* (New York: Praeger, 1984).

Dror, Y., *Major Israeli Strategy* (in Hebrew) (Jerusalem: Leonard Davis Institute and Akadamon, 1989).

Drori, A., ed., *Book of the Fourth National Conference of the Herut Movement* (Tel Aviv: Herut Movement Secretariat, 1957).

Durkheim, E., *Suicide* (New York: The Free Press, 1951).

Eban, A., *Life Story* (in Hebrew) (Tel Aviv: Maariv, 1978), vols. 1,2.

Eitan, R., *Story of a Soldier* (in Hebrew) (Tel Aviv: Maariv, 1985).

Ely, J. H., *War and Responsibility: Constitutional Lessons of Vietnam and Its Aftermath* (Princeton: Princeton University Press, 1993).

Erikson, R. S., and N. R. Luttbeg, *American Public Opinion* (New York: John Wiley, 1973).

Etzioni, A., *Demonstration Democracy* (New York: Gordon and Brench, 1970).

Evron, Y., *The Middle East: Nations, Superpowers, and Wars* (New York: Praeger, 1973).

——, *Israel's Nuclear Dilemma* (in Hebrew) (Tel Aviv: Yad Tabenkin, 1987).

——, *War and Intervention in Lebanon* (Baltimore: Johns Hopkins University Press, 1987).

Feld, M. D., *The Structure of Violence: Armed Forces as Social Systems* (Beverly Hills: Sage Publications, 1977).

Feldman, S., and H. Rechnitz-Kijner, *Deception, Consensus and War: Israel in Lebanon* (Tel Aviv: Jaffe Center for Strategic Studies, 1984).

Fogelson, R. M., *Violence and Protest* (New York: Doubleday, 1971).

Frears, J. R., *Politics and Elections in the French Fifth Republic* (New York: St. Martin's Press,1977).

Freedman, R. O., ed., *The Middle East after the Israeli Invasion of Lebanon* (Syracuse: Syracuse University Press, 1986).

——, *The Intifada: Its Impact on Israel, the Arab World, and the Superpowers* (Miami: Florida International University Press, 1991).

Fromm, E., *The Sane Society*, trans. Weissman, Z., et al. (Jerusalem: Rubinstein Publishers, 1975).

Gazit, M., *The Peace Process* (in Hebrew) (Tel Aviv: Hakibbutz Hameuchad Publishers, 1984).

Geist, B., "The Six-Day War" (Ph.D. diss., Hebrew University, Jerusalem, 1974).

George, A., *Presidential Decision Making in Foreign Policy: The Effective Use of Information and Advice* (Boulder: Westview Press, 1991).

Gerner, D. J., *One Land, Two Peoples: The Conflict over Palestine* (Boulder: Westview Press, 1991).

Giddens, A., *The Nation-State and Violence* (Cambridge: Polity Press, 1985).

Gluckmann, M., *Custom and Conflict in Africa* (Oxford: Basil Blackwall, 1956).

Goldberg, G., G. Barzilai, and E. Inbar, *The Impact of Inter-communal Conflict: The Intifada and Israeli Public Opinion* (Jerusalem: Leonard Davis Institute, 1991).

Goren, D., *Communication and Reality* (in Hebrew) (Jerusalem: Keter, 1986).

Graham, G. J., "Consensus," *Social Science Concepts*, ed. G. Sartori (Beverly Hills: Sage Publications, 1984).

Grosser, G. H., ed., *The Threat of Impending Disaster* (Cambridge: MIT Press, 1971).

Gurr, T. R., *Why Men Rebel* (Princeton: Princeton University Press, 1970).

Habermas, J., *Observations on the Spiritual Situation of the Age* (Cambridge: MIT Press, 1984).

Har-Even, A., ed., *Israel Toward the Twenty-First Century* (in Hebrew) (Jerusalem: Van Leer, 1984).

Herzog, Haim, *The People Shall Rise Up Like a Lion* (in Hebrew) (Jerusalem: Edanim Publishers, 1983).

Herzog, Hanna, *Political Ethnicity* (in Hebrew) (Tel Aviv: Hakibbutz Hameuchad Publishers, 1986).

Hewedy, A., *Militarization and Security in the Middle East: Its Impact on Development and Democracy* (New York: St. Martin's Press, 1989).

Horowitz, D., "Is Israel a Garrison State?" *The Jerusalem Quarterly* 4 (summer 1977): 58–75.

———, "Military Thinking and Civilian-Military Relations," *Israeli Society and Its Defense Establishment* ed. M. Lissak (London: Frank Cass, 1984).

———, "The Permanent and the Fluid in the Israeli Security Concept," *War of Alternative*, ed. Yariv, A. (in Hebrew) (Tel Aviv: Jaffe Center for Strategic Studies, 1985).

Horowitz, D., and M. Lissak, *From Yishuv to State* (in Hebrew) (Tel Aviv: Am Oved, 1977).

———, *Distress in Utopia* (in Hebrew) (Tel Aviv: Am Oved, 1990).

Horowitz, D., E. Sivan, Y. Porat, et al., eds. *The Superfluous War—Questions and Answers on the War in Lebanon* (in Hebrew) (Tel Aviv: Sha'al, 1983).

Inbar, E., *Israeli Strategic Thought in the Post-1973 Period* (Jerusalem: Israel Research Institute of Contemporary Society, 1982).

——, "War in the Jewish Tradition," *State, Government and International Relations* 26 (spring 1987): 1–14.

——, *War and Peace in Israeli Politics: Labor Party Positions on National Security* (Boulder: Lynne Rienner, 1991).

Inbar, E., and G. Goldberg, "Is Israel's Political Elite Becoming More Hawkish?" *International Journal* 44 (summer 1990): 631–60.

Joll, J., *Europe Since 1870* (New York: Penguin, 1983).

Keren, M., *The Pen and the Sword* (Boulder: Westview Press, 1989).

Kerkheide, V. W., *Anthony Eden and the Suez Crisis of 1956* (Cleveland: Ph.D, diss., Case Western Reserve University, 1972).

Key, V. O., *Public Opinion and American Democracy* (New York: Alfred Knopf, 1961).

Kimmerling, B., "Prominence of the Israeli-Arab Conflict as a Social Indicator, 1949–1960," *State, Administration and International Relations* (1974): 100–26.

——, *The Interrupted System* (New Brunswick: Transaction Books, 1985).

Kimmerling, B., and J. S. Migdal, *Palestinians: The Making of a People* (New York: The Free Press, 1993).

Klieman, A. S., *Israel and the World after 40 Years* (New York: Pergamon, 1990).

Kriesberg, L., *Social Conflicts* (Englewood Cliffs: Prentice-Hall, 1982).

Kuhn, T. S., *The Structure of Scientific Revolutions* (Chicago: Chicago University Press, 1962).

Lahav, P., "Rights and Democracy: The Court's Performance," *Israeli Democracy Under Stress*, eds. Sprinzak, E. and Diamond, L. (Boulder and London: Lynne Rienner Publishers, 1993).

Lane, R. E., *Political Man* (New York: The Free Press, 1972).

Lasswell, H. D., "The Garrison State," *American Journal of Sociology* 46 (1941): 455–64.

Lavi, Z., "The Editors' Committee—Myth and Reality," *Journalists' Yearbook—1987* (in Hebrew) (Tel Aviv, 1987), 63–77.

Levita, A., *Israel's Military Doctrine: Defensive and Offensive* (in Hebrew) (Tel Aviv: Hakibbutz Hameuchad Publishers, 1988).

Levy, J. S., "Domestic Politics and War," *Journal of Interdisciplinary History* 18, no. 4 (spring 1988): 653–73.

———, "The Diversionary Theory of War: A Critique," *Handbook of War Studies*, ed. Midlarsky, M. I. (Boston: Unwin Hyman, 1989).

Liebman, Y., "The Religious Component in Israeli Nationalism," *Gesher* 2/113 (winter 1984): 63–78.

Lipsitz, C., "The Study of Consensus," *International Encyclopaedia of the Social Sciences*, ed. Sills, D. L., vol. 3 (1968).

Lissak, M., "The Social Price of the Wars of Israel," *The Price of Power*, ed. Offer, Z. and A. Kovar. (in Hebrew) (Tel Aviv: Maarakhot, 1984).

Lustick, I., *For the Land and the Lord: Jewish Fundamentalism in Israel* (New York: Council on Foreign Relations, 1988).

Lustick, I., *Unsettled States, Disputed Lands: Britain and Ireland, France and Algeria, Israel and the West Bank-Gaza* (Ithaca: Cornell University Press, 1993).

Maoz, Z., and B. M. Russett, "Normative and Structural Causes of Democratic Peace, 1946–1986," *American Political Science Review* 87, no. 3 (1993): 624–38.

McClosky, H., "Consensus and Ideology in American Politics," *American Political Science Review* 58, no. 2 (1964): 361–82.

Medlicott, W. N., *Contemporary England* (London: Longman, 1978).

Meir, G., *My Life* (in Hebrew) (Tel Aviv: Maariv, 1975).

Menuhin, Y., and D. Menuhin, eds., *The Borderline of Obedience* (in Hebrew) (Tel Aviv: Yesh Gvul Publishers, 1985).

Midlarsky, M. I., *On War: Political Violence in the International System* (New York: The Free Press, 1975).

Migdal, J. S., *Strong Societies and Weak States* (Princeton: Princeton University Press, 1988).

Mikunis, S., *In These Tempestuous Times* (in Hebrew) (Tel Aviv: Maki Central Committee Publishing House, 1969).

Miliband, R., *Class Power and State Power* (London: Verso, 1983).

Mills, C. W., *The Power Elite* (New York: Oxford University Press, 1956).

Mintz, A., "The Military-Industrial Complex: The American Concept and the Israeli Reality," *State, Government and International Relations,* no. 26 (1987): 15–31.

Morris, B., *The Birth of the Palestinian Refugee Problem, 1947–1949* (Cambridge: Cambridge University Press, 1987).

———, *1948 and After* (Oxford: Oxford University Press, 1990).

Mueller, J., *War, Presidents and Public Opinion* (New York: John Wiley, 1973).

Muller, E. N., *Aggressive Political Participation* (Princeton: Princeton University Press, 1979).

Nakdimon, S., *Toward Zero Hour* (in Hebrew) (Tel Aviv: Ramdor, 1968).

Naor, A., *Government in War* (in Hebrew) (Jerusalem: Hebrew University, Jerusalem, 1986).

Naor, M., *The War after the War* (in Hebrew) (Tel Aviv: Publishing House of the Ministry of Defense, 1970).

Neeman, Y., *Open-Eyed Policy* (in Hebrew) (Ramat-Gan: Revivim, 1984).

Neuberger, B., ed., "Three Israeli Approaches," *Diplomacy in the Shadow of Confrontation* (in Hebrew) (Tel Aviv: Open University, 1984).

Ofer, Z., and A. Kovar, eds., *The Price of Power,* (in Hebrew) (Tel Aviv: Ministry of Defense, 1984).

Ornan, U., "The War and the Peace," *From Victory to Downfall,* ed. Ratosh, Y. (in Hebrew) (Tel Aviv: Hadar, 1976).

Pappe, I., *The Making of the Arab-Israeli Conflict, 1947–1951* (London and New York: Tauris, 1992).

Peled, S., "Stability and Changes in the Structure of Israeli Public Positions from the End of the Six-Day War to December 1970," (Ph.D. diss., Hebrew University, Jerusalem, 1976).

Peled, Y., "Ethnic Exclusionism in the Periphery: The Case of Oriental Jews in Israel's Development Towns," *Ethnic and Racial Studies* 13, no. 3 (1990): 345–67.

Peleg, I., *Begin's Foreign Policy 1977–1983: Israel's Move to the Right* (New York: Greenwood Press, 1987).

Peleg, I., and O. Seliktar, eds., *The Emergence of Binational Israel: The Second Republic in the Making* (Boulder: Westview Press, 1989).

Peres, S., *David's Sling* (in Hebrew) (Jerusalem: Wiedenfeld & Nicholson, 1970).

Peres, Y., *Ethnic Community Relations in Israel* (in Hebrew) (Tel Aviv: Sifriat Poalim, 1977).

Peres, Y., and E. Yuchtman-Yaar, *Trends in Israeli Democracy* (Boulder and London: Lynne Rienner, 1992).

Peretz, D., *Intifada: The Palestinian Uprising* (Boulder: Westview Press, 1990).

———, "Early State Policy toward the Arab Population, 1948–1955," *New Perspectives on Israeli History*, ed. Silberstein, L. J., (New York: New York University Press, 1993).

Peri, Y., *Between Battles and Ballots* (London: Cambridge University Press, 1983).

Popper, K. R., *The Open Society and Its Enemies*, 5th ed. (Princeton: Princeton University Press, 1971).

Prothro, J. W., and C. W. Grigg, "Fundamental Principles of Democracy: Bases of Agreement and Disagreement," *Journal of Politics* 22, no. 2 (1960): 276–94.

Raanan, Z., *Gush Emunim* (in Hebrew) (Tel Aviv: Sifriat Poalim, 1980).

Rabin, Y., *Service Log*, vol. 2 (Tel Aviv: Maariv, 1979)

Rafael, G., *Privy to the Secrets of Nations* (in Hebrew) (Jerusalem: Edanim, 1981).

Ravitzki, A., "The Future and the Possibilities," *Israel toward the Twenty-First Century*, ed. Har-Evan, A. (in Hebrew) (Jerusalem: Van Leer, 1984).

Raviv, I., "Israel's Security in the Third Year since the Six-Day War," *Maarakhot*, no. 204, January 1970.

Riftin, Y., *Guardianship* (in Hebrew) (Tel Aviv: Sifriat Poalim and Kibbutz Ein Shemer, 1978).

Rosen, S., "War Power and the Willingness to Suffer," *Peace, War, Power and Numbers*, ed. Russett, B. M. (Beverly Hills: Sage Publications, 1972).

Rossiter, C., *Constitutional Dictatorship* (New York: Harper & Row, 1963).

Rubinstein, A., *A Certain Degree of Political Experience* (in Hebrew) (Jerusalem: Edanim, 1982).

Russett, B. M., *Controlling the Sword* (Cambridge: Cambridge University Press, 1990).

Russett, B. M., and G. Barzilai, "The Political Economy of Military Actions: The United States and Israel," in Mintz, A., ed. *The Political Economy of Military Spending in the United States* (London and New York: Routledge, 1992).

Russett, B. M., and T. W. Graham, "Public Opinion and National Security Policy: Relationships and Impacts," *Handbook of War Studies*, ed. Midlarsky, M. I. (Boston: Unwin Hyman, 1989).

Schieff, Z., and E. Yaari, *The Garden-Path War* (in Hebrew) (Jerusalem, Tel Aviv: Schocken, 1984).

Schiffer, S., *P.G.C. Snowball, Secrets of the Lebanese War* (in Hebrew) (Tel Aviv: Edanim, Yediot Ahronoth, 1984).

Segal, Z., "Military Censorship: Powers, Judiciary Criticism of Its Actions and Draft for an Alternative Arrangement," *Iyunei Mishpat* 15, no. 2 (July 1990): 311–42.

Seliger, M., *Ideology and Politics* (New York: The Free Press, 1976).

Seliktar, O., *New Zionism and the New Foreign Policy System of Israel* (Carbondale: Southern Illinois University Press, 1986).

Shafir, G., and Y. Peled, "As Prickles in Your Eyes: Socioeconomic Features of Rabbi Kahane's Voting Sources," *State, Government and International Relations* 25 (spring 1986): 115–30.

Shamgar, M., "The Observance of International Law in the Administered Territories," *Israel Yearbook of Human Rights*, vol. 1, pp. 262–78.

Shamir, M., and A. Arian, "Ethnic Voting in the 1981 Elections," *State, Government and International Relations*, vols. 19–20 (1982): 88–104.

——— , "The Intifada and Israeli Voters: Policy Preferences and Performance Evaluations," *Elections in Israel—1988*, ed. Arian, A. and Shamir, M. (Boulder: Westview Press, 1990).

Shamir, R., "The Political Role of the High Court of Justice" (in Hebrew) (master's thesis, Tel Aviv University, 1989).

Shapiro, Y., *Democracy in Israel* (in Hebrew) (Ramat-Gan: Massada, 1977).

——— , *An Elite without Successors* (in Hebrew) (Tel Aviv: Sifriat Poalim, 1984).

——— , *To Rule Hast Thou Chosen Us* (in Hebrew) (Tel Aviv: Am Oved, 1989).

Sharett, M., *Personal Diary* (Tel Aviv: Maariv, 1978).

Shavit, Y., *Restraint or Response 1936–1939* (in Hebrew) (Ramat-Gan: Bar-Ilan University Press, 1983).

———, *The Mythology of the Right* (in Hebrew) (Tel Aviv: Bet-Berl, 1986).

Shaw, M., *War, State and Society* (London: Macmillan Press, 1984).

Sheehan, N., *The Pentagon Papers* (New York: Finer, 1971).

Sheleff, L., *Conscientious Refusalism Out of Civil Loyalty* (in Hebrew) (Tel Aviv: Ramot, 1989).

Shiloah, Zvi, *A Great Land for a Great Nation* (in Hebrew) (Tel Aviv: Otpaz Ltd., 1970).

Shiloni, I., *Three Circles of Lebanon* (in Hebrew) (Tel Aviv: Yosef Sherbrak, 1986).

Shils, E., *Center and Periphery: Essays in Macrosociology* (Chicago: University of Chicago Press, 1975).

Shlaim, A., *Collision across the Jordan* (New York: Columbia University Press, 1988).

Simmel, G., *Conflict* (Glencoe: The Free Press, 1955).

Skocpol, T., *States and Social Revolutions: A Comparative Analysis of France, Russia, and China* (Cambridge and New York: Cambridge University Press, 1979).

Skolnick, J. H., *The Politics of Protest* (New York: Simon & Schuster, 1969).

Sneh, M., *End of the Beginning* (in Hebrew) (Tel Aviv: Kibbutz Hameuchad Publishers, 1982).

Sorokin, P. A., *Man and Society in Calamity* (New York: E. P. Dutton, 1942).

Sprinzak, A., *Illegalism in Israeli Society* (in Hebrew) (Tel Aviv: Sifriat Poalim, 1986).

Stein, A. A., "Conflict and Cohesion," *Journal of Conflict Resolution* 20 (1976): 143–66.

Stein, K. W., *The Land Question in Palestine 1917–1939* (Chapel Hill: University of North Carolina Press, 1984).

———, "One Hundred Years of Social Change: The Creation of the Palestinian Refugee Problem," *New Perspectives on Israeli History*, ed. Silberstein, L. J. (New York: New York University Press, 1993).

Stohl, M., *War and Domestic Political Violence* (Beverly Hills: Sage Publications, 1976).

Sutherland, E. H., and D. R. Cressey, *Principles of Criminology* 7th. ed. (Philadelphia: Lippincott, 1966).

Swirski, S., *Israel—The Oriental Majority* (London: Zed Books, 1989).

Thomson, D., *Europe Since Napoleon* (New York: Penguin, 1978).

Titmuss, R. M., *History of the Second World War: Problems of Social Policy* (London: Longmans, Green, 1950).

Verba, S., "Public Opinion and the War in Vietnam," *American Political Science Review* 56 (1967): 317–33.

Vital, D., *The Survival of Small States* (in Hebrew) (Tel Aviv: Am Oved, 1973).

Wade, E. S. C., and A. W. Bradley, *Constitutional and Administrative Law* (London: Longman, 1985).

Wahl, N., *The Fifth Republic* (New York: Random House, 1959).

Weizmann, E., *Thine the Heavens, Thine the Earth* (in Hebrew) (Tel Aviv: Maariv, 1975).

———, *The Battle for the Peace* (in Hebrew) (Tel Aviv: Edanim, 1981).

Wright, H. D., *The Dissent of the Governed* (New York: Academic Press, 1976).

Yaari, E., and Z. Schieff, *Intifada: The Palestinian Uprising* (New York: Simon & Schuster, 1990).

Yaari, M., *Struggling for Liberated Toil* (in Hebrew) (Tel Aviv: Am Oved, 1972).

Yaniv, A., *Dilemmas of Security* (New York: Oxford University Press, 1987).

Yankelovich, D., *The Changing Values on Campus* (New York: Washington Square Press, 1972).

———, *The New Morality* (New York: McGraw-Hill, 1974).

Yariv A., ed. *War of Alternative*, (Tel Aviv: Jaffe Center for Strategic Studies, 1985).

Yellin-Mor, N., *Israel Freedom Fighters* (in Hebrew) (Jerusalem: Shakmona, 1974).

Yitzhaki, A., *Latrun—The Campaign over the Road to Jerusalem* (in Hebrew) (Jerusalem: Kanah, 1982).

Yuval-Davis, N., *Matzpen—The Socialist Organization of Israel* (in Hebrew) (Jerusalem: Hebrew University, 1977).

Subject Index

A

Agranat Committee, 119, 122
Agreements
　cease-fire, 111, 112, 121, 134, 186
　disengagement, 125, 128
　interim, 16, 126, 128, 181, 221–22
　peace, 22, 29, 34, 46, 47, 52, 86, 87, 91–92, 93, 96, 97, 107–08, 118, 124, 128, 198, 200
Agudat Israel and Poalei Agudat Israel, 20, 29, 38, 46, 48, 56, 88, 107, 127, 202
Ahdut Haavoda, 30, 47, 48, 52, 54, 56, 63, 67, 75, 93, 94
Al-Ard, 191
Anxiety-responses, 44–48, 56, 57, 67, 68, 160, 163, 167, 219. *See also* Fear-responses
Apathy, Political, 4, 6, 70, 200
Arab-Palestinian-Israeli Conflict. *See* Conflict, Arab-Palestinian-Israeli
Army, 4, 6, 8, 42, 53, 55, 73, 75, 143, 175–76, 188, 189, 204, 222, 223. *See also* Israel Defense Forces; Militarism and Militarization
Autonomy, 10, 157

B

Beirut, 89, 134, 136, 140–144, 147
Biosociology, 69
Bombardments, 36, 92, 93, 94, 97, 107, 108, 140, 144

Borders, 31, 32, 63, 84, 88, 89, 105, 116, 117, 127, 130, 133, 134, 137, 155, 160, 182
Brazil, 189
Britain, 4, 5, 206, 207, 213–14
　and the Suez Campaign, 5, 16, 31, 32, 36, 46, 49, 61, 194

C

Call-up. *See* Mobilization
Canaanites, 20, 86, 91, 97, 106
"Cause and Effect" Approach, 7, 11, 13
Censorship and Secrecy, 5, 8, 38, 41, 50, 95–96, 113, 139, 162–66, 178, 180, 191, 192, 221. *See also* Manipulation
Civilian Society, 19, 163, 221–23
Committee Against the War in Lebanon, 140, 145, 154
Committee for Peace, 44, 55, 60, 89–90
Conflict, 15, 33, 123
　Arab-Palestinian-Israeli, 28, 30, 31, 44, 49, 60, 88, 89, 96, 102, 109, 120, 126, 154, 171–72, 181, 188, 199, 200, 221–22. *See also* Palestinians
Conscientious Objector. *See* Disobedience
Consensus, 3, 4, 5, 6, 9, 10, 11–14, 16, 17, 19, 21, 188, 189, 193, 199, 203, 206, 209, 210–15, 217, 218, 220

291

292 Subject Index

Consensus *(continued)*
  and the Gulf War, 160–63, 165–66, 169
  and the Intifada, 173, 180, 181, 182
  and the Lebanese War, 131, 135, 145, 207
  and the Six-Day War, 67, 69, 71–73, 75–77, 78
  and the Suez Campaign, 38–49, 50, 51, 55–58, 202,
  and the War of Attrition, 83, 90, 92, 94, 95, 100, 198
  and the Yom Kippur War, 102, 104, 111, 113, 115, 116, 118, 121, 198
  affirmative, 79
  antidemocratic aspects of, 4–5, 95, 211
  artificial, 95
  basic or minimal, 15, 212–13
  positive and negative, 14, 213
  secondary, 78
Consensus concept, 11, 14
Consensus structure, 42, 56, 57, 78, 93, 94, 186, 207–07, 212. *See also* Governments and Ruling Coalitions; National Unity Government
Consensus values, 42–44, 50, 56, 57, 59, 71, 73, 74, 78, 97, 114, 121, 138, 139, 145, 146, 167, 180, 186, 188, 205, 209
Consent, 38, 114, 188, 196, 207
Criticism, 5, 32, 40, 50, 74, 76, 95, 107, 113, 114–15, 118, 119, 137, 139, 150, 164, 176, 180, 201, 205. *See also* Dissent; Opposition; Protest and Protest Groups

D

Decision-Making Processes, 12, 35–39, 41, 50, 57, 72, 76, 77, 94, 120, 122, 145, 165, 193, 201, 222–23

Delegitimization. *See* Legitimacy and Deligitimization
Democracy, 16, 18–20, 84, 85, 97, 98, 109, 118–120, 122, 154, 173, 179, 182, 186–89, 191–92, 199, 209, 212, 213, 216, 219, 223
  formal, 10, 20
  in Uniform, 55, 84, 143
  and war, 3–5, 7, 11, 16, 18, 50, 66, 68, 73, 78, 95, 96, 99, 150–51, 156–57, 167, 168, 169, 188, 191, 193–94, 203–05, 211, 220–21
  Western, 6, 10, 11, 12, 146, 188, 203, 205, 209, 220
Disasters, 69, 71, 160
Discipline. *See* Obedience and Discipline
Disobedience, 18, 124, 144, 145, 146, 173, 179, 189–90, 213. *See also* Opposition, public; Protest and Protest Groups
Dissent, 5, 6, 13, 14, 16, 19, 193, 199, 202, 203, 204, 205, 207, 208, 209, 210, 213, 214, 215–16
  and the Intifada, 180, 181
  and the Lebanese War, 123, 124, 128, 141, 143, 144–45, 146–47, 150–51, 153, 154–55
  and the Six-Day War, 64, 77
  and the Suez Campaign, 45, 58
  and the War of Attrition, 83, 91, 92, 98, 100, 101
  and the Yom Kippur War, 104, 118, 121
  retrospective, 52, 118
Dissent Concept, 12, 14

E

Egypt
  agreements with, 124, 127, 128, 132, 147, 200

Subject Index   293

and the Six-Day War, 61, 64, 65, 68, 69, 71, 75, 76
and the Sinai Campaign, 29–32, 34–54 *passim*
and the War of Attrition, 84, 90, 92, 93, 97, 102
and the Yom Kippur War, 103, 106, 107, 108, 109, 110, 112, 115, 116
Elections, 29, 32, 43, 85, 104, 114, 119, 122, 157, 191
Elites, 6, 8, 9, 14, 50, 73, 78, 95, 99, 100, 128, 135, 141, 150, 151, 172, 186, 188, 189, 192, 197, 200, 202, 205, 208, 209, 213, 217, 219, 221, 222, 223
  civilian, 8, 188
  economic, 12
  military, 8, 10, 29, 100, 113, 180, 188, 189. *See also* Military-Security Establishment
  political, 6, 8, 10, 14, 21, 29, 38, 55, 64, 70, 71, 73, 95, 101, 113, 116, 128, 147, 158, 159, 164, 168, 180, 189, 204, 209, 210. *See also* Political Establishment
Elitist School, 8, 13, 203
Emergency, State of, 7, 16, 18, 73, 113, 186–87, 188, 189, 203–04, 209, 210, 211, 213
  legislation in times of, 162, 178, 191, 196, 204, 207
Extra-Parliamentary Activity, 12, 14, 17, 18, 19, 44, 55, 58, 60, 65–67, 69, 74, 77, 86, 89–90, 91, 94, 97, 100, 101, 108, 115, 118, 119, 121, 122, 123, 124, 135, 138, 140, 145, 146, 151, 154, 155, 166, 187, 200, 204, 208, 209, 210, 211, 217, 221. *See also* Protest and Protest Groups

F

Fear-responses, 59, 67, 68, 69, 74, 77, 78, 98, 104, 111–12, 114, 121, 164, 166, 175, 186, 205. *See also* Anxiety-responses
Fighting Society, 8, 19, 73, 76, 91, 157, 189, 192, 197, 223. *See also* Society in Wartime
France, 5, 16, 32, 36, 46, 49, 57, 61, 64, 128, 147, 180, 187, 194, 203, 207, 214, 215. *See also* War, Algerian
Free Center, 86, 91, 97, 106, 111, 115

G

Gahal. *See* Herut/Gahal/Likud
"Garrison State" model, 73, 162, 167, 185, 188, 189
Gaza, 31, 36, 47, 49, 52, 54, 56, 58, 60, 67, 76, 140, 171, 174, 176, 180, 208, 221
Germany, 4, 190, 191
Governments and Ruling Coalitions, 6, 35, 37, 38, 40, 41, 42, 55, 56–57, 63, 67, 71–73, 78, 85, 91, 93, 94, 107, 114, 122, 125, 126, 127, 128, 129, 137, 147, 154, 173, 186, 207. *See also* Consensus structure; National Unity Government
Gush Emunim, 17, 120, 140, 151, 154, 158, 187, 200, 201

H

Haolam Hazeh, 60, 62, 65, 68, 76, 89, 91, 94, 97, 111, 121
Herut/Gahal/Likud, 24, 27, 29, 62, 63, 64, 187, 188, 192, 193, 196, 200, 221
  and the Gulf War, 161, 164, 170

Herut/Gahal/Likud *(continued)*
  and the Intifada, 157–59, 173, 174, 181
  and the Lebanese War, 124–125, 126–128, 129, 131–33, 135, 147, 149–50, 151, 152, 153, 154, 155, 199, 216
  and the Six-Day War, 64, 65, 67, 71, 72, 73, 74, 75
  and the Suez Campaign, 29–32, 36, 38, 40, 44, 47, 49, 52, 53, 54, 56, 58, 60
  and the War of Attrition, 84–86, 90, 91, 92, 93, 94, 100
  and the Yom Kippur War, 104, 105, 106, 112, 115, 116, 121, 122

I

Imperialism, 194, 195–96
Intercommunal and Interethnic struggle, 16, 18, 21, 33–34, 89, 123, 128, 130, 147, 160, 171–82, 201, 203, 211, 217, 221
Intifada, 16, 18, 157–59, 160, 164, 171–82, 193, 201, 202, 203, 206, 207, 213, 217
Intolerance, Political, 95, 153, 164, 217
Israel Defense Forces (IDF), 43, 77–78, 84, 85, 87, 90, 91–93, 103, 106, 107, 110, 111, 112, 115, 117, 124, 125, 130, 135, 136, 137, 141, 143, 144, 146, 147, 148, 149, 167, 189, 217

J

Jordan, 29, 30, 31, 32, 34, 38, 41, 45, 47, 48, 49, 61, 62, 63, 86, 87, 109, 127, 170, 220

K

Kach (Jewish Defense League), 115, 149, 154, 187, 191, 200
Kahan Inquiry Commission, 146, 151
Knesset, 21, 22, 29, 38, 43, 50, 56, 65, 68, 73, 75, 86, 91, 95, 111, 118, 119, 122, 125, 126, 127, 128, 135, 136, 138, 139, 142, 151, 162–62, 164, 165, 189, 191, 192–93, 204–05, 216

L

Labor. *See* Mapai/Labor/Ma'arach
Lasswellian model. *See* "Garrison State" model
Lebanon, 30, 123–24, 128–37, 141–143, 145, 147–48
Legitimacy and Delegitimization, 3, 4, 5, 6, 14, 19, 20, 49, 58, 80, 84, 85, 94, 97, 98, 104, 118, 145, 154, 187, 202, 211, 213, 216, 217, 219, 222
Liberals and Independent Liberals, 60, 61, 63, 65, 85, 88, 93, 100, 107, 116, 121, 122, 200
Likud. *See* Herut/Gahal/Likud
Limited Military Activity, 89, 90, 107, 108, 116, 124, 125, 129, 134, 135, 136, 137, 139, 155, 202

M

Maki, 24, 28, 30, 40, 42, 44, 50–51, 55–58, 60, 62, 65, 89, 100, 108
Manipulation, 5, 8, 95, 188, 205, 211, 213, 217, 222. *See also* Censorship and Secrecy
Mapai/Labor/Ma'arach, 17, 21, 22, 23, 29, 30, 61–63, 104, 188, 193, 198, 199–200, 221

Subject Index   295

and the Intifada, 157, 158, 159, 170, 173, 181
and the Lebanese War, 124, 125, 126, 127, 134, 135, 137, 138, 139, 141, 146, 152, 154, 207, 216
and the Six-Day War, 66, 67, 71, 72, 73, 74
and the Suez Campaign, 30, 35–38, 41, 42, 44, 48, 49, 51, 54, 55, 56, 57, 61
and the War of Attrition, 86, 87, 88, 90, 91, 92, 93, 94, 95, 96, 100
and the Yom Kippur War, 107, 109, 112, 115, 116, 117, 118, 119, 121, 122
Mapam, 17, 24, 27, 28
and the Intifada, 158, 173
and the Lebanese War, 134, 137–39, 154
and the Six-Day War, 65, 70, 71, 72
and the Suez Campaign, 30, 33–35, 37, 39–44, 47–48, 51–58, 60, 61, 207, 208
and the War of Attrition, 88, 89, 90, 92, 93, 94, 96, 100
and the Yom Kippur War, 107, 113, 114, 116, 117, 121, 122, 125
Marxism and Neo-Marxism, 9, 10, 11, 13, 28, 33, 203, 212
Mass Media, 5, 12, 18, 38, 42, 43, 50, 55, 56, 57, 66, 68, 71, 74, 77, 83, 95–96, 98, 110, 113–14, 124, 135, 136, 145, 147, 150, 161, 165, 180, 201, 205, 216, 217, 221
Matzpen, 19, 60
Militarism and Militarization, 8, 91, 156, 167, 189, 199, 204, 205, 219
Military-Activism, 29, 54, 63, 65, 66, 85, 86, 92, 105, 109, 124, 125, 127, 128, 129, 132, 136, 141, 153, 193, 195, 198, 202, 210

partial, 28–29, 30, 36, 38, 60, 63, 66, 79, 87, 92, 107, 109, 127, 130, 131, 134, 136, 139, 148, 195
Military-Industrial Complex, 8
Military Force, attitudes towards, 5, 10, 11, 17, 18, 20–24, 33, 46, 54, 59, 60, 65, 75, 79, 80, 85, 87, 89, 90, 93, 100, 105–06, 109, 114, 116, 125, 129, 130, 132, 134, 141, 142, 157, 158, 159, 172–74, 180–82, 187–89, 193, 195–97, 199, 202, 206, 208, 211, 219–20, 222
Military Passivism, 28, 60, 65, 96, 106, 109, 134, 159, 166, 168, 172–73, 193, 198, 210
partial, 28, 60–61, 66, 90, 96, 108, 109, 125, 127, 134, 138, 181, 193, 198
Military Security Establishment, 17, 39, 64, 67, 68, 77, 100, 110–11, 112, 113, 119, 144, 162, 175, 176, 188–89, 197, 204, 221, 222–23. *See also* Elites, military
Mobilization, 4, 5, 7, 10, 32, 50, 64, 71, 94, 113, 117, 145, 166, 168, 179, 188, 197, 213
Modernization, 199, 202
Moledet, 158, 164
Movement for Peace and Security, 90, 91, 97, 100, 108
Myth of Siege, 217

N

National Circles, 86
Nationalism 86, 202
National Religious Party (NRP), 35, 39, 46–47, 48, 57, 61, 70, 72, 88, 93, 100, 107, 127–28, 136, 141, 158, 160, 187, 188, 202
National Security, 15, 17, 27, 29, 54, 56, 61, 67, 68, 69, 71, 72, 73,

National Security (continued)
83, 84, 87, 88, 90, 95, 99, 103, 105, 110–11, 113, 118, 121, 124, 128, 130, 131, 161–62, 164, 165, 174, 189, 190, 195, 196, 197, 201, 219–22

National Unity Government, 60, 66, 67, 72, 73, 74, 86, 92, 93, 100, 101, 104, 123, 151, 152, 165, 172, 175, 200, 207

O

Obedience and Discipline, 7, 8, 166, 188, 214

Occupied Territories, 62, 63, 75, 76, 79, 83–90, 91, 96, 105, 106, 107, 108, 109, 111, 112, 114, 116, 117, 120, 122, 125, 126, 127, 140, 144, 146, 157, 158, 159, 168, 170, 171–82, 190, 193, 198, 199, 201, 202, 208, 218, 221

Operation Litani, 131, 132

Opposition
political, 38, 39, 40, 42, 45, 51, 55, 56, 57, 60, 66, 71, 74, 84, 93, 96, 97, 102, 107, 116, 117, 118–21, 128, 129, 135, 144, 148, 149, 150, 190

public, 4, 6, 7, 8, 38, 56, 66, 96, 99, 101, 111, 113, 118–21, 141, 145, 146, 147, 180, 205, 210. See also Protest and Protest Groups

to war, 4, 5, 6, 7, 8, 17, 37, 40, 42, 43, 44, 49–50, 51, 52, 61–63, 97, 101, 102, 114, 123, 135, 137, 138, 140, 150–52, 190, 199, 201, 205, 207, 210, 211, 214, 216, 217

P

Palestine Liberation Organization (PLO), 16, 107, 124, 129, 130, 132, 134, 137, 139, 142, 146, 147, 149, 153, 155, 157, 160, 161, 173, 175, 178, 202

Palestinians (Palestinian problem), 16, 18, 28, 60, 62, 84, 85, 89, 90, 91, 96, 107, 108, 124, 128, 129, 132, 134, 137, 139, 140, 141, 144–45, 147, 153, 154, 155, 157–58, 160, 163, 167, 168, 170, 171–182, 185, 187, 193, 195, 198, 199, 200, 201–02, 221–22, 223

Parliamentary Activity, 14, 21, 22, 29, 38, 43, 50, 56, 65, 67, 70, 73–74, 91, 95, 97, 101, 118, 119, 138, 192, 204–05, 210, 211, 216, 221

Parties
dominant, ruling, 17, 35, 37, 55, 56, 57, 61, 72, 73, 74, 77, 78, 95, 101, 107, 118, 120, 128, 152, 153, 189, 199, 200, 204, 208, 212, 214, 215, 216

opposition, dissenting, 52, 86, 91, 93, 134, 135, 139, 141, 146, 147, 153, 208

peripheral, non-axial, 50–51, 56, 75, 111, 199, 200, 214

radical, 5, 94, 191, 214, 215

Peace and Security, 150

Peace Now, 17, 138, 140, 144–45, 146, 151, 158, 168, 190, 200, 201

Pluralism, 5, 11, 13, 42, 73, 95, 203, 211, 213

Political Behavior, 3, 4, 5, 40, 41, 43, 44, 50, 52, 53, 65, 85, 125, 138, 144, 204, 211, 222

Political Culture, 5, 12, 17, 42, 51, 57, 84, 102, 122, 151, 188

Political Discourse, 104, 160, 163, 181, 186, 197, 219

Political Establishment, 3, 5, 8, 9, 13, 57, 63, 64, 67, 68, 86, 87, 88, 91, 93, 94, 95, 98, 101, 102, 110–11, 119, 121, 128, 134–35, 138, 147, 150, 162, 163, 175, 176, 180, 181, 188–189, 217. See also Elites, political

Political Extremism, 104, 149, 154, 187, 191, 199, 200, 201, 222
Political Power, 4, 5, 8, 9, 13, 41, 55, 63, 66, 67, 71–74, 86, 88, 118, 119, 121, 124, 130–31, 153, 154, 181, 194, 199, 200, 210
Political Stability, 6, 11, 17, 64, 71, 199, 211, 216, 220
Preemptive Strike 28, 45, 47, 49, 71, 77, 78, 87, 107, 110, 111, 113, 125, 126, 152–53, 202, 220
Press. *See* Mass Media
Preventive Strike 45, 133, 153, 155
Progressive List, 20, 173, 192, 200
Progressive Party, 35, 37, 46, 48, 56, 57
Protest and Protest Groups, 12, 17, 66, 67, 84, 91, 97, 98, 99, 101, 104, 116, 118–22, 123, 124, 141, 144–45, 146, 147, 148, 150–51, 154, 166, 182, 186, 201, 209. *See also* Disobedience; Extra Parliamentary Activity; Opposition, public

R

Rafi, 61, 63, 66, 67, 71, 72, 194, 200
Rakah, 75, 76, 90, 138, 139, 140, 146, 154, 217
Ratz (Civil Rights Movement), 20, 114, 121, 139, 140, 154, 158, 166, 173, 200
"Refusal" states, 128, 132, 160
Revisionist Party, 21, 23, 24
Rights and Freedoms, 5, 8, 18, 20, 84, 120, 157, 173, 178, 187–89, 190, 191, 192, 204, 205, 209
Rule of Law, 162–63, 172, 178

S

Secrecy. *See* Censorship and Secrecy

Self-Defense, 33, 53, 61, 62, 64, 69, 97, 136, 166, 191, 223
Sexual Stratification, 209, 217, 222
Shinui, 119, 120, 121, 135, 140, 173, 200
Siah, 20, 90, 91
Social Rifts, 3, 5, 6, 153, 201, 215
Social Stratification, 9, 12, 66, 79, 209–210, 222
Society in Wartime, 90, 156–57, 189–90, 204, 205, 209, 219, 221. *See also* Fighting Society
Sociology of War, 7, 71, 73
Sociopolitical Order, 8, 10, 11, 12, 13, 14, 15, 18, 19, 57, 59, 60, 64, 65, 66, 72, 77, 79, 80, 87, 95, 96, 115, 124, 162, 172, 180, 182, 192, 204, 209, 211
Soviet Union, 22, 32, 34, 53, 54, 61, 92, 93, 94, 96, 97, 106, 109, 112, 126, 131, 132, 133, 136
State List, 88, 107
Supreme Court, 177–78, 190, 191–93, 204, 221
Syria, 31, 62, 63, 64, 65, 68, 69, 75, 103, 105, 107, 108, 109, 110, 115, 116, 124, 127, 128, 130, 131, 132, 133–34, 135–37, 140–41, 147–48, 152, 160, 172, 220

T

Tehiya, 124, 135, 149, 151, 154, 155, 164, 187, 192, 200, 202
Terror, 46, 49, 62, 64, 65, 85, 86, 87, 88, 89, 105, 107, 108, 128, 129, 130, 131, 132, 133, 135, 136, 141, 142, 147, 148, 155, 159, 177, 198, 220
Threat-concepts, 48–49, 56, 57, 58, 59, 78, 92, 93, 96, 97, 112, 121, 167, 175, 180, 186, 206, 219
Transfer, 164, 168–69

U

United States, 5, 6, 11, 22, 31, 32, 53, 61, 64, 68, 70, 93, 97, 106, 107, 110, 112, 126, 127, 132, 133, 147, 157, 158, 160, 175, 180, 187, 194, 206, 209, 213, 214, 215, 216, 223

V

Violence, 73, 123, 124, 151, 159, 174, 175–76, 177, 181, 187, 188, 190, 201, 216, 222
  governmental, 8, 9
  political 151, 163, 216

W

War
  Algerian, 147, 180, 187, 203, 207, 214, 215
  of Attrition, 16, 17, 83–101, 104, 106, 108, 121, 128, 131, 148, 197, 198, 202, 203, 205, 206, 207, 213, 215, 217
  First World, 4, 5
  Gulf, 16, 156–170, 180, 194
  of Independence (1948), 16, 21, 23, 49, 103, 112, 148
  Iran-Iraq, 133
  Korean, 5,6, 194, 205
  Lebanese, 16, 18, 19, 96, 117, 123–55, 180, 189–90, 196, 197, 198, 199, 201, 202, 203, 205, 206, 207, 210, 212–13, 214, 215, 216, 217, 222
  Second World, 4, 5, 7, 11, 194, 203, 206, 214, 215
  Six-Day, 16, 17, 59–80, 84–5, 86, 88, 89, 98, 104, 106, 126, 128, 190, 193, 198, 206, 214, 215
  Suez Campaign, 5, 6, 16, 17, 27–58, 60–61, 67, 77, 104, 128, 134, 194, 197, 202, 203, 205, 207, 208, 213, 215, 217
  Vietnam, 3, 5, 6, 8, 12, 13, 147, 180, 187, 194, 205, 209, 214, 215, 216,
  Yom Kippur, 16, 17, 96, 102–22, 124, 125, 128, 153, 176, 193, 197, 198, 200, 203, 206, 207, 213, 216, 217
Wars (characteristics and types of)
  antidemocratic aspects of, 4, 5, 8, 156, 162, 169, 189
  defensive, 28, 33, 48, 62, 75, 97, 142
  economic issues in, 8, 9, 10, 12, 54, 62, 100, 103, 154, 166, 169, 194, 196, 197, 204, 209
  of initiative, 30–32, 35, 36–39, 45, 47, 48, 49, 52, 62, 142
  just or unjust/justified or unjustified, 6, 33, 36, 48, 51, 52, 53, 75, 88, 90, 91, 92, 95, 97, 138, 140, 187
  "no alternative," 98
  offensive, 16, 30, 34, 41, 48, 53, 61, 65, 84, 107, 145, 153, 195, 202
  preemptive, 70,
  preventative, 16, 46, 49, 54, 139, 142, 143, 152, 153
  public behavior and, 4–7, 12, 13, 19, 65–66, 67, 69, 73–74, 75, 76, 78, 90, 96, 98–100, 113,180, 208
  total, 7, 47, 89, 90, 91, 112, 127, 129, 130, 135, 144
Wartime society. *See* Society in Wartime
West Bank (Judea and Samaria), 23, 24, 30, 61, 63, 76, 88, 104, 116, 127, 128, 132, 140, 141, 146, 171–72, 174, 176, 180, 187, 193, 200, 201, 208, 221

Y

Yesh G'vul, 145, 154, 213
Yishuv, 16, 20, 21, 23, 186, 204

Name Index

A

Alon, Yigal, 38, 72, 73
Aloni, Shulamit, 121, 139
Altman, Arieh, 23
Amit, Meir, 70
Arafat, Yasir, 161, 178
Aran, Zalman, 35, 37
Arens, Moshe, 153
Ashkenazi, Motti, 119
Avneri, Uri, 117

B

Bader, Yochanan, 30, 38, 153
Bar-Lev, Haim, 92, 119, 137
Barnett, Michael N., 10
Bar Yehuda, Israel, 37, 38
Barzilai, Israel, 34, 35, 37, 39, 41, 69, 70
Begin, Menachem, 23, 30–32, 38, 53, 54, 64, 66, 67, 72, 85, 104, 105, 112, 116, 126, 130, 132, 133, 135, 136, 143, 148, 149, 152–53, 154
Ben-Aharon, Yitzhak, 115, 137
Ben-Gal, Avigdor, 152
Ben-Gurion, David, 22, 28, 35, 36–39, 41, 45, 55, 57, 63, 66, 72, 200
Bentov, Mordechai, 33, 37, 39, 41, 69, 70
Berman, Yitzhak, 136–37, 146
Brecher, Michael, 64

Burg, Avraham, 161
Burg, Yosef, 37, 38, 136

C

Cahana, Kalman, 38
Carmel, Moshe, 37
Chomsky, Noam, 163
Cohen, Geulah, 153
Coser, Lewis A., 7, 162

D

Dayan, Moshe, 63, 66, 67, 72, 73, 75, 92, 94, 95, 101, 106, 107, 113, 116, 117, 118, 119, 122, 125, 131, 132

E

Eban, Abba, 68, 70, 92, 94, 137
Eitan, Rafael, 132, 143, 152
Elazar, David, 107, 119, 122
Eliav, Lova, 101, 200
Erlich, Simha, 136–37
Eshkol, Levi, 37, 63, 64, 66, 67, 68, 70, 72, 73, 75, 77, 78, 200
Etzioni, Amitai, 12

G

Galili, Israel, 38, 94, 95, 106, 110
Geist, Benjamin, 65, 70

Geva, Eli, 144
Goldman, Nahum, 97
Greenberg, Uri Zvi, 23
Grigg, Charles M., 212
Gur, Mordechai, 131, 137, 140

H

Haber, Eitan, 201
Habermas, Jurgen, 163
Hammer, Zvulun, 146
Hausner, Gideon, 112
Hazan, Yaakov, 34, 39, 41, 60, 69, 70, 72, 88, 109
Hillel, Shlomo, 140
Horowitz, Dan, 204
Hurewitz, Yigal, 117
Husayni, Faysal al-, 178
Hussein, King (of Jordan), 32, 86
Hussein, Saddam, 159, 160, 161, 168, 170

J

Jabotinsky, Zeev, 23, 86, 195

K

Kahane, Meir, 115
Kimmerling, Baruch, 204

L

Landau, Haim, 38, 65, 105, 109
Lasswell, Harold D., 8, 73, 162, 167, 185, 188, 189
Levi, Moshe, 144
Levin, Hanoch, 91
Levin, Yitzhak Meir 38, 46
Levy, David, 136, 141, 152
Lissak, Moshe, 204
Luz, Kadish, 35, 37

M

McClosky, Herbert, 209
Meir, Golda, 37, 41, 45, 66, 68, 92, 93, 94, 95, 97, 101, 106, 107, 112, 116, 119, 122, 125, 153
Mikunis, Shmuel, 114
Meir, Yehuda, 176
Mills, Wright C., 8
Milo, Roni, 163
Mintz, Alex, 204
Mitzna, Amram, 144
Moda'i, Yitzhak, 152

N

Naftali, Peretz, 37
Namir, Mordechai, 37
Nasser, Gamal Abdel, 31, 32, 49, 52, 64, 92, 93, 97, 102
Nathan, Abie, 178-79
Neeman, Yuval, 153
Nusseiba, Seri, 164

O

Ofer, Avraham, 101

P

Peres, Shimon, 63, 134, 136, 137, 138, 146, 165, 170, 173, 181, 207
Peri, Yoram, 204
Prothro, James W., 212

Q

Qadmoni, Assa, 119

R

Rabin, Yithak, 130, 137, 138, 152, 154, 173-74, 176, 181

Rafael, Yitzhak, 47, 112
Ratosh, Yonatan. *See* Shelah, Uriel
Riftin, Yaakov, 40, 41, 42
Rimalt, Elimelech, 65
Rosen, Pinhas, 37
Rubinstein, Amnon, 135, 141–42

S

Sadat, Anwar, 102, 132
Sagi, Yehoshua, 152
Sapir, Pinhas, 35, 37
Sapir, Yosef, 67
Sarid, Yossi, 137, 140, 161
Schieff, Zeev, 201
Shamir, Yitzhak, 153, 164, 165, 166, 173
Shapira, Moshe, 37, 38, 136
Shapiro, Yonathan, 204
Sharett, Moshe, 35–37, 41
Sharon, Ariel, 132–33, 135, 142, 145, 146, 149, 151, 152–53, 158, 196
Shaw, Martin, 163
Shein, Yaakov, 190
Shelah, Uriel (pseud. Ratosh, Yonatan), 86
Shem-Tov, Victor, 137
Shitrit, Bekhor Shalom, 37
Simmel, Georg, 7, 162
Skocpol, Theda T., 10
Skolnick, Jerome H., 12
Sneh, Moshe, 108
Sorokin, P. A., 7
Stohl, Michael, 8
Swirski, Shlomo, 209

T

Tabenkin, Yitzhak, 38, 63
Tamir, Shmuel, 86, 115, 127

V

Vilna'i, Matan, 176

W

Weizmann, Ezer, 105, 131–32
Werhaftig, Zerah, 136

Y

Yaari, Ehud, 201
Yaari, Meir, 35, 39, 41, 43, 47, 69, 70
Yadin, Yigael, 66
Yankelovich, Daniel, 12

Z

Zadok, Haim, 125
Zippori, Mordechai, 136, 141
Zur, Yaakov, 137
Zussman, Yoel, 191